What readers say about
Invisible Means of Support

"I believe that the psychic vibrations in *Invisible Means of Support* are nothing less than overwhelming. The book acts as a kind of psychic data link—a transceiver for all of the mental energies of its author, its readers and everyone else who has an interest in it. My philosophy is 'If you stop learning, you die.' You will never stop learning after you read this book!"

—*Bob Grahn, Psychotherapist, Educator*

"What makes *Invisible Means of Support* so special is the combination of its extraordinary spiritual breadth and the concreteness of its themes which are cast in contemporary circumstances with meaning for us all. It is a baby boomer's cornucopia of creative insights on how to live with spirit in an overly material world."

—*Judith Lessow-Hurley, Professor, Multicultural Education,*
San Jose State University

"I found [the] description of the shadow-side of the medical and legal professions to be eye-opening, and I was charmed by the on-going inner wisdom dialogue with Hippocrates. In fact, *Invisible Means of Support* has much that is most illuminating."

—*Fran Dorff, Founder of The Center for Process Spirituality*
and Author of The Art of Passingover

"A moving and insightful account of one person's journey of self-discovery. Augustine has crafted a deeply personal and practical guide for all spiritual seekers. At the same time he has given us an inspiring real life story of encounters with the invisible world."

—*Michael Toms, Co-founder, New Dimensions Radio,*
Author of At the Leading Edge

"A work like no other! *Invisible Means of Support* puts the reader within the writer's skin and lets him experience the peaks, the tough decisions and the pitfalls in the quest for enlightenment. The author presents strong evidence on how seemingly incidental coincidences are actually planned into our lives, and how events and people are placed in our path on purpose to help us understand our life's intended direction. A pleasure to reread again and again."

—*Anthony Hoffman, Real Estate Entrepreneur,*
Past-president Optimist Club, Santa Clara, Ca.

INVISIBLE
Means of Support

A Transformational Journey

A Tribute to Joseph Campbell

Dr. Dennis F. Augustine

Golden Gate Publishing
San Francisco, California

Copyright © 1994 by Dr. Dennis F. Augustine

This book may not be reproduced in whole or part, whether by printed, electronic or other means, without prior written permission from the publisher. Exceptions are limited to reviewers or the media who may quote brief passages. Address all queries to Golden Gate Publishing, P.O. Box 2043, Saratoga, CA 95070.

This book is sold with the understanding that the information contained herein does not constitute professional psychological advice. This book is autobiographical. However, many of the names and other identifying details have been changed to protect the privacy of the individuals involved.

Cataloging-in-Publication Data

Augustine, Dennis F.
    Invisible means of support : a transformational journey / by Dennis F. Augustine.
    p. cm.
    "A tribute to Joseph Campbell"—T.p..
    Includes bibliographical references.
    ISBN 0-9636736-0-2
    1. Self-realization.   2. Spiritual life.   3. Augustine, Dennis F.
4. Podiatrists—Unitied States—Biography.   I. Title
BJ1470.A94 1994   158.1'092
Library of Congress Card Catalog No. 93-078398

Text design by Cypress House, Fort Bragg, CA 95437
Cover design by Mark Gatter
Cover photo by Kitagawa II/Superstock, Inc.

Permission to quote from *The Power of Myth* by Joseph Campbell © 1988, and *Illusions: The Adventures of a Reluctant Messiah* by Richard Bach © 1977 by Richard Bach and Leslie Parrish-Bach. Used by permission of Delacorte Press, a division of Bantam Doubleday Dell Publishing Group, Inc.

Permission to quote from *The Unstruck Bell* (formerly *Mantram Handbook*) by Eknath Easwaran © 1993, courtesy of Nilgiri Press, Tomales, CA 94971

Permission to quote from *The Art of Passingover* by Father Fran Dorff © 1992, courtesy of Paulist Press, Mahway, NJ 07430

Permission to quote from *Man's Search for Himself* by Rollo May © 1953, courtesy of W.W. Norton & Co. Inc., New York, NY 10110

Permission to quote from *Father, The Figure and the Force* by Christopher P. Andersen © 1982, and from *Quiet Desperation* by Janice Halper © 1987, courtesy of Warner Books, Inc., New York, NY 10020

Permission to quote from *Uncommon Wisdom* by Fritjof Capra © 1987, and *Transformations* by Roger L. Gould, M.D. © 1978, and from *Zorba the Greek* by Nikos Kazantzakis © 1953 by Simon & Schuster, Inc. Copyright renewed © 1981 by Simon & Schuster, Inc. Reprinted by permission of Simon & Schuster, Inc.

Printed in the U.S.A
First edition

Dedications

One day, when I was lost as lost could be, I randomly flipped through the TV channels and came across what proved to be the most popular series of shows ever aired on public television—*The Power of Myth*—and witnessed the following conversation between Joseph Campbell and Bill Moyers:

Moyers: Have you ever had sympathy for the man who has no invisible means of support?

Campbell: Who has no invisible means? Yes, he is the one that evokes compassion, the poor chap. To see him stumbling around when all the waters of life are there really evokes one's pity.

Moyers: The waters of eternal life are right there? Where?

Campbell: Wherever you are. If you are following your bliss you are enjoying that refreshment, that life within you, all the time.

That series had a profound impact on my life. And those particular words inspired the title of my book, *Invisible Means of Support*.

Because of the enormous contribution Joseph Campbell made to my life and to the lives of many others, I dedicate this book to his memory.

This book is also dedicated to the memory of Lewis Diaz, a benevolent Jesuit priest who was killed in the Netherlands by a deranged assassin whom he was counseling while on leave from the Catholic Church.

And to my father, Frank Augustine, whose early departure from the seminary of the Maryknoll Fathers to lead a secular life made it possible for me to be a part of this great world, without which this book could not have been written. It is from my father that I inherited my curiosity about life.

Acknowledgments

My special thanks to my wife, Cecile, who has shared the roller coaster of life with me for the past twenty years. Her tremendous support, love and friendship have been a stabilizing factor in my life.

To my children, Jason and Michelle, for their unconditional love and for helping me restore the childlike wonder that had been missing from my life.

To Lynn Grincewich of Lynn's Secretarial Services and Robert Bowles II for their valuable assistance.

To the Microsoft technical phone support team for their patience and expertise in helping me format and fine-tune this document.

To the staff at the Saratoga Library for their patience and guidance over the past few years and for providing a secure environment which helped me recollect and compose my thoughts.

My undying gratitude goes out to the many people who took the time to review and critique my manuscript. They include Philip Kavanaugh, M.D., Michael Holland, Matthew Fox, Bob Grahn, Judith Lessow-Hurley, Fran Dorff, Anthony Hoffman, Kelly Ross, Michael Toms, and Thupten Tsering.

I want to acknowledge all the life guides I have mentioned throughout this book, living and deceased, for their inspiration and wisdom. I consider them to be my co-authors in this venture.

I also want to thank my past adversaries in my professional and business life. Unwittingly, they taught me that events and circumstances are never one-sided, and that the push and pull of life always provides opportunities for growth.

A heartfelt thanks to my editor, Colin Ingram, a highly skilled literary surgeon, who made the precision cuts and sutures in my manuscript as painless as possible. His invaluable editorial services and faith in this most challenging project helped to make this book and my dream of sharing it with others a reality.

And finally, thanks to all the invisible, unnoticed people whose contributions have undoubtedly brought me to where I am today.

Contents

Throughout all his writings and lectures, my husband's lifelong study of human cultures, from the Paleolithic to the present time, describes a unity of spirit beneath the vast differences of culture which he found revealed in the symbolic arts, and which he hoped would also have value for others in their quests for self-fulfillment. *Invisible Means of Support* is a realization of his hopes.

— *Mrs. Joseph Campbell*

Introduction

I first met Dennis Augustine in May, 1989, when the rabbi of my synagogue asked us to organize a speaker's series on spirituality for the congregation. At our first meeting Dennis presented a detailed outline for the series that touched on philosophy, science, psychology and theology.

I remember thinking, "Who is this guy?" He seemed an unlikely participant, packaged as he was in the slick veneer of a Silicon Valley entrepreneur. Yet he had a startling breadth of knowledge of ideas and issues related to spirituality.

As we began to get to know each other, I invited Dennis and his wife to my home for a visit. As we talked, I began to make a pot of tea. Dennis was telling us about a festival they had recently attended at Stanford, called *Vesak,* or Buddha Day.

"One of the rituals included the bathing of the baby Buddha in sweet tea," he recalled. "It's a Japanese tradition especially geared for children."

Dennis also mentioned having had tea recently with a friend at the tea garden in the nearby Hakone Gardens.

"This seems to be tea week," he commented, with a gentle smile.

"Even more so," I said. "My son has just been telling us of the Japanese tea ceremony that he learned about in his social studies class."

No sooner had I made that remark than the tea cup I was about to hand Dennis literally exploded in front of us. We were all momentarily stunned as the shattered cup and its contents fell to the floor.

Dramatic as it was, a freak phenomenon is normally left unexplored and quickly forgotten. But on this occasion Dennis provided a curious explanation.

"Had Carl Jung been alive and watching, he would have characterized this event as a 'catalytic exteriorization,'" he said. He then explained how the grand master of the psychoanalytical world theorized that such an event is the result of a burst of mental energy propelled into the physical world during times of heightened creativity. "I guess we just got too creative," Dennis joked.

Since then, Dennis has become a good friend, but he is still a mystery to me. His soft-spoken, gentle demeanor is tempered by a rock-hard quality of Hoboken, and he continues to amaze me with his knowledge of religion and spirituality.

Dennis has known the heights of professional and commercial success, and has plumbed the depths of failure and personal tragedy. In *Invisible Means of*

Support, he candidly holds up his own life as a mirror in which we can see our own. He passionately weaves eternal truths with a street-smart perspective of someone who has been through it all. This book is about exploding the pervasive modern day myths that bind us and discovering the ancient mysteries that have the potential to liberate us.

From this book we learn how we have become lulled into complacency and have become prisoners of outdated beliefs that no longer serve us. Through Dennis' eyes we see first-hand the price tag that accompanies the ongoing process of enlightenment. The book teems with visionary experiences, synchronicities and playful homilies about the eternal human struggle.

Stories of spiritual journeys have been told and retold, and bookstores overflow with volumes recasting ancient wisdom and mythology. What makes *Invisible Means of Support* so special is the combination of its extraordinary spiritual breadth and the concreteness of its themes which are cast in contemporary circumstances with meaning for us all. It is a baby-boomer's cornucopia of creative insights on how to live with spirit in an overly material world.

Read it, and don't be surprised if this book changes your life. Coincidences you have overlooked, life guides you have ignored and ideas you have discarded will begin to play a significant role in your own, personal journey.

There is meaning and wisdom in the space once occupied by the shattered teacup. The energies within this space are invisible. But they have been made understandable and accessible by *Invisible Means of Support*.

Judith Lessow-Hurley, Professor,
Multicultural Education, San Jose State University

Foreword

The *Net of Indra,* the warrior god of the Hindu pantheon, is a magnificent form so vast it covers creation. To gaze upon it from afar is to witness a single, shimmering brilliance. But to view it more closely reveals countless threads. All the threads crisscross each other, and at each crossing point there is a gem.

These are not ordinary gems. Each is lit by an internal flame that radiates light outward in all directions from its multi-faceted surface. This light is reflected from gem to gem until the most distant partakes in every other gem's luminescence.

The gems have another notable quality. As the light from other gems strikes it, each gem's own brilliance is excited and enhanced. Thus each gem in the net brightens all the other gems until each has become a source of light that contributes to and sustains the brilliance of the whole.

The patient observer of the *Net of Indra* will also discover that the gems are not alike—some are brighter than others, and each gem has its own distinct color. Those with a certain purplish tint reflect streams of purple light that connect more eagerly with other purple gems. The same is true for the colors of all the other gems. Careful observation uncovers that each gem in the net—while sharing its light—appears to be more intimately connected with others of its own kind.

These connections are not merely mechanical. There is a sense of preference, of intent, as though the gems are not bound to reflect their own color but wish to do so. Further observation reveals that the threads that hold the gems are not still but vibrating. And as one thread vibrates, its motion flies along its length until it meets another thread, which vibrates in response. Like the reflected light of the gems, each thread reciprocates the pulse of all the other threads. Like the gems, the threads of this extraordinary net have a special quality. As they are touched by a vibration, they become excited and vibrate more strongly. Vibration is imprinted upon vibration and excites further motion.

The vibrating threads cause the gems to quiver so that their light begins to shimmer until it becomes a dance of scintillating colors, never still, intensely alive. The *Net of Indra* seems to have no end. The number of its gems and threads is beyond counting, and the light that dances across the net is infinitely reflected.

Early on, I dimly sensed the existence of the *Net of Indra,* but it has taken me a long time to begin to understand my role in the web of creation. I have been amazed to discover that I radiate my own light and that I receive and reflect the light of everyone I have ever encountered or ever will encounter; that I shake all the threads of creation and am, in turn, shaken by them.

It has been a fascinating journey, filled with forward and backward steps—bliss and despair; all the drama of life—yet it has had a definite, overall direction.

The concept of the *Net of Indra* comes from the Hindu Vedas and while it can be thought of as myth, metaphor or scripture, depending on one's individual interpretation, for me it has a corollary in reality. I have been learning to live within this reality, learning to sense and to flow with the invisible support, energy and guidance that the net of life offers.

One of the ways I have been guided by the invisible forces that surround us is in learning to share. Not just sharing in the practical sense, but in the sharing of my innermost self. Like many other writers, I had doubts about spending years of my life writing a book about my own intensely personal experiences. Who would be interested? And hasn't it been done thousands of times over by others on their own journey? So why bother?

The answer came to me when I understood that real knowledge and wisdom are not imparted at one sitting. We need to hear stories of spiritual growth over and over again, each time from a unique, individual perspective. And like the gems in Indra's net, I hope that my particular experiences will resonate with others'. All of our individual stories matter and have their place among the chronicles of the world.

Who shakes the *Net of Indra* and causes the light to shimmer and dance? We are all shakers and we are all gems, bound together in ways we barely imagine. By writing this book, I, together with the invisible forces that support me, shake a thread, a single thread that is connected to all other threads in wondrous creation. If I am able to excite and brighten the light of one single soul, it will have been worth the effort.

Dennis F. Augustine
Saratoga, California
January, 1994

There is an environment of minds as wells as space. The universe is one—a spider's web wherein each mind lives along every line, a vast whispering gallery where...no news travels unchanged and ...no secret can be rigorously kept.

—*C. S. Lewis*

Work in the invisible world at least as hard as you do in the visible.

—*Rumi*

There is an invisible way across the sky,
Birds travel by that way, the sun and moon
And all the stars travel that path by night.

—*Kathleen Raine*

CHAPTER 1

Someone to Watch Over Me

How do you lead a good life, a good, moral, ethical life, when everything
around you works the absolutely opposite way?

—*Martin Scorcese*

In 1842, P.T. Barnum began a huge promotional campaign for a Wild West
Buffalo Hunt to be held in Hoboken, New Jersey. He wrote letters from
fictitious readers to newspapers throughout the region, feigning excitement
over the great event-to-be. Newspaper editors picked up the theme and, with
the aid of a massive poster campaign, the Grand Hoboken Buffalo Hunt
became the biggest news item of the year.

On the day of the "hunt," a huge crowd of tens of thousands gathered at
Hoboken Raceway. When the animal shed was opened, the crowd saw a dozen
or so scrawny bison that Barnum had bought and shipped to Hoboken. They
had been so ill-fed they could hardly move. When Barnum's hired "cowboy"
rode around them, trying to excite them, they didn't budge. The contrast
between their expectations and this sorry sight made the crowd erupt with
jeers and shouts.

As it increased to a deafening uproar, the sound of the huge throng so
frightened the bison that, in spite of their condition, they stampeded and
headed for the crowd, tearing through fences and railings as if they weren't
there. In response, thousands of onlookers panicked and ran in every direction. The screams of the crowd kept the bison moving and the whole scene
became a bedlam of chaos and hysteria which lasted for several hours.

Miraculously, no one was killed or even seriously injured. Barnum got all the publicity he had wanted and went on to become a master con man. For its part, Hoboken began to develop a reputation for scheming and corruption that lasted a century and a half.

If I turned out to be a failure, I could always blame it on Hoboken. Unlike other cities, where dark undersides are masked by modern buildings, attractive landscaping and litter-free streets, my Hoboken was so thick with crime you could feel it in the air. Bookmaking, theft, loan sharking and political corruption were everywhere, and assassinations were not uncommon. Many city legislators were organized crime leaders, and the Mafia was protected by corrupt cops. Almost everyone seemed to be on the take, and stolen TVs, golf clubs, typewriters, suits and dresses were as available as cigarettes, liquor and drugs.

The culture of Hoboken was a study in contradictions. We were taught in school that honesty is the best policy, that lying is a sin and that the Golden Rule is the way to live. Yet it was clear that in real life lying, cheating and stealing were the means to success. We were taught that we were all equal, but jokes and references to "polaks," "niggers," and "queers" defined the real world. In fact, we knew culture equaled conspiracy; only the tough, the corrupt and the politically connected got ahead.

Very few outsiders came to Hoboken, so everyone seemed to know each other or be related in some way. While some of us were college bound or apprenticing to become blue collar workers, and a few were heeding a special call to be priests, there were also guys being groomed for the rackets. They were looked upon like any other in training for a career.

Some of my friends' fathers were known criminals. Sophia was a girl my age who lived just up the street. Her father was Frank "The Vise" Simone, and he looked as hard and tough as his name. With very few heroes to look up to, we all looked up to the shiny Cadillacs owned by the mobsters and, for a while, I was driven to school each day with Sophia in The Vise's Cadillac. Sophia was a precocious, hazel-eyed brunette with a model's looks, but I never even thought of making a play for her because of who her father was. I enjoyed the prestige of riding in the Cadillac, but it ended abruptly. Frank was found sprawled on the streets of Fort Lee, his head blown off by a shotgun blast.

School was dreary and I got around the boredom by being the class clown. I was always getting into trouble and, periodically, I would be suspended until I returned to the principal's office with a parent. One time, my father came with me, but instead of listening to Mr. Pinto, the principal, Dad began upbraiding him about what he perceived to be favoritism and corruption within the system. Many positions in the school were patronage jobs, and Dad wouldn't let him forget it. He ranted and raved about the poor job the schools were doing and how he was paying for it with his taxes. Dad completely missed the point of the meeting—disciplining me—and the purple-faced principal just sat there and took it, unable to get a word in.

On the way home Dad and I both laughed about how he had told off the principal.

"You were just like Perry Mason on TV, Dad," I told him.

"Yeah," he said, "you can't let these hypocrites get away with this stuff."

Episodes like this had a strong effect on me: never take responsibility for your own actions, it's always someone else's fault. Being raised in Hoboken taught me that there was little difference between mayor and mobster, cop and thief—the thing was to look out for yourself and get what you can.

Had I lived my childhood exclusively in Hoboken, I don't know what would have happened to me, but there was a totally different world as well, a wonderful world, although, ironically, my escape from crime-ridden Hoboken was Sicily, the fabled home of the Mafia. I spent several summers there, living with my grandfather and grandmother.

The town of my mother's birth was Roccalumera, a fishing village on the Mediterranean coast. It was a place of hard work and much poverty, but to me it was paradise. Balconies on either side of the alley-like streets displayed endless varieties of vines and fragrant, hanging flowers. Fruit trees were plentiful; apricots, apples, figs and prickly pears were there for the taking.

The Mafia was there, too, but it wasn't present in the day-to-day affairs of the people—you had to look closely to find it.

While my life in Hoboken had been constrained to a dozen or so city blocks, here I explored the foothills on my uncle's motor scooter, and discovered colorful villages, hidden canyons and spectacular views. The warm, sunny days cried for adventure, and the blue sea and majestic purple mountains beckoned constantly. The ocean was my second home, and I would snorkel for hours in the clear waters, searching for octopus and crab.

Although I spent several summers in Roccalumera, I was always the "American kid," or, more accurately, the "crazy American kid." I stood out because I was taller than most Sicilians and because of my pranks. One of my favorites was to sneak into the rooms where women were sewing on their machines, grab the ends of their thread and run down to the beach, a block away, still holding onto the threads. They'd chase after me, shouting, "Crazy

American kid," while the whole town turned out to watch the spectacle. Fortunately, they were a tolerant people—at least with a wild and boisterous boy.

Aside from the beauty of Roccalumera, I appreciated a quality I had never known in Hoboken. Maybe it was because the streets were so narrow and the houses so close together that the townsfolk had no choice but to live with each other. Maybe it was the climate or the slow pace of life. Whatever, the Sicilians in Roccalumera exhibited a spontaneous friendliness toward each other that was as invigorating as the clean air. I made many friends there, and each time I returned they would not only remember me, but welcomed me with open arms and unlimited hospitality.

The beauty of Sicily and the warmth, kindness and generosity of the people were in sharp contrast to my life in Hoboken. Roccalumera offered me hope for a better way of life. But at summer's end I would be back home, once again playing to the hilt the role of tough street kid. Without that hope, I don't think I would have made it.

When I was in high school, I carefully cultivated my tough-guy image. It was mostly bluff, but I liked the attention and respect it brought me. Life after school consisted of drinking and gambling, fights with rival gangs, general rowdiness, and outwitting the police. One of our favorite pastimes was to go down to the Hudson River piers and untie the barges so that they would drift downriver. The Coast Guard would then sound the alarm and, while they were in hot pursuit of the barges, the police would be in hot pursuit of us. Running away was mostly for the fun of it, because when we did get caught, there was little chance of being arrested. A police captain's son, a lieutenant's son and two sergeants' sons were part of our gang. If they arrested us, they would have to arrest their own sons, and that never happened.

The street wasn't all bad—I learned to be self-sufficient, to use my wits and to think quickly when I had to. The street taught me how to read people, to know what made them loyal or disloyal. I learned how to make deals and the importance of keeping your word. I learned how not to get suckered, especially since I'd watched my own parents being "taken" by everyone in town on repairs, guarantees and inflated charges.

Uptown, a tough-acting gang that all the neighborhood kids looked up to was called the Blackhawk Juniors (I never saw the Blackhawk Seniors, if there were any). For several months I worked hard at getting into that gang and, when I was finally accepted, it was great—an honor. I felt like I'd made it into the elite of society. We all acted tough and all the kids in our part of town respected us. Mostly, we played basketball or poker or just hung around, drinking and doping.

Alcohol, marijuana, LSD and heroin were plentiful. I did most everything except heroin. There were heroin junkies all over the place, and I saw how they would do anything—literally anything—for a hit. Somehow, I had the sense to know that I couldn't handle heroin, but I frequently drank too much.

One evening after drinking with Kevin O'Toole and Joseph Langer, one of these friends suggested we roll some drunks. I went along with the idea—it wouldn't be cool to say no—but I hoped we wouldn't find any.

By the time we got to River Road down by the Hudson River, it was dark and the whole area smelled dank and musty. Litter and empty bottles were everywhere. A little way ahead of us, sitting under the bridge, two winos were holding bottles and muttering to themselves. Kevin and Joseph both picked up empty beer bottles. I did, too, but I had a sinking feeling in the pit of my stomach that this was grossly wrong. Why was I here? Why was I doing this? So far, my "crimes" hadn't really hurt anyone...they were more like pranks. But deliberately, intentionally, injuring other people, helpless people, was no prank. What kind of "tough guy" bashed harmless winos?

I didn't say any of this aloud. I didn't say or do anything. Kevin leaned forward and hit one of the winos with his beer bottle, but it didn't break. "Shit!" Kevin said and hit him over and over again until it smashed. The sounds were dull thuds and then a sharp crack of breaking glass. Then Joseph did the same with his victim. It was a game, the rules for which kept them going until their bottles broke. The winos were so drunk they didn't defend themselves. One groaned and sank to the pavement. The other fell silently in a heap.

I couldn't believe that my friends had actually gone through with it. For the sake of appearances, I pretended to hit them with my bottle, actually striking the pavement instead. "Did you get 'em, Augie?" Joseph asked—calling me by my nickname.

"Yeah, I did." It was so dark the other boys couldn't tell what I had done.

The two winos were still moving, writhing slowly on the ground, and I hoped that they hadn't been injured seriously. Now that the "fun" was over and it was getting cold, we kicked at empty bottles as we walked back toward our own neighborhood.

For the first time in my life, a matter of right and wrong had struck me between the eyes. Previously, I'd been able to rationalize my acts, but here there were no grays—this was all black and white, all wrong. It was wrong to have gone along with the idea in the first place. It was wrong not to have stopped it. I knew then that I would never do anything like that ever again.

Hanging out on a street corner that night with nothing to do but smoke cigarettes and pot, drinking and shivering in the cold, I realized I had to get out of there. But where could I go? It was time to leave Hoboken, but what was there to replace being a tough guy?

During my summers in Sicily, I had seen another world, a world of clean skies and friendly, warm, compassionate people. Somewhere, even nearby, I knew there must be people like them, people who could show me a way out. But how could I find them?

> You can and you can't,
> You will and you won't;
> You'll be damned if you do,
> You'll be damned if you don't.
> —*Lorenzo Dow*

The nuns at Our Lady of Grace School had killer aim when throwing erasers and chalk. If you acted up there was instant retribution—a twist of an ear, a knuckle to the head or a paddle to the butt. You couldn't count on your parents to intercede, and there seemed no limit to the sisters' ability to inflict pain when they were confronted with disobedience. Once, Antoinette Rubino was criticized by Sister Annunziata for teasing her hair in class. Antoinette had the temerity to reply, "You can't tell me what to do; you ain't my motha." The sister responded by pouring a handful of rice onto the floor in the corner of the room and forcing Antoinette to kneel on it. Sister Annunziata knew how long it would take before Antoinette's knees started to bleed.

Sister Assumptor was the toughest nun at our school, possibly the toughest nun that ever lived. She wore a black habit down to her ankles, but she could move quickly. Her tight, clipped voice, her hooked nose and glasses, and her rapid movements made her seem like a falcon, always looming and ready to strike. She carried an umbrella even when it wasn't raining, and once, during a fire drill, she caught me in the heinous act of whispering. She smacked my thumb so hard with that umbrella I carry a scar to this day.

The kids were all terrified of Sister Assumptor, and we addressed her in respectful tones. We were all "yes, sister" and "no, sister," so when Jim, a tough eleven-year-old boy, glared at Sister Assumptor and said "fuck you" to her, I couldn't believe it had happened. Nobody ever talked back to Sister Assumptor, let alone use foul language in her presence. For a long moment there was utter silence, then the falcon recovered. She smacked him in the face and on both sides of the head. Then Jim did something even more unthinkable. He hit her back! He hit a nun. We couldn't believe this was happening! It was not only wrong, it was blasphemy. Striking a nun was like hitting God!

We waited breathlessly for what would happen next. Sister Assumptor grabbed Jim's collar with her talons and shouted, "I'll teach you a thing or two, you foul-mouthed little ruffian!" Then she dragged him away down the hall to some ominous office. I don't think I ever saw him again. Had he been sent straight to Hell or gotten beaten with the umbrella first? I wasn't sure about Hell, but I certainly knew about the umbrella.

I had come to Our Lady Of Grace elementary school when I was six years old. My parents transferred me from public school in order that I have a more structured, less chaotic environment. It certainly was more structured. From the first grade to the second year of high school, I wore a school uniform—blazer, white shirt and necktie. No kid liked wearing a school uniform, and I couldn't wait until school was over to tear off my necktie. On the other hand, I didn't have to worry about what to wear to school each day.

The atmosphere in Catholic school was generally militant. The first and primary thing we learned was blind obedience to the lay teachers and nuns. After blind obedience, the most important things were faith in God and faith in sentence structure and punctuation, both of which were learned by rote.

Mr. O'Neil, my high school Latin teacher, had a raspy voice, glasses, a round face and a W.C. Fields nose. It was fun to bait him but to do it in such a way that you couldn't be punished. One time, Mr. O'Neil was conjugating a Latin verb on the blackboard when I whispered, "I shit, you shit, he shits, they shit." My classmates heard me, but so did Mr. O'Neil. As he turned to face me, his glasses began to steam and his eyes bugged out. Best of all, his nose enlarged and turned purple as he attempted to restrain his anger. Mr. O'Neil looked like a volcano about to explode, which was the effect we all wanted to see.

From the outside, the school building was much like any other school, but the church was different from any other I had seen. Inside, it was very ornate, with wood and stone statues, carvings on the walls, and painted figures. But why was everyone so solemn? Elderly women dressed in black knelt in prayer.

Sometimes tears flowed down their cheeks. Were they in pain? Where was the joy the sisters always talked about? If anyone in the church felt joyous, they kept it very well hidden.

During mass, ushers held long poles attached to collection baskets. As a basket paused for a moment in front of each person, it presented an opportunity to give, but it also offered an opportunity to take. I knew better than to seize that opportunity. God would instantly get me. A thunderous lightning bolt would come crashing down and strike me dead on the spot! And if He didn't get me, the Mafia would. They were very loyal to the church and were known to track down petty thieves who stole from it. If word got out that someone had been stealing from the church, he was likely to disappear and never be seen or heard from again.

After the baskets had been passed along the pews, the ushers would take them to the front of the church and dump the money into a collection box. In addition to paper money and small envelopes, there were always piles of coins. The clinking of coins tumbling into the collection box echoed through the church, and it sounded like the jackpot winnings from a slot machine. I visualized that money. Where was it all going? The church was raking it in! What a racket, I thought, and I dreamt of the fortune I would claim for myself someday in whatever career I followed.

In addition to the regular curriculum, the sisters pounded into us that the Catholic Church was the One True Church, the Only True Church. The overall tone of the church's teachings seemed to be a never-ending series of threats that increased in intensity as I grew older, until it included all the terrible things that would happen to me if I had lustful or evil thoughts, if I lied, if I ate meat on Friday, if I used profanity, or if I smoked or drank or took drugs.

The good sisters took advantage of every possible way to embarrass us into exercising restraint. One time, in the seventh grade, a stern-faced Sister Delphine publicly told me, "Take your hands out of your pockets, Mr. Augustine, before you get yourself in trouble." Masturbation was considered a terrible sin, and the mere suggestion of genital contact, no matter how innocent or benign, was discouraged. It was the church's equivalent of preventive medicine. Nevertheless, I couldn't understand how something that felt so good could be bad for me.

Everyone took ritual very seriously. One day a nun warned us, "Never chew on the Eucharist (the wafer given at Holy Communion) nor desecrate it in any way. Just swallow it. If you do chew on it, not only is it sacrilegious—it will bleed." I never knew anyone who was willing to challenge the theory. Back in third grade, a girl had asked, "What happens if after taking Holy Communion you have to throw up?" It was one of those questions we all wondered about but were too afraid to ask. Sister Delphine answered, in all seriousness, "You can't clean it up yourself. It still has the consecrated host in it. You must get a priest to clean it up." The girl worried about it day after day and it became a self-fulfilling prophecy. The following week, she threw up on the way home from Mass. Embarrassed and too afraid to tell a priest what had happened, she may have felt guilty over it for years.

Of course, there was an escape from all my "sins"—I could avoid God's punishment through the confessional. But I never really believed that just confessing could wash away my misdeeds. Why would God set up a system where I was absolved of guilt through confession, and then let me go out and do it all over again? The apparent contradiction bothered me a lot, and no one ever resolved it for me. There was also the fear of sudden death. What if an accident happened and I died without absolution? Would I really be punished for all eternity? And if so, why would God allow that?

If one of the purposes of organized religion is to inspire and uplift Mankind to a more joyous life in God, why has the Catholic Church imbued its adherents with such pessimism? As a boy, I felt doomed from the start. I was somehow to blame for past sins not of my doing, as well as for all the daily sins caused by natural urges and passions.

Meanwhile, I wondered about the God we all prayed to. Was frightening people His only way of relating? I never felt I had a direct relationship with God, or that He had ever heard me pray. Gradually, I began to hate the constant fear of punishment. There was no way I could measure up to the church's high standards, no way I could live the saintly life demanded by the sisters. Because I was frequently breaking church taboos, and because as I grew older it wasn't "cool" to do church activities, I felt more and more distant from the church and from the God it described. My mother tried to get me to continue going to Mass, but I usually played basketball instead, and I spent the quarter she gave me for the collection basket on a soft drink or ice cream cone.

Some of the sisters were nice; some were compassionate; but they all seemed sad. They wore their solemnity like a blanket, and I watched them pray as if possession by the Devil himself was imminent. More than any other quality, many sisters seemed always to be afraid. I think they were afraid of not being good enough, of not pleasing God enough, and their fervor was not only directed at God and Jesus and Mary, but forced them to make sure that their students were also afraid. They rarely shouted, but their stern looks and cold voices said it all: "Keep it up, Mr. Augustine, and God will punish you. When you are feeling the fires of Hell burning your soul, then you'll remember what I told you. You will be damned for sure if you continue doing what you're doing."

The priests were inaccessible, formal robots who repeated the same ritual words and gestures. The devout Latin phrases passed from their lips as if they were actors reciting from a script. Occasionally, a chance meeting with a priest informed me that they were, in fact, real people with individuality and, sometimes, wisdom. Once, after I had accompanied my grandmother to Mass in Sicily, we were talking with the priest and the conversation got around to swimming in the ocean. He said he never went swimming because there were sharks in the water. I asked him, "Won't God protect you?" and he replied, "Yes, but one doesn't tempt the Lord."

At St. Michael's High School, I became aware that science and the church had fundamental disagreements on such things as how the universe was formed, the age of the earth, and evolution. How was I to make sense of things? I remember being taught how I carried the burden of original sin and how I had to redeem myself for something I hadn't done. Sure, I was a cut-up, and I gambled and drank, but I had never deliberately hurt others. Was I really to blame for the fall of mankind? Could an all-loving, all-benevolent God leave such a legacy? And where was the joy and the gladness they all talked about? I knew the nuns and priests were devout, but if they harbored some secret inner joy, it didn't show and none of it ever spilled over onto me.

And yet, I believed. I sensed that behind the ritual, the traditions and the devoutness, the church was connected to something really important. Perhaps the years of listening to church doctrine, perhaps the words that seemed so repetitive, awakened a knowledge I carried within myself, for I believed there was really a God somewhere. I knew nothing about His form or His attributes, or how to make contact with Him, but it didn't seem to matter. I knew that I couldn't live up to the high, strict standards of the church, so I decided to be my own person and go my own way, whatever this elusive God thought of me.

How does a street kid react to the mysteries? Probably the same way as any other kid—they are not very important in his life. But in my case some seed of recognition was sown. Something inside of me said, "Yes, yes, this may be important, but not now, not now." That's how it was for me. I grew distant from the church and from all things religious. God was on "hold, "where He would remain for a long time.

I'd never actually heard one of those inner voices out loud before, but they were there, to be sure, driving me, whipping me, urging me on.
—*Allan Brennert*

The street was everything, playing field, meeting hall and battleground. Home was where we ate and slept and performed a few necessary tasks, but the street was our life. We owned the portion of it that had been won and held by our gang. The smell from the Maxwell House coffee plant, where my father worked the night shift, wafted through the air. Dad worked just a block away but it was a world apart.

We were playing wiffle ball. The fluorescent street lights provided enough illumination so that the circular sewer covers on the corners could easily be seen and used for bases. I had just come to bat. I was sixteen, and I was drunk.

The bat was light and made of hard yellow plastic, and I waved it, anticipating the pitch, when two older Puerto Rican boys, maybe eighteen or twenty years old, arrived on the scene, conspicuously out of their neighborhood. Staying within your borders was an unwritten rule of street life. Crossing that imaginary line was an act of aggression.

This kind of thing wasn't new. Our gangs faced each other off on many occasions, but the police always broke up the fights before they got really violent. It was crazy and dangerous, living on the edge, but it was fun and I loved it.

That night, the two Puerto Ricans weren't just walking, they were strutting their stuff, daring us by their body language to fight. At least that's how I perceived it in my drunken stupor.

"What the hell are those spics doing here?" yelled Anthony ("Miggy") Mignoli. I felt brave from alcohol and because of our numbers. There were ten of us. The pitch came and, as I swung at the ball, I let go of the bat on impulse, sending it flying in their direction. The yellow bat rose in the air, spinning, in a high arc that brought it down on the other side of the street, startling the Puerto Ricans. Bobby Shannon ran over to retrieve it.

Maybe it looked different to them. A bat had been thrown at them and one of our guys was running toward them. Or maybe they'd planned it. But before any of us could move, they grabbed Bobby and one of them held a knife to his throat.

"They got Shannon!" someone yelled.

I'd wanted to be a tough guy, had worked at it, cultivating the image of "Idol," played by Marlon Brando in the movie *On The Waterfront*. I'd done more than my share of taunting, stone-throwing and fist-fighting. Now, suddenly, it was no longer fun and games. Bobby just stood there, paralyzed, afraid to move, eyes bulging, looking scared as hell, the knife point poking into his throat.

The bat was still lying on the ground, and I ran across the street to retrieve it. Eyes darted back and forth, anticipating the next move. I thought, if I hit the guy hard enough with the bat, it'll stun him, knock the knife out of his hand and he won't stab Bobby.

"Everything's cool, Bobby," I said. I picked up the bat and swung it as hard as I could toward the Puerto Rican with the knife. I caught him in the back of the neck but he jammed the knife into Bobby's throat. I hadn't seen the second Puerto Rican moving fast to my blind side and before I could back away his knife plunged into my lower abdomen. As I was falling I was stabbed again in my right thigh by the one who'd got Bobby. *"Vamonos!"* he said, and then both Puerto Ricans took off as fast as they could. Crazy Jake ("the Snake") Jacobsen grabbed a metal trash can—we had no weapons—and flung it at the retreating Puerto Ricans in a vain attempt at vengeance. But, for me, time had stopped.

Bobby and I were on the ground. I was in shock. It was like being in some kind of limbo. I didn't feel pain—I wasn't even aware of the stab wounds. I felt something warm and wet on my leg. I looked down. My whole side was covered with blood. I assumed the matter was serious and that I would die shamefully in the pool of my own blood. Above me, but seeming very far away, I could hear shouts of "Call the police, get an ambulance!"

"Hold on, Augie!" someone said, "everything will be all right." I could hear Bobby nearby, holding his throat, gurgling up blood and trying to keep from choking.

I remained in limbo until the police finally came. Then I was lifted into the back of a police car and rushed to St. Mary's Hospital. While lying in the back of the police car, I began reliving the event. I saw myself falling backwards in slow motion, never quite hitting the ground. As I fell, I noticed there were stars everywhere in the black night sky. A voice seemed to come from a distance. "Look what you've gotten us into now, you idiot!" I saw the translucent image of a person above me—it looked like me.

"You aren't real," I said. "I'm delirious. Leave me alone, can't you see I've been severely injured?"

"If I'm not real," it said, "why are you speaking to me?"

"I'm Dennis Augustine. There's only one of me."

"Your name has merely been lent to you, and I'm part of you whether you like it or not."

"Oh yeah? Then how come I'm lying here bleeding, and you're up there?"

"I'm a messenger."

"A messenger? Who sent you?"

"Your other selves."

"What do you mean, my 'other selves'?"

"Look, we don't have time right now—I've got to give you the message."

"Okay, what's the message?"

"Your being stabbed is the message. It means that you can't go on being the Dennis Augustine you've been. You're holding up your other selves. Your messing up the best parts of all of us. Do you get it? You're messing it all up, and you've got to start listening."

Strong arms grabbed me and placed me on a gurney. I seemed to be back in the world. I was glad to be back; I didn't like what I'd heard. Now there was a great deal of frenzied activity around me as I was wheeled into the emergency room. Anxious faces peered down at me. A young doctor examined me, looking into my eyes and examining my wounds, while a nurse checked my pulse and blood pressure. Then my mother was at my bedside, crying and shrieking uncontrollably, her face contorted, repeating over and over, "Why…why?" and pounding her chest with fury. She believed I was dying, and it seemed much more important to console her than to worry about whether or not I would live.

The next day I had to undergo exploratory surgery to see if there was any organ damage or internal bleeding. Fortunately, the knife had missed my vital organs. But in addition to the knife wound, the surgery resulted in a large, disfiguring scar that would serve as a reminder of my folly for the rest of my life. And, in spite of morphine and other medication, the pain was intense. However, I made it and, later that day, I learned that my friend Bobby would also survive.

Toward the end of my hospital stay, I fell into a depression of mourning, not wholly for myself. It was as though I had somehow connected with others, unknown to me, who were also in pain and anguish. I did not know what to make of this except that I sensed I was not alone in my suffering—and that helped.

There was lots of time to reflect while in the hospital. I had almost succeeded in getting myself and my friend killed by attempting to prove how tough I was. I could admit to myself that I had initiated the whole episode, but my invitation to brawl had not been meant as a fight to the death. In fact, I had nothing in particular against Puerto Ricans. They were just the newest ethnic group in town and consequently the lowest on the social ladder, just as we Italians had been before them when the Irish gangs were dominant. But they were not part of our gang, and that made them enemies.

One of the Puerto Ricans, whose name was Emilio, proved to have a long history of stabbing his victims. Emilio had been looking for trouble as much as I had. The difference was that he was looking to draw blood, while I didn't have that killer instinct. I had just gotten in over my head in the constant bluffing game we all played.

My anger toward Emilio made me promise something to myself. It wasn't a resolve to be a better person. No, I would make it up to everyone by becoming successful—not modestly successful, but hugely successful. I wasn't just a delinquent kid who always got into trouble. I would show my eighth grade teacher who told me I would never get past high school or amount to anything. I would prove to my parents, my neighbors and my friends that I was smarter than they thought. I would show the world that I was "somebody!"

The physical effects of the stabbing stayed with me for many years—pain, muscular weakness and a diminished athletic ability. The emotional effects are with me still. What caused this series of events to unfold? Why was I at bat just at that critical moment? If it was a meaningful coincidence, what was the meaning? For all my bravado, I had never wanted to really hurt anyone. So why was God punishing me? For years I lied about the event, describing my actions as being taken solely to protect my friend Bobby. It was hard for me to see that the whole episode was the result of my penchant for courting excitement and danger, the culmination of years of trying to be a tough guy.

Although the events I have described occurred, at least in part, through a teenager's foolishness, I remember sensing that there was also some other reason that this violence had happened to me. I was unable to fathom why, but I sensed that a part of me had died that night. I had lost the innocent belief that I was exempt from misfortune.

After the stabbing, I became more serious, more cynical and less trusting of life. I felt myself to be an unworthy person because of the pain, the shame and the anguish I had caused myself and my family. My weapon of revenge became my absolute determination to succeed.

Oh, let my eyes be opened wide,
That I may clearly see,
How often in another's guise,
God walks the road with me.

—*R. H. Grenville*

When you're lying on the bottom of a swimming pool, about to drown, the sounds of other children are muted by the water, but you can still hear their screams, shouts and laughter. Then there is a terrible, crushing pressure filling your head, and awareness starts to fade away.

I was ten years old, and it had been a hot, humid day in Hoboken. Without telling my parents, I decided to go to the local pool to cool off. Jumping up and down in the water felt great, even though I couldn't swim, but then a little thing happened. Just a little thing. On one of my jumps, I tilted a bit to one side on the way down. Nothing very dramatic. Except that I slowly tilted more and more until I lost my balance and smoothly slid down to the bottom of the pool, looking up.

With my last, fleeting consciousness, I was dimly aware of something grabbing my skinny arms and pulling my limp body to the surface. Then I was frantically choking, coughing, sputtering and gasping for air. It was a wonder anyone had noticed me among all the other bodies in the water, but some sharp-eyed older boy had. After I recovered, my dominant feeling wasn't fear—it was embarrassment. The water hadn't been over my head; all I'd needed to do was get up. But, instead, I laid on the floor of the pool, immobilized by fear and inexperience.

Life is like that, somehow. When we're immobilized by fear, the obvious is overlooked. A similar thing happened when I was in my teens. I was hiking in the mountains above the Hudson River with some of my friends when the trail ended abruptly at a narrow chasm. It was only four feet across but a 600-foot sheer drop down. I was the last one to jump across. It wasn't that difficult a feat, but I panicked and landed on the far side with one foot on firm ground and the other foot on the vertical face of the chasm. Unable to find a hold, I started to slide downward, and there was no way for me to raise myself. My friends hadn't waited for me, and they were too far ahead to help. As my strength failed and I started to slide faster, I suddenly felt a strong hand grab my wrist. I looked up, and above me saw a man I had never seen before. I grabbed his arm with my free hand and slowly he pulled me upward to safety. Again on flat ground, I thanked him profusely and then he left. I hadn't seen anyone else on the trail, but a man appeared on the scene at just the right time, and I am alive to tell about it.

Most of us are touched every day by the hidden hand of some stranger, at times in a dramatic way, like the hand that saved my life. Sometimes it is a subtle touch, unnoticed or just casually acknowledged. And sometimes the effect does not occur for years and years after the event. Often, others have an effect on us that is less dramatic but that, with hindsight, we see as having profound importance in our lives.

John Dempsey had that kind of influence on my life. John was a close, high-school friend I looked up to and would have followed practically anywhere. Unbeknownst to me, John applied to, and was accepted by, Northwestern College of Oklahoma. I followed his lead and was also accepted. I spent two years there as a business and accounting major. Without John's influence, I don't know if I would have received more than a high school education. After I returned home from Oklahoma, I began dabbling in marijuana dealing. And then I met a fine human being named Bob Goldsack, who got me a job at the local A & P supermarket and acted as a surrogate father when I was confused and heading downhill.

Bob was a family man who was also an alcoholic, but he was my friend, guide and confidante—a secret sage. The smile, the gleam in his eyes, the laughter he inspired in me made me revere him, once I looked past what society called a character flaw.

Bob Goldsack had had a hard time of it. One day he told me, "After I got out of the service, I went to work as an on-line engineer for the Melba Toast Company. I set up their mechanical operations. It was a good job—paid well, with good benefits. One day there was a malfunction on the assembly line. I started to repair it without realizing that I had forgotten to turn off the main switch and pull out the fuse. I don't know what I was thinking. Well, anyway, before I knew it, wham! I'm flying through the air into a vat of batter. Part of my goddamned right hand was sliced off. The doctors tried to sew it together as well as they could, but it was a real mess. The good news was that I lived!"

Bob started laughing and coughing at the same time, a hacking, smoker's cough. "The bad news was, I lost my job. Who's going to keep on a cripple? It put me out of work for years and years." He took a swig of liquor from his shiny, pocket-size, stainless steel flask and continued. "Then the A & P hired me. I was so grateful for the opportunity to work that I did whatever they asked me, without complaint. What else could I do? I work as often as they'll have me—seven days a week if I'm needed."

After a while I lost touch with Bob. Later, I found out from his son that his drinking had begun to interfere with his work and he was let go at age fifty-six. Somehow, he landed a job as a security guard, and he stayed at that until he died of cancer a few years later.

Bob was not able to follow his own advice, but he dispensed wisdom and encouragement as though there was no limit. "There are friends and there are friends," Bob would say. "Some will want to drag you down with them. Be careful. Open your eyes! In the end you'll need to move ahead without them."

I loved Bob. When I tried to tell him how talented and gifted he was, he would shy away as if the compliment was too painful to bear. "It's too late for me," he would say, draping his arm over my shoulder, "but you have your whole life in front of you. Don't waste the opportunity like I did."

"But you're not that old," I protested, "and besides, it's never too late. You even said so yourself."

"That's true, Denny, I did say that. But you'll find out someday that your path in life is not so much governed by your decisions as by how you decide to live with the decisions you have already made." I didn't understand his words very well at the time, but his meaning eventually sunk in.

Bob was an anomaly, a man who had given up on much of life and yet was a good provider for his family and a true friend to many. While he couldn't help himself, he helped many others. It's interesting how people with vices and addictions can still add to the quality of other people's lives. It makes me think of the artists, poets and writers who, in spite of their addictive personalities, have inspired, enlightened and entertained people all over the world.

To some, Bob Goldsack was a frog. To me he was the Frog Prince.

There were others. Like the old man in the park who fed the pigeons and smelled the flowers; the grizzled longshoreman who, in his off time, wrote poetry; the magician who loved to dazzle the audience with his tricks when the fair came to town; or my friend Wayne, who loved ballet and stuck to it in spite of taunts from his peers.

As a boy. I found these variations of the human character oddly beautiful. It made me question the criteria, the standards and the rules by which we judge what is beautiful or ugly, right or wrong, worthy and worthless. I admired and respected rogue personalities. To me, they were somehow more alive and more real than "normal" people.

In spite of these positive influences, I still saw no way out. Living in Hoboken was very frustrating for anyone with initiative. Business was tied up, politics was tied up, and capital was tied up. To get ahead, you needed a powerful sponsor. Everyone knew the system was corrupt, and the only way to succeed was to have connections. No connections, no advancement. And I had none. My incidental claim to fame was that, before he married, my father lived two doors down from Frank Sinatra and his family.

And then there was Carmine. He was from my mother's village of Rocca-lumera, and I had heard him mentioned as a kind of honorary uncle. My mother had told me to go see him, that he could help me. But who wanted to see another Sicilian? We were Sicilian and so were many of our neighbors, and it didn't take long to know that Sicilians—contrary to the Hollywood image of the Mafia—were the blue collar workers, the hard-working, uneducated laborers who busted their backs for a lifetime and never got anywhere. Sure, a few of them had made it in business by pulling themselves up by their own bootstraps for decades, but they were the exceptions.

There seemed no way for me to go, either. Since I had nothing to lose, I agreed to see Carmine. I vaguely remember seeing him as a young child, and I had heard the terms "il professore" and "il dottore" used occasionally, but I had never paid much attention. When I entered Carmine's office in Union City, I met a tall, fair-skinned man with blue eyes and a perfectly-tailored suit, the complete opposite of what most Sicilians from the old country looked like. He exuded confidence and authority. This was Dr. Carmine Sippo, friend of the family, professor, college dean and recipient of a double doctorate in business and education.

In addition to his position as dean at Wagner College on New York's Staten Island, Carmine operated a service for placing aspiring students into medical schools in the U.S. and abroad. He went through my school records, which showed I was an average student. He quickly saw that whatever career plans I had were naive and, from a series of incisive questions, he also saw that I had an anti-establishment attitude and a strong, entrepreneurial spirit. I needed to be my own boss. But I believe that what tipped the scales in my favor was my determination to succeed. Whatever it was, he decided that I had real poten-tial, and he was willing to back me.

Carmine recommended that I enter the field of podiatric medicine. Podia-try was then a young and still relatively unknown field. It was growing rapidly, and there was room to forge ahead and make a name for yourself. Carmine determined which courses I would need to complete before applying to medical school, and he laid out a program for me to take at Wagner College. I went into his office without a goal and left thinking that I, a troubled and confused kid with no connections, could be admitted to medical school and become a doctor. Carmine had that ability. Nor was his vision utopian. He had the knowledge and the contacts to open doors. What an opportunity! I didn't hesitate—I went for it.

For my interview at Wagner College, I was determined to make a good impression. Carmine had told me to cut my long hair before going, but I still had a spark of individuality, a disinclination to cave in to the system. A lot was at stake here, so I decided to compromise. I wouldn't flaunt my individuality, but I wouldn't cave in either. I wore a short-hair wig to the interview, and I was accepted!

I took a heavy load of difficult classes, because I was a man in a hurry. One class in particular, a summer school course in physics, was very tough. I was afraid I was going to fail. I studied like crazy, and near the end of the course, I pleaded with Professor Jensen to give me a passing grade. I told him I'd really worked hard at the course and needed to pass it in order to get into medical school. I offered to do anything he suggested to improve my grade.

With the compassion of a drill sergeant, he replied, "It's too bad. If you can't pass my course, maybe you don't belong in medical school."

I know you, I thought. *You're the same type as Mr. Maus, my eighth grade teacher, who told me I would never make it past high school. You are the ones who use your positions of power to knock down dreams. You are the ones that see the letter of the law and never the spirit.* I hated him at that moment; oh, how I hated him!

I got a D in the course, the only low grade I received. I had labored and studied like mad for the whole year, given up pleasure and fun to do it. *What a waste,* I thought. The system was stacked against me.

Carmine Sippo tried to reassure me. I was made of good stuff, he said, and one grade was not going to hold me up. He was like that. There was no room for pessimism or self-pity. And he was right. Through Carmine Sippo's good offices, and his confidence in me, this Italian-American street kid, former gang member and pot dealer, was accepted into the Illinois College of Podiatric Medicine.

Not many people are aware that teachers like Dr. Carmine Sippo exist, teachers who specialize in matching students to medical schools. Although many medical schools can choose from an overabundance of student applications, there are also many schools which, at times, need more students. A matchmaker in the best sense, Carmine didn't just look at grades, he looked at the whole person—the actual person and the potential person. His expertise and understanding totally changed my life, and I will always be thankful.

Carmine Sippo had a profound effect on my life. He appeared at a critical moment just when it seemed there was no hope. A phrase in the Old Testament says, "Remember to welcome strangers in your house. Some did and welcomed angels without knowing it."

Are there really guardian angels that drive events through the agency of human beings? If not, why do certain people have such an impact on others' lives, and what, if any, is the invisible force that guides them? Are we a part of a highly sophisticated communication network that is operated by our own subconscious selves?

"Meaningful arrangements" is a nice phrase. I think there are meaningful arrangements in our lives, and in my own life I have experienced enough spectacular coincidences to believe they were intended and planned. I don't know if ethereal guardian angels have been involved, but I do know that people have intervened in my life at critical times and with great beneficial effect. I call these persons "life guides." Although they are alive in the flesh, they, too, are guardian angels.

In the past, people seemed more aware of the guardians around them. Harriet Beecher Stowe was one when she wrote these lines in *Slavery—Busting Uncle Tom's Cabin:*

> Sweet souls around us watch us still,
> Press near to our side.
> Into our thoughts, into our prayers,
> With gentle helping glide.

CHAPTER 2

Joining the Revolution

What is the difference between "I want food" and "I want sex"? Consent.
—*Hugh Prather*

When I drove from Hoboken to Chicago to attend the Illinois College of Podiatric Medicine, I didn't know what to expect. I'd lived around crime and gangsters most of my life, but Chicago was the Big Time. I had seen so many gangster movies about Elliot Ness and Al Capone, I suppose I expected to see black cars careening around corners, guns blazing from the windows. Actually, it was a delightful city, fast-moving and filled with energy.

And here I was, an Italian street kid from Hoboken as a first-year medical student in Chicago, and doing pretty well at it. On the way, I'd almost drowned; I'd been stabbed; and I'd been saved from falling off a mountain top. A guardian angel was certainly watching over me. A special sort of guardian angel must watch over our sex lives, too, because during my first year at medical school I had another close call. In the telling, it sounds funny, but at the time I was scared out of my wits.

My roommate Phil was a pleasant, mild-mannered young man who worked part time at Cook County Hospital's Mental Health Center. He had an unusual friend, Crazy Jack Malone, who was also enrolled in the podiatry college even though everyone who knew him considered him a certifiable maniac. Crazy Jack was muscular, about six feet three inches tall, a better-looking version of the Incredible Hulk, with his hair styled in the manner of Elvis Presley. Jack could crush an average human with his bare hands and think nothing of it. He had a hair-trigger temper, and everyone who had to deal with him in any way was afraid of him. He frequently told his instructors to go fuck themselves and threatened to beat them up if they even hinted at giving him a failing grade. The school administrators did nothing to restrain Crazy Jack's behavior—they evidently feared for their lives more than they did the prospect of a sociopath becoming a doctor.

Now, Crazy Jack was married to a stunning beauty named Jasmine, the lead stripper at the Pink Panther Club in Chicago's Gold Coast district. Jasmine was a femme fatale, and her sexual teasing didn't stop when she was offstage. To goad Jack and create excitement, she would flirt with almost any man, although no one would dare risk sparking Crazy Jack's rage by responding. Not only did no one mess around with Jasmine, no one wanted to be anywhere near her. If Crazy Jack even imagined that a man was coming on to Jasmine, he was as good as pulp.

One Sunday morning, Jasmine called Phil on the telephone and started whispering seductively to him. This so terrified Phil that he began stuttering badly, and he handed the phone to me. Jasmine started telling me how she was all alone and wanted to come over to see us; she was going to come over to our place—she had to see us, she just *had* to see us. I was terrified, too, and told her not to come, but she said she was coming anyway and hung up.

A little while later, Jasmine knocked on our door and said that if we didn't let her in she would make a scene and tell Crazy Jack we had been mean to her. That was tantamount to a quick death, so we let her in.

Jasmine didn't waste any time. She went into her stripper routine, which was the sexiest thing I had ever seen. She had an exquisite figure that was soon covered only by her G-string. Phil was staring at her with his eyes full of both desire and fear. Then Jasmine moved close to me.

I didn't feel particularly brave. In fact, I was every bit as afraid as Phil. But throughout my first year at medical school I had taken my studies very seriously. That, plus working two part-time jobs, left little time for female companionship. When Jasmine's beautiful, near-nude body pressed against me, and when she kept asking me to embrace her, my hormones won out and I threw caution to the winds, Crazy Jack Malone or no Crazy Jack Malone.

Moments later, Jasmine pulled me into the kitchen and sat on the counter. She raised her legs, spread them apart and pulled me against her, pressing my face against her voluptuous breasts. It wasn't long before we were locked together in passionate, frenzied motion that didn't stop until a dramatic climax, with Jasmine laughing, moaning and screaming in turn.

Just then I noticed that Phil was staring at us from the kitchen doorway, open-mouthed, a look of disbelief on his face. A few seconds later, the phone rang. It was Crazy Jack, wanting to know where his wife was. Even if the sky had fallen, it could not have dampened my ardor more quickly. Crazy Jack Malone was coming—was on his way.

Jasmine swore that it would be our little secret. She promised she would never, never tell Jack, not even hint that we had done anything. We quickly scrambled into our clothes, and a few minutes later, Crazy Jack Malone was at the door, anger in his eyes, bellowing "What the fuck's going on here?" in a voice that could be heard a block away. He turned to Jasmine first, shouting insults at her and demanding to know why she had come and what had happened. Jasmine was angry too, but she knew she was safe—Crazy Jack always took his anger out on other men.

Jasmine, that paragon of secrecy and integrity, told Crazy Jack that we had made love in the kitchen, reveling in describing every last detail as she watched Jack boil. Then she grabbed her coat, cursed him, and screamed "Oh, I forgot to tell you, Jack. It was terrific with Dennis. He's much better at it than you are!" Then she ran out of the apartment.

Crazy Jack turned and looked at me. I knew I was a dead man if I didn't act quickly. I had grown up on the streets of Hoboken, and one thing I had learned was how to bluff when in a tight spot. That experience came to my rescue. I said, "Jack, Jack, c'mon. I wouldn't dare to even touch your wife. You'd tear me to pieces. Jasmine was drunk, and she forced her way in here. She isn't attracted to me; she really loves you. It's just that when she's been drinking, she likes excitement and wants to get you all worked up by concocting these wild stories."

Crazy Jack looked at me for a long time without speaking. I even managed a smile. He had been known to beat up people terribly on much less suspicion than this. I knew my fate was hanging in the balance and that Phil would not be able to save me. Crazy Jack clenched his muscles several times and just looked at me. Then, unexpectedly, he walked up to me and very quietly, very pointedly, said "Okay. Augustine, but if I ever find out otherwise, your ass is grass, understand?"

"Sure, Jack," I said, "no problem. Nothing happened, nothing for you to worry about."

I lived in fear for a while, expecting a sudden visit from Crazy Jack Malone, but it never came, and later Phil told me that Crazy Jack had made up with his wife and had forgotten all about the incident.

When Crazy Jack came into my apartment, Jasmine and I did not look innocent. Our clothes were rumpled and looked like they had been hurriedly put on—which they had been. Our faces were flushed and I was still breathing heavily. It would have been hard to miss, and I think Crazy Jack knew that I had made love with his wife.

Crazy Jack Malone was a man who struck first and asked questions later. It didn't bother him if he mistakenly sent the wrong person to the hospital. It wasn't like him to restrain himself. If he typically beat up others whom he only mildly disliked, what would he have done to me, and would I have survived? What caused this perennially jealous brute of a man to let me go? Once again, destiny or a benevolent God had intervened and saved me from a dangerous, potentially fatal event.

Oh, Jasmine, Jasmine, I still think of you from time to time, but not with desire—only with the memory of my fear. And Crazy Jack, I hope among your various pastimes, you never chance to read this story.

The meeting of preparation with opportunity generates the offspring we call luck.

—*Anthony Robbins*

During my second year in the Windy City, I enjoyed a streak of fortunate "coincidences." I was able to find an apartment very close to the podiatric college even though the housing situation was very tight. Then, almost next door to my apartment was an A & P supermarket. Back in New Jersey, I had temporarily worked for A & P and I still had my Retail Clerks Union card. It turned out that they did need some extra part time help, and, because of my previous experience with A & P, I was hired at a higher-than-customary wage. And then one day at work, while I was stocking shelves, a dapper black gentleman who looked to be in his sixties, asked me for assistance.

A hundred other people had asked me for assistance in the A & P and then had gone about their way. But this man, for some reason, asked me if I was going to school. I told him I was a student at the nearby podiatric college. He then handed me his business card, from which I learned that Dr. Milo Turnbo was a podiatrist who had been practicing just around the corner from the A & P for thirty-five years. We became good friends, and I visited him from time to time, taking advantage of the opportunity to observe and learn more about my new profession. What good fortune it was to meet a practicing podiatrist and to be able to learn from him to augment my studies.

Back in Hoboken, Dr. Carmine Sippo had destroyed my stereotypes about Sicilians by proving to be articulate and successful. Now Milo was doing the same for my stereotypes of blacks. I'd thought I was free of ethnic prejudices, but then why was I surprised to meet a black man who was educated, successful and gracious?

Milo loved good bourbon, and he would often arrive at the A & P well-lubricated but with perfect manners. There was a glow of youthfulness and vigor about him, even though he must have been in his mid-sixties. When he saw me, he would come right up to me as though meeting me was the highlight of his day. "Dennis," he would say, "how good it is to see you again." His smile was infectious—he was one of those persons with whom it is simply impossible to be sad. Everyone liked Milo. We talked about everything from his medical practice to the price of canned goods, and this sophisticated, white-haired gentleman made me feel like I was his equal, that I was on a par with him.

At the time, I believed that I was creating opportunities for myself by sheer power of will. That it was my determination and my shrewdness that was the catalyst for my successes. Have you ever had a stalled car and been pushed by another car behind you? You feel your car accelerate and, unless you know better, you might think it was your own engine speeding you onward. In reality, the power comes from another source. That's what was happening. I was being pushed by another power source, and I sat there, holding onto the steering wheel, steering a course, secure in the belief that I was the means of locomotion.

Nevertheless, I did considerable pushing on my own. I knew that many of the other students were sons and daughters of podiatrists. All they had to do was get through medical school and there would be a practice waiting for them. Others came from wealthy families, who would set them up in practice. I decided that in order to get what I wanted, I would have to study harder and make more sacrifices than everyone else. And I did. I supported myself by working two jobs in addition to continuing my studies. In addition to the A & P job, I worked as the night admissions clerk at the McKesson Emergency Industrial Clinic on Chicago's south side, where I was once again confronted with the seedier side of life I had left behind. The neighborhood was an urban war zone, and the customers were drug addicts and victims of stabbings, gunshot wounds, concussions and abrasions. Several of them looked capable of inflicting some of these on me as well. At night, when the buzzer sounded, I would look through a plate glass door to see who our next customer was. Some of them looked so potentially violent or acted so erratically that I wanted to shout, "Go away!" I couldn't do that, but there were many nights when I was glad to get through my shift in one piece.

My life was one of deliberate self-denial. I rarely ate, and my weight fell until I looked emaciated. There was little time for socializing, especially with women (other than a few one night stands). The A & P was in a well-to-do neighborhood; how many sophisticated young women in that exclusive area were going to be attracted to someone in a red A & P apron? No matter. I needed to teach myself discipline. I had spent my youth indulging in fun times. Now life was serious business. I had an agenda, a mission, and I was going to get through medical school. I realized that part of me was still the kid from the streets of Hoboken; I couldn't, just couldn't screw up this opportunity.

Hitch your wagon to a star

—Ralph Waldo Emerson

Leonardo Da Vinci once described the human foot as a masterpiece of engineering. Where the chiropodists of earlier days were limited to trimming corns and bunions, at medical school we were gaining an arsenal of information, including biomechanics. A modern podiatrist could not only diagnose the cause of foot abnormalities and determine corrective measures, he could also predict in advance what deformities an individual was prone to develop.

The third and fourth years of medical school were busy and exciting times. I was chosen for a four-month externship (like an internship, but rotating at clinics outside of the teaching facility) by three prominent podiatric surgeons on staff at Northlake Community Hospital. Two of my classmates and I not only got to see patients in a private practice setting but we had the unusual assignment of consulting with and operating on prison inmates at Statesville Prison in Joliet. This was a sobering experience. I can still remember the prison bars being slammed shut and locked behind us as we proceeded down a long corridor, accompanied by a guard to the prison's medical clinic.

My first surprise was how easy the inmates were to work with and how cordial most of them were. Having no place else to go, they relished the opportunity to talk to someone—anyone—from the outside.

Working at Statesville probably affected me more than my fellow doctors-in-training—Mike Di Carlo and John Dinkins. Mike grew up in Middle America, while John, the son of a surgeon, grew up safe and secure in a Chicago suburb. I, on the other hand, had lived in the turbulent, inner city of Hoboken. It wasn't farfetched to imagine that, given a few bad breaks, I could have spent time behind bars.

Statesville prison brought back memories of my marijuana dealing days during the late 60s. What if I had chosen the low road—a life of crime? What if my friends and acquaintances had ratted on me to save their own necks? After all, they had the connections at City Hall, their fathers were police officers, not mine.

Perhaps it was my own teenage flirtation with crime that allowed me to relate so well to the inmates. At least I understood them. The sad thing is that even if they wanted to change, the system wouldn't allow them that luxury. Once labeled an ex-con, they were marked for life. It would take an extraordinarily strong person to overcome this dilemma.

Some of the inmates were just plain old rogues. They had no desire to redeem themselves or change their lives. I remember hearing about how the notorious Sonny Jackson had robbed a jewelry store. We were working in the prison clinic when a special report aired on the local radio while the robbery was in progress. Sonny was a crazed stick-up man who somehow managed to escape the maximum security prison. An hour after we heard the report, he was returned to the prison hospital, his body riddled with bullet holes like a slice of Swiss cheese.

I saw him lying on a stretcher, dripping blood and moaning in pain while in a state of delirium. It brought up visions of the old James Cagney and Edward G. Robinson movies, not to mention the real-life gangland slayings that had occurred in Hoboken. It was a scene I'll never forget.

When we saw patients, they were usually restricted to a guarded waiting room. One day, while looking for a patient, I inadvertently found myself alone with the prisoners in an unguarded room. Then the door closed shut behind me. Panic. I was alone in a room of hardened criminals. *What if I'm taken hostage?* Would I fight back? Could I do to them whatever it took in order to save myself? Or was it better to finesse it, to talk my way out of whatever developed?

Nothing bad happened, but I breathed a sigh of relief when I emerged from that room.

The orderlies at Statesville, as in other prisons, had special privileges because of their model prisoner status. How a former ax murderer becomes a model prisoner was too spooky to think about. But, presuming that anyone can change if he wants to badly enough, I tried to withhold judgment.

Nevertheless, many of the orderlies behaved more like adolescents than grown men. One day, a prisoner named Jud Williamson filled a syringe full of water and squirted his fellow inmates. Jud, and all the other orderlies, were dressed in white medical uniforms. It was like a scene from *One Flew Over the Cuckoo's Nest*. There was Jud, right beside me, taunting and joking with his buddy, Big Al Rhodes who stood across the table from us.

Al drew some water in his syringe and attempted, for the third time, to squirt Jud in retaliation. Just then, a fluke happened. From the pressure, the needle somehow flew off Al's syringe and landed, a perfect bull's-eye, into the pupil of Jud's right eyeball. I had never seen anything like it. The odds were probably a million to one against such a thing happening.

When the needle hit him, Jud let out a bone-chilling scream that ran right up my spine. He jostled about in what looked like an epileptic seizure and was able to pluck the needle from his eye. We bandaged him temporarily until a general physician could be called in.

Adolescent behavior was common, but one of the things I remember most about Statesville was the pecking order among the prisoners. One hears accounts of VIP prisoners who receive special treatment. Carlo Barzini was one such fellow. Carlo was a reputed underworld figure who was serving five to ten for grand larceny. He was the only one among the prisoner-patients who wore a dapper robe, and he was escorted around the clinic in a wheelchair like some medieval potentate. Considering the fact that Carlo was in no way disabled, this demonstrated the respect—albeit out of fear—with which he was treated.

Carlo and I got along extremely well. He always referred to me as one of his *paisani*, an affectionate Italian term for a countryman or kindred friend. We chatted about Hoboken, New York, Italian cuisine and, as to be expected, about unions and rackets. When my externship period ended, Carlo's closing statement to me was right out of Hollywood.

"Augustine, you set your practice up in Melrose Park and I'll take good care a ya."

"Thanks, Carlo, I'll remember that."

All my life I had looked in awe at guys like Carlo. Interacting with them at Statesville Prison was like joining large carnivores behind the bars at a zoo. They had a brute charisma, a sense of power in their bearing, and I realized that I had always wondered what it would be like to live in their world, where decency and virtue is crushed and aggression and violence is rewarded.

When I left Statesville Prison after completing my externship, I realized that being inside a prison had given me a tantalizing view of the darker side of myself. But, while I acknowledged that darker side, it did not have to direct me. I continued to be fascinated by organized crime figures. but the books that had once been my staple reading no longer held my interest.

I had made it out of the streets, I was in hot pursuit of a profession, and, unlike the prisoners at Statesville who were serving ten years to life, come June I would be a free man.

During this period, a series of fortuitous events occurred, one after the other. Through my chance meeting with Dr. Milo Turnbo, I was given the opportunity to observe firsthand how a practicing podiatrist functions. Then, thanks to Milo, who coaxed me into attending a student party, I met a wonderful, pretty woman named Cecile. Through Cecile I came to know her cousin Victor, a practicing podiatrist in Chicago. And through this chain of circumstances, I was introduced to Dr. Jay Seymour.

Dr. Seymour was the image of a self-made man. He wore an impeccably tailored suit, a silk shirt, and a custom-made gold bracelet with a matching bracelet-watch. He had neatly manicured nails and perfectly-groomed hair, beard and mustache. His manner was playful, with a devilish grin and an infectious laugh. At the same time, he was a caring physician, going to lengths to greet his patients warmly and personally.

Men felt at home with him and women adored his style and grace. When I first walked into Dr. Seymour's office, I was struck by the Oriental decor and dim lights. It was like walking into someone's private den. This was Seymour's inner sanctum, and I was star-struck. I felt privileged to be there. His office was comfortably furnished with soft leather couches and sitting chairs, a coffee table made of rich Brazilian wood, exotic oriental lamps, sculptures, artifacts, and an ornate Chinese desk which was more for show than for use. No expense had been spared.

Jay preferred sitting on his plush, soft leather couch. This is where deals (real estate investment trusts, investment in ski chalets, nursing home deals, securities transactions, banks and other tax shelters) were struck between patient schedules. Jay enjoyed his work and his pioneering flare every bit as much as he did the wealth and privileged status it brought him. Patients never seemed to mind. They were as attracted to him as I was.

Dr. Seymour was at the time a prominent albeit controversial podiatrist, one of the pioneers of minimal-incision foot surgery, or MIS, as it is called. Hundreds of practitioners came from all over the country to observe Dr. Seymour's revolutionary procedures.

Traditional podiatry had come a long way. Dysfunctional feet could now be corrected and patients could walk normally again, but to do this, traditional surgical procedures were followed: a general anesthetic and IV hookup were required, large incisions were made, bones reset and reshaped, and steel supporting pins were often inserted to keep them in place. With general anesthesia, an anesthesiologist must be present in addition to surgical assistants, and there is always a danger of complications, even fatal complications. Lengthy stitches were required to sew everything up again. For the patient, foot disorders frequently meant severe pain, expensive hospital stays and prolonged periods of recovery during which the patient could not work.

Dr. Seymour's methods were in stark contrast. I recall the first time I observed him. A fifty-six-year-old lady, Wanda Rutledge, limped into his office, supported by her husband. She was obviously in pain and was no longer able to work as a hostess in a local restaurant. Mrs. Rutledge had a large callus on the bottom of her right foot, and years of trimming it with a razor and wearing store-bought pads no longer helped.

X-rays showed that one of the metatarsal bones had dropped below its normal position and was creating friction and pressure on the tissue beneath it. "The callus," Dr. Seymour said, pointing to Mrs. Rutledge's foot X-ray, "is nature's warning signal and has developed in response to this pressure. Once the bone is repositioned, the callus will gradually disappear by itself and normal, pain-free walking should be restored. However, as I tell all my patients, there are no guarantees."

"I understand, Dr. Seymour, do the best you can. This thing is killing me."

The woman was seated comfortably when Dr. Seymour took Mrs. Rutledge's hand in his, gently reassured her once again, and began the procedure. The operating room looked like a comfortable dentist's office, with a tray of miniature surgical instruments, the like of which I'd never seen before. Nitrous oxide was given to relax the patient, and a local anesthetic was carefully administered. Then a tiny incision, less than $\frac{1}{8}$ inch, was made on the top of the foot. Blood flowed freely from the incision, no tourniquet was applied, and no attempt was made to stop it. (I later learned that this was deliberate; the blood flow acted as a natural form of irrigation to constantly cleanse the interior and wash away debris.)

Using his delicate instruments, Dr. Seymour quickly and expertly began to alter the supporting tissue around the bone. During the procedure, he chatted lightly with the woman and asked, "Do you feel any discomfort now?" I was amazed when she said, "I can't believe it, doctor, I don't feel a thing."

I could hardly believe what I was seeing! By this time, I had performed a fair number of surgeries myself, following standard procedure each time. This meant raising the affected leg and applying a tourniquet to stop blood flow into the foot. Then I would cut open the foot, tie off any bleeders, retract the vital nerve, muscle tissue and skin edges off to each side so that the bone was clearly exposed. When cutting bone, I would use what amounted to a miniature chain saw. The surgical procedure required an operating room team and usually took about forty-five minutes plus surgery preparation time and several hours of post-surgical recovery.

Watching Dr. Seymour was like watching an artist at work. He was so familiar with the anatomical landmarks of the foot and so adept with his hands that he was able to change the abnormal alignment of the metatarsal bone by manipulating his instruments through a tiny opening—without actually seeing the inside of the foot he was working on. It was like watching a master craftsman construct a miniature sailing ship inside a bottle, except that in this case the bottle was opaque—the craftsman could not see what he was doing; he had to feel it!

I timed the procedure and stared at my watch in disbelief. From the time of the incision to the time it was closed with a single stitch took slightly less than five minutes! Then Mrs. Rutledge's foot was carefully bound in such a way that the binding supported the new position of the bone—no pins or other devices were needed inside the foot. Once again, Dr. Seymour inquired if there was pain or other discomfort and Mrs. Rutledge replied that she felt fine.

An hour after she had entered Dr. Seymour's office (most of which was taken in filling out forms), she walked out, unassisted by her husband and on her own two feet. I was absolutely stupefied! What I had just seen negated almost everything I had learned about surgery in the last three years. The whole procedure had been so efficient, so matter-of-fact, that it was over almost before I could grasp what had happened.

The contrast between a hospital surgery and Dr. Seymour's office was equally amazing to me. In a hospital, formal and elaborate procedures were carefully followed, and the atmosphere was formal and tense. In contrast, Dr. Seymour's office was comfortable, casual and filled with warm, smiling faces. The lack of discomfort from the procedures and the immediacy of the positive results definitely lifted the spirits of the patients and the staff. Dr. Seymour enhanced this mood by his light and conversational manner. He made each patient feel a guest in his home, someone to be treated with affection and respect. It was also obvious from the way that they beamed at him that his patients were in awe of his skills.

I observed several more surgical procedures that day with similar results. Dr. Seymour was not only a skilled surgeon, he was a superb showman. He knew the mysterious effect his procedures had on those practitioners who had never seen them, and he also knew that his studied casual air enhanced the effect.

"I bet they don't teach you anything like this at podiatry college," he said with the confident air of someone who had discovered the fountain of youth.

"I've never seen anything like it!" I said, "It's absolutely revolutionary."

"This is the wave of the future, Dennis, and how podiatry should be practiced."

In between procedures, he would sit in his plush office, discussing investments and business deals on the telephone. With his nurses preparing patients, Dr. Seymour performed three to four surgical procedures per hour. In a single day, he completed as many procedures as traditional podiatric surgeons were able to do in three months.

Word had spread within the professional community about Dr. Seymour's innovative procedures, and podiatrists from many different regions arrived in his offices to observe and learn minimal incision techniques. Many of these doctors would interrupt Dr. Seymour with questions at critical moments— "Why are you doing it that way…?" When I was observing, I tried my best to be helpful and to keep quiet except at appropriate times. I wasn't about to blow a once-in-a-lifetime opportunity.

Apparently, I was successful, and my sincere desire to learn came through, for a wonderful mentor-protégé relationship developed between us. I was given the extraordinary opportunity to participate in state-of-the-art medical techniques that not even my professors knew much about, and to learn from one of the foremost practitioners of this new art.

Over a two-year period of working with Dr. Seymour while I was still in medical school, I learned just about every aspect of running an innovative and hugely successful podiatric surgical practice, leapfrogging over the years that it normally takes to gain such proficiency. It meant that I, too, would become part of a pioneering medical fraternity, which was what I so desperately wanted. Dr. Seymour was providing a wonderful service to people at a much lower cost to them, and he was quickly growing rich in the process. That seemed to me an ideal combination, and I resolved to become a part of the podiatric revolution.

The events that led me here were magical. Some people insist that fortunate events are simply a lucky draw, and that for every individual like me there are a hundred less lucky and less fortunate. Others attempt to identify the process behind events as due to a positive mental attitude, visual imagery, etc., that stimulate the individual to bring about his or her own good fortune.

I prefer to think we are all life guides to each other. Cecile's cousin, Dr. Victor Conway, did me the immense favor of setting up a meeting with Dr. Seymour. I, in turn, was able to engage Dr. Conway in philosophical discussions, which he dearly loved. We were good for each other. Meeting Dr. Seymour was a wonderful opportunity for me, but he needed a protégé to teach and to help spread word of his techniques every bit as much as I needed a mentor.

Are these opportunities always the right ones? If not, how do we know which ones to act on and which to ignore? My single-minded drive to be something in the world, to gain monetary and professional success at all costs, did not allow for such speculation. Anything that furthered these goals was right, and anything that hindered them was wrong.

And, in following the lead of Jay Seymour, and associating myself with the nonconventional procedures of minimal incision surgery, I was setting myself up as a revolutionary, with all the promise, the uncertainty and the agony that accompanies all revolutions.

CHAPTER 3

Defining the Mountain

Here was a living energy that called out to me, "Here is your chance."

I had long felt the lure of California. California! What visions the name conjures: land of golden sun, beauty, opportunity and riches! An American who traveled extensively got into a conversation in England one day with a woman from London. He waxed eloquent about the awesome English cathedrals so steeped in history, the magnificent old colleges, and the thatched roofs and gardens of the English countryside. When he had finished his eulogy, he asked, "Aren't you content to spend the rest of your life here?" She cut him short with, "What are you talking about? Everyone in their right mind wants to live in California!"

During Christmas break of my fourth year in medical school, Cecile and I decided to visit California. We arrived in San Diego, crossed into Mexico, and then drove up to central California through the coastal towns of Morro Bay and San Luis Obispo. It was magnificent! Lush landscapes, incredible, towering trees and a wide, colorful assortment of flowers. Hundreds of miles of picturesque ocean views and soaring, sculptured cliffs. The sheer size, the scope of it was incredible! In the flatlands of New Jersey or Chicago, even out in the country, the vistas were limited. Along the California coast, space came alive with enormous hills, receding one after another into the distance. Steep, shadowed canyons studded with giant oak trees flowed downward to vast stretches of sandy beach as far as the eye could see. Here, beaches were not mere flat stretches of sand—each beach was different, with individual varieties

34

of rocks, cliffs, dunes, rivers and pounding surf. The coast seemed limitless; you could walk all day and not come to the end of the beach. Driving across the Golden Gate Bridge and meandering up and down the hills of San Francisco, I understood for the first time what Tony Bennett meant when he sang, "I left my heart in San Francisco."

It's hard to explain California to someone who has never been there. So much is wrong with it: the crowding, the droughts, the earthquakes, the endless, tasteless land development. But I recognized a quality that I had not been aware of since I was a boy in Roccalumera, Sicily. It was as though all nature—the land, the air, the sea and sky—was not something to endure and protect yourself against, but something to be part of, to enjoy, to revel in.

More than clean air, warm sun and sheer beauty was an incredible freedom, a sense that everything was possible. In California I found an energy, not tension but a laid-back, comfortable vitality that was almost tangible. It beckoned, urged you onward and proclaimed, "Here is your chance! Whatever you want to do, here is where you can do it!"

During my four years of medical school in Chicago, by working at part time jobs and living a Spartan life, I managed to save up enough money, I hoped, to start my practice. A few months after our trip, I returned to California and put a down payment on a lovely old ranch house in San Jose that could be converted into an office. After fours years of intense learning, of holding down two part-time jobs, eating barely enough to sustain myself, and denying myself almost every pleasure normal to a young man, I was Dennis Augustine, doctor of podiatric medicine. I had the pleasure and honor of having my mentor, Dr. Seymour, bestow upon me the certificate granting me the right to practice medicine. It should also have been a time to celebrate, to give credit to my accomplishment, and to pause and reflect on how far I had come. But I had no time for that, having completed only one more necessary step on the road to success. Whatever that success was to be, I was certain it would occur in California.

Whenever the notion of starting a medical practice cold is mentioned, it sends shivers up the spines of newly-established doctors.

Park Avenue in San Jose, California is a lovely boulevard, lined with large and majestic maple trees. Lush, manicured gardens separate the old Spanish and Victorian style houses from the road. In the heart of a thriving metropolis, it is a throwback to a more elegant, slower-paced era. This is where, after much work and bureaucratic frustration, we changed our modest ranch house into a podiatric treatment center. I disliked the modern, stark white medical buildings that were cropping up everywhere. Like Dr. Seymour's practice in Chicago, I wanted an office where my patients could feel at home without an imposing clinical veneer. I wanted them to feel they were visiting a friend as well as a doctor.

Most new physicians associate themselves with existing medical groups or form partnerships because of the difficulty in starting a new practice for themselves. Those who can afford it may purchase an established practice, but starting from scratch gives pause to even the most courageous doctors.

Self-sufficient, I was up for the challenge. I wanted to start out boldly with my own office and my own patients. Besides, it's common knowledge that to purchase another doctor's practice means to lose between one-third and one-half of the existing patients, who are unwilling to be treated by the new doctor in town. Mainly, however, existing podiatric practices were traditional, and patients were expected to come back every few months for the rest of their lives to have their corns and calluses trimmed. I didn't want to keep foot problems in check; I wanted to correct them. I wanted to specialize in minimal incision foot surgery. By doing this, I would be competing for patients with all the traditional podiatrists and podiatric surgeons in the area.

In life, one person's loss is frequently another person's gain, and the gains kept coming my way. A local podiatrist became disabled and began referring his patients to my office, an enormous piece of good fortune that enabled me to get a running start. My first surgery was on Mercedes Gottlieb, an elderly, obese lady with diabetes. I had performed many surgical procedures in my last year of medical school and during my externship at the Statesville Prison Medical Facility. However, Mrs. Gottlieb was the very first on my own, without another surgeon in attendance.

Diabetes can cause complications in foot surgery, but tests showed that Mrs. Gottlieb's circulation and glucose levels were normal. She had a painful corn on the tip of the third toe on her right foot. Through a tiny incision, I performed a routine bone spur removal.

I still remember the way Mrs. Gottlieb, a pleasant, accommodating woman told me about her problem. "You know, dokteh, ven yur feet hoyt, you hoyt all over," she said. "Bat, vat ah yuh gunna do?"

Although this was a rhetorical question, I told Mrs. Gottlieb precisely what I was going to do.

"Vatever you say, dollink, yur da dokteh."

I had observed Dr. Seymour perform so many similar procedures in Chicago that I could have done it with my eyes closed—which is essentially what I did, since I could not see the bone spur I was correcting. Within minutes, I completed the procedure without incident.

"How are you doing, Mrs. Gottlieb?" I asked.

"I'm fine, dokteh, haf you stotted yet?"

"Actually, I'm all finished."

"Oh, Got bless you, I deedn't feel a ting."

But a few days later, when she came into the clinic, the tip of Mrs. Gottlieb's toe had turned black. "So vattya tryink to do, dokteh, toyn me into a schwartze?" she said playfully.

Like many people of her generation, Mrs. Gottlieb wore her prejudices comfortably.

"It appears you have a hematoma, which is a little pooling of blood in the area. We'll keep a close eye on it," I said warmly, but something wasn't adding up. Soaking it, as well as other noninvasive procedures, did nothing to solve the problem. There was no infection; her pulses were normal; she had no pain; skin temperature was normal; what could it be? I was dismayed—would I have to call on another surgeon to get me out of a jam on my first procedure? *No,* I told myself. *You're a trained podiatric surgeon—use your training!*

A close examination revealed the answer. I pressed against the bottom of her foot, simulating a walking step, and the third toe contracted, pointing downward. An overly tight ligament and tendon were causing the hematoma by traumatizing the tip of the toe with each step Mrs. Gottlieb took. The painful corn, and the bone spur that created it, had masked a secondary condition that was brought to light only by the initial corrective surgery. A five-minute procedure corrected the ligament and tendon, and within a week, her toe had returned to normal color.

"Dokteh, you deed a vunderful chob. I can vair all my shuz now vit no prablum."

My worst fear had been that her hematoma might have developed into gangrene, a possibility made more likely by her diabetes. If I had not discovered the problem quickly, there was a possibility she might have lost a toe, or even a foot.

"…a vunderful chob," she told me.

It was dramatic, wrought with the same potential disaster as a thrilling movie, but with a basic difference: I did not reveal the drama. Mrs. Gottlieb's condition was corrected without burdening her with anxiety. I hid my own anxiety, confronted an unusual situation and passed a critical test without someone looking over my shoulder. I was now responsible for my own actions, and I assumed the responsibility proudly.

It was important for me to earn a living. It was important to stand on my own two feet yesterday—not tomorrow.

—Hal David

Money from my practice started coming in much sooner than I'd anticipated, much sooner than anyone had predicted. I'd long ago started reading every book I could find on how to get rich. I read about the lives of Conrad Hilton, J. Paul Getty, Aristotle Onassis, John D. Rockefeller and scores of other notables to see how they got their wealth. I read books by George Bockl, John Allen, Edward Rybka, Joseph Schwartz, Tyler Hicks, William Nickerson, Al Lowry and many others that promised riches through the magic of real estate investing. And I read countless inspirational books on gaining self-confidence. If they could do it, I could do it. Before I turned twenty, I began boasting to my friends that I was going to be a millionaire.

In accordance with the advice to think big, I'd convinced my parents to co-sign for a $5000 bank loan, and we borrowed another $2800 from the family life insurance policies. Together with some poker winnings, I had enough for a modest down payment, and in December of 1970, at the age of twenty, I'd bought a ten-unit apartment building in Jersey City. I did not know it at the time, but I was using "creative financing." Boy, was I proud!

I was a kid who had gotten into trouble several times, a kid with no experience, a kid who was asking his parents to trust him with their savings. I wanted so badly to prove myself to them. I've heard psychologists say that many successful people have succeeded because of a neurotic urge. That was me, but my urge began to give me direction, and almost anything was better than remaining a nonstarter in Hoboken.

It wasn't as easy as the books made it sound. It took lots of hard work and the willingness and fortitude to deal with vindictive tenants and corrupt city inspectors. I kept the property for fifteen years, and the cash flow helped finance my education, but I couldn't have gotten by without dealing marijuana.

Ethics never entered into my decision to deal pot, although at the time pot was not considered harmful. I did what I thought I had to do in order to survive.

As a typical teenager, I was a walking contradiction. On one hand, I was starting to get serious about getting ahead in life. On the other hand, I was exposing myself (and my parents, since I stashed my pot at home) to the risk of getting busted and having a permanent police record. I was addicted to dealing. I wanted to stop, but the money was too good and I was on a winning streak. I rationalized my dealing by telling myself that I would be able to pay for my own education, and not be a burden to my parents.

By chance or fate, I never got caught dealing. What a difference that would have made! Some of my friends did get caught, and their first serious brush with the law created a momentum that brought them into ever more serious conflict with society and its rules. One day, I suddenly realized that I, too, was racing towards a dead end. I have no idea where this realization came from or what prompted it. All of a sudden, it was there, and I couldn't squirm away from it. I had to stop dealing. Not later, but right away. And I did. All at once, and forever.

While attending college, I made money playing poker and made sense of things by taking LSD and peyote. Under the influence of drugs, I felt connected to all things. I dropped tabs of acid on weekends as routinely as I took holy communion wafers as a parochial school student. If it was good enough for Timothy Leary, I reasoned, it was good enough for me. I'd met the controversial professor once at Newark Airport during school break. He autographed a yellow piece of paper which read "LSD melts in your mind, not in your hands," below which he wrote, "Stay High. Love God." Whatever shards of allegiance to my birth faith remained were completely severed by my experiences with hallucinogens, and the slogans of the pied piper and high priest of psychedelia supplanted the monotonous promises of redemption and salvation offered by parish priests. Having a direct experience with a powerful, creative force, I felt I'd gotten as close to heaven as possible, and I turned my attention to money-making schemes.

Years later, with my podiatric practice nicely underway, my entrepreneurial spirit still yearned for quick success. Even though my practice was starting to bring in a significant income, it wasn't enough. I had a heavy debt load from buying the equipment I needed and from paying off my medical school loans. I wanted to pay them off quickly. Maybe that's why I got into commodities trading. At any rate, I was in the market, the proud but temporary owner of gold, silver, corn, wheat and pork bellies. You've probably heard stories like this before—mine went something like this:

"Why are commodities such an attractive investment?" I asked my broker.

"Because of the leverage. You can control $100,000 worth of goods for only $10,000. If the price goes up 10%, you've just made $10,000 and doubled your money."

"Sure, but can't you lose it just as fast?"

"Not really," he told me, "because there are safeguards built into the system. If the price drops more than a certain small amount, trading stops until the price stabilizes."

I was hooked. In addition to wanting to pay off my debts, much of my motivation was simple greed. So I invested. The trouble began with gold, whose price at the time was very volatile. Political turmoil in Zaire, which might affect the economy, might also affect the number of workers in Botswana, which in turn might result in an increase of mine workers in South Africa, could possibly lead to increased gold production and lower prices. On such heady information do commodity prices rise and fall.

Anyway, the price of gold suddenly went down. And, just as my broker had told me, trading on gold stopped for the day. I had a sell-short order placed on my gold. That is, if the price dropped below a certain level, my gold would automatically be sold, limiting my loss, or so I believed. But when the price actually dropped, there were thousands of sell-short orders ahead of mine waiting to be executed. When the first wave of gold was sold from these other automatic sell-short orders, the price dropped again, and, once again, trading was halted.

I watched the price drop day after day. My investment dwindled, and I wasn't able to sell. I had bought the gold on margin for 10% of its full value. When its value dropped and the margin call came, I had to come up with additional funds or sell the gold at the current price. Like most other naive commodities investors, I didn't have the extra cash to put up more margin, and I was forced to sell my gold at a great loss. Experienced traders were waiting to buy at a low price—they could afford to wait until the price rose again.

To recoup my losses, my broker suggested that I get into wheat, corn, soybeans and pork bellies, which I did—blindly. I didn't know, at the time, that my broker was "churning" my account—buying and selling so he could make commissions, while my funds dwindled. I wound up losing more than $10,000. I did everything wrong: I chose a broker on someone else's recommendation—I didn't know anything about him myself; I bought on the broker's recommendation—I didn't know anything about commodities trading; I used money I could not afford to lose; and, worst of all, I convinced Cecile to cash in her portfolio of blue chip stocks in order to increase my available funds, and I lost her money as well.

My ego took a real beating. I felt like an absolute fool. I had dragged Cecile into this blunder because of my greed and impatience. For once and for all, I had to learn that I was no longer a kid playing poker on the streets of Hoboken. I needed to learn patience, to invest wisely, and not to risk what we could not afford to lose. It was a good lesson.

A soulmate is someone who has locks that fit our keys, and keys to fit our locks. When we feel safe enough to open the locks, our truest selves step out and we can be completely and honestly who we are; we can be loved for who we are and not for who we are pretending to be.

—*Richard Bach*

I made a fool of myself more than once with women. The first time I proposed to Cecile, I got cold feet and backed out. Although I disappointed her, it was a private matter, between us. But it was different when I proposed to her a second time. As soon as Cecile told her family, her mother began to plan a huge, traditional Jewish wedding. I had just finished reading *The Art of Selfishness* by David Seabury and *How I Found Freedom in an Unfree World* by Harry Browne. Marriage was one of the many traps the authors identified, and in spite of my love for Cecile, all my fears came to the fore. This was it—the end of my dreams, an anchor around my legs. Once again, I backed out, feeling like an ass about the whole thing, and once again Cecile stood by my side, putting up with all my fears and quirks, all the while remaining my loyal friend and lover.

In March of 1977, I proposed to Cecile a third time. We were in Reno, having driven from the San Francisco Bay Area up through the foothills of the Sierra Nevada, over the high passes and down into the Nevada desert. The department of Reno City Hall reserved for civil weddings had been designed by someone able to combine ugliness and discomfort with bland colors. Several couples were waiting, and others kept coming and going. It was like being on an assembly line—impersonal and efficient. A sign said, "take a number." We took a number and waited our turn. The man next to me asked, "Is this your first?" I nodded, and he chuckled, "This's my fifth." That was the extent of our conversation, but it was enough to frighten me even more than I already was.

When our number was called, we found ourselves facing an indifferent justice of the peace with an equally indifferent deputy at his side as witness.

Side by side, we faced them. I looked at my lovely bride-to-be and thought, "What in hell am I doing here?" I was about to swear my life away to a woman who would steal away my freedom and drag down my career, my years of determination and sacrifice. *Say something, Dennis,* I thought. *Get out of this. Now, while there's still time.* My mouth opened, but I couldn't speak. After so much pulling back, after so much irresolution, after so many flip-flops, I had finally agreed to be married. Could I now, once again, say no to the woman I loved and who loved and had done so much for me? *Hurry, Dennis,* I thought, *it's now or never, for God's sake! There is more at stake here than pride and compassion!*

My pattern with women for a long time had been to enjoy love and companionship, avoid commitment and keep success as priority number one. Was it really my determination to succeed or did it go back farther than that? When I was fourteen, I had a girlfriend named Terry O'Brien. She had long blonde hair and pretty blue eyes that promised pure love. I had opened my heart to her without reservation, given all I had to give, and she had rejected me. How could that be? I had the curious belief, so common among the lovelorn, that those you love with all your heart are obligated to love you back. But Terry didn't, and, oh God, how it hurt.

It's funny how the mind doesn't dwell on the beauty of a former relationship, only on the sorrow of parting, as though parting were the only thing worth remembering. And I was dwelling on it. I felt like my insides were being twisted and squeezed, that the hurt was trying to invade and overcome me. I couldn't stand it.

It's hard enough to deal with at any age, but a fourteen-year-old can't just write it off as "something that happened." There had to be a reason. Someone had to be held responsible. It was Terry's mother, who had never liked me. It was a cruel and unfair "fate" that had deliberately targeted me. It was my own failure: I wasn't good enough, manly enough, competitive enough to keep her.

I hated being alive. My insides churned with pain. My mother had a collection of pills in her medicine cabinet. I took several out and watched myself in the bathroom mirror as swallow them. I waited to die. It was a long wait. There were no sedatives in the handful of pills I had taken, and the only effect was an upset stomach. Nevertheless, I felt that by my symbolic deed of daring, by my attempt to reject life, I had purged myself, had sufficiently punished myself for failing with Terry.

I vowed never again to trust a relationship with a woman. Over the years, I'd had brief affairs with various women, but the issue of total trust and commitment had never come up until I met Cecile in Chicago.

I had been invited to a party. Typically, I declined parties, and on this Friday evening I was exhausted after a full day of medical school, followed by five hours of wrapping and weighing produce. But I had met Dr. Milo Turnbo while I was working at the A & P, and he encouraged me to go.

"All work and no play..." Milo had said, giving me his sparkling smile. Something about his suggestion played on my mind, and I decided to pay a brief courtesy call and then leave. But after I arrived, I met a young woman who had come to the party with a blind date. Her date was off somewhere and she was alone, and we began to talk. My impression of Cecile was that here was someone special. She had a warm, friendly manner, a lovely face and an attractive figure. But what really caught my attention was the way she talked about a trip she had taken to Rome and Venice. She had a sense of history, of aesthetics, and she was able to bring the old world charm of the places she had visited come to life. I shared with her some memories of Sicily: the people, the open air cafes, Italian ice cream. We spent most of the evening with each other.

A slow and cautious relationship developed, one that was warm and deep at the same time. There were many similarities between us. For one, we looked alike. Even though I was Italian and Cecile Jewish, strangers thought we were brother and sister.

One of Cecile's childhood experiences paralleled the stabbing I'd experienced when I was sixteen. The pain I suffered during recuperation had been intense and prolonged and accompanied by many hours of soul-searching. Cecile had experienced something similar when she was sixteen. One quiet evening, she began telling me about it:

> I remember the date—the morning of September 10, 1965. I was sixteen years old and on my way to school. It was cool, and I was wearing

an olive green raincoat. When the stoplight turned green, I started across the pedestrian crossing. A moment later I looked up to see a huge semi truck bearing down on me. The driver had run a red light, and I frantically tried to run back to the curb. Too late. With one foot on the curb, I suddenly felt the impact of this monstrous machine.

The front tire hit me and I lost consciousness almost immediately. I was later told my body had been pushed for about ten feet along the pavement. My raincoat was torn to shreds, and so was the skin on my back. My cousin was a witness to the accident, and she said, 'That girl is dead. No one can survive something like that.'

I *was* almost dead. When I regained consciousness several minutes later, I was still under the wheel of the truck. The pain was horrendous. As it turned out, my ribs had been crushed and my lungs had collapsed. I tried to breathe shallowly, but the effort and pain were so intense I knew I couldn't keep it up.

Somehow, my parents had learned about what happened and were there before the ambulance had arrived. Lying there, I managed to gasp to them that it wasn't my fault. Crying uncontrollably, I heard them say, 'We're not blaming you, honey.'

Then some paramedics arrived, and I was given oxygen and rushed to the hospital. I was barely able to expel air from my chest. I knew I had to keep breathing in order to live, but the pain was so excruciating that each time, over and over again, I had to decide to live and force myself to do it.

I never saw the truck driver, a person who entered my life for an instant and changed my life entirely.

When I was sixteen, recuperating from being stabbed and in intense pain, I mourned for something beyond my own suffering. At the same time, Cecile was in a hospital, undergoing corrective surgery for her life-threatening injuries.

Do people mourn for the suffering of their soul mates whom they have not yet met? If so, does that suggest a knowledge of the future? Or is it that these relationships are already full and mature from events long past, and are simply awaiting the right circumstances to flourish once again?

From the time I first met her while I was in medical school, Cecile had been my faithful friend, lover, nurturer and chief supporter. This woman now at my side, waiting to take her vows, had come to me when I had nothing, was nothing. She helped me through countless hard times, and her faith in our mutual love was strong enough to allow her to leave her family and friends in Chicago and come with me to California, unmarried and with no commitment. She had asked for nothing more than my love. And what had I done in turn? I had proposed and reneged twice, and still Cecile had been faithful and understanding and had never pressed me on the issue.

I had accomplished my goal of becoming a podiatrist and starting a successful practice. I had no more excuses. I finally had to face the fact that it was time to grow up, to leave behind the old hurt of rejection. It was time to see Cecile, not as a threat, not as someone who could hurt me, but as the wonderful, loving woman she was. Cecile was the best thing that had ever happened in my life. In *The Bridge Across Forever*, Richard Bach puts it this way:

> Until you make room in your life for someone as important to you as yourself, you will always be lonely and searching and lost....[1]

The walls I'd built around myself to keep from getting hurt didn't really protect—they isolated me.

Cecile would have loved a large, formal wedding, but in 1977 it was difficult to get rabbis and priests to perform interfaith marriages. Besides, we were wary of how our Catholic and Jewish families would get along. And so we decided that a civil ceremony would be best. No, I'm not being totally candid; that was only part of it. The biggest part was that, although I had finally agreed to marriage, I wanted to avoid any hassles and keep, as much as possible, our marriage from the public eye, as though this might lessen my entrapment and my embarrassment at being "caught."

The justice of the peace began to intone the familiar words and, in spite of myself, my right cheek began to quiver uncontrollably. I turned and looked at Cecile. She was quietly jubilant. I had never seen her face so filled with love and devotion—for me. Maybe it was the look on her face, or perhaps it was a higher grace, but for the first time in my life, I was able to really see beyond myself and understand the meaning of selfless giving. For some, it may be fighting a courageous battle; for others, it may be forgiving a wrong inflicted upon us; for me, the greatest sacrifice I had ever made was saying "I do."

I did it. And a new chapter of our lives began.

Fear of commitment had been my weakest point, and the feelings it aroused made all other sacrifices seem feeble. Finally, I had to face my greatest fear—entrapment—and, like others before me who have done the same thing, that fear, once faced, lost much of its power.

There was something else about Reno. We were surrounded by casinos. Brilliant neon lights flashed on and off. Drinking, gambling and risqué floor shows went on twenty-four hours a day. Why did people come here to get married? To tie the knot before objecting parents found out? To marry quickly because a baby was due? To marry as cheaply as possible? Whatever the reason and in spite of the impersonal, assembly-line wedding, when a man and woman stand next to each other and pledge their vows, the same universal sacrament unfolds.

When Cecile stood next to me, she was every bride, with every bride's longing and fulfillment. When we were joined by pledges and kissed as man and wife, the drab surroundings became a grand cathedral, a profound stage where one of life's most significant dramas was enacted.

A feast is made for laughter, and wine maketh merry; but money answereth all things.

—*Ecclesiastes 10:19*

The Vietnam War was coming to an end. As the soldiers returned, I counted my blessings. My years of school deferment plus a lucky draw in the draft lottery had kept me out of the conflict. Compared to wartime tragedies, my investment blunders seemed insignificant. If soldiers could survive the tribulations of that terrible war, then I could surely survive some investment losses. Besides, I was just warming up. To get back on course, and not repeat the same investment mistakes, I repeated the Lowry-Nickerson real estate course that I had previously taken in Chicago. If I was going to become a millionaire by the time I was thirty, I had my work cut out for me.

After fifteen months, my practice was pulling in $100,000 a year. This was unheard of in medical circles; it usually took years and years to pay off debts and begin making a profit. I was already making more than most executives in nearby Silicon Valley. The income from my practice, together with our frugal lifestyle, provided the investment funds I so badly wanted.

One of my heroes was E. Joseph Cossman, a living legend of aggressive but ethical marketing. His course, *How To Make Money,* said it all. Following the advice of Cossman and others, by leveraging my available funds to the limit, I was able to acquire five properties.

As my portfolio expanded, I planned future conquests. Each new acquisition was a trophy, a badge of achievement, a new hotel on my Monopoly™ board. I didn't allow myself to enjoy these stepping stones of advancement. *"Not yet, not yet,"* I told myself. *"Wait until I really make it big."*

On the professional side, I pulled out all the stops. I joined the Academy of Ambulatory Foot Surgery and the American Podiatry Association. I published public information packets on foot care. I became involved with local service groups, served on public health education committees, and organized the largest foot-screening program for senior citizens ever attempted. I appeared on several radio shows and did many presentations for civic groups on the new techniques in foot surgery. In addition to a real public service, these activities all provided terrific publicity. The exposure and subsequent media coverage brought in large numbers of new patients, and my practice grew still more.

To help establish my professional credentials, I wanted to become a board-certified surgeon. The lion's share of this effort was made by Cecile. Sitting on the floor (we still had little furniture) and using an old manual typewriter, she typed up the required fifty case-history reports, complete with preoperative and postoperative X-rays and photographs. In 1977, I was the youngest podiatric surgeon to be awarded the status of Diplomate of the American Board of Ambulatory Foot Surgery.

It felt like there was no stopping me. Later that year, as our income continued to increase, Cecile and I gradually loosened our self-imposed frugal lifestyle. As a symbol of our burgeoning success, I bought my first Mercedes. It was my first adult toy. I remembered how people in Hoboken had looked up to anyone with a Cadillac. I'd wanted to know what it felt like to be the driver of a prestigious car. It felt good.

Since childhood, I'd romanticized "success" and identified with the self-made entrepreneur. In *Transformations, Growth and Change in Adult Life,* Roger Gould states, "The status system patently tells us, as men, if we can get enough power, money or fame, we will reach the magical state of bigness!"[2]

I believed there was a magical state of "bigness" which automatically produces happiness and fulfillment—the state where, once you get there, you finally have enough. I didn't know how much it would take to get me there, and there wasn't time to ask whether or not success brought inner contentment. I only knew I wasn't "there" yet.

But in rare quiet moments, I remembered the frightened, angry kid lying in his hospital bed, recuperating from stab wounds. I could hear him saying he would show his parents, his friends and his neighbors that he was smarter than they all thought. He was not just a delinquent. Godammit—he was going to be "somebody!" *not for its own sake, but as an act of vengeance against an unjust world.*

Success was not an option. I had no choice.

> That elephant ate all night
> That elephant ate all day.
> For all we could do to bring him food
> The cry was still, "More hay!"
>
> *—John Cheever Goodwin*

CHAPTER 4

The Med Wars

I feel that tradition is a kind of a conspiracy to keep anything new from happening.
                                                            —George Lang

Podiatrists joke about the difference between DPMs and RDs, between doctors of podiatric medicine and "real doctors." This humorous self-deprecation is caused by the fact that the rest of the medical profession, even to this day, knows little about our work. Many MDs do not know that our medical education and training is every bit as comprehensive and rigorous as theirs. In 1977, the California Podiatry Association was still working to get podiatrists admitted to hospitals as part of the surgical staff. Traditional podiatrists wanted foot surgery to be treated like any other surgery—that is, a serious procedure that should be done in a hospital. All the podiatric surgeons who favored simpler, in-office surgery were clearly bucking the trend, and the traditionalists didn't like it one bit.

There were other problems. After meeting with senior citizen groups and realizing that consumers were not getting the information they needed through traditional channels, I put together a packet of information on foot and leg exercises, a shoe-fitting guide, and a booklet called *The Main Causes of Foot Disorders, A Consumer's Guide to the Most Common Foot Problems*. I made this packet available without cost to the senior citizen community, but the gesture was not appreciated by some of my colleagues, for I received another reprimand from the ethics committee of the local podiatric society.

It was the booklet that caused them concern, and the fact that my name was printed on it as author. Although the U.S. Supreme Court had a year earlier affirmed the right of physicians to advertise, this right had not been accepted by many conservative medical societies. My podiatric society was against doctors handing out any information with their name on it.

There was also another complaint against me. Since many senior citizens were unable to find convenient transportation in order to come in for treatment, I had recommended to the ethics chairman that our local society provide free transportation to senior citizens. I felt this was a badly-needed public service as well as an effective marketing tool to bring in patients who would not otherwise seek treatment. The program was never instituted, so I decided to offer the service myself. This brought us many new and grateful patients, but was also seen as going against traditional behavior. The conclusion of the ethics committee of the podiatric society was that I be officially reprimanded. However, since I had notified the society of my plan and they hadn't responded, I was technically off the hook. It was made clear to me, however, that if my activities continued, I would be subject to immediate expulsion.

The podiatric society had other methods of intimidation. I began to hear rumors that traditional podiatric surgeons were feeling threatened by me. Other podiatrists who were performing in-office minimal incision techniques were doing so quietly, if not secretly. I was in the public eye, blatantly going against the traditionalists.

One day, the peer review committee for the Northern California society began requesting volumes of information on all my Medi-Cal and Medicare surgeries. This was to be handed over to the government examiners, delaying my reimbursements. My cash flow was hit hard.

My adversaries hoped to find claims for surgery I had not performed since, as a result of efficient, minimal incision techniques, our office was performing a very high number of procedures—more in a single day than a hospital-based surgeon was able to do in a month. No doubt there were unscrupulous practitioners who billed for surgeries they hadn't performed, so this was a legitimate inquiry. However, we had carefully documented all our procedures, and no irregularities were found.

The second part of the inquiry had to do with the sequence of procedures. For example, hospital-based podiatrists, using traditional surgical techniques, often operated on both feet at the same time, believing that their patients, in pain and laid up for extended periods, would balk at having their other foot corrected and would not return. Also, considering the high cost of hospital treatment, it made economic sense to do all procedures at the same time.

Minimal incision procedures, however, were more suited to a dental approach to foot surgery. The corrective work was performed in two to six sessions spaced one to two weeks apart. This allowed time for some healing to occur and generally minimized trauma to the foot. By spacing out the corrective procedures, the patient could be up and around. The method also reduced the chances of infection or other complications, since the operating time would be minimized.

Doing corrective surgery in stages is foreign to traditional podiatric surgeons. My adversaries, moreover, were looking for any way possible to denigrate my work, so they claimed that by performing and billing for several procedures I was doing unnecessary work in order to increase my fees. This was in spite of the fact that the patient's overall costs were very much lower than comparable procedures done in a hospital.

Their strategy was clear: by continuing to probe my procedures, my colleagues believed they could get me to buckle under from the general hassle and the delayed Medicare and Medi-Cal payments. I was given subtle hints to use the local hospital for procedures instead of my office, to halt my practice of providing transportation for senior citizens, and to stop disseminating consumer information.

Friends often asked, "If your procedures are so great, why haven't all podiatrists adopted them?" Minimal incision techniques require a high degree of manual dexterity and visualization skills, since the procedures are done mainly by feel. Although these techniques look easy to perform, they are difficult for the novice or occasional practitioner. In fact, many traditional podiatrists tried minimal incision surgery with poor results, due to lack of proper training. They would then describe the procedures as worthless, even though thousands of patients around the country were benefiting from them.

The public believes that medical professionals adhere to high standards of ethics and integrity—these qualities are almost synonymous with practicing medicine. In fact, many doctors are strongly motivated by money. By attracting large numbers of new patients to my office, I threatened my colleagues' income. I was perceived as an upstart; an influence that was reducing their patient load, and they weren't about to stand for it.

Pressure from the podiatric community put me in a difficult spot. I desperately wanted to fit in, to become part of the mainstream. After all, becoming part of the mainstream was a part of my vision of success. But I couldn't give up the procedures which I knew benefited so many people. I took the Hippocratic oath seriously where it says, "physician, do no harm."

In addition to being places of healing and corrective treatment, hospitals are potentially dangerous to one's health as well as one's pocketbook. To watch my clients heal and become well again without undergoing discomfort or great expense was marvelously satisfying. In addition, my early years as a street fighter in Hoboken imbued me with the ability to stand up under pressure. I was on the verge of entering a holy war, but I didn't know it.

Like Prometheus, we blame the gods and ignore our complicity in creating our fate.
                                        —*Sam Keen and Anne Valley-Fox*

The pressures of my struggle to maintain momentum and defeat my medical detractors were starting to get to me. I didn't like the continuous battle, the waiting for the next ax to fall. To reduce my anxiety I enrolled in an est training program. At the guest seminar I attended, it was clear something was going on. The est staff had a glazed look that indicated inner peace or numbed brains. I wasn't sure which, but I was uneasy enough in my own life to give it a try.

Training was held in a large, elegant, hotel conference room. The setup seemed traditional enough—about two hundred chairs were arranged in a semicircle around a raised platform for the speakers. Before entering, we were told to take off any timepieces we might be wearing and not to talk unless specifically directed to do so. After picking up our name tags we were directed to begin taking seats in the front rows—shy persons were not allowed to hide in the back. The trainers were expressionless—no friendly greetings or small talk.

The chief trainer began by insulting us for a prolonged period. "All of you here are assholes! If you weren't assholes, your lives would be working for you and you wouldn't be here. You are all assholes because you keep lying to yourselves that everything is okay, that the things you believe in are right, that the things you do are right. Only assholes go around, year after year, feeling so messed up but still believing that what they're doing is right!

"I don't want you to believe anything that I will be saying this weekend. Have you got that? Have you all got that? If you believe what I'm saying, you're just staying stuck in your belief systems!"

Encouraged to respond, a man asked, "Then why should we be here?"

"Because it's important that you listen! Because it's important that you experience what is going on!" the trainer shouted and told a story about laboratory rats and cheese. "In a laboratory, there is a rat in a maze. The maze has four tunnels. The scientist in charge of the experiment puts cheese in the first tunnel and lets the rat loose. The rat wanders around and finally finds the cheese. Then the handler puts more cheese in the same place and lets the rat loose again. This time, the rat finds it more quickly. By the fifth or sixth time, the rat goes directly to the first tunnel to find the cheese. Now the scientist puts the cheese in a different tunnel. The rat is confused, and wanders up and down the first tunnel, looking for the cheese. Eventually, it starts sniffing and looking elsewhere, and finally it finds it. That rat has some intelligence. It stopped searching the first tunnel after it was convinced there was no cheese there.

"The difference between that rat and you assholes is that you can't stop searching in the first tunnel. You are convinced that the first tunnel is the cheese tunnel. You label it the Cheese Tunnel and you believe in it. No matter how long it is empty, it is still where you search.

"That's how you live your lives. You make it right to wander up and down the first tunnel whether there's cheese there or not. You would rather be right than find the cheese! That's why you are all assholes, because you are filled with beliefs about tunnels that no longer work!

"In the laboratory, just to make things more complicated for the rat, the handler will put some cheese in the first tunnel again. The rat sniffs it out and finds it. After the cheese has appeared in a number of different places in the maze, the rat learns to rely on his sense of smell. He no longer wanders up and down a single tunnel—he points his little snout into the air and smells! And that helps him find the cheese! He has ceased having a belief system, and has learned to rely on his experience.

"Now look at your lives. Once in a while, by accident, you find some cheese—some terrific thing happens in your life. Great! Wonderful! And what do you do? You want it to happen again. You can't let go of it, so you construct a new belief system about how to keep getting it. And it doesn't work! You assholes keep looking for where the cheese was last time, and you don't understand that the guy in the white coat—whether you call him God or fate or karma—isn't playing your game. He keeps moving the cheese! You can't find the cheese—you're not enjoying your life, and the more you search for the cheese, the worse you feel!"

I needed to know more about this, and I raised my hand. "Yes, Dennis, stand up."

I said, "If I want something, why does that make it harder for me to get it?"

"What do you want?"

"Well, I want to reach my professional and financial goals."

"Fine, go ahead and reach them."

"But why will my attachment to my goals keep me from enjoying my life?"

"Because," the trainer shouted at me, "you're hung up on a belief system. You're living in your fucking mind and you don't know how to live in real life. All of you assholes are spending your lifetimes waiting for cheese that isn't there, and you don't know how to enjoy the cheese that is there!"

Later in the weekend of training, I asked about the responsibility for being mugged.

"You are the sole source of your experience, Dennis."

"Okay, I get that I'm responsible for everything I do, but if I get mugged, how am I responsible for what the mugger does to me?"

"Who is the source of your experience, Dennis?"

"The mugger."

"Really? Is the mugger creating his image in your mind?"

"Well, no, I'm the one who sees him, but he's real—he's there."

"Dennis, who got you out of bed this morning, brushed your teeth and ate your breakfast?"

"I did."

"So you take responsibility for those actions?"

"Yes."

"How about for being on 47th Street in New York, or wherever this mugging is taking place? You responsible for being there?"

"Yes."

"Responsible for seeing the mugger approach?"

"Well, I guess it's my eyes that see him, so I'm responsible."

"Good. Now who is responsible for making a crime out of this little action?"

"The mugger. He's the one committing the crime."

"No, Dennis. He's accepting your money. You are the one who has determined it is a crime."

"But I didn't give him my money willingly. He demanded it! He threatened me!"

"What would have happened if, before he could say anything, you approached him and offered to give him one hundred dollars? Would he have 'mugged' you?"

"Probably not."

"No? Then who is choosing the kind of experience it is? You are the one who chooses to make it a crime. You are the one who decides to give him the money, regardless of the reason. Nobody else does this for you. You didn't create the mugger, but your reactions, which are your choices, determine what your experience will be. Do you get it? Do any of you get it?"

"You're saying I'm responsible for everything I experience."

"Right. Dennis, as long as we're talking about New York City, have you ever seen a weird-looking, homeless person wandering around, talking aloud, say, to God? Ever seen anything like that?"

"Yes."

"We label him nuts—off his rocker. We avoid him if we can. Nobody wants to be near him. But in some societies, people like that are venerated. They're cared for, cherished and looked up to because they're thought to have a pipeline to the divine that others don't have. What causes the different reactions? Perception. And a different perception means a different personal experience.

"There's more. That weirdo we're talking about has his experiences, too. Do you think it will affect him differently if society treats him like a holy man or like dirt?"

"Sure."

"Then your experience of that weirdo, your experience of that mugger, affects his experience, too. You're responsible! Do you get it?"

The main theme of the est program was learning to take responsibility, and thus control, over your own life. This matched my own independent, go-it-alone streak. But the other side of the coin was less easy to accept. If I assumed responsibility for everything that happened to me, I could hardly blame my medical peers for my problems. I would have to give up the belief that I had been forced by my detractors into a position of defending myself. I would have to admit that I had caused all this strife myself.

I came away from the est training with the knowledge that all the choices I'd made since childhood had brought me to this moment in my life—to these circumstances. I had chosen to be where I was, comfortable or not. All my life I'd believed it was not possible to attain success without a struggle, so I'd created one. In fact, I'd created everything—I was in control of my own, individual universe. It was my free will that created my need to be financially independent at an early age. It was me who chose to become a maverick podiatric surgeon and go it alone, not only in medicine but in my whole life.

And it was also me who insisted on becoming number one in my field, which set me up as a target for my peers.

It was my fault I'd been stabbed in a street brawl in Hoboken. I accepted it. Now, my adversaries were grown up and "civilized," so the methods they used were more subtle. Legal maneuvering, peer pressure and character defamation had taken the place of guns and knives. But, once again, I had created the situation. This realization was both sobering and painful. I could no longer blame someone else for my problems, not even the adversaries attacking me. I had to take full responsibility for causing them to react the way they did, because I had challenged their hard-core beliefs and threatened their livelihoods.

My est experience awakened the memory of being whacked with an umbrella by Sister Assumptor in Catholic school for talking during a fire drill. I could accept the responsibility for precipitating the action by talking when I was supposed to be quiet, but was her action a "right" action? What is the relationship between being responsible for something, and the propriety of the consequences? Previously, I had condemned Sister Assumptor's act; but if I am responsible to some degree for everything that occurs to me, how could I continue assessing right or wrong to anything done to me?

Est led me to an understanding of the courage and rewards that come from sharing intensely personal feelings in an open forum. The willingness of so many people to share their tribulations was a revealing and a beautiful thing to me. For the first time in my life, I didn't feel so alone or isolated. There were other people with problems just like mine. They'd been there all along; I'd just never really noticed them before.

The trainers talked about many of the things I'd heard from the Catholic Church in my youth. With est, however, spiritual concepts had a strong, logical foundation. They didn't demand unthinking allegiance to implausible doctrines. But the spirituality I felt with est was temporary, much like my early experiments with LSD and other drugs, a force that titillated rather than satisfied and allowed a faint acquaintance but no deep relationship. There were no drugs involved with est, but there was that same sense of a shallow, or premature, awakening, like shaking green fruit from a yielding tree.

I couldn't accept from est the view that life is a mere game, or an illusion that masks some greater reality. Life seemed too important and intense for that. Nor could I "be here now" and still plan for my ambitious future. How could I plan ahead? How could I stay a step ahead of my adversaries without attempting to anticipate their moves? I could accept that, like Prometheus, we blame the gods and ignore complicity in our fate, but I could not accept that we are totally responsible for creating our own reality. That would mean that children napalmed in Vietnam or blown to bits in Bosnia brought their fate upon themselves.

Nor was I interested in finding a father-figure or guru to worship. As I took more advanced est programs, I saw that the higher up one was in the est organization—and therefore, the closer to its evangelistic leader—the more Werner Erhard was eulogized. I also did not like being the target of aggressive est marketing.

Many of the positive feelings I got from est did not last past the training. I could accept est theories—for example, *everything we resist persists and problems dissolve when we cease resisting them*—but I could not apply them to my life and my concept of success. When I thought about my life, I realized that to be "successful," I'd have to continue to live in a world of adversity. To stop resisting meant giving up my goals, and I simply wasn't willing to do this.

Nevertheless, est helped me. What stayed with me was the understanding that I could take charge of my life. If I could not stop fighting, at least I could determine how the battle was to be fought.

Doctors are haunted by two paralyzing fears. They're terrified of malpractice suits that could wipe them out, financially, and of being labeled a "nonconformist" by their associates. If it comes down to prescribing an accepted treatment with questionable benefits or suggesting a more advanced approach that shows great promise, most doctors will play it safe.

—*Julian Whitaker, M.D.*

You're a good doctor, so the first time you're sued for malpractice it comes as a real shock. After all, you've had such a warm, satisfying relationship with your patients. You smile and welcome them; they smile and thank you. You see their concerns in their eyes and hear it in their voices, and you feel for them. You do everything you can to minimize their discomfort and aid their recovery. You explain the risks—there are occasional failures in all types of surgery—and you only proceed when they have acknowledged the risk, signed a release, and are ready to continue. When they sue you, you don't understand how they can do it.

The first time it happened to me, suit was brought by a thirty-four-year-old welfare mother who accidentally bumped her foot after surgery, which temporarily weakened her toe. I explained that it would heal in time, but she lost confidence and someone "got" to her. Vengeful competitors and malpractice lawyers wait in the wings like vultures preparing to feast on the remains of a fresh kill.

I was worried because I was "bare"; that is, I had no malpractice coverage. Because of sharp cost increases, I'd elected not to buy malpractice insurance that year, although I'd at least had the good sense to buy legal defense insurance, and this would cover up to $10,000 of legal costs. Furthermore, my documentation on the case was in order.

Aside from doing good work, documentation—keeping accurate records of everything he does—is a doctor's primary means of protecting himself from losing malpractice suits. To make sure all bases are covered, the doctor may order additional tests, X-rays, etc., that serve no useful purpose other than to bolster his protective documentation. The fact that the tests may be uncomfortable or expensive is not sufficient deterrence. A doctor quickly learns how the game is played, and knows he will get into serious trouble sooner or later if he does not play by these rules. To complicate matters, more testing often provides more income to the doctor, and while this is certainly welcome, it causes guilt, and the doctor may feel he is prostituting himself for money.

There was little chance I'd lose the case, but in order to avoid spending time in court I settled for $3000. My insurance paid the legal charges, almost exactly $10,000, which was the limit of my coverage. I escaped with little more than a financial scratch, but the hounds of the medical establishment were still sniffing and eagerly awaiting their next chance.

Another episode was when one of the "old guard" practitioners issued a complaint against me to the local podiatric society. It began at a meeting of the society when I saw Dr. Berringer and told him that I'd operated on Juanita Sanchez, a patient of his. Mrs. Sanchez was an elderly Hispanic lady who'd had foot problems for years. Her condition had been treated conservatively by Dr. Berringer, and, in my opinion, she had never been totally cured. When Mrs. Sanchez came to see me, however, she told me she was not under any other doctor's care, and I proceeded on that basis. After I'd performed corrective surgery, Mrs. Sanchez did not return to my office for her final follow-up appointment. When one of my staff members called her, we learned for the first time that she had been a patient of Dr. Berringer and had returned to his care for an unrelated, minor foot condition because he was located closer to her home. Unfortunately, Mrs. Sanchez further complicated the situation by not telling Dr. Berringer that she'd been treated by me. She informed us that she felt too embarrassed to tell him. It was an awkward situation, and I wanted to set the record straight.

It's a "no-no" for a doctor to treat a patient who is under the care of another doctor, so at a society meeting I told Dr. Berringer what had happened. Dr. Berringer became agitated and asked for Mrs. Sanchez' medical records so he could update his file. I sent them to him and forgot about the matter.

I was reminded of it when the local podiatric society asked me to attend an informal meeting of the ethics committee. I was very dismayed that Dr. Berringer had chosen to make an issue of it, but I was led to believe the committee did not consider the matter of Mrs. Sanchez very serious—just a technicality to be amicably dispensed with. But the "informal" meeting turned out to be a tribunal, with charges brought against me that had not been previously disclosed. I was attacked, harshly interrogated, and humiliated.

Because minimal incisions heal quickly and leave virtually no visible scar formation, and because Dr. Berringer had little knowledge of these procedures himself, he had convinced himself and others that I had not performed any surgical procedures whatsoever on Mrs. Sanchez (in spite of the fact that her condition was alleviated and her walking was now improved).

I stood accused by my peers (but not by the patient) of assault and battery, uninformed consent, fraudulent billing and falsifying records—any charge of which, if proved, would have been enough to end my career. The vicious attack took me completely by surprise. I did not understand Dr. Berringer's motive. Could Dr. Berringer have done this because he had lost a patient? It was no secret that young practitioners before me had left the area because they refused to kowtow to the conservative guardians of foot care whose fervent desire was to maintain the status quo.

Following this "informal" meeting, formal hearings were held. Though these hearings were supposed to be fair and impartial, I found them to be a total sham. The decision to "get" me had already been made. I felt like the sacrificial lamb that would teach other young upstarts not to commit the sin of challenging the old taboos and rituals handed down from our podiatric predecessors.

The conventional practitioners of these proceedings were the duly consti-tuted board of review. Rather than being unbiased referees, they were the ones who were most threatened by the new surgical techniques and by the rapid growth of my practice. It was as if I was on trial for banishing rainfall, and all the judges were umbrella manufacturers. And yet these well-established practitioners thought themselves to be the conscience of podiatry. They had been doing it for thirty years—how could they be wrong?

The charges against me were so spurious and exaggerated, and so completely refuted by my documentation, that I was incredulous when found guilty and expelled from the local society. The expulsion did not mean much in practical terms. I could still practice and I was still a member in good standing of my supporting national organization, the Academy of Ambulatory Foot Surgery, yet I was determined to right the wrong that had been done to me. I consulted an attorney and made plans to appeal my expulsion to the state podiatric association.

Peer review boards, composed of practicing doctors, are empowered to act as unbiased overseers of the medical professions, but some doctors exercise undue influence on board decisions. Standards of practice, like biblical scriptures, are subject to broad interpretation. Thus, the guidelines for medical practice are malleable and can be twisted to serve the needs of an empowered faction. As with religion, if you dare to challenge the established order, you are targeted for retribution and held up as a warning to others.

Over the years, I have seen the scenario repeated; the "butchers" of the medical profession go unscathed because they are good old boys, members of the "club." They scorn anything that is innovative if it does not coincide with their personal interests. Threat of malpractice looms so large over a modern-day doctor, especially a surgeon, that it has driven some of the finest people out of medicine. Ironically, it is not so much vindictive patients that are at the bottom of this but avaricious lawyers and competing doctors with low ethical standards.

Doctors know that it is bad publicity for any doctor to have lawsuits pending against him—the larger the number of lawsuits, the worse the publicity and the more easy it is to scuttle a good reputation. Envious, vindictive doctors help initiate frivolous lawsuits to undermine competitors who threaten their income. It doesn't matter who is at fault, or whether the lawsuits have any merit; having a large number of lawsuits initiated against you is sufficient to cloud your name.

Some doctors have turned legal proceedings into a lucrative sideline. There are doctors who do this legitimately, who provide a public service as unbiased experts, but there are others who are willing to take adversarial positions against their colleagues, regardless of the facts of the case. These doctors are the hired guns of the medical profession.

There are many ethical, principled lawyers, but there are also lawyers who consistently initiate lawsuits they know to be without merit because they realize that the physician either cannot take the time off to defend himself in court, or is willing to settle rather than receive the bad publicity stemming from a trial* Ironically, when doctors are willing to go through court proceedings, statistics show they typically win most of their cases.

All ethical physicians are in favor of patients who have been injured through gross malpractice being compensated for their losses, the truth is that the majority of lawsuits have unethical motives. The winners in the malpractice game are the lawyers. The losers are doctors and patients. The doctors lose because they can be driven out of business (or out of their minds, with litigaphobia—the fear of lawsuits); the patients lose because they're the ones who pay to compensate for doctors' high insurance costs and for unneeded procedures that doctors must have to help defend themselves against litigation. The system is in dire need of fundamental change.

Courage is not the absence of fear, but the judgment that something is more important than one's fear

—Gnosis Magazine, Fall, 1991

To the chagrin of my medical colleagues, instead of ceasing my professional marketing efforts, I increased them. It was my experience that people were hungry for information on foot care. So, in 1979, I purchased a prerecorded audio library called "Foot Facts On Tape," along with the equipment that would allow interested persons toll-free phone access to it twenty-four hours a day. Upon request, a free informational brochure was also sent to the caller. If they wished, they could call me or any other doctor they chose. It was an instant success. We received upwards of forty calls each day and were booking patients right and left. At about the same time, I changed the name of my

---

* Interestingly, in Athens of the fourth century B.C., Crito, a prosperous friend of Socrates, complained: "For at this very time, there are people bringing actions against me not because they have suffered any wrong from me but because they think I would rather pay them a sum of money than have the trouble of long proceedings."

practice to the "Park Avenue Foot Clinic." A good marketing move, the name was immediately identifiable, and I jokingly told my patients that I had always wanted to be a Park Avenue doctor but had to settle for San Jose.

The public appreciated the information and responded accordingly. They informed me that they were fed up with the traditional Yellow Page listings that didn't say anything or give a clue as to what the doctor was like. *How could my marketing efforts be termed unethical,* I thought, *when my patients are so satisfied?* The clinic began operating at an unprecedented level. I was coming closer to my vision of having one of the most successful foot clinics in the country.

I was ready to go still farther, but one month after starting the phone system I was contacted by the Medi-Cal office of the state of California. They informed me I was being investigated. On the surface, the investigation had nothing to do with my marketing efforts, but it was hard to believe that this wasn't a punitive response from disapproving colleagues. It was soon apparent to the investigators that, while our billings were among the highest in the state, they were all legitimate. Nevertheless, having to respond to the charges cost me time, money and anxiety.

In the midst of all this, somehow I managed to write and publish the book, *How To Market Your Professional Services.*[2] This, I felt, was the future of medicine. The government wanted to create competition within the medical field, and consumers wanted a change as well. I would be one of the first doctors to test the waters of competition. I didn't realize the degree to which I was setting myself up to be an unwitting martyr. After all, I was aggressively marketing my practice; I was pioneering new ground in ambulatory foot surgery; I was rendering much of hospital-based foot surgery obsolete; and I was providing consumer information that had been withheld from consumers before. Whenever professionals attempt to demystify their profession, there is a price to pay.

Meantime, my expulsion from the local podiatric society was overturned by the California Podiatry Association. Dr. John Reid, with whom I'd experienced repeated conflicts during his tenure as the ethics chairman, was found to be lying under oath, and my membership was reinstated. The old-guard podiatric surgeons were furious. I was still a "wanted" man, but I was also wanted by the public. After I was interviewed in a national tabloid, our office was flooded with new bookings. I grossed a quarter of a million dollars that year, more than any of my accusers with their years of practice, but they weren't about to give up. I received more threats, and another meeting on my status was scheduled. I was becoming an infamous celebrity among my peers, but constant anxiety over the proceedings, sleepless nights, the countless hours I had to spend reviewing my records lest some minor slip strengthen my enemies' case were all getting to me. Still, outwardly, I appeared the pillar of calm.

Some people become willing symbols for a cause; I was a very reluctant martyr. Deciding that demonstrating success, was the best revenge, I purchased a bright red Mercedes 450 SL convertible, sending an unmistakable signal: *"Eat your hearts out, guys. This is what I do, and I'm here to stay whether you like it or not."*

If these self-righteous zealots wanted a battle, that's what they'd get. Before the next meeting, I hired a private investigator who wired my briefcase for sound so I could record the proceedings. It was amazing how candidly my opponents spoke out against me, just as if I weren't there. One said, "What can we do to get this guy?" Another said, "I know of several ways we can generate complaints against Augustine and get them to the BMQA (Bureau of Medical Quality Assurance). Once they receive them, they'll have to investigate." My opponents were spinning enough rope to hang themselves and were unaware of it. If I was being set up to take a fall, there appeared to be enough incriminating evidence to take my enemies down with me.

Christmas of 1979 had pretty much been ruined for me by the continuing attacks by some of the traditional practitioners—now I would reciprocate by giving them a New Years Eve present. Nick Rice, my investigator, and I decided to attend the next regularly scheduled meeting of the society at an elegant restaurant, Villa Felice. In my childhood summers in Sicily, I had heard how Mafiosi would send their enemies a platter of fish to put them on notice that they had made a serious transgression against The Family. Recalling this custom, we arrived in the middle of their dinner, and Nick served the members of the ethics committee with subpoenas to appear in court. At first they thought it was some kind of prank, but it slowly sunk in that they were being sued for four million dollars each for malicious prosecution, unfair competition, defamation and infliction of emotional distress!

I wanted them to feel what it was like to be on the receiving end, to have their livelihoods jeopardized, to be hunted and humiliated in front of their peers. If nothing else, they knew I meant business! Now they would have less time to initiate further actions against me. Now they had to deal with having a major lawsuit on their hands. Whenever they applied for consumer credit, they would have to disclose that they had been sued. They would have to check their insurance policies carefully to see if they were covered for all their actions in their capacities as committeemen of an association. And they would have to hire expensive attorneys to defend themselves. They could no longer do battle from the sanctity of their privileged positions—their actions would be exposed to public scrutiny in the courtroom and in the media.

For the past two years, these individuals had misused their power to cause me and my family considerable grief and expense without justifiable cause. They had forced the aggressive warrior, the darker side of my personality, out of the closet. Now I could play out a symbolic Sicilian revenge. My opponents had turned what was essentially a turf battle into what had become, for me, a holy crusade—a just war. In addition to preserving my own career, I would not allow them to turn back the clock and prevent the implementation of modern foot care. Not only would I not knuckle under to their unrealistic demands, I further aggravated them by writing a second book, *The Foot Care Revolution: How To Walk Away From a Foot Operation on Your Own Two Feet.*[3] It was a labor of love, and my good friend and supporter, Dr. Ed Marlowe, the first president of the Academy of Ambulatory Foot Surgery, honored me by writing the foreword.

Never before had the officers of a professional medical society been sued by one of its members. No one had ever had the chutzpah to take on the establishment before. In response, the state podiatric association, to protect its officers in a local dispute, established a legal defense fund for the eight defendants. This upped the ante. I was no longer fighting eight individuals; now I was up against the entire California podiatric establishment.

As word of the impending lawsuit got around the country, tensions rose within the national podiatric community. We were stirring up a hornet's nest, and my name was becoming known to my peers nationwide.

On November 1, 1980, the Academy of Ambulatory Foot Surgery filed suit against the American Podiatric Medical Association and the American Board of Podiatric Surgeons. The suit alleged that an elitist group of 300 hospital-based podiatrists were attempting to obstruct and restrain the practices of 2,000 minimal-incision podiatrists in the United States. A large insurance company was named as co-defendant for several discriminatory practices (including restricting reimbursement to minimal-incision podiatrists at the recommendation of the hospital-based board whose members monopolized the American Podiatric Association). The suit filed by the AAFS against the APMA and the hospital-based board gave considerable support and credence to my own lawsuit. The timing couldn't have been better! I was no longer alone. My individual slingshot had been transformed into a ballistic missile.

The battle was joined. Near the end of 1980, I received notice that I was to be audited by Medicare, the federal health program. It appeared that my enemies had once again exerted their influence. In spite of my lawsuit and the AAFS lawsuit that helped to support it, I felt discouraged. The audit meant more wasted time, more wasted money, and the possibility of being prosecuted for some minor technicality. There was no time for my family, for relaxation or recreation. From the moment I arose to the time I slumped exhausted into bed, each day was fraught with anxiety. My life had a single focus—fighting the Med War.

When you have a big name, you pay a big price because you have to adhere to a higher standard than doctors who are not as prominent. In a government program such as Medicare, all it takes is a missing lab test sheet, failure to properly document a dosage amount in a prescription, or failure to record a physical therapy session that you have performed. You may be liable even if you've done all procedures correctly, if you haven't recorded them all perfectly. The omission admits the possibility that you may not have actually done the procedures for which you have billed Medicare.

And, so, I was greatly relieved to learn that I passed the inspection with flying colors. No significant violations were found. In 1981, my opponents caved in. The officers of the local and state podiatric associations came to my office to negotiate a settlement. Had I pursued the lawsuit, I probably could have bankrupted my opponents and the local podiatric society. But I did not have a killer instinct. It was enough to win vindication for myself and freedom from future harassment. If I could do that, I would have opened the way for all my fellow practitioners to offer their services without interference from the medical demagogues.

The settlement included public acknowledgment that I was innocent of all charges that had been brought against me, along with a printed public apology. Henceforth, I would be treated like any other member in good standing with local and state societies. The practitioners of minimal incision surgery would no longer be discriminated against. And the peer review procedure would be overhauled to make it fair and free of conflicting special interests.

One month after my settlement, I read that another Dennis—an ophthalmologist named Dennis L. Brooks—had filed a $5 million antitrust lawsuit against the San Diego Academy of Ophthalmology. Two years later, he filed a second lawsuit against the American Academy of Ophthalmology plus ninety-five individual members. Like me, Dr. Brooks' new, more effective methods had been a threat to his more traditional colleagues. His lawsuit was the largest antitrust suit in medical history in the United States. I have since read of other, similar actions that have had a sobering effect on the paternalistic grasp of the entire medical community.

During this stressful period, I enjoyed the support of my wife, my staff and a few loyal colleagues who stayed with me even when their own positions were threatened. That we could have defeated a powerful, monopolistic establishment seems, in retrospect, amazing. This is perhaps the only country in the world where an individual has an opportunity to take on the established power structure and win. I have credited the people around me and my own stubbornness, but, in hindsight, I see that the invisible web of supporting forces were also at play in these events. As Ralph Waldo Emerson said, "Every secret is told, every crime is punished, every virtue rewarded, every wrong redressed in silence and in certainty."[4]

It was a bittersweet victory. "Athletes sometimes have a strange reaction to a great victory. Some call it 'morning-after sickness.' An Olympic gymnast who has trained for fifteen years wakes up the day after her gold medal performance feeling oddly depressed. An even more pungent feeling may hit those who prevail in personal disputes. The man who wins a crucial court case is stabbed by sympathy for those he defeated."[5]

Two years later, the United States Federal District Court in Washington D.C. approved a successful settlement of the class action suit by our national association against the American Podiatric Medical Association. It had taken six years of hard work and $300,000 in costs, but it resulted in board-certification of all qualified podiatrists, irrespective of whether they were hospital-or office-based. For the first time, out-patient foot surgery was accepted and officially recognized by all the professional associations, government agencies and insurance companies. We had done it.

CHAPTER 5

The Dark Side of Success

The wheeler-dealer is a man or a woman who moves ahead—forges ahead—in his chosen field of endeavor by the most extraordinary means …not waiting for his turn in line, he pushes ahead with speed, ambition and guts, leaving in his wake the unmistakable impression of flamboyance.
                                    —*Martin S. Ackerman and Diane L. Ackerman*

I knew that the media was important, but I don't think I grasped how powerful it could be until after a conversation with Marsha Bevins, who came to me complaining of a painful bunion. During the course of her treatment, Mrs. Bevins mentioned that she hoped to be able to do some walking within a few days because she was going to visit her daughter "at the television studio."

A buzzer went off in my head when I heard that. "Oh sure," I told her, "you'll be able to walk on this foot in a couple of days. By the way," I said, "what studio does your daughter work at?"

"She's at KPIX TV. She's the producer of the *Evening Magazine* show…are you familiar with it?"

Oh, Jesus, did I know it? It was the most popular entertainment program in the San Francisco Bay Area! "Yes," I said. "In fact, my wife and I both watch it religiously." I paused and, with as much casualness as I could muster, asked: "I wonder if your daughter would be interested in filming a segment on minimal incision surgery?"

"Why, I don't know, but I'll certainly ask her."

Almost before I knew what had happened, someone from *Evening Magazine* called and said they'd like to do a fifteen-minute piece hosted by Richard Hart and profiling me and my work at the Park Avenue Foot Clinic. Not only did we land one of the most successful TV shows in the San Francisco Bay Area, but it cost us nothing! The crew filmed for several hours, choosing representative patients. Of course there was lots of excitement at the clinic, and it slowed us down, but my patients couldn't have done better if I'd coached them. Corrine Piazza stated on camera, "I love to dance, and now I can not only walk comfortably—I can dance again." And she performed a little dance number right there to prove it! Another young woman said, "I haven't been able to wear high heels for the last four years. Now I can wear them again. And the procedure didn't even hurt!"

The show aired locally and on stations around the country in February of 1982; again, several months later; and later still was rerun. The results were stunning. Patients phoned from all over California and from other states as well. We were overwhelmed, and my hard-working staff frantically tried to accommodate the influx. By asking new patients how they'd learned of us, I tracked the results of my PR efforts. The income from several airings of that single show over the next few years resulted in additional income of $500,000!

During this time, I was traveling around the country, giving lectures on surgical techniques as a board member of the AAFS. My newfound celebrity status and my office walls covered with photos of me with famous people had another salutary effect. When patients came into our office for the first time and saw them, they felt almost as though they already knew me. They liked the fact that their doctor was active in community events, and our doctor-patient relationships began with a high level of good will and trust.

I had learned to play the media game. Some of my colleagues had also learned it. For example, Dr. Jerome Snyder, an aggressive, business-minded podiatrist, placed ads in the same newspapers I did, directly adjacent to mine. When I changed the day my ads appeared, he changed his, too. Where my ads were educational, informing the public about the availability of new procedures, Dr. Snyder's ads warned the public about the dangers of what he called "blind" or "peephole" surgery. He established an on-going, paid-for newspaper column on foot care, published under the guise of objectivity and public service. One of his headlines read: "New bunion surgery: innovation or rip-off?" He lost no opportunity to label MIS techniques ineffective while defending older, outdated techniques.. Snyder's ads had some effect, and we lost some patients as a result, but I simply had too much momentum going to be stopped. In 1982, my clinic earned $600,000 and was clearly among the most successful podiatric practices in California.

Our culture covers doctors with sanctity. In fact, they are mostly ordinary people with ordinary fears, resentments and jealousies, and with perhaps an extraordinary interest in making money. Doctors don't like to talk about this with anyone outside the profession. But when they get together among themselves, the conversation almost inevitably drifts to money and how to make more of it. Ironically, in spite of their preoccupation with money, most doctors are poor businessmen and are notorious for making bad investments.

I sometimes wonder what Hippocrates, the author of the Hippocratic oath taken by all doctors, would say about contemporary doctors. Actually, he might not be surprised. In his own time, a poet said:

> How little you know about the age you live in if you believe that honey is sweeter than cash in hand.
>
> —*Propertius Sextus, Roman poet, 50-16 B.C.*

In October of 1982, I took two courses in laser surgery. Hospital lasers, which a few years earlier had cost $500,000 were now available for in-office use for $30,000, and I purchased one as soon as I could. I realized if I didn't move quickly to capture the Northern California market, someone else would. I didn't want to battle my colleagues, I wanted to outflank them. The laser service we provided was an instant and whopping success, and it further enhanced the high-tech reputation of the Park Avenue Foot Clinic. Once again, the publicity and new patients I received after introducing laser treatment enraged my peers. Their lawyers scrutinized my ads for possible irregularities and sent copies of them to the podiatric licensing board for review.

None of this gave me pause. My next progressive step was to start a physical therapy program, utilizing electrical muscle stimulation and ultrasound, which sped up the healing process and reduced post-surgical complications. Then I had nitrous oxide installed in all five of my operatories. This eased patient anxiety about surgery. We even provided Sony Walkman headphones to further relax our patients and make them feel comfortable.

To keep up the momentum, I continued to build up my professional image. As a result of frequent speaking engagements, TV show appearances, various awards and honors, I received the Outstanding Young Men of America

Award in 1983 and appeared in *Who's Who In California*. I displayed these icons of achievement on the "ego wall" in my clinic office. The display had started out as a symbol of my ability to help my patients, but somewhere along the way it had become ego gratification. I personified a service, and my market share was based on the public's perception of me. If the procedure of deliberately marketing one's image seemed contrived and false, it was also impossible to maintain a high-volume medical practice without continuing publicity.

One day, in a skull session with publicist Pat Cassidy, we noted that Queen Elizabeth II would soon be arriving on a tour of Silicon Valley and had been reported as complaining that her feet were hurting her. If we could figure out a way to ease the queen's foot problem, we could gain beneficial publicity.

For some time, a colleague had been trying to get me to prescribe his newly-developed silicon insoles. The silicon molded itself to the shape of the foot and relieved pressure spots better than any material previously used. The queen and the silicon insoles seemed a terrific match. We played around with phrasing and came up with, *Silicon insoles from Silicon Valley—fit for a Queen.* I got the insoles and Pat had some satin lace insole covers made up and placed them in a velvet-lined, walnut jewelry box adorned with a royal crest.

Pat planned a photo-op to coincide with the queen's visit, and reporters and photographers were present when I appeared in front of a chauffeur-driven, vintage green Rolls Royce in my surgical smock and cap, holding the box of insoles. We had previously notified the British Consulate in San Francisco that we would be presenting a gift to the queen, and they were waiting for us when we drove into the city and presented them with the insoles. I didn't get an audience with the queen, but I did get several newspaper write-ups, including this one in the San Jose Mercury News:

> San Jose podiatrist delivered to the British Consulate yesterday a velvet-lined box complete with royal crest, containing just what every good queen needs for schlepping through Silicon Valley—silicon insoles. Dr. Augustine is National Chairman of the Public Education Committee for the Academy of Ambulatory Foot Surgery, a title exceeding in length only that of the Defender of the Faith herself.

Some of the lectures I gave on minimal incision surgery were held in Chicago, and each time I was there, I was able to visit my in-laws, old friends, and my mentor, Dr. Jay Seymour. A visit to his facility was mind-boggling. Dr. Seymour's patients formed lines that extended along the corridor to the lobby of his offices, and even to the outside. It looked for all the world like a line of people waiting to buy tickets to a popular performance, with one difference—everyone in line had foot trouble of some kind, and so they were all seated.

As Dr. Seymour's stature grew, jealous adversaries did everything possible to discredit him, but he was politically well connected and had the financial resources to keep his opponents at bay. Moreover, his entire operation was so big and successful that he seemed invulnerable. He also appeared to relish controversy and being at the cutting edge of his specialty.

As successful as Dr. Seymour's practice was, there was one podiatrist whose high fees made him look conservative by comparison. Dr. Louis Needleman's office was located on Madison Avenue, in Manhattan. He was a master at generating positive publicity, and his waiting room was covered with signed photographs of celebrities, including Hugh Downs, Jessica Tandy, and Anne Bancroft. They were happy to pay a premium for services rendered. After all, this was Madison Avenue. In many cases, however, Dr. Needleman would have to take on the insurance companies on behalf of his lesser-known clients to make sure they were properly reimbursed.

Most people believe it isn't possible to fight for higher insurance reimbursements from the company that covers them. But if an insurance company cut the reimbursements on Dr. Needleman' surgical fees, claiming they were above the customary fee level, he'd bring the company to its knees by having patients file lawsuits in small claims court. He often agreed to act as their expert witness and provided substantial documentation to justify a higherreimbursement. In most cases, the insurance companies paid rather than have someone spend time in court. If Dr. Needleman was filing the claim for himself, he would often file it in the middle of Harlem and often won by default.

A continuing need for publicity is not normally associated with operating a medical practice, but I was running a super practice, not a normal practice. Whenever I didn't appear on television or deliver talks to civic groups, etc., our patient volume quickly dropped off. Even my twenty-four-hour dial-a-tape service didn't generate enough patient bookings by itself. In order to play in the league of Drs. Needleman and Seymour—that is to say, at the very top—I needed to intensify my publicity efforts. In August of 1983, I hired a sophisticated New York City public relations company to develop a high-exposure program for me.

Meanwhile, I had to deal with criticism that minimal incision surgeons constantly faced from traditional surgeons: we were operating blind; we couldn't see what we were doing inside the foot and, consequently, we weren't able to do accurate corrective procedures. Never mind that I and many others had trained intensively for this type of surgery and were so familiar with the anatomy of the foot that we could quite literally do the procedures blind-folded; never mind that our positive results confirmed this; many of the traditionalists were still unconvinced.

Then, in November of 1983, I was able to order a state-of-the-art imaging device just approved by the Food and Drug Administration and the state of California. It was called a lixiscope, and, thanks to computer-aided imaging, it enabled us to view the bone being operated on while the surgery was in progress.

After success with the lixiscope, I was driven to move faster than anyone else. The Copley News Services, with over 400 newspapers around the country, did a feature story called "Put Your Best Foot Forward" in which I was quoted extensively. Then a popular tabloid did a series of features on state-of-the-art foot care, and each story was accompanied by a photo of me demonstrating the new procedures. *Harper's Bazaar* also did a story on my work, called "Keeping In Stride," followed by articles in *USA Today* and *Prevention Magazine*. During this time I co-authored a new book, *Holistic Foot Care*, and it was an unexpected surprise to tune in to the David Letterman Show and see him holding a copy of my new book, mentioning it to the millions of viewers in his audience. Serendipitous media events like these were pure gold; they kept our phone lines steadily busy with inquiries and did not cost us a cent. Being prominently covered by the media was intoxicating; no matter how I tried to take it in stride and treat it casually, I could not help feeling exhilarated. I was riding the crest of a magnificent wave; all I had to do was to stay with it.

One media personality said I was getting more coverage than President Reagan, but the more publicity I received, the more I wanted. It was like a drug addiction. I was getting high from fame and success, and I couldn't get enough. Although I wouldn't admit it to anyone, I wanted a shot at *20/20* and *The Johnny Carson Show.*

> ...those who make fame and the opinion of others their life's goal are always panting after it like a thirsty dog. They never find peace. Glory and others' opinions of oneself are as changeable as clouds of a stormy sky.[1]   —*Martin Gray*

Of course, I justified my panting. I told anyone who would listen that I wasn't interested in fame per se—it was just the means to an end. The formula was simple: the more famous I became, the more clients I would obtain and the more income I would receive. I said this so many times I almost believed it myself.

The lixiscope brought a quantum leap to minimal incision surgery. Prior to its introduction, we would have to shoot an X-ray onto Polaroid film and wait three to five minutes while it developed to ascertain if more work was required. The lixiscope gave on-the-spot, instant images while the procedure was performed. This enabled us to do more precise corrections and to do them more quickly, resulting in an even higher percentage of good results.

Many of my minimal incision colleagues were critical of this new device. They claimed it was a useless, high-tech gimmick. However, the ever-present fear of lawsuits was really at the basis of their criticisms. They believed that if the lixiscope were accepted, and they didn't employ it in their own practice, they could be sued for malpractice for not using it.

Given the choice of being trained to use this revolutionary new device or slandering it in the hope that it would not become widely used, many podiatric surgeons adopted the latter course. Ironically, among these were several minimal-incision surgeons who had complained bitterly that their hospital-based peers were narrow-minded and had closed their eyes to the future.

It is easier to forgive an enemy than it is a friend.

—*Mme. Dorothee Deluzy*

The successful settling of my lawsuit against the officers of the local podiatric medical society had several positive results. Not only was I vindicated and free to practice as I chose, l was seen as a dragon-slaying medical folk hero. But before I had much chance to savor my bittersweet victory, another kind of war—a more personal kind—had begun.

My good friend, teacher and staunch supporter, Dr. Ed Marlowe, had recently relocated to San Jose from Chicago. With the help of my real estate broker he had found an old home and turned it into an office, just as I had done. Later, as he became more established he even bought a newer version of my bright red 450 SL Mercedes sports car. He had asked me if it was okay, and I had said yes. After all, Ed Marlowe, twenty years my senior, had been like a wise old uncle to me, and I had relied on him for advice when things got tough. We had also become good hang-gliding buddies. How could I, in good conscience, stand in the way of such a simple request?

Ed had read my book on how to market professional services. He had all the ingredients necessary to become a podiatric celebrity—he was handsome, charismatic, outgoing, energetic, and he knew how to put people at ease and make them laugh. Ed learned quickly, and as time went on, he hired a public relations firm to launch his own marketing program.

Problems started when I was advised that Ed had somehow convinced the producer to keep me from appearing as his co-guest on *People are Talking,* a popular Bay Area television talk show I had had my sights on for some time. They were aware of my book, *The Foot Care Revolution,* and knew that Ed had written the foreword. I found out later from Ed that he had no desire to share the limelight.

Imitation may be the sincerest form of flattery, but Ed's actions did not please me. When he began competing with me, using the same media and other marketing techniques I had developed and wrote about, I found myself getting very resentful. I told myself, *Well dummy, you wrote the book on the subject for all to see; what did you expect?* For some reason, I'd had the naive and romantic notion that Ed would never compete with me. We were comrade in arms in The Foot Care Revolution. That all ended when he went public.

From Ed's side, perhaps it was just friendly competition, and there was room for both of us to be doing the same things. But from my side, it was a declaration of war. After all, as I understood it, marketing was war. For the first time I understood how my adversaries in the local podiatric medical society must have felt. Although they were not my personal friends, they must have felt betrayed by me, a colleague who chose to do his own thing without regard for the effect it would have on their livelihoods.

In *Quiet Desperation,* Jan Halper quotes Rollo May:

> This type of individual competitiveness—in which for you to fail in a deal is as good as for me to succeed, since it pushes me ahead in the scramble up the ladder—raises many psychological problems. It makes every man the potential enemy of his neighbor, it generates much interpersonal hostility and resentment, and it increases greatly our anxiety and isolation from each other.[2]

To some winning is more important than caring; competition holds a higher priority than friendship. Perhaps I was so wound up in succeeding that even the possibility of a threat constituted an actual one. How many among us remain decent, caring persons when our vital interests are threatened?

My son Jason was born on June 23, 1981, two months after the successful settlement of my lawsuit and one month after Ed's appearance on the popular afternoon TV show, *People Are Talking*. Cecile's pregnancy had been a difficult one, compounded by an inflamed heart condition that occurred only during pregnancy. It was a joyous occasion, holding my son in my arms. It should have been more joyous, except that I felt guilty for not "being there" for Cecile during a difficult time for her. I had been so wrapped up in my struggles that it seemed there was no time for anything else—a familiar refrain in my life.

My old friend, fear of commitment, was there, too. Was I ready to be a father? Did this mean more obligations? Now I was really trapped, with no way out. I looked at Jason, trying to fathom who he was, what he represented and what he would become. It was a new chapter in my life, but an unknown one whose contents I could not completely control—that was the real fear. I sensed that, in spite of all my energy, drive and abilities, this event would decide its own destiny. That was the scariest part.

When Cecile and Jason were ready to come home from the hospital, we were met by a white Rolls Royce, complete with flowers and champagne, compliments of Dr. Ed Marlowe and his publicist. Ed had gone ahead of us to meet us at our home where he would take pictures of our arrival. What a class act that was! It forced me to acknowledge that friendship can exist with competition—at least for some of us.

Ed may have forced me into competing with him, but I soon discovered that I needed the tension the competition provided. It forced me to shape up and improve my own practice. The improvements I was forced to make paid off handsomely, so, like it or not, Ed actually did me a favor by competing with me.

Where is the line between friendship and contending positions? Can these elements coexist for any length of time? Not with me, not at that time. Friendship and trust could not be apportioned into individual segments—yes on this one, no on that—at that time they needed to be all yes or all no.

In the past I had spoken out for the freedom to practice, and I had fought hard when my peers tried to deprive me of it. Could I in good conscience now deprive Ed of the same opportunity? No, I could not. But there is a big difference between respecting another's right to compete, and being able maintain a close friendship at the same time.

Yet, when I took time to reflect, I sensed that Dr. Ed Marlowe was a Life Guide, someone who had been placed there at the right time to influence my life and keep me on track. Are Life Guides always comfortable to be with? Do they, themselves, have to be perfect in order to help others? I didn't think so. Maybe Ed's message to me was that friendship and trust somehow must be reconciled with selfish interests. Or was the message that trust and friendship are sacred, there are only a limited number of slots available, and not everyone can fill them. We best hold on to what we got.

Somehow, it was too late for that. As a result of our prolonged competition, Ed and I grew distant—or at least I grew distant. I knew, intuitively, that we had to remain allied in our professional pursuits, but the price of competition was, for me, a loss of a close friendship.

In every field of human endeavor, he that is first must perpetually live in the white light of publicity. Whether the leadership be vested in a man or in a manufactured product, emulation and envy are at work...The reward and punishment is always the same. The reward is widespread recognition; the punishment, fierce denial and detraction.
—*Action Letter, Academy of Ambulatory Surgery*

In some professions, any publicity is good publicity. Not so in medicine. In July of 1984, in the midst of a tremendously successful, thriving practice, Dr. Seymour was approached by Pamela Zekman, an investigative reporter for a CBS affiliate station in Chicago. Dr. Seymour was no slouch at verbal debate and felt he could hold his own with Ms. Zekman. Against his attorney's wishes, he agreed to a series of filmed interviews.

Dr. Seymour didn't know that Ms. Zekman had a friend who developed complications as a result of surgery he performed, and she wanted revenge. The television series was titled, "The Walking Wounded."

By the sheer number of procedures Dr. Seymour had performed, there were bound to be some dissatisfied patients. There was an army of conventional podiatrists—bitter enemies—waiting for the opportunity to destroy him. In fact, Ms. Zekman boasted during one program, it was easy garnering disparaging remarks about Dr. Seymour's work from his colleagues.

A few patients were interviewed. One complained of pain while walking; one endured a severe infection; another claimed a recurrence of the problem.

No mention was made of the thousands of people who had been greatly helped by Dr. Seymour.

The television cameras had a perfect target. Dr. Seymour's late model Mercedes, his elegant mode of dress and his bluntness aided in his portrayal as an incompetent, arrogant, greedy wheeler-dealer.

Dr. Seymour wasn't a pushover; he fought back, but the negative publicity was overwhelming. The enemies he had made over the years came back to haunt him, and malpractice lawyers in the Chicago area went on a feeding frenzy. CNA Insurance, the professional liability carrier for members of the Academy of Ambulatory Foot Surgery, suddenly found itself liable for millions. While most of the cases were nuisance lawsuits that would have been dismissed in court, CNA felt it could save litigation costs by settling the cases as quickly and cheaply as possible out of court. That's how the game is played. But Dr. Seymour knew how to play, too. He immediately filed a major lawsuit against CNA for breach of contract. His claim was that CNA failed to have the cases reviewed by the peer review of the Academy to see if they were justified before making out-of-court settlements. Dr. Seymour believed he had no choice but to do this. Because CNA was settling out-of-court by paying off each claim, his policy coverage limits would soon be exceeded and he would have been personally liable for the remaining lawsuits being filed against him.

Legal maneuverings went on, but CNA just wanted out. Whichever way it went, the negative publicity surrounding Dr. Seymour and the hospital-based podiatrists represented too much of a financial risk. CNA canceled its entire coverage with our Academy, and all the members had to find new insurance coverage on their own.

A lifetime of service was destroyed. To some, Dr. Seymour may sometimes have appeared arrogant, and he may have flaunted his opulent lifestyle, but there is no doubt he was one of the great pioneers of foot care who developed innovative techniques and assisted and inspired many others in the field. Eventually, the negative publicity emboldened Dr. Seymour's enemies enough to influence the Illinois licensing board to withdraw his license to practice, and he was forced to retire. Other minimal incision surgeons felt chastened by his demise. The same thing could happen to any of us. A cloud over our entire movement has lingered ever since. One investigative reporter with circumstantial evidence, aided by the staff members of a TV station who didn't present both sides of the story helped to end the long and brilliant career of a medical pioneer and weaken and delay a national movement to provide modern foot care.

Compared with Dr. Seymour's experience, my experience with malpractice lawsuits seemed trivial. Nevertheless, I took each one seriously. Over six years of practice, I had incurred only six suits. Four were dismissed after I won in arbitration. The remaining two were settled for nuisance value. However, each case takes an emotional toll. Then, in 1984, I was sued eight times. Three suits were dismissed or dropped, one was won in arbitration, one dragged on with no activity or resolution, and three were paid off for nuisance value. As a ratio of surgical procedures, this was extraordinarily good, but the record offered little comfort. I could never get used to being sued.

Throughout my years of practice, I was conscious of potential lawsuits and extremely careful. By 1988, after thirteen years of practice, the cumulative total of settlements in my malpractice cases was only $165,000, a mere pittance compared to the million-dollar-plus judgments awarded by juries for cases of alleged negligence. But I was always fearful of the "big one."

When you are sued, the potential for disaster hangs over you like a guillotine. Even if you win all your cases, a stigma attaches to you just because you've been sued. One effective trick that malpractice lawyers use to intimidate doctors and scare them into submission is in asking for a high punitive damage award. Punitive damages are separate from damages for actual losses the patient may have suffered; they are awarded if the judge or jury believe that the doctor's negligence or misconduct is very serious and payments in addition to the actual losses are justified. This strategy is effective because punitive damages are not covered by insurance. Therefore, the doctor is sorely tempted to settle a case for damages that are covered, rather than risk the possibility that he might lose everything he owns from a high punitive award.

Most malpractice cases that go to court are won by the doctor. However, it's a rare surgeon who is willing to give up $10,000 to $30,000 for a week's work in order to defend a nuisance claim paid for by an insurance company. There is a myth in this country that doctors stick together to protect each other, even when malpractice has occurred and doctors are aware of it. This happens occasionally, among doctors who are close friends or who are part of a medical cartel, but more often nothing could be further from the truth. Most malpractice cases are either initiated or encouraged by a critical peer. In manufacturing and in other service industries, competition is recognized as healthy. There are ethical limits that businessmen do not transgress, so it is ironic that many medical professionals, usually held in higher esteem than businessmen, do not recognize these same limits.

Dr. Richard Drummond was the new maverick on the medical horizon. An up-and-coming plastic surgeon, in a few short years he had built an empire on the fashionable upper East Side of New York City. In a major feature story in *Manhattan Magazine,* Dr. Drummond was reported to have become a giant in the plastic surgery market by spending $35,000 per week on advertising. The piece claimed that Dr. Drummond would gross six million dollars that year! In September of 1985, I wrote to Dr. Drummond. After convincing him that our differing medical specialties would preclude any rivalry, and that I might be able to offer him some ideas on marketing, he agreed to let me visit his plastic surgery center. In November, Cecile and I flew to New York.

When we approached his facility, we were greeted by a uniformed doorman with the words "La Posh Cosmetic Surgery Center" emblazoned on his hat. Exiting the elevator, we entered a smartly decorated, expansive waiting room that was filled with patients from many different ethnic groups. Several attractive staff members were busily answering questions and directing patients.

Dr. Drummond was a tall, elegantly-dressed young man with a neatly manicured beard. At thirty-three, he was two years my junior. After introductions in his private offices, we were allowed to tour the operatories where his staff surgeons were working. As a podiatrist, I didn't feel qualified to judge the quality of the surgeries being performed, but his claimed rate of about one hundred surgeries per week seemed incredible. Dr. Drummond hoped to capture over fifty percent of the plastic surgery market in the United States by opening franchises across the country.

Because of the business he was taking away from his peers and his attempts to establish franchise operations around the country, Dr. Drummond had made enemies. Judging by the trouble I had run into with far less volume than he was doing, I could see the handwriting on the wall. Based on his current volume, if he had a typical failure rate of five to ten percent, I felt this man was going to have some dues to pay. Nevertheless, during our visit, we shared ideas, problems and possible solutions.

Dr. Drummond was pleasant enough, but Cecile and I sensed something about him that wasn't right. Later that day, he invited us to an elegant restaurant, and when the waiter gave us less than optimum service, Dr. Drummond publicly and loudly criticized him. When someone from management approached, he yelled, "I'm Dr. Drummond, and nobody treats me or my guests like this!" From our standpoint, the performance was totally uncalled for, but as his guests we felt it was not our place to protest.

When we parted company later that day, Dr. Drummond offered us the use of his chauffeured limousine to take us to my parents' home in New Jersey on the other side of the Lincoln Tunnel. The rush hour traffic was made worse than usual by an accident, and we were in slow traffic in a slum section on the Manhattan side of the Lincoln Tunnel when the car telephone rang and Dr. Drummond demanded that the chauffeur drop us right there—in the rain—and return to take Dr. Drummond's patients home.

He could have gotten another limousine service or called a cab for his patients—after all, he had an image to maintain—but it seemed he lacked the courtesy to do either. The embarrassed chauffeur apologized profusely, but he couldn't refuse his boss's direct order. So he left us to fend for ourselves in a rough neighborhood. Fortunately, we were soon able to hail a cab, and after we had gotten over our indignation, we started thinking that if this was how Dr. Drummond treated restaurant waiters and guests, how did he treat his patients? What made a man like Dr. Drummond tick? And for that matter, in wanting to learn from him, how much like him was I?

The things we admire in men, kindness and generosity, openness, honesty, understanding and feeling, are concomitants of failure in our system. And those traits we detest, sharpness, greed, acquisitiveness, meanness, egotism and self-interest, are the traits of success. And while we admire the quality of the first, we love the produce of the second.

— *John Steinbeck*

I had little time for such thoughts. In 1985, I'd chalked up 1.6 million dollars in income. But before I could congratulate myself, I once again asked myself, *"Have you reached your peak or can you go higher?"* The answer came as another thought: *"Well, Dennis, how much pressure can you take?"*

"Is the game of life measured by who can take the most pressure?" I asked.

"Maybe I don't have to answer that," I thought. *"Maybe if I'm just more careful, more cautious than the others..."*

As a story goes, if you place a frog in boiling water, it will instinctively jump out, but if you place a frog in cold water, and ever so gradually increase the heat, the frog will stay there until it boils to death.

CHAPTER 6

The Hole in the Top of the Mountain

The toughest thing about success is that you've got to keep on being a
success.   —*Irving Berlin*

Success was not my ultimate goal. I still believed in the magical state of
"bigness," the state where you finally have enough prestige and possessions
to produce happiness and fulfillment. So, in 1979, in the midst of my med
war, I bought an interest in a fifteen-unit apartment building and, with
minimal down payments, purchased six more rental homes in Sacramento. In
1980, I traded the apartment building for a forty-eight-unit building that
occupied almost an entire city block. My goal was to accumulate $10,000,000
worth of real estate investment properties. I figured that at a 10% annual
return, I would make a million dollars a year even without the income from
my practice. I had become a millionaire—at least on paper—at the age of
thirty, while most doctors were still grinding it out in residency programs
without a practice of their own.

Now, I no longer had time to search for good investments, so I hired an
experienced and well-recommended business manager, Mike Maglia, who
devised a plan that combined maximum asset growth and tax-free income. It
was a sophisticated program that included tax-exempt annuities, trust deeds,
equipment leasing and even cattle-feeding projects; it also involved converting
my employees to an independent staff leasing system. The financial planners

I talked with all put it this way: would you rather pay Uncle Sam and get nothing in return, or put your tax dollars in a sheltered program that could reap additional gains and allow you to defer taxes indefinitely? I didn't need much convincing, believing it absolute heresy to pay income tax that could legally be sheltered. Whenever my CPA hinted at paying some tax, I would look at him as if he were a government agent who was unethically trying to confiscate my assets.

Mike found a restored historical building in San Diego that qualified for additional depreciation deductions because of its historical status. Called the Onyx Building, it was located in the Gas Lamp Quarter of San Diego, an ongoing historical renovation area of the city. The anchor project of the area was a new convention center, which the city estimated would be completed in two or three years. I also invested in the reconstruction of two nineteenth century hotels in San Diego, the Grand Sadderly and the Horton Grand. Taken apart brick by brick and stored in a warehouse, they were be put together again on a different site in the Gas Lamp Quarter.

There was certainly risk involved. Until the space was rented, I would be carrying a $20,000 per month loss on the Onyx Building alone. I also had a 1.5 million dollar balloon payment coming due on my forty-eight-unit apartment building. With my high leveraging, I was way out on a limb and had to rob Peter to pay Paul to keep everything going. But 1983, was extremely prosperous. I doubled my total income and there seemed no limit to what I could produce.

It is a heady feeling when money comes in so fast you have to invent ways to spend or invest it.

> To be handed a lot of money is to be handed a glass sword, blade-first.
> Best handle it carefully, sir, very slowly, while you puzzle what it's for.[1]
> —*Richard Bach*

Cecile and I discovered a magnificent estate in the hills of Saratoga, near San Jose. Using proceeds from the sale of our previous home, the equity for which in California's booming real estate market had appreciated to over $300,000, we put a substantial down payment on the million-dollar-plus estate. We were now really on the top of the mountain, but living in luxury was a relatively small part of my satisfaction. The bigger part was knowing that I had bested my competitors, who could only dream of such grandeur.

Unfortunately, the satisfaction of being on the top was short-lived, for the challenge of climbing was replaced by the challenge to keep the empire intact. I knew my competitors were not going to roll over and play dead, and I'd read that material success was not a guarantor of happiness, but I hadn't anticipated the fear. I was terrified that it would all be taken away from me, and that I would once again be a nonentity. The thought of becoming mediocre, insignificant and ordinary was almost too much to bear.

There was only one way to keep the empire intact—achieve more. The more credentials I could collect, the more positive publicity I could garner, the more books I could publish, the more lectures I could deliver, the more real estate I could acquire, and the more income I could generate, the more protection I would have from the forces threatening to take it all away.

I continued to pursue material acquisition while the intensity of my fear of loss increased with each achievement. I believed that money and possessions insulated me from the threats of the outside world. But in insulating myself, I was all the more alone, and the more alone I was, the more vulnerable I felt.

By American standards, I was an outstanding success. I looked around and saw two beautiful Mercedes, an elegant home, and a net worth in millions, and yet I was more insecure and filled with self-doubt than I had ever been in my life.

All religion begins with the cry 'Help!'

—*William James*

Psychologists tell us that success is more than having wealth and possessions, more than gaining prestige. They say that true success comes from enjoying the process of creating and moving ahead, not just from keeping score of accomplishments. But enjoying the process is not always easy in our modern, competitive culture. In my case, the process itself was destroying me.

The process involved my taking on more and more responsibility. It meant living a leveraged lifestyle with enormous debts whose servicing required an uninterrupted high level of income. I couldn't let up because I needed the income to keep making payments. I was in constant consultation with advisers, all of whom had different, conflicting ideas on how I should spend, protect and invest my newfound wealth. I had no time for anything but the process itself.

I rarely saw family or friends—every moment was needed just to keep things going. Through the constant attention to business, I became isolated, an isolation magnified the belief that no one else could understand my problems or the heavy load I was carrying. After a while, I found myself just going through the motions. I was on a treadmill, becoming wealthier and more prestigious, but never feeling satisfied.

Slowly, the charge and excitement of building higher and higher, bringing in more and more, began to wear off, but the responsibilities didn't go away. With never enough time in the day to finish everything, you feel trapped in a routine that's no longer a challenge but a drudge. When this happens, you lose your sharp edge, the finely-honed skills that have brought you this far. You lose some perspective and make some bad decisions. Self-doubt creeps in, and the high-pressure routine leaves you fatigued.

Exasperated, you consult your closest colleagues and find they're experiencing the same thing, pursuing the same dreams and making the same mistakes. Your role models, are suffering, too. Their families are coming apart. Scandals, costly litigation and other calamities engulf them. For a moment, you think: am I worshipping the wrong idols?

But how can that be? You're at the top of your field—an absolute, unqualified success. Peers want to discover your secrets. You are constantly in the public eye. Can you remain there, surrounded by jealous enemies who continually attack you? Can you remain sane?

You feel alone, but that's the nature of the game. As you approach the mountain top, you discover there's no room for others. Something's happening, but you don't know what it is. You can't give up; you haven't reached the very top, the place where at last you'll be unassailable, where no one, absolutely no one can reach you.

But you're stuck. You can't bear the thought of continuing, and you can't consider giving up and losing what you've gained. In the absence of understanding, it's easier to keep going than to stop. So you keep going, robot-like, until something happens, until something happens to stop you.

Something happened.

Snorkeling in St. Thomas in 1985 was a treat. The warm waters reminded me of summers in Sicily. We looked forward to returning to Saratoga and a home surrounded by gardens and perennial sunshine.

My marriage was happy and we had a wonderful five-year-old son. My podiatric practice was making 1.6 million a year, and I had an impressive real estate portfolio. I had achieved local celebrity status as a surgeon, was Secretary of the Academy of Ambulatory Foot Surgery, and a sought-after national lecturer. The street kid from Hoboken had made it big, a multi-millionaire at thirty-five, but something was wrong with paradise.

On the eve of our departure from Miami Beach, I felt restless. I had a series of bad dreams and woke up in a cold sweat. As I lay there, I reminisced about what I'd accumulated through the years—the money and the status—and in the very process of acknowledging my accomplishments, I began to feel very anxious. My emotions were tightly coiled up within me. I never allowed them out. I took pride in this perverse accomplishment. How cool I seemed, under pressure. Everyone who knew me admired my ability to remain detached no matter what was happening. I was not only an American Success Story, I was unflappable.

But my mentor, Dr. Jay Seymour, the personification of the hard-driving, successful celebrity/physician, had fallen from grace and was facing potential financial ruin. And shortly before our Caribbean trip, my father-in-law had died. Harry had been a wonderful man and I loved him dearly. Kind and considerate to all but himself, Harry had worked himself to death.

I sensed these were two warning shots across my bow, but why should I dwell on them? I was only thirty-five years old; was it already time for a mid-life crisis? *How foolish!* I suppressed the feeling of foreboding flooding through me and countered with rational arguments. *It's only natural for me to be anxious,* I thought. *I have been attacked again and again by medical peers. I have juggled a large number of investment projects, with their demands and risks, and some of them had gone bad. My career and my investments have required me always to be alert, on guard, and in tight control of my affairs. And I will continue to be. I have to be.*

But something odd was happening. I felt like I was coming apart. It's not as though I never had feelings. Sure I had them. I was as sentimental and romantic as anyone. During movies, when Cecile would shed tears freely, I came close to tears myself. But I bottled it up, fighting the evidence that I felt anything. My feelings were a private affair, to be felt if necessary, but never displayed.

Then an irrational fear, one that reached back to my childhood, popped up. My repressive Catholic upbringing entered my thoughts and I wondered if God was punishing me for something I'd done wrong. I remembered the sisters telling me, "Dennis, you'll go to hell if you continue like that," and "Feel God's wrath, Dennis, then you'll be sorry for what you've done!" I tried to force the fears out of my mind and bring my thoughts back to the practical world, pretending that this wasn't really happening to me. I had so many responsibilities, so many things to control. If I didn't control them all, I'd lose them. But was it worth the endless struggle for more publicity, more patients, more investment ventures, higher returns, safer profits, more shelters to avoid taxes?

Lying in bed, I suddenly felt tired, very tired. I had the urge to cry. I hadn't actually cried since I was a small boy. Now, I felt the pressure of tears welling up. I sat up in bed and suddenly could no longer control myself. The dam broke, and I was a little boy again, crying out my hurt, shuddering and sobbing, powerful feelings coursing through me like a tornado rushing across the plains.

Cecile awoke from a sound sleep and gaped at me. In all the years she had known me, she had never seen me like this. I cried to her that I was a failure, a weakling hiding behind a mask of strength, a dumb bumbler who thought he had all the answers. I cried that I couldn't go back to it, couldn't do it any longer, couldn't hold it all together anymore. Still sobbing, I fell into a troubled sleep, fraught with images. I was cornered in a deep pit and forced to watch the residue of my past experiences flitting across my vision. Long lost memories and unresolved needs were like wash to be hung out to dry and then sorted.

In that deep pit, I died and left everything behind me. It was more real than the most immediate of waking experiences. Then I awoke again to find myself suspended; one part of me was dead and the other unable to be born. I was once again in the now, but with a clear visual image. I saw myself as part of the immense puzzle of creation, but the pieces—the people and events in my life—were being pulled away, the puzzle was coming apart; no, wait, the puzzle wasn't coming apart; the puzzle piece which was my life was separating. It was like a strip of land breaking off from a continent and becoming an island. I saw myself floating out to sea. The world that had always surrounded and defined me was leaving. A rush of fear scrambled through my mind, telling me I was now to be cast adrift, homeless.?

I don't know how long I cried. My body felt like a limp rag, and as I started to feel sorry for myself, I noticed something else that was new to me—my mind had stopped. The ever-present mental chatter had halted. And in its place was a deep sense of peace and contentment. Then I felt an urge, an urge to ask for help, but from whom? Suddenly I remembered a passage from *The Three Pillars of Zen:*

"I am dying," I sobbed. "I have killed all my gods. I have no key to resurrection. I am totally alone." Stark fear and utter despair possessed me and I lay on the floor for I don't know how long until from the pit of my abdomen a cry came forth: "If there is any being in the entire earth who cares whether I live or die, help me, oh help me!"[2]

I repeated these words, whispering into the cosmic ear, repeating the last ones like a mantra, over and over: *help me, help me, help me!*

Those who have more or less normally expressed their feelings all their lives may find this account melodramatic. After all, everyone has an emotional catharsis from time to time. What's the big deal? But this was my very first time as an adult. I had always been in control, my feelings always subjugated to my will. When my feelings broke loose and ran from captivity, it was an incomprehensible, terrifying experience. It felt as if an alien had totally taken over my body and mind.

When the tide of emotion had ebbed, a ray of hope made itself known in the peaceful stillness of the afterglow. It was a moment of wisdom and attunement. Fears were cast aside, and mind and heart, together, glimpsed the true nature of existence. It augured movement but did not divulge direction.

There is an atmosphere of irresistible fascination about the figure that appears suddenly as guide, marking a new period, a new stage in the biography.
—*Joseph Campbell*

It had been an unusually long day. I had seen forty patients and performed seven surgeries. I was exhausted, not just from this day but from a month of depression and fatigue. Several weeks had passed since my cry for help, and my stoic demeanor had been shattered. As far as I could tell, no help was forthcoming. The last thing I needed at the close of office hours was the sudden arrival of a new patient, someone without an appointment who demanded to be seen. Apparently, he had a badly infected toenail and was in a great deal of pain. As tired as I was, I simply couldn't ignore his plight. Telling the staff that I would handle this last patient myself, I asked my receptionist to bring me the patient's form before she departed. I slumped in my office chair and rubbed my eyes for a moment.

When I opened my eyes again, the form (with "Welcome To Our Office" printed across the top) was in front of me. The words seemed blurry, and at first I was unable to make out the patient's writing. Then my vision cleared and I did a double-take as I read the patient's name: Hippocrates. Just beneath it, he had entered his address in a finely-scrolled handwriting—Cos, Greece. I could appreciate a joke as well as anyone, but I felt so drained that the last thing I needed was to treat a crackpot who thought he was the legendary Greek physician. I'd refer this "Dr. Hippocrates" to the Valley Medical Center's emergency room and then go home.

As I walked into the treatment room, I expected to find some downtown wino, so I was surprised to see an aristocratic-looking man with a neat beard and wavy white hair, wearing an obviously well-tailored suit. He was short and spoke in a soft voice with an accent I couldn't place. His manner was courteous and cultured. If he was a crackpot, he certainly was not a typical one. Trying to shed some light on what was happening, I said to him, "Now really, what kind of work do you do? Are you a professional actor?"

"No," he said, "I'm a doctor." I asked him to describe his background, and he said, "I was a contemporary of Socrates and studied medicine under my father, Heraclides. If I may say so, I was a fairly diligent student of the prominent atomist, Democritus, and I am proud to add I was also an Asclepiad, a member of the guild that was inspired by the God of healing."

Whoever he was, he had done his homework and seemed to know his way around ancient Greece. I had no idea what was going on, or the reason for it, but I was intrigued and some of my tiredness left me. "Okay, Dr. Hippocrates," I said, "it's time we addressed your problem."

His right foot was propped on a treatment chair, and it was evident that the infection in his big toe had been bothering him for some time. "What treatment do you recommend?" the self-proclaimed Hippocrates asked. My professional reflexes took over and, as if I was speaking to a real physician, I said, "First we need to clear up the infection. Then a $\frac{1}{8}$-inch section of your ingrown nail will be removed under local anesthesia and the area will be incised and drained to get rid of the exudate." He nodded reassuringly, and I continued. "Then I will put you on an antiseptic soaking solution program, culture the wound and prescribe a wide spectrum antibiotic. After that—"

Hippocrates interrupted me to say, "After that, you'll wait seven to ten days for the infection to clear up and then you'll cauterize the root of the toenail border...possibly with your CO2 laser, so the condition won't recur."

I stared at him without speaking. I felt curiosity, fear and awe. In a whisper, I said, "How did you know that?"

"I have been keeping up with my studies since I left my practice," Hippocrates said casually. "I'm particularly fascinated with your laser. In my own day, we used a rudimentary magnifying glass to intensify the sun's rays and we were able to remove small superficial growths and cauterize them without anesthesia. Nothing like what you have, of course. But then again, we had healing agents that worked much more quickly than those you have today."

I wasn't in the mood to challenge him, and I fell back on my professional demeanor. I cleaned the infection site and quickly wrote out a prescription for an appropriate antibiotic and handed it to him. "Here. Fill this prescription as soon as you can and start taking these pills tonight. You must come back tomorrow so I can remove the portion of your nail that is ingrown."

I walked the dapper gentleman to the lobby and unlocked the door for him. I was so flustered I forgot to present him with a bill for my services. Then Hippocrates or whoever he was, raised his right arm in some kind of salute and said, "Thank you, Dr. A. Until tomorrow." Then he left.

There was a heavy load of patients next day, so I was glad when the last patient and the staff had gone. In spite of myself, I had been anticipating Hippocrates' return all day and was disappointed that the elderly gentlemen had not yet made an appearance. Just then I heard a sharp tapping on the lobby door and went to open it. There he was, dressed in a different but equally stylish suit and tie.

"Sorry to be so late, Dr. A., but I had some…uh…difficulty getting here." He followed me into the examination room and sat down. Remembering the poor condition of his toe, I challenged him:

"If you're really a physician, why did you allow your condition to go unattended for so long?" With a look of total innocence, Hippocrates said quietly, "What condition?" And casually removed his shoe and sock.

I looked down. The toenail which a day ago had been badly swollen, obviously infected, and severely ingrown, was now perfectly normal. I examined it for traces of infection but there were none at all—it had completely healed. I felt the blood drain from my face, and I sat motionless as I watched Dr. Hippocrates slowly put back on his sock and shoe.

There was no possibility of pretense through makeup or other artifice—I had seen too many badly infected toenails to be deceived in that way. Trembling slightly, I looked at Hippocrates and asked quietly, "Who are you and why are you here?"

"Remember that night in Miami last month," Hippocrates said, "when you were in a state of uncontrollable anguish? Remember how ashamed, how mortified you felt at the sudden display of emotions you'd been suppressing for so long?"

This was too much. I shouted, "All right, who are you, really? What right do you have to meddle in my personal life?"

"You asked for help, don't you remember? You prayed for guidance and forgiveness. You asked to be released from the chains of bondage that were weighing you down. Am I paraphrasing you correctly?"

It was numbing to realize that he spoke the truth. I hadn't divulged my emotional turmoil to anyone but Cecile, so there was no way Hippocrates could have known this by ordinary means.

"How did you heal your toe?" I asked.

"Let's just say it was a technique I learned a long time ago," Hippocrates said, "and I've had a few thousand years to perfect it."

"But that's impossible!"

"Is it really? You mean to tell me you don't believe what you just saw with your own eyes?" he said. "Now you sound like your medical adversaries who claim your own procedures are impossible, or unsafe, or unsound, when you know that they work."

He had nailed me on that one. It was the narrow, biased disbelief of my peers that had caused me and my close associates so much trouble through the years.

"Look," he said, "the toe was just to get your attention. What you think of me isn't important. It doesn't really matter whether I am who I say I am or a skilled charlatan. What is important is that you understand the message. The issue to be resolved here is what to do with the rest of your life. How are you going to free yourself for what you really want? I'm simply here to help you. It's going to require a lot of hard work—mostly on your part."

I don't know if I started to believe at that point or not, but I was impressed. He was saying things I needed to hear, and the source didn't matter. As if listening to my thoughts, Hippocrates continued, "No, I'm certainly not God as you think of Him—far from it. But I am a god in the sense that we are all gods, that we are all a part of divinity…at least until we lose ourselves in the pursuit of worldly things."

"As I have done?"

"As you have done."

Again silence. Maybe it was my fatigue or maybe it was being confronted by the plain, unvarnished truth, but I felt tears flooding my eyes. I bowed my head and sobbed silently. I felt a gentle hand on my shoulder.

"Dr. A," he began (that was what my office staff called me…another thing Hippocrates couldn't have known), "what matters is now. I've been chosen to help you because we are alike in many respects. My work was controversial, just as yours has been, and I, too, was deeply involved with the politics of medicine of my time.

"My real passion was teaching philosophy and spirituality, you know, but I gave all my time and energy to medicine. Not that there weren't rewards— there were, over the ninety years that I lived on earth, but I never followed my true calling. And I've had plenty of time to regret it.

"Now we both have a chance. I'm here to assist you in following your true passion. Most of the work will be yours, for you have to discover your real passion and you have to find the determination to follow it. My job is to give you occasional hints to keep you on the right track."

"What do you mean when you said we both have a chance?" I asked.

"This is my opportunity to follow the passion that I denied myself a long time ago, Hippocrates said. You are as much my opportunity as I am yours." He paused for several seconds, then said "I must be going now."

Hippocrates placed his hand firmly on my shoulder, then withdrew it. "Oh, excuse me," he said, "this is how you do it now," and he extended his hand to shake mine. Then he said "Good-bye," turned and rapidly walked out.

I remained immobile for a moment, then ran out the door to the waiting room. There was no one there. I checked the exit door—it was locked. Then I ran back into my office. It was still, and I was alone. I picked up his patient registration form and read it more closely. On it, for patient's age, was the number "2446."

Are visitations real? And what is "real?" Hippocrates' foot certainly felt tangible when I examined it. So had his hand when we shook hands. Even the chair he sat in had squeaked. I still have the patient form with his writing on it, but what does that prove? It's easy to be skeptical about mystical experiences until they happen to you. In the few minutes (if time was still operative) that Hippocrates was in my office, I changed from total skeptic to…to what? I know that something had happened that was important. After leaving the office, I felt lighter and more confident. My problems and my burdens didn't miraculously disappear, and the correct path for my life didn't suddenly and dramatically make itself known to me. But I sensed that it would come, that I had made a start. And that was enough for the moment.

CHAPTER 7

Introduction to Wisdom

Here is Edward Bear, coming downstairs now, bump, bump, bump, on the back of the head, behind Christopher Robin. It is, as far as he knows, the only way of coming downstairs, but sometimes he feels that there really is another way, if only he could stop bumping for a moment and think of it.

—*A.A. Milne*

Hippocrates told me to find direction and said he'd be able, from time to time, to guide me, but what was I supposed to do now? I cast around, weighing different directions, but I had single-mindedly gone one way for so long that, somehow, all my casts landed in the same place—a place called "more." It seemed out of the question to come to a halt and reverse my direction. Wouldn't a relatively small change suffice? Maybe that's why I went to see Dr. Gary Wyatt, in Los Angeles.

Gary was one of the most successful podiatrists in the United States, the principal mover and shaker behind what was rumored to be a multi-million dollar medical corporation. His facility produced more income than Dr. Seymour's or Dr. Needleman's, but where they were flamboyant and combative, Gary was cool, calm and totally focused. Five podiatric surgeons worked for him, and his Los Angeles facility was a certified surgical center, or surgicenter (i.e., something between a doctor's office and a hospital surgery where outpatient procedures are performed in a well-equipped, safe environment whose costs are considerably lower than those of a hospital). A surgicenter has considerably more profit potential for the surgeon than a doctor's office. In addition to the podiatrist's bills for procedures rendered, a surgicenter is reimbursed by insurance companies for the use of operating rooms, nurses, IV's, anesthesia, etc., effectively doubling the surgeon's income for services rendered.

Dr. Wyatt's surgicenter was low key, quiet and superbly efficient. I thought I had a lucrative practice and was one of the highest of high-rollers in my profession. Now I realized I had fallen into the same trap of complacency that had snared my competitors. The surgicenter was the wave of the future, and I had completely missed it.

I left Gary's offices more excited than I'd been in years. Here was the answer I needed to give new direction to my life! I could hardly contain myself. Hippocrates had told me to find my true passion, and now it felt like I had. This was my passion, to achieve more wherever there was more to achieve. It would be another "first" for me—the first podiatric surgical center in the San Francisco Bay Area, and the crowning jewel of my career. As soon as I got back to San Jose, I would start drawing up plans for a new surgicenter.

In the science of mechanics, momentum is defined as the property of a moving body that requires a specific amount of force to alter its speed or direction. It takes force, or energy, to slow an object, and even more to bring it to a complete stop and reverse its direction. Mental momentum has different properties. It seems that the longer we've been moving in one direction, the more energy it takes to alter our course. Mental momentum also seems to possess a built-in booster. When we encounter bumps along the road of life—even those that are attempting to teach us a lesson—our booster kicks in and propels us forward even faster. Perhaps that is why we're so good at ignoring lessons and why we continue to do the very things that do us harm—more eagerly, more efficiently and more rapidly than before.

Without being aware of it, I participated in the "greater fool theory," which states that in inflationary times there is always a greater fool to pay a higher price for a property. Of course, when inflation slows down, the theory dissolves, and the person holding the property at the time the bubble bursts becomes the greatest fool.

In the early months of 1986, rumors began to circulate that the Federal Government was about to pull the plug on tax shelters. Too many frauds and abuses had come to the attention of legislators. When the Tax Reform Act of 1986 was passed, a number of well-heeled investors started to run scared. The new tax laws primarily affected investors like me, those carrying large, negative cash flows on their properties. Leverage is a wonderful tool when things are going well, but when the economy declines, the highly-leveraged investor is the first to bite the dust.

My eyes had been opened by visiting Dr. Gary Wyatt's podiatric surgical center in Los Angeles. After my return, my eyes were opened again—this time, to my investment naiveté. The Onyx Building, which I had bought in San Diego three years earlier, had never been fully leased, and was now costing me $15,000 each month. I had paid over 2.2 million dollars for the Onyx, and I'd also paid for many improvements. Now, with a soft real estate market, a delay in the building of the adjacent convention center, and a delay in the building being granted historical status for, I discovered it was worth only 1.3 million at best.

The hardest part was acknowledging that I had made a mistake. In spite of all my real estate studies, despite picking the smartest, most reliable advisers, I had goofed. I gritted my teeth. *"Goddammit, I am not a loser,"* I thought. *"My road is up, not down!"* My reflexive response was not to cut my losses, but to figure out how to make enough money to more than compensate for them. I was like a degenerate gambler who had a continuing need to up the ante. Meanwhile, there was a surgicenter to build, the prospects of income even beyond what I had thought possible, and a new element in my life.

At about 4:30 on the afternoon of December 3rd, 1986, Cecile gave birth to our daughter, Michelle Ilyse. This joyous event almost didn't happen. When she was pregnant with Jason, Cecile suffered a serious heart inflammation and had terminated a subsequent pregnancy at the recommendation of her doctor. Although it had never been confirmed, Cecile felt the unborn child was a girl, and she badly wanted to try again. However, our internist was strongly against it, and advised us to end this pregnancy. "Cecile, you shouldn't risk it," he had said, "but if you insist on trying, I'll try to find an obstetrician who will deliver the baby." Because of his pessimistic attitude, we decided to change doctors to an OB/GYN specialist working out of Stanford.

After a comprehensive evaluation, Dr. DiSilva felt confident that Cecile could have a successful pregnancy if she refrained from all physical labor and literally stayed off her feet. That's all we needed to hear. The contrast in attitude between our previous internist and our new doctor was amazing. The Stanford physician and his team were not only highly competent, they had total confidence in themselves and in us. It reminded me of my own medical optimism and the confidence I instilled in my patients when competing surgeons said something couldn't be done.

My beautiful daughter, Michelle, was proof of the validity of that optimism.

After Michelle had spent some time bonding with Cecile, she was cleaned off, wrapped in a soft blanket, and handed to me to take to the nursery. As ecstatic as I was, some of my old doubts about added responsibilities came flooding in. I suppose it was laughable, being anxious about another mouth to feed when our net worth was in the millions, but it felt real to me. From that small point of anxiety, my thoughts ran to the present and my plans for the surgicenter.

There I was, walking down a hospital corridor holding my infant daughter and thinking about the surgicenter when a doctor in a light green surgical smock and cap fell in step alongside me. He had snowy white hair and a distinguished look, managing somehow to look dapper even in his surgical outfit. "Congratulations, Dr. A."

My mouth dropped open, and I stopped abruptly. "Hippocrates, what are you doing here?"

"My, how quickly we forget," he said. "I see you're about to get yourself in trouble again. Didn't you learn your lesson that night in Miami?"

"I'm not in trouble. In fact, I've found a new goal."

"Really," he said dryly, arresting me to look into my eyes, his face close to mine. "Here, let me hold her for a minute." Before I could protest, he took Michelle from me and started cooing to her for all the world like a proud grandfather.

I wasn't going to let him change the subject. "With a surgical center I can gain more income and more prestige. Plus it will be a benefit to my patients."

"Really," he said.

"I'll reach a level where I'll have no peer. Besides, the practice will be more efficient with a new, larger facility."

"That's fine, Dr. A. Just fine," he said, thrusting Michelle back into my arms. "Be seeing you." He started to walk away.

"Wait a minute," I said, rocking tiny Michelle, who'd started to cry, "I guess I'm not really as sure of this as I sound."

He came back. "Well, at least that's something. Don't you remember that you were going to seek your true passion. You were going to set yourself free to follow your true calling. A 'surgicenter,' as you call it, is your true calling? For Zeus' sake, Dr. A., wake up!" Once again, he started to walk away.

"But, Hippocrates, how can I tell when I find my true calling?" He was halfway down the corridor when he turned to call out, "You'll feel it. And the closer you get to it, the more you'll know when you're on the wrong track." Then he was gone and I entered the nursery more confused than ever.

Michelle was a blessing for us. She made our family seem whole and complete, and we all adored her. I was immensely proud of Cecile and the way she had made it through the complete term to deliver a healthy baby. But in spite of a new baby in the house, the surgicenter occupied my mind. After granting me preliminary approval, the City of San Jose rejected my plan for the new center. Had Hippocrates known about that in advance? No matter, I wasn't about to just sit back and accept it. I felt like I was being pushed, and, as usual, I decided to push back.

Help me, Cassius, or I sink!
—*William Shakespeare, Julius Caesar*

Reluctantly, I went to see Bob Goodheart. Believing that each individual should be able to handle his own affairs, coming from a family that regarded the seeking of professional help tantamount to an admission of insanity, I was careful to tell acquaintances that Bob was a business consultant—I couldn't bring myself to admit he was a shrink.

Nothing seemed to be going right. Many of my investments were souring and my plans for the surgicenter had been denied by the city of San Jose. Perhaps I should have been used to adversity by now, but I just couldn't muster the determination to go on fighting. Much of the sparkle and pleasure had gone out of my life, and I couldn't make decisions anymore. Each day seemed to increase my apathy and melancholy. And so, in January of 1987, I went to see Bob Goodheart.

The setting was unusual. Bob's office occupied the entire top floor of a converted church. Unlike typical offices, Bob's single, large office spread across several different working areas with no walls or other barriers to separate them. The high, ornate cathedral ceilings were reminders of the building's past. It seemed significant to me that people were now coming to an abandoned church and seeking help in a counseling chair—a modern-day confessional. Oddly enough, I never saw any other patients in Bob's office and there were no secretaries to take his calls. For that matter, there were no calls—the phone simply never rang.

I was filled with a sense of mystery but also a sense of serenity. I couldn't help but think of the many parishioners who had come here to hear sermons, partake of ritual and share fellowship. It reminded me that I hadn't attended regular church services since I was an adolescent.

To ease my embarrassment, we started out talking about my investments. For a considerable time, we analyzed what I had done and then I complained that if I attempted to sell any of my properties, I would be required to pay all the taxes I had been able to defer for years. Bob put that in perspective. "Look Dennis, you've enjoyed living off the taxes that you didn't pay all those years. You hedged your debts in favor of using tax dollars for purchasing other investments and for living a higher life style. And you were able to do both."

It was true. I had made enormous gains—gains that I could not have done without playing the deferment game. My problem was that I had never looked at the possibility of having to pay the piper. I had kept trading my properties up, putting them in a family trust, with the intention to defer taxes indefinitely. I had never given any thought to my priorities changing or to the government's changing the tax rules mid-game.

"You became a willing partner," Bob told me, "in a game that's run by the rules of capitalism. And when you play the game, you derive some benefits from your participation. When you exit the game, you can't just quit and cash in your chips. There are consequences. You have to pay a fee to get out; think of it as an exit visa. But that's not the most significant point, Dennis. Everyone makes mistakes or, rather, errors in judgment, and most of us learn from them. Your problem is twofold. First, you're blaming the government and your advisers for your own naiveté."

POW! That hit me hard. Bob was right. I'd gotten sucked into the victim mentality, seeing myself beset by outside forces that were trying to do me in. It brought me back to my est training, and what I had learned about assuming responsibility for the events in my life.

"The second part of your problem—and this is the more important part," Bob went on, "is not that you made a mistake and blamed others for it…it's that you thought you were invincible!"

It's amazing how a few words can sometimes cut through years of fuzzy thinking and cause a profound shift in attitude. It was all true. I had signed up for the game of capitalism, without realizing that there were dues to be collected, and that the rules could be changed at any time by the game manager—the U.S. government. In a flash of belated insight, I realized the trap I had set for myself and that it would not be easy to escape. Most of all, I realized then and there that I no longer wanted to play.

"The irony of all this," I said, "is that I had planned to be financially independent by the time I was forty. I had pretty much accomplished this until recently. Now I don't know what's going to happen—and, quite frankly, I'm scared."

"What are you so scared of?"

"Well, I have this fear of losing everything. Plus, I expected to climb higher on the financial ladder. For another, I've always prided myself on getting around any obstacles that were placed in front of me."

"So, this is one time you didn't have your way, and it's burning at your craw. Some of your marbles are being taken away by the big bullies down the street, and you're angry."

"I am. And I feel beaten down. It's been a humbling experience. I get these outbursts of emotions at odds times of the day or night. I'll be sitting alone for a moment, and, suddenly, it's as though I'm watching a tearjerker movie."

"Dennis, it costs something to be more open. These mood swings are part of the price you pay for becoming a fuller person."

So far, even though I'd been jolted with new insights, the discussion had been on understandable, familiar, comfortable turf. We went on to talk about truth, and I told Bob I'd been trying to discover what was right for me but was unsure how to proceed. I was careful not to mention Hippocrates—that was part of my experience I wanted to keep to myself. Then Bob introduced a concept that was new to me.

"In the Western view, the only way to know the truth is to draw from your experience. This has a severe limitation, because the only way to know the whole truth is to experience everything. But that's impossible. Therefore, you can never know the whole truth. That's been a part of your problem, Dennis. You've relied on your experiences for your sense of truth and rightness. Your experiences as a kid on the streets of Hoboken, fighting your medical competitors, these have been marvelous teaching tools, but they aren't everything—they don't contain the whole truth.

"Look at it this way," Bob said. "What we have all around us are people living with partial truths. Each individual goes on collecting experiences and charting his course based on those experiences. His decisions are based on reason, but reason is limited to those things he has experienced or can logically construct. So he goes his own way doing the best he can, never knowing the whole truth about what he is doing or why he is doing it."

I couldn't figure out what Bob was getting at. How else can we learn other than from our experience? As if reading my mind, he continued, "There is another possibility. The Eastern view is to take one object and peel off its layers like an onion, layer by layer until you get down to the core of the matter. At the core of any matter is the essence of all matter."

This kind of talk was stimulating, but it made me feel a bit uneasy, although I wasn't sure why. "That's interesting philosophy, Bob, but what's the point? What has it to do with my life?"

"What it means, Dennis, is that by dealing with an object, or an event, by focusing on it and understanding its central core, its essence, you can know the entire truth within all matter and within all events. By understanding that essence, that universal truth, you can best deal with all other experiences."

"Wait a minute, wait a minute, Bob. You just made a big leap. How does knowing the truth of one thing lead to the truth of all things?"

"Well, take particle physics—you know, where physicists try to find the ultimate nature of matter by searching for an ultimate, indivisible particle. In a broader sense, every bit of matter, every thought, every event has an essential quality that defines it. If I can make a crude analogy, it's as if you could look into someone's eyes so deeply that you are able to understand not only everything about them, but about the entire human race as well. When you begin to understand the essential nature of one thing, you will begin to understand the essential nature of everything."

"Okay, suppose I go along with that for the moment. How do I peel the layers off the onion? How do I get to know the essence of a thing?"

"Start with intuition. Let's use the example of a guillotine. Imagine lying with your head in a guillotine. Above your head hangs the sharp blade. You have one chance to survive. There is a rope by your left hand and a rope by your right hand. One of those ropes is unattached; the other drops the blade. Observation—that is, reason—won't tell you which rope to pull. What do you do?"

"I don't know."

"There's nothing to go by, but if you can muster the 'cool' to do it, you try to 'feel' the answer, feel which rope is unconnected and which linked to the blade. You can't arrive at the answer by reason alone. You need to 'feel' the answer by employing your own deep intuition—something like Luke Sky-walker did by trusting the 'force' in *Star Wars*."

"You mean, take any issue, evaluate it for the questions it poses, and let my intuition find the truth of the matter? What if I don't believe in intuition?"

"Then you're mucking up the whole process. You have to begin with a small, a very small act of faith."

Now I knew where my feeling of uneasiness was coming from. I'd had a sense about where this was heading. Faith. I hadn't had a lecture on faith since Catholic school, and I wasn't sure I wanted one now. I admitted to Bob that I didn't know how to get to the spiritual side of things. Theology was not one of my favorite subjects, and blind faith was not part of my vocabulary. There had been too many abuses and frauds committed in the name of religion.

"No, no, Dennis, don't get hung up in religious dogma. I'm not talking about that. When I say faith, I simply mean faith in yourself. Just enough faith to allow yourself to begin to trust your intuitive judgments."

"I've always relied on my judgment in the past. But what about now? Part of my judgment insists I overcome the obstacles to building a surgicenter (maybe I could change the site, appeal the city's decision or revise the plans) while another part tells me that I don't want any part of it. Which do I follow?"

"The best way I can express it," Bob continued, "is that when you listen to your heart peacefully, quietly and without expectations, your true self will speak to you, and you'll know what you really want. Listening to oneself is a skill that most moderns have lost. It needs to be regained."

Bob's words could have been spoken by Hippocrates, and I wasn't completely certain that they weren't, since I'd had a feeling the Greek was aware of what I was doing even when I couldn't see him.

"Sometimes," I admitted, "when I listen to myself in a quiet moment, it hurts. I don't like the outpouring of emotions."

"Dennis, it's not necessary to like them, or to be comfortable with them. All you need is a bit of faith (that word again) that the strong emotions you feel are a part of growing, of maturation, of being alive. Quit trying to figure everything out. Just begin by having faith that you are getting in deeper touch with your humanity and that a highly intelligent part of you is becoming free to guide you in the right direction."

"The idea of paying attention to what you're really feeling and really doing relates to what I've read about the teachings of Gurdjieff."*

"Yes, but Gurdjieff was talking about ultimate knowledge of what we are

---

* Georgy Ivanovitch Gurdjieff, born on the Russo-Turkish frontier (thought to be around 1866), a mystic and spiritual teacher who postulated that people are no more than machines run by forces outside their control.

and why we are here. According to Gurdjieff, it took him and twenty other people in his life who were partially awake to assist each other continually in realizing what was really happening. The tendency toward self-hypnosis was so strong, he felt, that most of the time we act like machines."

As we came to the end of a long and, for me, illuminating session, this erudite psychologist who, I came to learn, gave a lot of credence to myths and legends said, "According to the Old Testament, Solomon started off as king of the Jews. As he was about to assume the reins of power, he prayed to God for divine guidance. Because he was righteous and had asked on behalf of all his people, God bestowed on Solomon enormous power and wealth. God empowered him to act on His behalf, for their benefit. But Solomon got caught up in wine, women and song, and the entire *Book of Solomon* recounts his despair when he veered off course from his mission. This is the story of a guy who stopped listening and stopped growing, who was too busy gratifying himself to hear anything or learn anything.

"Solomon could have had it all if he'd understood that the money and power wasn't really his—he was only the channel through which they flowed. The lesson I get from this is that money and power come and go, and we can enjoy them while they are here, but they aren't attached to us. When we try to attach ourselves to them, to cling to them, we forget who we are and our purpose in living."

"I see your point, Bob, but Pearl Bailey also has a point. I remember she once said, 'Honey, I've been rich and poor, and rich is better!' Maybe if I can just play the financial game better, everything will turn out all right."

So my old friends, "bigger" and "more" remained at my side. We continued to cling to each other because we thought we were all we had.

How Bob Goodheart and Hippocrates must have groaned when, despite their arguments, I reverted to my habitual ways. Was I unique in this regard? How many times must we bang our heads painfully against a wall before we realize we should stop? Are we such stubborn creatures of habit that we will continue to endure pain rather than change our nature? Apparently so. Gurdjieff said that we are mostly asleep, even when we think we are awake. He said that even the best and most determined of us go through life reacting like robots to events, and that extreme and dramatic circumstances are required to awaken us. If this is so, then perhaps my descent into unhappiness had been too gradual—it lacked drama. Or is it the quantity of suffering? Must we experience a minimum amount of suffering before we are jolted out of our old habits? I think the need for a dramatic lesson is the correct interpretation, for aren't there many of us who remain moderately unhappy for years, even lifetimes, and never even consider changing our courses? If so, what triggers the cosmos to call forth the dramatic event that will, finally, capture our attention and force us to change? And why does it only happen to some of us?

I felt more comfortable the next time I met with Bob Goodheart, and I opened up about a frustration that had been plaguing me for many years. "You know, Bob, since I first opened my practice, as successful as it's been, it's also been a constant battle. There hasn't been a single day during these twelve years when I haven't felt beleaguered by my professional enemies. I'm just so tired of it. What is a person supposed to do when it seems impossible to have a meeting of the minds, or at least a truce?"

"Well, I think I know what you shouldn't do. You're a leader, Dennis, and for you to back away from an active life won't help you any. Leadership requires many attributes, and you've got intelligence, courage, perseverance and creativity going for you. Maybe what you lack is sensitivity."

I bristled. "You mean sensitivity toward peers who are trying to hurt me? Am I supposed to turn the other cheek?"

"Dennis, if you can learn to be sensitive to the needs of your peers, I suspect you won't have frequent occasion to turn your cheek. What would you do if you were walking down the street and met a disabled man who needed your help crossing an intersection?"

"I'd help him."

"Of course you would. But why?"

"Well, because he needs my help and he can't manage by himself. And because I care about him."

"Right. Now let's take it one step further. Suppose, as you approached, that same disabled man started shouting, 'Damn curbs! Why do they make these curbs so high? I pay taxes, too! How am I supposed to get across?' What would you do?"

"I'd still help him because I'd know he needed help in spite of his ranting."

"Exactly, Dennis, exactly. Now the trick is to learn to view your competitors as you would that disabled man. They're shouting too, and behind their belligerent words, they're really crying, 'Help!'"

Bob can cut through a lot of stuff to arrive at the truth. I knew he was right, but it was awfully late in the game for me to change. I had solidified my "to hell with them" attitude over many years, and it wasn't easy to drop it that suddenly and undo the hard feelings. If someone has been throwing stones at you for years, even if you understand the motivation you remember the stones.

Before we broke up for the day, Bob told me a story about the artist, Gauguin, and his escape to Tahiti. "You know, Dennis, many people think of Gauguin as a hero for rejecting what he believed to be a corrupt bourgeois society and following his artistic vision. His life in the tropics was, at first, an adventure in paradise. But, as you may recall, he later strove, unsuccessfully, for recognition from the very society he rejected. Finally, his spirit was broken by the debilitating and ultimately fatal disease he had caught in Tahiti.

"Gauguin's biographers have probed deeply into his personality, and they claim that his flight from European society had less to do with dedication to art and more to do with his self-loathing and irrational expectations. In other words, he was trying to escape from himself. It's a long road to the end of one's obligations."

Bob paused to let it sink in. I picked up the discussion. "I can identify with Gauguin—I sure feel like running away from my responsibilities. I think what I'd like most to do right now is nothing! I want to read you something." I groped in my pocket for a piece of paper containing a short poem by James Kavanaugh. "It's called 'Someday'":

> Someday I'll walk away
> And be free
> And leave the sterile ones
> Their secure sterility.
> I'll leave without a forwarding address
> And walk across some barren wilderness
> To drop the world there.
> Then wander free of care
> Like an unemployed atlas.[1]

"That's how I really feel, Bob!"

"That's okay, Dennis. but you sound so apologetic, as if taking time off is morally wrong. Remember, you're in good company. Christ did it, and so did the Buddha, Mohammed and many of the Hindu sages. They all took time off for a well-deserved sabbatical to reflect on and contemplate their lives."

Sabbatical. It has a nice sound and a pleasant connotation—not a running away but a temporary leave-taking. A time of inspiration and replenishment. On a whim, I looked it up in my dictionary and found that the word is derived from Sabbath. Among the ancient Jews every seventh year was a *sabbatical year.* According to Mosaic law, during the sabbatical year the land and vineyards were to remain fallow and debtors were to be released from their obligations. Even in modern times, many colleges and universities follow the ancient tradition and grant extended leave to faculty members every seven years.

Why did I feel I had to apologize for wanting a time for contemplation? If sabbaticals were given every seven years, I was overdue. Besides, a sabbatical was not an ending, it was a pause before continuing. It was also a nice way of avoiding a decision.

In hindsight, however, I think my problem really had little to do with escaping responsibilities. Even the continuing fusillade from my peers, while causing some anxiety, was not the real motivation. How can you stop when you are near the top of the mountain? It beckons to you, leading you on even though each time you get close you see that there is a still higher peak. When you have the demonstrated ability to earn a million or more dollars a year, it is very hard to stop doing it; it seems almost criminal to stop doing it. What a waste not to make that next million!

As with any addiction, what's really hard is stopping.

CHAPTER 8

Burnout and Repaying the
Cosmic Debt

There is an evil I have observed under the sun, and a grave one it is for man, that God sometimes grants a man riches, property and wealth, so that he does not want for anything, but God does not permit him to enjoy it. *—Ecclesiastes*

Bob Goodheart's retelling of Gauguin's escape stayed with me for some time. At one point in our conversation, Bob had said, "The Gauguin Myth that escape ends all problems is a lingering testament to the tremendous power of the fantasy that seduces the misguided romantic. It's a myth that is still carried out by males in modern society."

I had a benchmark for escape fantasies: my sister-in-law, Sherry, and her husband, Jerry, had dropped out of a successful restaurant business and left for the Virgin Islands, near St. Thomas, where their new home was a sailboat. For a few years, I enviously watched how their lives were faring. When their money finally ran out, they leased property to start a new restaurant on a resort island near Tortola, in the British Virgin Islands. That was still pretty idyllic, but when they were unable to renew their lease they wound up with a fast-food restaurant in South Carolina. Selling kosher hot dogs to conservative southern Christians proved less successful than they had hoped. Sherry and Jerry's fate seemed to confirm that conservative moves to improve my life were safer than blindly casting my fate to intuitive winds. I could get by with small changes and still keep moving in the same direction. That way, I wouldn't have to give up very much.

One of these small but pleasant changes was to take time off with my family to vacation in Hawaii. Sunsets, cloud formations and volcanoes instilled in me a sense of awe and mystery. Each island has a definite character all its own, and the sand and lava beaches are magnificent. Hawaii is a paradise that never fails to inspire me. Relaxing on the beach, playing with my four-month-old daughter, I felt less overwhelmed. Maybe, everything would be all right if I took occasional vacations, eased up on my work hours and cut back on my leveraged investments. I was feeling good physically. While on the Fit For Life diet, I had lost twenty pounds and I now felt lean, trim, and healthy. I wasn't about to gain it all back on this trip, so I headed for a workout at the weight room of the condominium complex where we were staying. How insignificant it seemed at the time. Just a faint popping noise in my lower back and a momentary sharp pain down my right leg which quickly subsided. No big deal. But two hours later, lying in the sun, the pain came back. I tried to loosen it by swimming, but that didn't help. Well, it wasn't going to interfere with my vacation! I viewed it as just one more enemy to be overcome, and I continued enjoying the superb strawberry daiquiris in this daiquiri capital of the world.

Three days later I could barely get out of bed. A therapeutic massage helped slightly, as did a visit to a local chiropractor, but then things got worse. Starting to feel desperate, I went to a traditional medical clinic. X-rays showed no abnormalities and I was released with only a prescription for pain medication. By now, I could only enter and exit a car with the greatest of difficulty. When it was time to leave Hawaii, Cecile, the children and I were all whisked around the normal check-in procedures. I had been strong and healthy all my life; now I sat in a wheelchair with people staring at me and trying to figure out what was wrong with the vigorous, healthy-looking man. I didn't like the image of being crippled, and I had to fight the urge to yell out to passersby, "Hey, I'm not really like this—this is just temporary!"

Arriving home, I tried to return to my usual routine—but I couldn't. In spite of misgivings, I had to delegate my tasks at the clinic to Dr. Reaper, my assistant, and to other staff members. I was in too much pain to do much of anything myself, although it was almost as painful to give up control of the clinic.

I had been a doctor for many years and had tried to empathize with my patients' pain and minimize it as best I could. But there is nothing like personal experience to place things in perspective. The pain was all-pervasive, part of everything I did, day and night, everywhere. It could not be ignored. Every thought, every impulse was shaded by the cloud of pain, and this helped feed my anger and despair. Some people experience injury and pain with a degree of tolerance, or acceptance. I could not. Where others might view their plight as a severe but fairly common back problem, mine was a tragedy. I searched for causes, for someone or something to blame. I had paid my dues in life by sheer hard work, and I didn't deserve to have this happen to me now. Everything I did, everything I'd accomplished, was by pushing hard, by forcing the world to accommodate my goals. Even when the world pushed back at me and gave in only grudgingly, I was in control. I was the one calling the shots. Now, in acute pain, I was no longer in control. I could analyze and calculate, I could work harder or faster, and I could push and shove relentlessly. But no matter what I did, the pain didn't go away.

Large payments were coming due on my real estate investments, and the Onyx Building in San Diego was still costing me almost $15,000 per month. I needed continuing cash flow to help pay for all my leveraged investments, and the cash flow came from my practice. I was walking a flimsy financial tightrope where one false slip could send me tumbling into financial ruin. If I couldn't perform, how could I keep everything afloat?

The pain was debilitating enough; what energy remained was drained away by my preoccupation with the question, "Why did this happen to me?" And because I could see no justification for experiencing this injury, I answered for the universe and its maker: *"Because you wanted to screw me!"*

To what extent, if any, are diseases, injuries and accidents self-imposed? Do we somehow force them upon ourselves when our egos are so resistant to change that nothing else will stop us? It's difficult to imagine that there are lessons so unique they can only be learned through sickness. Is it better to believe that the outside world has randomly or even maliciously imposed misfortune upon us? If we believe that, it enables us to wallow in our pain, expending what energy we have left in blaming someone or something outside of ourselves.

I also cursed my body for failing me when I needed it most. It never occurred to me to ask what this experience was trying to teach me. The call for change had come—from my emotional catharsis in Miami, from Hippocrates and from Bob Goodheart. And as I had with everything in life that didn't go my way, I got angry and resisted.

Somehow, it is not enough to just experience pain. We give life to it and empower it by conceptualizing it. It becomes not just pain but "the thing that happened to me." Why did it happen, why has the world turned on us, or what did we do to bring it on ourselves? Thus we not only bear the pain, we also feel that something is terribly wrong with the world or with ourselves. I was like that, tormented not only by a severe back injury but by the belief that it never should have happened, my healing energy dissipated by an endless debate on the callousness of fate.

After returning home from Hawaii, I consulted an orthopedist who diagnosed my condition as a slipped disk with nerve damage. He recommended physical therapy and estimated that it would take anywhere from a few weeks to six months for it to heal. Gradually, my back and leg pain improved from excruciating to merely awful, thanks to therapy, special pillows, a back brace, and the use of stiff, straight-backed chairs. But the continuing combination of pain and frustration made me increasingly irritable. And although I was still incapable of performing most of my former duties at the clinic, it was still hard for me to delegate responsibilities.

Objectively speaking, my problems were considerably milder than many people I knew. For example, Dr. Drummond, the rude plastic surgeon Cecile and I had visited in New York—the one who was setting up franchises in order to become the IBM of plastic surgery—had been indicted by a grand jury on felony charges of defrauding insurance companies and aiding the unlicensed practice of medicine. His wife had left him; he'd lost all his possessions; and he'd filed for bankruptcy. When I last heard of him, he had 212 malpractice lawsuits pending against him. For all his rudeness and aggressive marketing, Dr. Drummond's fall symbolized another highly successful medical practitioner who had been toppled from his pedestal. It added to my overall apprehension.

Perhaps this was my future, too. I had grown too fast, too soon. Whatever perspective I had acquired vanished. It was as if all the positive things that had happened in my life never occurred. I was living in the "now," and the "now" was bad. Though I had just come off a vacation, I felt I needed a long rest and no responsibilities. *"Why me, why me?"* I kept asking myself, occasionally responding, *"Why not you?"*

I wanted to see Bob Goodheart again, and on a typically warm, sunny day in May of 1987, I drove through the twisting curves of the Santa Cruz Mountains to his office. It had been a harrowing week. Whether prompted by back pain or because I was simply fed up with the pressure of performing, I was in great emotional turmoil about my life style. My shiny Mercedes 450SL with its vanity license plates had, until recently, seemed like a well-deserved reward for my endeavors. Now I began to despise it and all it stood for, as an assault on the sensitivities of those less fortunate, those people who would never come close to affording a car like this.

Where I had previously arrived at Bob's office filled with the pride of ownership, this time I was embarrassed and was glad no one was in the parking lot to see me. As I approached the converted church that housed Bob's offices, my shame at having to consult a counselor returned. I kept thinking to myself, *"Great, Dennis, just great. So you're now paying someone to have a conversation with you. Maybe you should call these visits rent-a-friend, especially now that you keep coming back. What's next? Got any other ways to waste your money?"* I was also glad there were no passersby to see me walk in. I felt as though any stranger seeing me in these circumstances would somehow know I was a troubled man coming to seek help.

But for all these negative thoughts, I was in trouble and knew I needed to be here. I opened the front door, and my thoughts were quickly dispersed by Bob's bearded, smiling face. He greeted me as if I was a close friend coming to dinner. We walked up to his spacious office that, for all its contemporary decor, felt like the inside of a church.

There was a natural ease about Bob, a politeness of the heart. His presence filled the room but, somehow, it allowed for others to have their own, individual space as well. I launched directly into my problem. "In spite of my painful back and in spite of receiving all kinds of other hints to get off the treadmill, I don't seem able to do it. But at the same time, I can't stand the pressure and the responsibility any longer, and I want out. I despise my possessions and what they represent, and I still want more of them. If it weren't for the voice of reason that goes on in my head, I'd go around destroying everything I own. Christ, Bob, I'm stuck, and everything around me looks dark and dismal. It's like being shot with a slow-acting poisoned arrow. You don't recognize the deterioration in the beginning but gradually the toxins begin to take effect. After a while you find yourself reacting badly to almost everything—even things that never used to bother you—and you don't know why."

Bob studied me for a long moment, in silence. Then he asked, "Have you ever seen the movie *Dr. Zhivago?*"

"Yes, but it's been a while."

"There's a line in it that's relevant: 'Your health is bound to be affected if, day after day, you say the opposite of what you feel, if you grovel before what you dislike and rejoice at what brings you nothing but misfortune.' That's part of the addiction process. I believe you are an addict. An achievement addict. You press yourself to your limits, and sometimes beyond, and that gets you to a higher level of achievement. But you can't allow yourself to enjoy that achievement, you see, because that would make you content, complacent, and that would rob you of the need to achieve more. So in order to sustain ever higher achievements, you can't allow yourself to be happy with any of them—you have to keep going. Do you see?"

I knew Bob was a very skilled counselor. Now he seemed more than skilled; he was brilliant! He had cut through multiple layers of my personality and hit the proverbial nail on the head.

"Remember, Dennis, when you told me about your early experiences with drugs, how they gave you your first real spiritual experience? I've had enough experience counseling druggies to know that, in addition to all the bad trips, they are getting some peak spiritual experiences from them. What's happening is something like this: As a human organism, you have the capacity to perceive your oneness with creation and the unity with all things. You also have the capacity to see the differences, the disconnectedness in life. What happens in a drug-induced experience is that the pills turn up your unity volume and decrease your capacity to see differences.

"Now the pills don't contain truth, they don't contain happiness within themselves. They are a catalyst for a biochemical process that enhances one of your capacities and diminishes another. When you're on a high, your sense of the unity of all things, of the divine source, is greatly enhanced. The problem is that it is an artificial enhancement—it can't be sustained, at least not without larger dosages of drugs.

But drugs are expensive, and the addict has to work harder and harder to get more and more of them. All of his energy, all of his effort, whether legal or illegal, goes into obtaining more drugs. Finally, the body has become so desensitized to the drugs that, no matter what the dosage, the original experience cannot be regained. Yet the addict keeps trying megadoses, because he still gets some temporary relief. He is desperately unhappy but doesn't know how to stop. Do you see where I'm leading?"

"I'm like the drug addict, only I'm hooked on achievement."

"That's right. Look at your achievements. In a short period of time, you've accomplished things that most people can't do in a lifetime. But it isn't enough. You're now like the addict in the latter stages of his addiction. You've been making superhuman efforts to achieve more and more even though you're unhappy. Like the drug addict, when you gain money, property or prestige, you get some relief—but it's only temporary. You keep pushing and pushing like a steam roller but there's less and less energy available. Just think of it as trying to use too much energy from an inadequate source. Finally, you're not getting any happiness from it at all—in fact the pressure's tormenting you—but you don't know how to stop."

"Okay, Bob, okay. How do I learn to stop? Can I learn to stop?"

Again there was a lengthy pause. "What's called for, Dennis, is for you to begin using your abilities, your energy, your enthusiasm in other ways, ways that will balance your life. An acquaintance of mine was the youngest person ever to become chief of surgery at the local Kaiser facility (I temporarily stopped listening as I tried to figure out who the 'friend' could be, and I had to ask Bob to repeat himself). This acquaintance became so obsessed with his work and his prestigious image that he moved his bed into his office. He took sleep courses at Stanford so that he could get by with just two to three hours of sleep a night. Like yourself, but to a more extreme degree, his zealousness caused him to tap into his superhuman resources. He was also having several love affairs on the side. His wife couldn't take this for very long, of course, and she divorced him. On the professional side, this man made great, rapid strides, but at what price? Now the question I have for you, Dennis, is why would a person want professional advancement so badly that he would be willing to lose not only his wife but all other enjoyable activities in life?"

Spontaneously, without really thinking it through, I said, "He's not getting what he needs in his life, and he's trying to make up for it professionally." As soon as I said it, I knew the words applied to me as well. It was something I had known, deep down, for a long time, but it had taken Bob's story about someone else to pierce my stubborn shell of denial.

We sat quietly for a few minutes to let it sink in. Then I mentioned a recent decision I had made. "I'm going to get rid of the Onyx Building—whatever it takes."

"Dennis, you're making progress. By your decision, you're saying, 'If this building weighs on my mind much longer it will increasingly affect other parts of my life. So this is the best possible action for me at this time.' There's only one problem with that—while you're starting to eliminate the negative things in your life, you have nothing positive—or better yet, thrilling—to replace the void."

"Well," I said, "I'll just have to work on that, won't I?" I could almost hear Hippocrates sigh in my ear and whisper a faint 'Amen.'

"Come on, Hippocrates," I said aloud, my voice filled with sarcasm, "you weren't around when 'amen' came into usage."

"Wasn't I?" came the whispered reply. "I suspect we have different notions of time."

Had I spoken out loud? I looked at Bob, but he just smiled and gazed innocently away, looking for all the world like he was in on the game.

He had stood firm before every trouble...he could no longer look misery in the eyes...It was like the dying away of the swing of a pendulum which no one had noticed while it became steadily slower and whose stopping now came over one as something sudden.   —*Martin Buber*

When I was a kid, my dad frequently commented that I was racing against time, afraid that I might miss out on some fun. Now, it had slowed to a melancholy crawl. One day, when everything around me seemed particularly bleak, I became aware that I was staring at the Atmos clock. The Atmos was a beautifully-crafted, gold-plated Swiss instrument that ran without an apparent power source—no batteries, no springs, no sunshine. It appeared to be a perpetual motion machine, but it ingeniously utilized small changes in air temperature—as little as 1°—to power itself. It's mysterious, spinning pendulum was a hypnotic focal point—except that it had just stopped.

The identification plate on the base of the Atmos read, "Frank Augustine, in recognition of twenty-five years loyal service to General Foods Corporation, presented on June 26, 1975." A few years after his retirement, my father gave it to me as a gift. When Dad had given it to me, I wasn't sure how to accept it or if I even wanted it. We had a strained relationship. I felt awkward, being given something of strong sentimental value. "Are you sure you want me to have this?" I asked at the time. "Yes," he answered, "it will look good on your mantle."

Dad had long before relinquished the family purse strings to Mom and didn't give traditional gifts. He rarely, if ever, went shopping but would quietly observe whatever possessions of his I seemed interested in. Then, when he felt it appropriate—it didn't require a special occasion—he would bestow it on me as a gift. Since the gifts were neither new nor exciting, I had never appreciated them. In fact, I had never appreciated him.

"Twenty five years at the same job," I thought. *"How could he have settled for such a mediocre job, whose only reward after twenty-five years of loyal service was a gold clock, an honorary dinner and a modest bonus? What a waste! Never, never in a million years would I settle for that kind of life,"* I thought, as I sat in the comfortable surroundings of my prosperity. Of course, I grudgingly admitted, there were some differences between us.

We never had a lot of money, but somehow we always managed to get by. We were a solid family, but there was no denying that Dad had quite a different childhood experience than most people. His mother had been institutionalized when he was six years old and his father was unable to care for five young children. Dad was put up for adoption, but a family could not be found, so he was placed in a school for boys in Pennsylvania where he remained until he was sixteen. Then he enlisted in the army, spent a year with the Civilian Conservation Corps (CCC), and re-enlisted in the Army where he became a chaplain's assistant.

When I was growing up, my dad was never there for me emotionally. How many fathers are? His gift of the clock seemed a belated payoff, something to make up for not being there when I needed him most. As I stared at the precision mechanism of the Atmos clock, it began to dawn on me that I had never forgiven Dad for his imperfections. Like most children, I failed to see that he was a good person who had stayed with my mother through many tribulations and had provided me with a stable home (however much we might have argued). And I remembered how willingly he and my Mom had gone out on a limb for me when I was still a kid. They had borrowed money from their life insurance policy and had cosigned for a bank loan that allowed me to buy my first apartment building—my first investment.

The Atmos clock was no longer as accurate or precise as it used to be. Like the clock, my life malfunctioned occasionally. I hadn't believed the clock would actually stop, but now it had come to a grinding halt. I could almost hear my Dad's voice, admonishing me, "Why didn't you get it fixed?"

"I didn't know who to call," I answered lamely, but the truth was that I was too busy to make the effort. Then, Hippocrates interrupted me with: "Just as you were too busy building your empire to look at the rest of your life."

"Dennis, has always moved faster than everyone else, always afraid he'd miss out on something," my father said.

"Wonderful," I thought, *"they're holding a conversation with each other in my head."*

Hippocrates ignored my sarcasm. "Look at your feelings, Dr. A.—pay attention. Look at the hatred you developed when you were younger, the humiliation and the shame and hurt that nourished it. And most of all, look at the fear that continually feeds it. Do you understand what you were so afraid of, and why you were in such a hurry?"

"I...I was afraid of not making it, of being a failure."

"That's right, but why such a strong drive? Why was it so important to you?"

"I needed to show that I was smarter than..."

"Than what, Dr. A.?"

"Smarter than my dad gave me credit for."

"But what did you really want from him?"

"I just..."

Hippocrates said softly, "You just wanted him to love you."

There was another silence. I didn't say anything. I didn't have to. After a while, I heard Hippocrates' voice again. "You didn't feel that your dad loved you, and ever since then you've been in such a terrible hurry to prove that you don't need him—over and over and over."

I remembered a conversation I'd had with Jason when he was six years old It was one of the rare occasions when I spent time with my son. We were playing Nintendo; I was every bit as addicted to the game as Jason was. But after I'd played a game of Super Mario Brothers, rushing around secret passageways, castles, mazes and such, and trying to avoid being killed, Jason said something that caught my attention.

He said, "I like playing Duck Hunt and Zelda better than Super Mario, Dad, 'cause there's no hurry." When I asked him why that was so important, he said, "When you go real fast you miss all the fun secrets that you can find if you take your time."

My small son—my six-year-boy—had told me that, in life, there are secrets and treasures along the way, but if we don't take the time to notice them, we miss them. A tremendous wave of sadness and regret washed over me then, as I realized how much we might have learned from each other if I had taken the time.

"Maybe you can be better with Jason than I was with you," Dad's voice spoke softly. "There's still time."

What is time? How then can we describe its passage? In Greek, *chronos* means time as we usually think of it, but there is another Greek word for time—*kairos*, which refers to those times when eternal values of the cosmos plunge into the fate and destiny of the world and forever alter the life of individuals. In this sense there is another way of measuring time, and that is by watching something grow, perhaps, or watching something fade.

There's still time, Dad's voice had said. Time. That illusive dimension. So many people I knew had remarked that time sped up as you grew older, and I had felt it too—days just zipping by in an endless stream. But the stopped Atmos clock symbolized my life right now. I was malfunctioning and had ground to a halt.

"Don't take it so hard, Dr. A. Stopping for a while has its advantages." Hippocrates' voice was gentler than usual. "It helps you to notice things."

When Jason was born, a shift took place in my attitude towards my dad. Perhaps I was beginning to understand that it is not always easy to be a father. I started to read books on fathering and father-son relationships. In particular, I was struck by the insights in *Father, the Figure and the Force.*

> The adult male who is close to his mother, but has never been able to get past a strained, formal status in his dealings with his dad, is commonplace in this country. Our affection for mom only serves to complicate matters, for we must at once concede that we—subconsciously at least—wanted her all to ourselves, and that she was the oft-unwitting cause of our rift with father and of the anxieties that followed.[1]

That really hit home to me. Not only had I favored my mother all my life, I realized I had, until recently, viewed my dad through the lens of her disapproval of him as father and husband. One of the last holdouts of my lingering resentment toward my Dad has been that we were emotionally distant—he certainly never confided in me, and I never confided in him—and that it was his fault. After all, if a father could not extend himself, how was an immature son expected to do so? Since then, I have read many books on father-son conflicts but until *Father, the Figure and the Force,* remained only partially satisfied with their explanations.

> Finding father is nothing less than the odyssey of self-discovery. We have learned to cast off the idealized image of father as benevolent patriarch, but that is a small step towards understanding how much a father survives in us. He did not make it easy. We have not made it easy for him. It was not part of father's nature to communicate with the rest of the family, and indeed, we did not invite him to share his hopes and fears, his dreams and doubts, with us. He was emotionally isolated and the degree of isolation had as much to do with the role mother wished him to take as it did with the kind of father he might have wanted to be.[2]

My father's gift of his elegant clock represented a changing of the guard—the passage to a new generation. And that changing of the guard gives us the opportunity not only to take over where our fathers left off, but to liberate ourselves and future generations from old world, conventional values that have kept us father-bound to the traditional roles of provider, outsider and absentee disciplinarian.

For all his provincialism, Dad had given me a hand up and out into the world without my even knowing it. And for that, I was both ashamed and happy that I finally realized his contribution to my life.

"There's still time," the voice of my father had told me, but what good was time if I could not make use of it? Hippocrates had said that I had slowed down enough to begin to notice things. What he hadn't mentioned was that I would not like the things I saw.

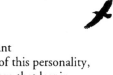

What I most want
is to spring out of this personality,
then sit apart from that leaping.
I've lived too long where I can be
reached.   *—Rumi*

In the spring of 1987, my architect informed me that the San Jose building department had again turned down my request to build a new surgicenter. I had spent thousands of dollars on plans, revision fees and other modifications to meet the city's criteria, and I had been previously assured by both my architect and the city planners that there would be no problem gaining approval. Several local politicians owed me favors, and I considered calling in their marker, but I had no more fight left in me.

At one time, everything I touched had turned to gold, and my sheer will could overcome all obstacles. Now, everyone was saying "no" and slamming the door in my face. It seemed that everything I touched turned to ashes, and I bitterly resented it. Despite the est training I'd received and all the words of wisdom from Hippocrates and Bob Goodheart, I was once again caught up in blame.

Damn it all, it wasn't fair! The Onyx Building was a loser, my surgicenter would never happen, the changed tax laws had screwed up my investments, and my back hurt like hell. I moved like a zombie. There were dark circles under my eyes and I had an ashen gray skin tone. Even my formerly-strong voice was reduced to a whimper. When I gave instructions to the staff at the clinic, their alarmed looks showed they knew something was wrong. When I saw patients, I did my best to disguise my condition and to pretend everything was normal. At home, I couldn't contain it.

I was constantly angry at Cecile and would start an argument at the slightest provocation. "Is there anything I can do?" she'd ask. "Are you angry at me?"

"I'm dying, for God's sake, and you're going about business as usual, as if nothing's wrong! My back is keeping me from doing what I need to do at the clinic, the Onyx Building is draining money, house payments keep coming due, the landscaping is costing more than it should, the house furnishings still need to be done—everywhere I look I see obligations and I can't get rid of them. We're close to losing everything, my health is failing, and you walk around like everything's normal!"

"Don't you think I know that?"

"No, I don't think you do!"

"Well, what do you expect from me? You're seem so full of bitterness all you can say are hurtful things. Nothing I say or do seems to help. And somebody has to take care of the kids. Do you want to get them involved with this? What would happen if I fell apart, too? Then what would we do?"

She was right, but I didn't want to hear it. Part of me was jealous that the kids were getting all the attention, and I resented Cecile for putting on airs of normalcy even though it made sense.

The clinic was going downhill and I couldn't stop it. I was failing miserably at being a husband and father. I had never felt so alone and so misunderstood in all my life.

Dinner conversation between Cecile and myself was nonexistent. Fortunately, the desires and the problems of Jason and Michelle, now six months old, broke the silence and made the meals less intolerable. Immediately after dinner I would sequester myself in our bedroom, glad to be away from all human contact. No one understood what I was going through, except maybe Hippocrates and Bob Goodheart, and they weren't around to help. At night, I slept erratically and had frequent nightmares. I don't know which was worse—the nightmares of my dreams or the living nightmare of each day.

In Jean-Paul Sartre's starkly realistic play, *No Exit*, three people are trapped in a room. Although they can speak to each other, they are incapable of communicating their mutual distress. Hell, for Sartre, is a world where no one understands, or tries to understand, or takes the time and trouble to help us bear our suffering.

You got to walk that lonesome highway,
You got to walk it by yourself.
Nobody else can walk it for you,
You got to walk it by yourself.

—from an American Spiritual

One night, I felt a presence in my room. It wasn't just a voice, this time, but the figure of Hippocrates, sitting on a chair near my bed. He was facing me. Seeing him there scared the hell out of me. It was one thing for him to walk normally into my clinic or to see him in a hospital corridor, and quite another to have him materialize three feet away from me in the dark.

"How did you get here?"

"Like I said before—"

"I know, I know, there are other ways of traveling."

My nerves steadied, and I ventured, "You might at least let me know when you're coming, Hippocrates."

"It doesn't work like that, Dr. A. When I feel you hurting badly, I'm drawn to you whether I like it or not."

"You mean you don't get to choose whom you help?"

"Can you refuse to help a patient in distress? In theory you can, but in practice you never do."

The diversion from my immediate troubles was pleasant, and I asked, "Why are you drawn to help certain people, Hippocrates? Why me? Why someone in this century?"

"Why are you more attracted to certain periods of history than others, Dr. A.? Why does a certain person, out of multitudes, cross your path? Creation is too vast for anyone to know why."

"Anyone, Hippocrates? Doesn't anyone know why?"

"I presume you're referring to God, and I must confess that in spite of a wealth of experiences, I'm no closer to knowing that than when I was a physician in Hellas—Greece, to you."

"That makes me think of a quote I once heard: 'Just 'cuz you're dead don't mean you're smart.'"

"Indeed, Dr. A., I know quite a few dummies where I now reside."

"Which is?" I asked.

"Right here, Dr. A., in between your atoms. But I came here for a purpose, and we must get on with it. Last time we spoke we were recalling your early relationship with your son, Jason—incidentally, nice Greek name, that, I was hoping you'd go along when I chose it."

"You—"

"Forgive me, Dr. A., 'chose' is too strong a word; I merely suggested it. You and Cecile were totally free to do what you wished. Anyway," he continued before I could get another word in, "you realized how your preoccupation with your career had let a lot of years slide by without your paying much attention to Jason. What I didn't have a chance to tell you then is why you were in such a hurry.

"Since childhood, you have been struggling with self-esteem. Why a person with your abilities would need to do that is beyond me, but that's the way it was. You're very bright, and for some reason you've been blessed with vast amounts of energy. You combined both of those traits and became a financial success."

"I'm not so sure I—"

"Spare me the apologetics, Dr. A. Your pursuit of a career wasn't pathological, at least not at first. Force of will can accomplish many things, for a while. But if it isn't supported by heartfelt conviction, it eventually collapses on itself. That's what has happened to you. You were so powerful you forced events to occur without placing limits on yourself—without understanding that limits are a necessary part of living. To keep up the maddening pace that stupefied and overwhelmed your competitors, you borrowed and borrowed from your emotional resources until there was nothing left. And because your ego—not your heart—was driving you, your emotional resources could not be replenished and they dried up. You lost your perspective and became fixated on financial advancement.

"You aren't alone in this, Dr. A. I think it has something to do with living in America. Do you know the French writer, Alexis de Tocqueville, author of *Democracy In America?*[3] He wrote, 'He who has set his heart exclusively upon the pursuit of worldly welfare is always in a hurry, for he has but a limited time at his disposal to reach, to grasp and to enjoy it.' You've been accumulating a negative emotional debt in pursuit of fame and fortune. You've had enough power to ignore it for many years; now, that debt has come due."

"How must I repay it?"

"I can't tell you that, not because I don't want to, but because you will have to decide that. However, I can give you a clue: listen."

I listened, and a male voice began to speak in what sounded like a German accent.

> The way in which a man accepts his fate and all the suffering it entails, the way in which he takes up his cross, gives him ample opportunities— even under the most difficult of circumstances—to add a deeper meaning to his life. He may remain brave, dignified and unselfish, or in the bitter fight for self-preservation, he may forget his human dignity and become no more than an animal.*

"I understand. I may lose a million dollars or more, getting out of the Onyx Building. But today I decided that whatever means I use, they will be ethical and decent, no matter how much it costs."

"Good, Dr. A., that's a fine start. I expected that of you. Now how about the unexpected?"

I was about to respond by asking what he meant, but some part of me already knew. There was something within me trying to emerge, something new that was hard to articulate. Somewhere, in my quest to survive and conquer the competitive environment in which I had practiced, I had buried a part of myself that was now demanding attention. I looked up across the room and noticed that Hippocrates had disappeared. I couldn't resist a sarcastic comment:"In our time, it's customary to say good-bye when you leave, Hippocrates." Then, in a voice that seemed fainter with each repetition, I heard "good-bye... good-bye...good-bye..." It was a superb dramatic effect, as if Hippocrates was calling to me from a rapidly increasing distance. His voice was full of gentle good humor and it made me laugh—the first time I had laughed in...what? Weeks? Months? It felt wonderful.

Once again, the words of my small son came to me. "When you go real fast you miss all the fun secrets." And there was a vision of the Atmos clock sitting on my mantle, stopped. All of this had something to do with time.

"Hippocrates?" I whispered into the stillness of my bedroom, "Can you hear me?" There was no reply, but I continued to whisper to no one in particular, "I think the best thing for me to do is to take a medical leave."

"Go on, Dennis," I said, talking to myself.

"I want to take a sabbatical—by myself."

"Why?"

---

* Hippocrates never mentioned the author of these words. Two years later I discovered their source while reading *Man's Search for Meaning* by Viktor Frankl.[4]

"Lots of reasons. My assistant, Dr. Reaper, will be leaving soon and this will be my last chance to get away. Also, I need to think about the things I have learned in the last few months. I need a fresh environment to heal myself, and I'd like to visit Italy and Sicily and stay with my relatives. But most of all, I just want to do it!"

Listen! I will be honest with you.
I do not offer the old, smooth prizes
but offer rough new prizes.
These are the days that must happen to you.
You shall not heap up what is call'd riches.
You shall scatter with lavish hand
all that you earn or achieve.
You but arrive at the city to which you were destin'd.
You hardly settle yourself to satisfaction
before you are call'd
by an irresistible call to depart.
You shall be treated to the ironical smiles and mockings
of those who remain behind you.
What beckonings of love you receive you shall only answer
with passionate kisses of parting.
You shall not allow the hold of those
who spread their reach'd hands toward you.[5]

—*Walt Whitman*

I read the lines over and over, certain that what had beckoned Walt Whitman was beckoning me. I thought about the Life Guides who had helped bring me to this point—not only Hippocrates and Bob Goodheart but Bob Goldsack, Jay Seymour, Carmine Sippo, Milo Turnbo, Ed Marlowe, my wife Cecile, my son Jason, and so many others. The same, invisible force that had brought our paths together was now inviting me to find myself. I rolled over and fell into a deep sleep, free of nightmares and gnashing of teeth. I dreamed about traveling.

CHAPTER 9

Sabbatical

Lord, I am scorched earth,
cracked and dry;
a weary runner,
a tired spent man.
No flowers grow.
Send water, Lord, send sleep;
make flowers grow once more.

—*Archbishop John Quinn*

How do you tell your wife that you must take a trip alone for a month, especially when there is a six-month-old baby to be cared for? How do you explain your need without arousing suspicion or fear of infidelity? "It's not that I don't love you, Cecile..." Or, "No, I'm not searching for someone else..." How do you explain the intensity of your pain? "I've got to do this! I'm destroying myself—do you understand? It's no longer a question of why...I have no choice! I have to do something!"

When I told her of my trip plans, Cecile did not admonish me. She didn't try to prevent me from going. On the contrary, she helped prepare my itinerary and bought the few personal items that I would need to take with me. But her eyes revealed a great sadness over my departure. With our new baby daughter, Michelle, demanding almost all her attention, there was not much left for me. At the same time, I knew I had squeezed every drop of compassion and understanding that she was capable of giving. It was not that Cecile had so little to give; it was that I needed so much. Where was the man she had married? For the past several months, I'd been wimpy, complaining, angry, withdrawn, melancholy or unable to act. Neither of us knew what my state of mind would be when I returned.

In *Poetry and Mysticism*, Colin Wilson interprets the Faustian myth this way:

> Faust in his chamber, in a state of profound depression; too much study, too much effort, has frozen his enemies. The old mill of the mind, consuming its rag and bone, goes on grinding whether he likes it or not, and he has a sense of futility. Yet (Faust) still has insight enough to state:
> The spirit world shuts not its gates,
> Your heart is dead
> Your senses shot.
> This is the clear recognition that when man thinks he has exhausted the world, he has really only exhausted his own mind. Other realities lie out there; it is simply the doors of perception that are dirty.[1]

Wilson tells us that although Faust knew there were other worlds outside his own, he had lost all hope of finding relief. So he chooses what seems to him to be the only solution—suicide. As Faust raises his vial of poison, he hears the church bells ring and a revelation comes to him. He remembers his childhood, his emotional flood gates open and he bursts into tears and cries, "The earth takes back her child."

Now he sees that it was only his own mind that was "weary, stale, flat and unprofitable," not the earth. More important, says Wilson, is that "His exhaustion and despair were superficial; the immense springs of power are still there, in the realm of the robot, ready to be released by the necessary act of will. Faust luckily discovers this before he kills himself"[2]

Throughout my crisis I never considered suicide as an option; however, I would be less than candid if I didn't admit to an underlying, even subliminal, wish for a quick, painless death such as might occur in an airplane crash. But even if I had been courageous or cowardly enough (take your pick) to kill myself, I'd read too many stories about unsuccessful suicide attempts, and I remembered reading an article about people who had jumped off the Golden Gate Bridge and survived—it seems they all changed their minds about a third of the way down.

Heidegger said that the crises facing modern civilization are due to our own myopia. Through habit, we dig our own ruts, and the deeper we dig, the less we can see of the world around us. Thus we become stuck in our own insular world, convinced that there is no way out.

The notion that there is no way out is implicit in many of our expressions. My father often said, "When you make your own bed you have to sleep in it." I never asked him why I couldn't simply change beds, unaware that attitudes, desires and fears are not cast in stone.

Going alone on a sabbatical was my way of changing beds.

But where was I going? I had no desire to meditate in a dark cave or trek through the wilderness or escape from all human contact. For all my desperate need to get away, my intentions were traditional and undramatic. In pursuit of my goals, I had bitten off more than I could chew. Now, I simply had to get away from these self-imposed responsibilities and from my high, professional profile. I wanted to be among people, but I badly needed anonymity. I decided to attend a week-long course on international business being held on the Isle of Man—I had always been more stimulated around businessmen than other doctors Then, I planned to meet my mother in Rome and tour the Amalfi Coast of Italy with her.

Having worn a back brace for the last two months, it took me a while to get comfortable in an airplane seat. As the flight to London lifted off, I began to feel better. The weight of obligations began to slide off my shoulders. When I looked around—out the window or at a fellow passenger, I noticed that I was once again interested in things. Simple distractions were a pleasure. I began to wonder what all these people did—what their lives were like.

I engaged a nice looking Australian in conversation. Steve Horner was a tall, middle-aged man with elegant manners. The managing director of Lend-Lease, one of the largest publicly-traded real estate development companies in the world, Steve's company was involved with deals whose magnitude made Donald Trump look like a bush leaguer. When he told me what he did, my spirits sagged; I was running away from my own real estate investment problems—the last thing I needed was to talk about real estate.

I pictured Steve as a workaholic, someone who put business first and had no time for family or friends. But as we got to talking, Steve volunteered that each year he set aside seven weeks for vacations. He spent three weeks with the family, two alone with his wife, one with his ten-year-old son, hiking, fishing and camping, and the remaining week by himself, for peace and reflection. I was pleasantly surprised by the balance in his life, and I decided then and there to implement something like it with my own family. I also told myself that I would try to stop judging people before I knew them. Steve's appearance as my fellow passenger was so timely and serendipitous that I felt convinced that our meeting was no accident.

Conversation, good food and service, and an entertaining movie uplifted me in a way that nothing had been able to do for months. The movie, *Over the Top,* with Sylvester Stallone, was about overcoming family trauma. In one scene, Stallone and his estranged son are reunited, and I found myself teary-eyed. Warm feelings that I had suppressed all these years were beginning to bubble to the surface. Where I once feared these feelings, I now decided they were okay and nothing to be ashamed of. So I cried unabashedly and laughed at myself. When the movie ended, the passengers around me saw a man with tears freely flowing down his cheeks and laughing at the same time.

During my stay in London, simple things continued to affect me deeply. Sitting on a park bench in Hyde Park, watching squirrels scurry with their acorns to secret places was a wonderful experience. There were squirrels in my neighborhood back home, too, but I had always been too busy to notice them. One of the little furry creatures jumped onto my bench and looked at me. We stared at each other for a minute or so and I had the feeling that this tiny creature of supposedly limited intelligence could see right into my mind and read my thoughts. I imagined it saying, "Come on, Dennis, there are acorns to be found and trees to climb."

The next day I wandered through Petticoat Lane and stopped to enjoy a huge Sicilian sausage sandwich. Then I bought two sets of earrings for my Italian cousins, Claudia and Marianna, from a young street vendor who seemed nervous, fidgety. Suddenly, as if his life was in great danger, he took off and began running desperately down the crowded street, chased by a London Bobbie. As I watched, I saw myself as a young boy, buying and selling "hot" goods in Hoboken. It had been a way of life then, without many alternatives, and I understood the boy's plight. I hoped he escaped.

A few days later, I was having dinner at the Palace Restaurant on the Isle of Man when the maitre'd came up to my table and introduced himself. He had the typical air of an Italian maitre'd, with a thin mustache on a swarthy complexion, and a tuxedo worn as if he had been born in it. His name was Vincenzo and, as it turned out, he was from Agrigento, a small Sicilian village that I had once passed through on my way to visit my relatives in Messina.

We had a wonderful time sharing childhood memories about the old country. Then Vincenzo began to tell me how he had been betrothed to his childhood sweetheart in Agrigento and had then come here to the Isle of Man where he had been promised a job. While here, Vincenzo had fallen madly in love with a local girl and married her. Many years later he returned to his village to visit his ailing father and was snubbed unmercifully. His boyhood friends had all turned against him and, except for his family, he was unwelcome in the village. At this point in the tale, Vincenzo grew silent and stared out the window, seeing only the past. After a while, he turned to me, and with a sad little smile, he said, "What could I do? I was in love."

When Vincenzo said that, I understood perhaps more completely than ever before in my life, what it meant to be in love. For a moment, I was a hapless suitor who had fallen in love and was then spurned by his village. Vincenzo, meanwhile, had returned to his duties. I sat looking out the windows at the bay which formed part of the Irish Sea, and as if it were a new revelation I thought, "Everyone has a story."

When I was not caught up in the enthusiastic business environment, I dipped into a small book called *Formulas for Transformation* (currently titled, *The Unstruck Bell*) by Eknath Easwaran. During the past year I had begun reading many books on philosophy and spirituality, and this one seemed especially relevant. What I enjoyed about Easwaran was his eclectic view of spirituality—how all religious beliefs can contribute to it. He confirmed many of my own speculations with metaphorical passages like this:

> The sea is a perfect symbol for the mind. It is in constant motion; there is calm one day and storm the next. We see only the surface, with hardly any inkling of the strange creatures that lurk below or the tremendous currents that sweep through the depths. From where we stand on this shore, the far shore is so completely out of sight that we find it hard even to imagine that there is another shore.[3]

The little book delighted me, and there was a pleasant contrast between the energetic, creative, innovative seminars on business and my retreat to my private world of burgeoning spirituality. The two seemed neatly separated and classified. So I was surprised by two of the seminar participants, Patricia Murray and Nana Maynard, from Fairfield, Iowa. Both ladies had a gracious quality about them that instantly caught my attention. Patricia wore her hair in an "afro" and resembled a calmer version of Angela Davis, the black communist professor of the turbulent sixties. Nana reminded me of the soulful poet, Maya Angelou. We became acquainted during the social occasions organized by the seminar promoters, and I learned that Pat and Nana were teachers of Transcendental Meditation, popularly known as "TM." I was still suspicious of the cult stigma that came with meditation and other Eastern teachings.

Dr. Seymour was a TM practitioner. He told me he would never have gotten through the attacks on him without TM, so I was curious and interested in meditation and the word or mantra that is mentally repeated during the process. Easwaran's book gave me the most delightful explanation of why a mantra is needed that I have seen, before or since:

> In the Hindu tradition, we often compare the mind to the trunk of an elephant—restless, inquisitive and always straying. If you watch an elephant sometime, you will see how apt the comparison is.
>
> In our towns and villages, caparisoned elephants are often taken in religious processions through the streets to the temple. The streets are crooked and narrow, lined on either side with fruit stalls and vegetable stalls. Along comes the elephant with his restless trunk, and in one sinuous motion it grabs a whole bunch of bananas. You can almost see him asking, "What else do you expect me to do? Here is my trunk and there are the bananas." He just doesn't know what else to do with his trunk. He doesn't pause to peel the bananas, either, or to observe all the other niceties that Emily Post says should be observed in eating a banana. He takes the whole bunch, opens his cavernous mouth, and tosses the bananas in stalk and all. Then from the next stall he picks up a coconut and tosses it in after the bananas. There is a loud crack and the elephant moves on to the next stall.
>
> No threats or promises can make this restless trunk settle down. But the wise mahout, if he knows his elephant well, will just give that trunk a short bamboo stick to hold on to before the procession starts. Then the elephant will walk along proudly with his head up high, holding the bamboo stick in front of him like a drum major with a baton. He is not interested in bananas or coconuts anymore; his trunk has something to hold on to.
>
> The mind is very much like this. Most of the time it has nothing to hold on to, but we can keep it from straying in to all kinds of absurd situations if we just give it the mantra.[4]

Pat, Nana and I got into some wonderfully interesting dialogues about spirituality and personal growth. When I mentioned all the "mistakes" I had made in my life prior to coming to the seminar, Nana offered, "I've found that there are really no such things as mistakes. The idea of a 'mistake' is just something we've invented with which to torture ourselves. As I see it, when we pay attention, everything enlightens us."

Pat followed this up with, "I like the old Cherokee saying, that says, 'Every thing in life comes to you as a teacher. Pay attention. Learn quickly.'"

Sticking to one of my old habits, I had prejudged Pat and Nana before I got to know them, and I had presumed that people as interested in business as they were could not be interested in matters of the spirit. And yet, here I was, very much interested in both topics myself, realizing that I was also probably being prejudged by everyone around me.

As we got to know each other, Pat, Nana and I found we had many things in common. One day we got into a discussion of medicine and I was introduced to *ayurveda,* thought to be the most ancient of all health sciences and one that is practically unknown in the West. While *ayurveda* goes back thousands of years, it is remarkably modern in its approach to human health. In India today, there are more than one hundred modern *ayurvedic* medical colleges; and a detailed, holistic scientific literature exists, including a vast *materia medica* which provides the theoretical framework for classifying the therapeutic properties of all plants.

Although *ayurveda* deals with pathology—the disease process—it is more concerned with the characteristics of individual patients, and how they contribute to good health. An *ayurvedic* practitioner is trained to look at all aspects of the individual, including diet, life style and attitudes. The techniques of ayurveda are so sophisticated that, for example, a trained practitioner can diagnose diseases solely on the basis of "reading" a patient's pulse.[5]

I was delighted to be introduced to ayurveda and wasn't surprised when Nana, after looking closely at me for a moment, volunteered: "Of course, much of the foundation of modern medicine that we have inherited from the Greeks was actually derived from *ayurveda.* In fact, Hippocrates would feel quite at home with *ayurvedic* medicine."

I stared at Nana and almost blurted out my recent dealings with Hippocrates, but something held me back. Was that old codger in back of all these discussions, guiding them with his unseen hand? Or was Nana clairvoyant? There was a quality to her eyes that suggested she had found the secrets of inner life. And though we hadn't known each other very long, I had a sense that Pat and Nana knew and understood my innermost fears and longings. One day toward the end of the seminar, we were sipping drinks and enjoying some tasty hors d'oeuvres when Jeff Wright, a real estate developer and a partner in a gold mine joined us. Nana asked Jeff, "Do you know Dennis?"

"Yes, sure. Dennis is a very spiritual person."

I was taken aback. Why had he said that? I barely knew him, and we had never exchanged a single word except about business. Then, as though I wasn't there, Nana said, "Dennis is all right! He's just resisting being happy. As soon as he learns to let go, he'll be fine."

This comment was made matter-of-factly, with no hint of judgment—it sounded as though Nana was just stating the obvious.

Why were things like this happening in the midst of a business seminar? Who were these people, really, and why did they speak about me so intimately? Was I that transparent? Or had I secretly wished for this kind of relationship and helped it come to pass? Is this what it meant to operate at a higher level of awareness?

There were quiet times as well. Once I became wide awake at four o'clock in the morning. I decided to take a hot bath and became very relaxed. I found myself letting go of all the remaining troubles and concerns I had left behind, and allowing the silence to overtake me. A peaceful emptiness permeated my whole being. It didn't require me to do anything…just let go.

To many, silence is alien, even dangerous. They feel safer filling their lives with sounds that protect them from dealing with silence. Background music, constant chatter, incessant activity and unending entertainment enable them to avoid silence. They live in a noisy world of largely meaningless sounds to which there is no need to listen. In such a world, they begin to go deaf, and the ability to hear the subtle, unfamiliar sounds of life becomes a lost art.

> In the middle of the night, a dog barks outside the castle of the Little King. The king calls down to the guard outside, "Guard, get rid of that dog!"
> "But Sire," the guard replies, "the dog is protecting you."
> "What is it protecting me from?" asks the Little King.
> "From the silence, Sire."[6]

Random thoughts: A sabbatical is supposed to be a leave-taking, a process of rejuvenation, and it is based on the idea that a change of locale and activities is a useful means of sustaining high levels of performance over a long period of time. Thus, a sabbatical is more a getting-away-from than a going-to.

How does it differ from an ordinary vacation? Are restful contemplation and quietude necessary elements of the sabbatical or can the individual experience a frenzy of activities? Must a person leave his familiar haunts or can he remain at home? Must the time be spent alone? Can a sabbatical have a planned itinerary, or must there be an element of spontaneity in order to achieve its goals? And when we depart in order to get away from something, are we really leaving in order to seek that which we sense is missing?

"You pose some interesting questions, Dr. A," a welcome voice responded. "We had sabbaticals in my time as well. The word is derived from *sabaton,* which means to rest from labor. Of course, the Israelites will dispute that, since they claim it comes from Shabbat, their word for Sabbath."

"Oh come on, Hippocrates, the Hebrew word for the Sabbath goes back to Moses, and that makes it more than nine hundred years before your time."

"In case you've forgotten, Greek civilization did not begin in my time. It predates—but I'm getting off my point."

"Which is?"

"Which is about your asking, 'And when we depart in order to get away from something, are we really leaving in order to seek that which we sense is missing?' What I want to say to you, Dr. A., is that all life seeks that which is missing. Everything you do is done, ultimately, in order to find that which is missing. When we find what is missing, we call it 'healing.' In your generation, some of your practitioners have come up with the phrase, 'holistic healing.' That is a step in the right direction.

And this is our life, exempt from public haunt,
Find tongues in trees, books in the running brooks,
Sermons in stones, and good in everything.
　　　　　　　　　　　　　—William Shakespeare

I left London for Fumicino Airport in Rome aboard a flight filled with the poetic, musical chatter of Italian. The gestures and speech of the Italian people, with which I was familiar since childhood, seemed fun for its own sake.

Although I had been in Rome many times, I saw it all with fresh eyes. The lobby of my hotel, located a stone's throw from the picturesque Spanish Steps, was a museum, with antique furnishings, sculptures and paintings, but the people brought tears of joy to my eyes. In England I had somehow awakened to the uniqueness, the depth and the beauty in each person I met. It was as if we were saying to one another, "We have faced each other for centuries, wearing different masks; why have we not recognized each other before?"

Now, in Rome, the feeling became even more intense. Every time I passed a face and looked into someone's eyes I had an intense feeling of sacredness. I only had to look at someone for a moment to feel tears beginning to fill my eyes.

Nor was the feeling limited to people. Everything, especially the statues and paintings, was alive, full of wonder and reverence. Someone—something—had slowly removed all the screens between me and the world around me, leaving me to face all its pain and splendor. As I gazed upon the figures of Romulus and Remus sucking at the mother wolf's breast, I took nourishment from the great Western myths and felt the cultural blood of ancient Greece and Rome run through my Sicilian veins.

I belonged here.

My mother joined me in Rome and together we visited her home and childhood friends, driving first to Naples, and then to the quaint town of St. Agatha de due Golfo, which means St. Agatha of the two gulfs—referring to the nearby Gulf of Naples and the Gulf of Salerno.

I like the way Bon Appetit magazine described this region: "To say that the Amalfi Coast is scenic would be like saying that Pavarotti can carry a tune."[7] The slopes to which the coastal towns of Sorrento, Capri, Positano, Amalfi, Ravello and Cetara cling are so steep that the streets wind back and forth like switchback trails. You might be able to call to your neighbors fifty feet above or below you, but if you wanted to drive to their house, you would have to go half a mile up one switchback and half mile back another.

When we arrived, we were greeted by my mother's dear friend, Rose, and several family members, and ushered to private rooms on the third floor of a large but not luxurious villa. I no longer wore my watch, and it was wonderful to shed clock time and to allow events simply to occur. At Rose's villa, I savored leisurely baths instead of rushed, five-minute showers. I welcomed the beginning of each day and cherished each waking moment. I loved talking with the townsfolk as much as I did just sitting in the garden, contemplating the birds, trees, flowers and rows of vegetables. I spent hours alone at nearby Nerano beach, soaking in the warm sun and swimming in the clear waters.

I enjoyed real Italian cooking, spaghetti served al dente—for the teeth—rather than the soft, overcooked pasta served in the U.S. The fettucini was seasoned with an exquisite but subtle sauce, not covered in a heavy white sauce. There's no such thing as typical "Italian cooking." Northwestern Italy cooks with rice, butter and cheese; the Val D'Aosta region is famous for its wide variety of delicious soups; Lazio is known for its potato pasta; Calabria uses different varieties of cabbage in its dishes, and so on. What American think of as Italian food is the cooking of Naples, which specializes in pasta covered with tomato sauce.

I also enjoyed watching Rose's father, Franco. He was very old, around ninety-five, and he spent his days seated in his chair, his cane at his side, staring into oblivion. His back was permanently bent, probably from a lifetime of working his farm. Occasionally, he took short walks, appearing as an aging falcon ready to take flight. Occasionally, though, Franco would put on an ancient-looking pair of glasses and hold a newspaper close to his face. One evening, Rose's daughter, Claudia, brought the old man a bowl of ice cream. When he saw it, Franco's eyes lit up and all traces of senility left him. He deftly maneuvered his spoon and scooped up the ice cream with great precision. So efficient was he that he cleaned out his bowl before anyone else in the family, and then he let out a great sigh and returned to apparent oblivion.

The next day, when I returned from swimming in the warm Mediterranean, I noticed my mom sitting next to him. Franco was conversing with her in clear Italian and understandable English about his old days in Hoboken, before he returned to Italy. He talked with gusto and described some events with such vigor and wit that my mom and I burst into laughter.

If Franco was senile, it was selective senility. He did precisely what he felt like doing, and if that meant shutting out the rest of the world at times, so be it. It was refreshing to have my ego reduced another notch. Once again, I had made a snap judgment and attempted to fit a human being into a convenient category, only to be shown that I was naive and hasty.

I took a small, coastal cruise ship to the picturesque towns of Amalfi and Positano. In several calm places, the captain stopped the ship and allowed us to dive and swim in the aquamarine waters. On the return trip we were hit by an unusual, furious rainstorm. It was so windy and wet that everyone retreated below deck. I have always been enticed by nature's fury, and I often enjoyed standing out in the open in a driving storm to "feel" the elements. This time, behind the closed porthole, I gazed out at the swirling, pounding rain from my cozy sanctum. As I stared at the swirling cacophony, a strange thing happened. It was as if my spirit had joined with the spirit of the storm, and I felt a part of myself rushing through the air, unfettered, plunging headlong this way and that. For those moments, I was the rain and wind, pushed along by furious energy over which I had no control and over which I wanted none. I parted clouds and shoved them together again and made the ocean foam and swell. I felt immensely free, as if I were a performing artist whose dance was not limited by his physical body.

The storm disappeared as suddenly as it had come, and the warm Mediterranean sun returned. What, I wondered, happened to that immense energy? Was it hiding, secretly waiting its next chance to explode into being? I had witnessed and then participated in something very special, but I did not totally understand what it meant.

After a week at Rose's estate near Naples, Mom and I flew to Catania, Sicily and drove to my mother's village of Roccalumera. In Sicily, there's nothing quite like returning to the town of your ancestors. The whole town turns out to meet you and to pay their respects. I loved the ritual greetings. When we arrived, an entire procession was waiting for us and we had to pass along the greeting line, shaking hands and kissing each person on both cheeks. Even with individuals you didn't particularly care for, this formal means of greeting was always extended, and all differences of opinion were, at least temporarily, put aside.

The harbor at Roccalumera was filled with colorful fishing boats. They reminded me of my childhood summers spent with my nonno (grandfather), Concetto, who had died some sixteen years ago. Concetto was a commercial fisherman who loved to drink and gamble. When I worked with him as a boy, he was bald and had the biggest nose and ears that I had ever seen. Through his thick, horn-rimmed glasses, Concetto had an infectious, mischievous smile, and he was known throughout the town for his caustic wit and poetic skill.

As I looked at the boats lying in the sand, I thought of how far I had come from this way of life to my own in California. It's easy to romanticize the simple rural life, but when I compared life in Roccalumera to my high living back home, the scenes around me seemed much more attractive.

As quaint as it was, Roccalumera was not paradise. The streets were very narrow, and everyone always knew what everyone else was doing. It was like living in a fishbowl, albeit a friendly one, but it was beginning to get to me, and in terms of privacy at least, home began looking better. Yet there were more experiences in the offing. Cousin Cadina came to visit, with her two children, a seven-year-old and a seven-month-old. Her children's ages were similar to my own. I loved Cadina. She had been my secret childhood sweetheart, but I had never let on, and I don't think she had any hint of it. We used to jump up and down on her bed until we were both exhausted. Then we would lie down beside each other, recovering. It was a deep sensual experience for me at the time, although I didn't understand it. Now, I looked at this adult woman and could still see the little Cadina I had known. What separated us now? Was it the separate roads we had traveled, or only the whisper of time?

How arrogant we are to assign enormous importance to adult love and to laugh at puppy-love. We think that childhood love is transitory—it doesn't last long. But it does, it does! Once you love a person, you never stop loving that person. Deep in your heart, that love still lingers and has an continuing effect on the life of your beloved.

Entertainment in Roccalumera was rare but exciting when it occurred. One morning I watched a huge semi-trailer truck try to make it down a narrow street that could barely hold a small car. Traffic stalled, horns were constantly tooted by irate drivers, as though the volume by itself could resolve the problem. Pedestrians and occupants of the adjacent houses all chimed in with their strident opinions until the scene was a bedlam of shouting, gesturing, cursing people. It was wonderful. Finally, by clearing the sidewalks of potted plants and all other movable objects, and driving the truck onto the sidewalks and scraping the house fronts, the truck made it through. A tremendous cheer rang out from the gathered crowd. It was a real event in the life of the town.

As the time for our departure grew near, my grandmother began verbally assaulting my mother. "Why do you have to leave so soon? Why did you spend so much time at Rose's instead of here? How can you do this to your own mother?" she wailed, "How can you treat me this way when I have so little time left to live?" All this was accompanied by such melodramatic gestures and wailing that you would have thought we were torturing her. What marvelous technique she had to make my mom feel guilty!

On the day before our departure, I went to a nearby town to shop for some jewelry. I found a beautiful diamond necklace with matching earrings for Cecile. For myself, I had arranged to have a custom gold watch/bracelet made, and it was now ready. It was a gift of love to myself, congratulations for beginning to find myself. The store owner, Graciela, was unable to accept credit cards. I could have arranged a cash transfer but she encouraged me to make the purchases on credit that she would extend to me, personally. This was quite a gesture on her part, since I was leaving for the United States. Graciela set no time limit for her repayment, nor did she tack on any interest. She simply said, "Denniseh, whenever you have some extra money, send it in payment to me." Yes, she knew my family in Roccalumera, but they weren't responsible for my debts, and she knew that. Her trust in me was such that I could never, never give her cause to regret it.

I thought about the mountains of paperwork back home, credit applications, legal documents, forms, contracts, lawsuits and on and on. Why had society ordered our lives like that? They say our greatness derives from the fact that we are "a nation of laws and not men." But laws by themselves do not create mutual trust, kindness and respect. These come from the heart, and no laws have ever created a loving, caring society.

On our last day, we said good-bye to what seemed like the entire town. More hugs and kisses, lots of tears, little gifts that would make our luggage heavier. My feelings about returning home were mixed. I would be returning to responsibilities, but I had gained a great deal during my stays in England and Italy, and I had a sense that I would be able to take much of it home with me.

CHAPTER 10

Treasure in my Own Backyard

To Adam, Paradise was home. To the good among his descendants, home is paradise.   —*Hare*

Cecile hadn't been a party to my decision to drop everything and leave for a month. I didn't ask her approval because there was no chance of my changing my mind—I had to go. But no matter how I tried to explain, no matter how debilitated and depressed I seemed, she never fully understood— no, wait, that's not fair—she couldn't imagine doing such a thing herself, so it was hard for her to empathize with me. After all, one doesn't just pick up and leave a family, especially when a new baby is in the house. Moreover, since we were having cash flow problems, Cecile had to assume responsibility for selling some properties in addition to temporarily losing her husband, caring for the children and helping to run the clinic. She had a right to be angry and hurt.

Actually, Cecile had many reasons to feel resentful. During my sabbatical I had examined my past, including my past husbanding, concluding that I'd robbed my wife of her freedom and personhood. Under the guise of building security for our family, my own need to be nurtured, to have my opinions respected and my plans executed had directed our lives since the first days of our relationship.

It was time for a real partnership between us. Finding myself—or at least beginning to find myself—had the added virtue of making room for someone else. When I walked through the gate to our house, Cecile and the children were waiting, all smiles. After a long, silent embrace, the sheer joy of having a family bubbled up within me. A lot of mending had to be done to make up for my past behavior, but this was "home," this was where I belonged.

That evening in bed, I whispered to Cecile, "I wasn't sure if you'd take me back." Tears welled up in her eyes and she didn't say anything, but her face expressed a longing for love and intimacy that had been absent for a long time. For a moment outside of time, we inhabited a world where our spirits united. When it was over, we held each closer than we had ever done before.

What a relief it was to find that I could feel good again, that I hadn't sustained some irreparable psychic damage. I felt renewed hope and vision, that most necessary state of mind. My back still hurt, but it was now just an annoyance—all the overtones of self-pity and doom were gone.

It wasn't all hugs and kisses and the warmth of familiar surroundings; there was also a letdown accompanying my return to responsibilities. My assistant, Dr. Reaper, had remained until my return; now he was off to further his own career and I was the sole doctor. Actually, although I was apprehensive about losing my assistant; I could once again be intimate with my patients and learn at firsthand how each progressed. I also noticed I had become less uptight about a number of things. For example, I stopped the vigorous pursuit of uncollected accounts. If a patient didn't finish paying, I was more inclined to write it off than go through collection procedures. I still ran a pretty tight ship, but I was less finicky over small matters. My loosening up at the clinic now afforded me more free time, and it was delightful to be home in the evenings to tell my children bedtime stories. And when I awoke each morning, I did so without dread. Instead, I felt enthusiastic about the new day.

I decided once again to cross the Santa Cruz Mountains to visit my counselor and friend, Bob Goodheart. This time I entered the converted church that was his office without caring that I might be seen by someone. The fear of what others might think (about needing psychological help) had been left by the wayside, and good riddance.

I told Bob about rejecting my financial adviser's recommendation that I hire another physician and start a multi-disciplinary medical clinic. I was no longer interested in pioneering—I had done my share and more.

"You're getting clearer, aren't you?" Bob remarked. "You seem to be more precise now about what you want."

"Well, one nice thing that's happened is that now I realize everything I own is expendable. When we first started these sessions, I couldn't let go of any of my 'marbles.' I suppose that given enough pain, one is willing to part with almost anything."

"Isn't life a series of 'letting go's?' Remember some time ago we talked about the fact that knowledge without action is worthless. Now you're beginning to empower your knowledge by acting on your insights, and the benefits will start coming."

"You're right. It's as though everything we talked about, everything I learned on an intellectual basis, was recreated for me on my trip so that I could have it as an actual experience."

Bob's comments reminded me of something Fritjof Capra explores in his book, *Uncommon Wisdom, Conversations with Remarkable People*. In a conversation with psychotherapist Carl Simonton, Capra asks why people who don't act on their insights within a reasonable period of time simply cease having them. "Because the unconscious will give up?"

"Right!" Simonton says, "It will say: 'No good telling him, he doesn't listen anyway.'"

Then Capra says, "If all of a sudden I get a deep insight into what's going on in my life, it'd be a way of changing it, and if I don't change it, then I will stop getting these insights."[1]

I said to Bob, "After my trip began, I had this insight…it felt very profound…that everyone I met would be of help to me. Then as I went on, it felt good being with people. I learned from everyone, young and old, rich and poor. I related to people with whom I had nothing in common but our human bond, and I felt nurtured by everyone…no, wait—I felt nurtured by every-*thing*, whether it was alive or not. Plants and rocks and…and the earth and clouds and rain…I was nurtured by all of them."

"Right on," Bob said, *"vis medicatrix nature"*

"What?"

"Vis medicatrix nature," Bob repeated, "It was a phrase coined by Hippocrates in ancient Greece."

My jaw dropped open and I looked for a subtext while Bob continued. "Do you remember the book, *Zorba, The Greek*, by Nikos Kazantzakis? It was later made into a movie starring Anthony Quinn."

"Yeah, sort of."

"There is a passage from it that I'll never forget. It goes like this:

> Everything in this world has a hidden meaning… men, animals, trees, stars, they are all hieroglyphics…When you see them, you do not under-

stand them. You think they are really men, animals, trees, stars. It is only years later…that you understand.[2]

"*Vis medicatrix nature,* "Bob continued, "is based on the principle that every living thing is infused with its independent source of life energy that animates it and causes it to evolve through its life cycle, and that we can tap into that energy."

"What do you know about Hippocrates?" I asked.

"Well, I suppose no more than your average healing practitioner knows about him," Bob answered, "The famous Hippocrates for whom the Hippocratic Oath is named…the guy who used garlic to treat pneumonia and infected wounds."

"What? What did you just say?"

"Garlic, he used garlic to treat patients with pneumonia and infections. You probably know that long before antibiotics came onto the scene garlic was used to fight bacterial infections…it was very popular in combating tuberculosis as well. The history books are full of references to it."

"As a matter of fact, I thought it was just an old wives tale."

"What?" Bob laughed, "You of all people should be open to alternative forms of medicine after all you've been through."

"Touché. Tell me more. Do you know how it works?"

"There's a chemical in garlic called allicin which is the principal therapeutic agent known to kill two dozen or more strains of bacteria. It's very powerful stuff."

"If it's so good, why isn't it used more?"

"The extract is extremely unstable, and commercial attempts to stabilize it have been unsuccessful so far. It also smells to high heaven, and when you get rid of the odor, you lose the potency as well. Besides, unless you could come up with a unique process for stabilizing the extract, there's nothing to patent. Consequently, no pharmaceutical company is going to invest large sums in something they can't monopolize. Nevertheless, it's an incredibly valuable therapeutic agent. In fact, it was Charak, the father of Hindu medicine, who said 'But for its odor it would be costlier than gold.'"

"How do you know so much about garlic" I asked.

"I'm a student of folk medicine. My wife and I have our own herb garden and we occasionally attend seminars on homeopathy."

So that's how Hippocrates did it, I said to myself. When he left my office, after that first visit, he used a high-potency garlic extract on his infected toe. But why hadn't he told me? Wasn't it an interesting coincidence that Bob

Goodheart just happened to be an expert on garlic cures, and that he just happened to mention "Charak, the father of Hindu medicine?" For "Hindu medicine" was the *ayurvedic* medicine I had so recently learned about from my friends Pat and Nana on the Isle of Man.

The chain of coincidences was growing longer.

Our conversation continued, and Bob asked me about my homecoming. Then he said, "Many things have changed, all for the better it seems."

"I've let go of trying to model myself after all the rich and famous doctors I looked up to for so long. That was a big part of the problem—I set my sights on duplicating and even exceeding their success even though I was increasingly unhappy doing it. I knew that for the most part they were unhappy too—but I guess my drive for success prevented me from seeing that."

"You've come a long way, Dennis. One way of measuring that is to ask yourself, 'Would I trade places with the person I was before?'"

"No!" I answered decisively, "I wouldn't."

As I left Bob's office, I found myself thinking about a story I had read Jason the night before. Called *The Treasure*, it tells of a peasant named Isaac who has a recurring dream three nights in a row. In the dream, a voice tells him to travel to the capital city and look under the bridge by the royal palace. After the third night, Isaac can no longer ignore the dream, and he departs on a long and difficult journey through forests and across mountains. When he finally arrives, he seeks out the bridge and finds that it is guarded day and night. Isaac lingers nearby, wondering what to do, when the captain of the guard sees him and approaches him: "Why are you here?" he asks. Isaac tells him about the dreams he had and the captain breaks out laughing. "You poor fellow," he said mockingly, "What a pity you wore your shoes out for a silly dream. Listen, if I believed a dream I once had, I would go right now to the town you came from and I'd look for a treasure under the stove in the house of a fellow named Isaac."

Isaac again plodded through the forests and over the mountains to get home as fast as he could. Following the captain's advice, he proceeded to dig an enormous hole under his stove. Lo and behold, there he found the treasure for which he had traveled so far. Author Uri Shulevitz ends the story by saying, "In thanksgiving, he built a house of prayer, and in one of its corners he put an inscription: 'Sometimes one must travel far to discover what is near.'"[3]

CHAPTER 11

Tension of Opposites

Losses always seem sharper, more real, than wins. A loser is startled, dismayed, shook up. He is suddenly alert to his feelings. He stands stock-still, like a deer, listening to the sound of his disappointment.

—Adair Lara

For five years I had been making payments on the Onyx Building in San Diego, but the proposed Convention Center adjacent to it—the prime attraction for buying it in the first place—had never materialized. I had gone out on a leveraged limb on this deal, the limb was about to snap, and I was going to pay a monumental price for my error. I decided to stop making payments on the property and to look for a buyer to take it off my hands. This was an important decision on my part; it would be the first time in my life that I formally admitted failing.

The Bank of San Diego (BSD) held the loan on the Onyx, and they naturally wanted their money. They threatened to foreclose on me if I did not bring my due payments current. I tried to convince them to allow me to sell the property rather than to go through all the hassle of foreclosure. If they foreclosed, I said, it might take them quite a while to sell the building and recoup their money.

In common with several banks during the late 1980s, BSD had made some problem loans, and they did not need to take any losses on the Onyx Building. In fact, they wanted a complete payoff on my loan—to end their risk—and did not want to permit the loan to be assumed by another buyer. In a game of poker with millions of dollars at stake; they threatened foreclosure and I threatened to delay the process for as long as possible, meaning I would sink deeper into arrears and they would be facing a larger loss. The possibility of finding another buyer was a bittersweet pill for BSD to swallow; they would not have to initiate foreclosure, but they would need to trust that I would find a qualified buyer. Each month that I did not, their potential loss would be greater. Then, they would have to allow the buyer to assume my loan, meaning they could not rid themselves of it. As I said, it was high stakes, and both sides were looking at large risks.

John Lovett, a loan consultant, had been working on my behalf and negotiating with BSD to get me free of the project. John's progress reports were bittersweet for me also; we were getting closer to finding a buyer and getting BSD to agree that the loan could be assumed, but the closer we got, the sooner I would have to face a devastating loss in order to complete the deal. All I could do was hope and trust that my newfound sense of purpose would lead me in the right direction.

> If we are really honest about it, however, we may recall at least several instances in our lives in which it was not actually 'us' who let go. In those instances, we knew we were incapable of letting go on our own. We had reached our limit. What happened then surprised us. It was as though some bigger and more powerful source than our own 'I' let go from within us. It is often only in retrospect that we realize this. When we do realize it, we spend some time trying to name the bigger and more powerful source which we energized at that time. We may speak of it as...the mystery, the muse, the Yahweh, the Buddha Nature, life, grace, nature, God, chi, the spirit, love, the Messiah, the Tao, or many other such names. What the language is trying to describe is a personal contact with a reality that is bigger and more powerful than our individual self.[1]
>
> —*Francis Dorff*

Sometimes, if we are fortunate, we reach the point where almost all material things in our life are expendable. In the midst of my anxiety over the Onyx Building, I had a sense that my stately home, properties and high-rolling lifestyle were no longer the important things in my life. Now that I was spending more time at home, the love I felt from my wife and the adoration I received from my children more than compensated for any losses I might sustain.

I began to define how much was enough, and was surprised to find how much less it was than I had previously thought. And then the strangest thing began to happen. No sooner had I reconciled myself to less material wealth than it began flowing toward me. Our two Park Avenue properties in San Jose closed; we unexpectedly received several thousand dollars in incentive rebates from orthopedic suppliers.; and since we had stopped making the payments on the Onyx Building as part of the loan restructuring deal, we were able to retain several thousand dollars of rental income from it. We received another sum as a partnership distribution we hadn't expected. These individual strokes of good fortune were beginning to have a cumulative effect; good fortune was now becoming the rule rather than the exception.

There were still shadows from my past. In August of 1987, my immensely successful colleague, Dr. Louis Needleman of New York City, called to let me know he had finally gained one of his remaining goals—to appear on ABC's *20/20* show with Hugh Downs and Barbara Walters. Dr. Needleman and minimal incision surgery received very positive coverage, and I was glad that my colleague had finally gotten his wish and that our surgical techniques were once again receiving the coverage they deserved. But his call also reminded me of the constant striving, constant maneuvering for advantage and for increased publicity. That life seemed a long way off, and I had no desire to go back to it.

When I watched the *20/20* show, my attention was captured more by the segment that followed Dr. Needleman—the trial and acquittal of John Delorean. After a long and costly trial for conspiracy to traffic in cocaine, Delorean was now a free man. He had become another fallen idol of the Yuppie age. Delorean had everything—wealth, power, fame, prestige and a picture-perfect wife and child. Then came the collision with fate. "How did you get through it all?" Walters asked.

"Very clearly, my faith in God," answered.

After allegedly being set up by the government in a contrived sting operation, Delorean had been hounded by the press and stripped of all his material assets. How easy it is for the public to believe the worst about someone. Despite my own experience with media hype, I, too, had believed he was guilty. Delorean never had a chance. He was creative, ambitious and flamboyant in his rise to the top—a sure-fire formula for making enemies. It wasn't important whether he was innocent or guilty—he deserved a comeuppance and he got it. Yet here was a man who had shown courage and dignity in the face of overwhelming adversity, and he had come through his ordeal spiritually transformed.

On a much smaller scale, I had been in a similar position, and I identified with Delorean. Somehow, I'd been helped to turn the corner before real disaster struck. It made me very grateful and reminded me of the saying, "There but for the grace of God go I."[2] The *20/20* show also made me realize how much my interests had changed, for I had found a personal story of trial and transformation much more compelling than the care of feet.

Cecile's cousin Marcie was getting married, and Cecile and the children would be spending three weeks in Chicago for the preparations and festivities. Since I was now running the clinic without the aid of another podiatrist, I could only take time off during the final week for the actual wedding, which meant that I'd be celebrating my birthday alone. After I had seen wife and children off, I was surprised to learn that my staff wanted to help me celebrate my birthday. I had never gotten too close to them; there never seemed to be time, and I had thought it correct to maintain my "professional distance." Thinking about it, I realized I was hoarding my affection just like I was hoarding material possessions and personal achievements.

A dramatic visit by a well-developed young woman dressed in the uniform of an English maid set the stage. Before she began her routine, the maid sat close to me with her dress raised above her thighs, embarrassing me and inviting me to remove her red lace garter, to the great merriment of all the staff. Then she performed an assortment of voluptuous songs and dances while sensually stroking me with a multi-colored feather duster. The maid was a gift, compliments of Cecile, Jason and Michelle, a fun way of saying "Happy Birthday" from two thousand miles away.

Then my staff presented me with a bottle of champagne and a gift highly appropriate for a podiatrist: a booklet titled, *The Joy of Sox*, a parody of the well-known *Joy of Sex*. (Example: "How often do you need sox? Answer: Most people enjoy sox once a day, some like sox twice a day, but everyone agrees that sox just once a week stinks!")

After I'd blown out the candles and we'd finished off the cake, Barbara Naughton, a quiet, conservative, studious-looking receptionist from Iowa said she wanted to give me a gift of a numerology/astrology reading. This was the last thing I would have expected from her (whoops, there I was, stereotyping people again). What was also surprising was that the reading would be done by her husband, Todd, a former Protestant minister.

I knew nothing of numerology and little enough about astrology, aside from the usual stuff we all pick up. While I was curious and open enough to accept the offer of a reading, I was also interested in why Todd had dropped out of the ministry. When we were alone together I asked him about it.

"I just got disillusioned with the hierarchy and all the politics," Todd offered. "It stopped serving my spiritual needs. But even then I was interested in numerology and I've maintained my interest in it despite the cynicism that surrounds the concept."

"What is the concept?"

"The notion that the numbers associated with our lives have significance...deliberate significance. This includes letters by the way, because in numerology, specific letters are related to specific numbers."

"*Okay,*" I thought, "*I can at least accept the possibility of that.*"

"Numerologists put a great deal of stock in a person's name. From your name, and the significance of the letters that make it up, I would guess you consider yourself a person of high motivation and compassion, someone who feels part of a larger family—by that I mean the Family of Mankind. I also judge that you would be happiest in a vocation where you could take your compassion and apply it to that larger family...to a wider audience. Also, in your case, the vocation, or activity, will not be of a routine nature; it definitely suggests being involved with people on a very large scale."

As far as the larger audience went, it was true—I had always wanted to connect in some capacity with the public, and servicing the needs of my patients and publishing information for other doctors wasn't enough to satisfy the urge.

There wasn't much opportunity to ask questions during the reading—Todd kept going at a fair clip, covering aspects of my personality as he saw them. Although I wanted to be open-minded, I had really started out quite cynical about the whole business. Then Todd suddenly paused and said, "Have you written a book yet?"

"Well, as a matter of fact, I've written three of them...professional books, for doctors and for lay persons...about foot care."

"I don't mean that kind of book. Besides, I'm not talking about just any book. Your numbers indicate the ability and the urge to express your innermost self."

That caught my attention. I had been interested in various art forms, but I had never attempted to express myself except within the confines of my profession. Yet there was something inside of me wanting to come out.

Todd went on. "Your birthday is on the twenty-sixth which is one of the business numbers. So I would expect you to have a drive, or desire to create, that manifests in business ventures." Then he offered general statements such as I had heard many times before: "All great artists are people who have experienced a great amount of difficulty in their life and who are given the opportunity to overcome their difficulties." Statements like this are trite or profound, depending on the degree to which we identify with them. I was receptive to Todd's statement, but even more important, it struck a resonant chord with my professional work. I had always considered my minimal incision surgery to be an art form as much as a science.

Toward the end of our time together, Todd read to me an interpretation of my personality by the noted astrologer, Grant Lewi, using my date and time of birth as keys.

"You're a pretty detached person, and however much your romanticism and personal emotionalism may seem to make you otherwise, you're inclined to be cold and self-sufficient at heart. (True, true, but I would hope I could substitute 'aloof' for 'cold.') You view people in a very calculating manner and are capable of hurting those who are fond of you by the ease with which you break human ties and follow your own bend, whatever it may be." (Also true. It often suits me to go my own way, oblivious of others.)

"When you figure something out to your satisfaction, you expect everybody else to follow your logic which you may not go to the trouble of explaining." (I admit it. I do have the habit of mentioning just a few words or phrases of what I'm thinking about and then expecting others, especially Cecile, to read my mind.) "The detachment and apparently genial exterior that you present to the world makes you a good doctor (Todd stopped and smiled at that one), social worker, hospital attendant or teacher—any occupation where sympathy and understanding must be used but cannot be allowed to interfere with routine." (This was uncannily accurate—I had never taken the trouble to define the personality characteristics needed for my podiatric practice, but I could not have done better if I had done it myself.) "You are a somewhat suspicious person, critical and judicial, though tolerant of your own eccentricities." (Ouch! But probably true.) "If you're cold, you're also stable and can be a bulwark of help in time of trouble. You are able to observe the roles of others without being affected yourself, thus helping them in getting on their own feet." (True once more. I've always had a cool, calm sort of detachment that seems to have had a reassuring effect on others in times of trouble—at least until my own times of trouble!)

The accuracy of Todd's reading was impressive, but it dawned on me that it was a waste of time and energy to worry about the pros and cons of numerology, astrology or any other esoteric system that attempts to provide insights. The importance of "readings," it seemed to me, was not in how accurately they could portray someone, or the nature of the particular system used, but in how they stimulated us to view ourselves. And it was clear that, regardless of the ultimate source of the information conveyed, Todd's reading had awakened in me a sense of mystery and wonder about how knowledge is disseminated and about the amazing diversity of systems and tools that mankind has used for guidance throughout the ages.

The test of first-rate intelligence is the ability to hold two opposed ideas in mind at the same time and still retain the ability to function. One should...be able to see that things are hopeless and yet be determined to make them better.

—*F. Scott Fitzgerald*

In what direction should I now head? The business seminar on the Isle of Man had reminded me how much I enjoyed thinking up and developing new business ideas. I kept ordering more books on how to succeed. Ever since high school I had been drawn to this subject, and, in fact, much of what I learned about enlarging my own practice had come from these books. Now, in spite of everything that had happened, the old tapes were playing in my mind.

It was like having a split personality; one part of me craved my former, fast-paced, driven lifestyle and the other longed to hold onto my newly-evolving inner experiences. So back and forth I went, a machine out of synch, trying to somehow integrate the forces that were pushing me. *Doesn't it ever become clear and unambiguous?* I wondered *Are these conflicting urges a permanent part of living?*

When a strong urge takes us in what appears to be the wrong direction, we have a tendency to believe that urge is wrong and must be suppressed. But oftentimes, that urge springs from a positive source—it's just that we haven't yet discovered the right time or place to use it. We may go along for years, always fighting a part of ourselves. Then, one day, a situation develops that cries for that talent we have had to deny for so long. Then, finally, we understand that the many trials we have undergone have had a purpose: they have led us to this point. Now our suppressed talent begins to blossom and instead of pushing against constant resistance from the world, we are supported and encouraged. All frustrated talents and urges that lack direction are awaiting their time. It just has not yet come.

A new philosophy, a new way of life, is not given for nothing. It has to be paid dearly for and only acquired with much patience....
—*Fyodor Dostoevsky*

I decided to produce a series of special reports and tape cassettes aimed at the professional marketplace. As part of my plan, I retained the services of seven noted business, finance and insurance experts to supply their knowledge for my workbooks and tapes. Then I contacted a marketing firm, the Millionaire Consulting Service of Orem, Utah to assist me in marketing my books and tapes. The principals behind this firm were Richard and Robert Allen, the brothers who popularized the "no money down" real estate seminars.

With this publishing venture, I wouldn't just be hawking get-rich schemes to the general consumer but offering sound, hard-to-find information to a professional audience. That justified the energy and time I was putting into the project. Or did it?

No sooner had I posed this question than I could hear Hippocrates' response. In measured tones, with great formality, he said, "It's been two years since we first met, Dr. A. Do you recall my words to you then? Follow your passion...follow your passion."

Hippocrates' sudden entrances no longer startled me, and I replied, "Yes, but how do I know what my passion really is?"

"You know, Dr. A., you know. It's simply that you're afraid to look at it openly."

"Well, what about my urge to publish business books and tapes? I feel strongly about—"

"Forgive me for using the modern vernacular, but let us cut the crap, shall we?"

Hippocrates knew exactly how to press my buttons. His "cut the crap" expression was exactly what my father had repeatedly said to me as a child. Now, my automatic reaction kicked in, except that instead of being crudely defensive, I used condescension. "I had thought, Hippocrates, that our discussions were on a fairly high plane of—"

"I repeat, Dr. A., cut the crap and tell me what you really want to do!"

Hippocrates' voice had a sharp edge to it that made me angry. "Who the hell are you to—"

"Stop fooling around, for Zeus' sake, and tell me! What do you really want to do?"

"Okay, okay, I want to write a book!"

"What kind of a book?"

"A book, a book, you know, just a book!"

"Dr. A, I can't waste my time talking to a fool! What book do you want to write?"

"A book on…"

"Yes, yes, on what?"

"Well—on 'life.'"

"Whose life?"

"I suppose…my life." I answered, my voice a faint whisper.

"Well, thank you, Dr. A. It was like pulling teeth, but you got it out."

All the fight went out of me when I realized Hippocrates had been goading me to prompt my admission. "But who am I to write a book about my life?"

"Everyone has a unique story to tell, but that's not important. What is important is that writing about your life is what you really want to do. Now, how shall we begin?"

"We, Hippocrates? What do you mean 'we'?"

"Just kidding, Dr. A, just kidding. You're quite able to begin on your own." And as quickly as he'd arrived, he was gone.

Whenever Hippocrates departed, it felt like his presence gradually diminished in my head until he was a tiny point surrounded by blankness— then the point disappeared and he was gone. *"A book,"* I mused. *"A book about my life. Is that what's been the real driving force behind my other projects? And what can I tell people about my life, and why would they be interested in the first place?"*

Just then the doorbell rang. The postman handed me a special delivery letter from John Lovett and a serendipitous-looking envelope from the state of California. The letter from John Lovett was about the Onyx Building. In it, John said, "The latest round of negotiations have been difficult, Dennis, with offers and counter-offers, and every kind of intimidation, threat and bullying. But it now appears as though the bank and all principals are in agreement. Unless something unforeseen occurs, we can look forward to a closing on December 3rd."

There had been so many delays and complications, month after month, that I wasn't going to hold my breath, but here was a very bright light at the end of the tunnel. And what perfect timing! December 3rd was my little girl's first birthday. We would have two wonderful reasons to celebrate.

The letter from the state of California contained a tax refund check. With it, we could pay off more of our creditors and still have some left for fun. The timing on this was good too, since it was Cecile's birthday. A few months earlier, Cecile had caught me by surprise when she arranged for the seductive dancing girl to show up at my office birthday party. Now it was my turn. I faked taking her out for a nice, cozy birthday dinner at an intimate French restaurant. It wasn't until Cecile was right on top of all our guests in a partitioned alcove of the restaurant that she realized what was happening. "Surprise! Happy Birthday!" they all yelled in unison.

The dinner was excellent, and Cecile really liked the two designer outfits I'd chosen for her. I had never before attempted to purchase clothing for Cecile on my own, but I wanted to convey how much I appreciated her hanging in there with me. I'd given her a tough time for a while, and this was my way of saying thanks.

The following day I had an MRI (magnetic resonance imaging) scan for my back problem. The process is painless but is accompanied by loud, grinding noises caused by the repositioning of the scanning equipment. The noise is so bothersome that music piped through provided earphones. In spite of the earphones, I got a headache and, when I arrived home, took some Tylenol, accidentally dropping a milk carton in the process. Within a second, a sea of white had spread around me. As I began cleaning up the mess, I remembered that this was the second time in a week I had accidentally dropped something. *"What is it now?"* I thought, *"Either I'm getting old, clumsy, or both,"* I told myself, as I lay down to rest my pounding head.

The MRI scan confirmed that my back problem was due to degenerative joint disease and a slipped disk. It was now over six months since I had injured my back and it was beginning to look like I would remain partially disabled for a long time. To offset the bad news, we received a hefty federal tax refund. I was being tossed up and down and up as though I was riding on an endless roller coaster. Since it was impossible to predict when my car was going to rise or fall or bank into a sharp curve, the best thing for me to do was hang on and try to enjoy the ride.

December 3rd was Michelle's first birthday. Cecile had dressed her in a pink dress with matching pink bows. Looking at her, I realized how much I delighted in her existence. Again, I thought about Cecile's determination and courage to have a second child in the face of high risk. This baby girl was alive because of a decision we made. Or was it the other way around? Had we made our decision to have a second child because, on some level, Michelle had communicated to us that she wanted to come?

On the same day, we learned that the Onyx had really closed—it was a done deal. Although I ended up losing a million and a half dollars, Martin Luther King's words came to me and I cried, "Free at last! Free at last! Thank God we're free at last!"

One thing was clear. I had allowed my previous financial successes to separate me from the human condition, and it had taken a dramatic failure to sufficiently humble me. I had two dominant feelings. The first was immense relief. The second was the understanding that no matter how much I tried to go it alone, I was an integral part of the universe, subject to laws I only dimly comprehended. The feeling was very humbling.

I think I can speak for those who have thought of ending their lives because they cannot bear the loss of material possessions, even of the investors who jumped out of their windows rather face financial ruin during the Great Depression. Several factors are at work. One is humiliation. Without material means or prospects, life is hard but bearable. However, once you have known the status and comfort that wealth can provide, it is humiliating to lose it. You believe everyone you know, and who knows of you, will see you as a failure.

There is more than humiliation. When you look back at all the steps, all the sacrifices, all the hard knocks that it took to bring you to your success, it is overwhelming, even unthinkable, to contemplate having to do it all over again. So it is not just the loss of the value of your possessions that makes you contemplate such a dire act, it is the loss of your self-image and the unbearable weariness that overcomes you at the thought of having to do it all over again.

As Syrus said, "The pain of the mind is worse than the pain of the body."

On December 7th, we held a large birthday celebration for Michelle. There were over fifty guests, attendant clowns, giant marionettes and a piñata-bashing with toys and candy falling like rain. It was a smashing success and an event to remember, and that evening, with guests departed and the children asleep, sitting amidst an enormous mess from the day's activities, Cecile and I drank a quiet toast to ourselves.

I don't think I had ever said it in my life, not even to myself. It just came out. I lifted my glass in acknowledgment and whispered, "Thank God."

The stream is saved from the current by the perpetual opposition of soil through which it must cut its way. It is the soil which forms its banks. The Spirit of Fight belongs to the genius of life.

—*Rabindranath Tagore*

A few days after Michelle's birthday party, I was browsing in a book store and noticed a handsome, hardbound diary for sale. It strongly appealed to me, so I bought it. I'd been having flashes of insight lately. I'd be sitting down somewhere, and suddenly an idea would appear from out of nowhere. I wasn't committing myself to anything profound; I just wanted to record some of my thoughts and feelings, and the thoughts of others, in case they might be useful someday.

As I was admiring the diary, a voice said, "You're getting more and more in touch with your personal power, I see." I looked up to see Bob Goodheart standing before me with a book in his hand. "Have you read *Why Smart People Fail?* Listen. 'When you have lost money, self-esteem and approval in the eyes of others, what kind of power can you have?' Here's what it says:

You have the power of your mind.
You have the power to figure out what went wrong and correct it.
You have the power to reinterpret what happened to you and put it in the most enabling scenario possible.
You have options before you if you choose to see them, and therefore you have the power to change.
You have the power to reinvent yourself.
You have the power to declare yourself the judge of what you do. By changing the judgment of success and failure from one that others impose on you to one you impose upon yourself.
You have another important power; you have the power to forgive yourself.[3]

I thanked Bob, jotted a few notes in my new diary, and started to think about the idea of laws. I had recently become interested in the variety of laws that stretch across the entire domain of human existence. Some years back I'd put some thought into the concept of a vast, interconnecting web of events that binds us all together. Now I was going beyond connections to ponder how perceptions actually shape our lives. I had recently seen the movie *Wall Street* and remembered a great line of dialogue that clarified this point: "Wall Street is a place where you have to give up everything you ever believed in order to get everything you ever wanted."

I knew that I had set aside values, ideals and beliefs at an early age to get what I wanted. Back then, those values seemed naive and unable to fit in with reality...they were just high-sounding words that were tucked away in a closet, to be opened someday after all practical matters, like my career, were taken care of.

Later that morning I had an urge to talk more with Bob Goodheart about values. On a whim, I called him and was surprised to hear him say, as if on cue: "You want to talk more about *Wall Street*, right?"

"Yes," I responded, no longer surprised by what appeared to be an elaborate telepathic network operating around me. We talked more about the film, the Boeskyesque character, Gordon Gekko, who has ruthlessly and without conscience forced his way to the financial peak, and his young protégé, Bud Fox, who desperately wants to get there himself. My past reaction to films like these was consistent. After watching one, I'd be filled with turmoil and frustration.

"You mean your conscience would bother you?" Bob asked.

"No, no, not at all. I always wanted to be a corporate kingpin or a high-flying entrepreneur. The guys in the films are symbols of those who actually made it—why couldn't I?"

"So...was it different when you saw *Wall Street?*"

"Totally the opposite. I could see clearly where their greed had led them, how it had corrupted them. It was a relief to be able to watch it without envying all the riches and power they had."

"What's amazing to me, Dennis, is how we remain blind to truth until we experience it for ourselves. Somehow, we always manage to believe we'll outfox fate. A forty-year-old man named Gerald Winkerlin found himself homeless after losing his job. He talks about an event that still haunts him":

> I was in a cashier's line at the supermarket behind this young, healthy-looking black woman. When her groceries were rung up she pulled out a bunch of food stamps. I suddenly felt anger well up within me, and I said, "Hey, get a job! I'm tired of having money taken out of my paychecks for people like you." I expected a sharp answer, but instead, she looked embarrassed and said, "There's nothing I'd like better than a job, but nobody will give me one." "Bull," I shot back. Now, laid off and turned out of my house twenty years later, I'd like to find that lady and tell her

I'm sorry. Little did I realize that what happened to her could happen to anyone. It happened to me.[4]

"People's motives are often not how we perceive them. William James said, 'The total expression of human experience is beyond any narrow or ethical bounds. The real world is one of a different temperament and more intricately built than physical science allows. It is a world unseen.' What do you make of this, Bob?"

"Basically, that there's no absolute right or wrong. All of us are a complicated mixture of good and evil. Take war for instance," Bob said: "Even the ravages of war give birth to new things. I don't mean that we should sanction war, of course. But as conqueror and conquered are brought together, out of this marriage, born of violence, a new race springs up to create a new civilization. This new civilization creates bridges; it softens the boundaries that separate races and nations. I think that what James meant when he said '...the total expression of human experience is beyond any narrow and ethical bounds' is that nature doesn't judge.'"

Just then, Cecile came in to remind me that we had planned to go to the Anne Frank Exhibit in San Jose. I didn't really want to go—the thought of viewing the horrors of the Holocaust once more was too morbid—but after I wandered around a bit, I became aware that it wasn't the atrocities that held my attention so much as the courage and strength of that young Jewish girl. The heart-rending, inspiring story of Anne Frank had found immortality—meaning and purpose had been given to her short life through the agency of a diary.

Diary! What a fine coincidence it was that our trip to the Anne Frank Exhibit occurred on the same day that I decided to begin a diary of my own. If Anne Frank could give an accounting of her days and be an inspiration to the world, maybe I could account for mine and make a small contribution to human understanding.

That coincidence was just one of many synchronicities and omens. One weekend Jason and I were invited by an attorney, Martin Fenster, to join him and his son, Bryce, at their vacation ski chalet in Blue Lake, California. I was hesitant about accepting the invitation because I only knew him casually and wasn't sure what we had in common. One evening, as I entered the chalet bathroom, I noticed a brightly-colored book on the tank above the commode. It was *Man and His Symbols* by Carl Jung. As I began flipping casually through its pages, I found myself drawn to the book like a safety pin to a magnet. The reaction it promoted in me was startling, as though an alchemical change had occurred that brought me to a completely new level of understanding.

Through Jung, I was formally introduced to my own unconscious self—a fellow I had noticed lurking in the shadows but had never clearly seen. Jung showed me that the unconscious was not a bag of repressed desires and conditioning à la Freud but a rich repository of universal patterns of meaning and energy he called *archetypes*. Archetypes appear in dreams and in the creative processes, and it dawned on me that my fascination with mythical personalities such as Odysseus and Midas were symbols of universal messages sent to me by my own unconscious self.

Jung called the unconscious the "great guide, friend and adviser of the conscious." It was an invisible guide, and it spoke to me through images and through my interactions with others: *life guides*, I call them. *For the unconscious self in others is the same self in us all, and part of the greater self called God.* This single sentence burned into my mind, my bones, and my very soul. That our inner selves are united—literally—was such a powerful, such a *right* concept that I immediately knew it was true beyond all doubt.

A lifetime of platitudes, parables, proverbs and myths suddenly made sense!

Martin Fenster's wife was a family counselor, so it was not too surprising to find a book on Jungian psychology in their vacation home. What I did find remarkable was that it would *coincidentally* come into my life at this time, while I was at the apex of my internal struggles that were churning within me like cake batter in a high speed blender.

I could hear the voice of my namesake, St. Augustine, speaking to me: "Nothing happens at random in the world."

San Francisco during the '70s was headquarters for gurus and mystics, so it was not surprising when a series of billboards, prominently displayed alongside freeways, featured the face of Meher Baba, the Indian Islamic guru who had taken an oath of silence and who communicated with his disciples via a small chalkboard. Meher Baba had a large following at the time, and his mustached, broadly smiling face became well known to Bay Area commuters. Underneath Baba's face, in large, bold letters, was printed, "You and I are one." Of all the people who drove by those billboards and read Baba's words, how many understood—how many understand now—what he really meant?

There was so much to learn. Among the things I learned from Jung was why I had been veering back and forth for so long between material and spiritual inclinations (and would probably continue to do so for some time). He set out the challenge that faces Man when he said:

Trying to give the living reality of the Self a constant amount of daily attention is like trying to live simultaneously on two levels, or in two different worlds. One gives one's mind, as before, to outer duties, but at the same time, one remains alert for hints and signs, both in dreams and in external events that the Self uses to symbolizes its intentions—the direction the life stream is moving.[5]

The tension of opposites I had been experiencing wasn't a sign of weakness but a normal life process. Jung himself had gone through it. (There was some comfort in this; if one of the greatest thinkers of our time had experienced this conflict, I was in good company.) I suppose many people who have read Jung are impressed by the breadth of his thinking and intuition. I was too, but beyond that, I felt, "Here's a person who understands me."

Perhaps I was inspired by Jung, or perhaps my own intuitive self was beginning to operate more effectively. Either way, I now understood that spiritual unfolding was itself a creative process of great depth and magnitude—a micro-repetition of the original creation. This meant, among other things, that my growth was unending; that no matter how many times I let go when the occasion called for it, no matter how much I believed I understood, there would always be further changes and insights ahead.

Was there a role for *faith* in all this? St. Augustine held that faith illuminates the mind and enables reason to grasp the essential facts about all reality. He wrote, "I believe in order that I may understand." I had a dim sense that I had heard this before, under unfortunate circumstances, in my Catholic childhood. Visions of nuns, priests and impressionable young children walking in single file, dressed in clean, neatly-pressed uniforms filled my mind.

At the time I had been unable to accept the ideas that had been forced upon me. But I now felt that those experiences were not all bad. A few of the ideas might even be good.

CHAPTER 12

A Surgeon's Worst Nightmare

> We dance round in a ring
> and suppose,
> But the Secret sits in the middle,
> and knows.
>
> —*Robert Frost*

February 8th, 1988 was a *productive* day. A productive day is a doctor's way of saying he made a lot of money for services rendered. Private practitioners—especially highly successful ones—have a funny way of pretending that money isn't their primary concern. Money is incidental ("Oh, just check with the receptionist…she does the billing"). That day, I performed four surgeries and various other procedures and billed out over $8000. Of course, that wasn't all profit, but enough of it was to be one heck of a *productive* day.

Everything went smoothly except my right surgical glove didn't fit. I asked one of my staff about it. "Lydia, is this my size?"

"Yes, it is," she replied.

"I've been meaning to tell you that the right gloves have been feeling tight lately."

"Maybe it's a bad batch," she countered.

She could have been right. It wasn't the first time we'd received defective medical supplies.

"Please order some more," I yelled through my office door. Hands and proper gloves are, of course, very important to a surgeon, and my still-aching back was enough of a bother without being constrained by poorly-fitting gloves.

The Jimmy Swaggart sex scandal was unfolding, and it turned out to be one of the best soap operas on TV. There is probably no worse scandal than one involving a "fornicating minister." Jim and Tammy Bakker had been vilified in the media spotlight the previous year and instead of helping to save the Bakkers' ministry, Reverend Jerry Falwell had swooped in like a God-appointed corporate raider to take over the whole operation. There was something amusing/disgusting/depressing about the message of salvation coming from woman-chasing, money-grubbing, bible-thumping evangelists who didn't practice what they preached. It was even worse seeing the moral bullies fighting among themselves with accusations and counter-accusations, trying so desperately to bring each other down.

The media depicted these religious messengers as cartoon character buffoons, showing them for what they were and, in the process, depriving them of their humanity. I, too, had my personal prejudices, and I felt a sense of justice when I saw Swaggart being cut down to size. But as I watched, I couldn't help thinking that these people had feelings and problems just like the rest of us. And in spite of their reckless and immature actions, they were trying to live as best they could manage. I certainly wasn't in a position to cast any stones.

I heard from my old friend and colleague, Jeff Ryder, now in the Virgin Islands:

> *Just thought I'd drop you a line to let you know we're still alive. We're in St. Croix now and our son's enrolled in a private school. Life is sunny and quiet, and we're in a lovely marina. We are in the charter business and that's our brochure enclosed.*

The colorful brochure was a fantasy traveler's dream. Jeff and his family lived on their fifty-two-foot ketch. One photo in the brochure showed Jeff playfully throwing his son into the air; beneath it was the caption, "Children welcome—nanny available." Other scenes showed Sam's culinary specialties and the surprisingly spacious accommodations in three double staterooms, with stereo, TV, computer, telephone and washer/dryer on board.

At the end of his letter, Jeff joked, "Like to swap places for a few months?"

I was happy for Jeff and his family. Although they had experienced some difficult times getting their new lives straightened out, it seemed to have been the right decision for them. But whenever I heard from Jeff, it made me pause and reflect on my own life. Like Jeff, I could have taken off for the Caribbean, too. But we are all different people, and it was hard to imagine being permanently away from all the "action."

It is interesting to imagine oneself in an entirely different occupation in an entirely different place. What prevents us from being lion tamers, spies, actors or gourmet chefs? A friend recently told me about a timid, soft-spoken man who had written a daily newspaper column for thirty years. It was a question-and-answer column on how to repair your home appliances. After thirty years, the man suddenly quit his job to become a tour leader in the Middle East. He is now a travel expert on the region and speaks fluent Arabic and Hebrew. Most important, he is happy.

How many people are really happy with what they're doing? In the Seth books written by Jane Roberts, Seth talks about our multiple selves. There are a multitude of alternate selves concurrently living all the alternate lives we've ever wished to live. While one aspect of our self is busy being a lion tamer, another aspect is occupied with the drama and danger of the spy's life, and so on. Seth also says that these alternate aspects of ourselves are constantly communicating with each other on a subconscious level, keeping alive the spark of interest in all the other possibilities we have thus far avoided in our lifetime.

I was attempting to give birth to a new life, while far from understanding my direction. Unlike Jeff, I felt my new life was here. I didn't feel the need to weigh anchor and leave it all behind in order to find what I was looking for. My urge to explore new ideas and create new businesses was still prodding me.

As a boy in Sicily, I used to watch the women swabbing their faces with the juice from a local cactus fruit. The women claimed that it not only felt good on their skin, but that it reduced wrinkles as well. Since then, it had been in the back of my mind to market it in some form as a cosmetic. I was slipping back into my deal-maker persona again, and this latest one was becoming an obsession, complete with visions of grandeur. In spite of all the lessons I had supposedly learned, a refrain of "you can't keep a good man down" kept playing and replaying in my mind.

Was I once again plunging in a new direction in order to escape something? Escape what? Lying on my desk at home was a message. My elderly cousin, John Trina had died. John had grown up in my mother's hometown of

Roccalumera, Sicily and had emigrated to San Jose long before I arrived. We had been very close. Now his time on earth had run out.

I found myself wondering what it really meant to die. When would my own time be up? How would it happen? Would I suffer? Would I be a burden to my family? Did other people think about death or did they try to push it out of their minds? Why don't we talk to each other about it? Are we so afraid, or is it because we feel we have no answers?

I wanted to believe in an afterlife, but how much of us is our spirit, and if the spirit outlives us, does it remember who it was? Will my spirit know that it is Dennis Augustine, and will it retain my memories, my desires, my fears and everything that make up what is me? And if it does not, will it still be me?

The Eastern books I had been reading spoke of "merging" with the creator, with the universe. For a metaphor, they often spoke of a drop of water merging into the divine ocean. But no one seemed able to explain what happens to our individuality. What happens to the individuality of the water drop when it touches the ocean?

So, I pondered, what is the purpose of all our striving in life if we are all going to die? Why do we fight over ideas such as ideology, justice, money, power, religion? Why struggle, why bring children into a world where their ultimate fate is death?

Children don't accept death. They think they will find a way out. When I was young, I believed that scientists would discover the secrets of extending life—by freezing or some other method.

My meandering mind returned to my life and posed the question, "What's the point in rejuvenating oneself if it only prolongs the cycle?" Are we not like ants, constantly rebuilding our lives after some external force has intruded upon us, only to endure the same thing over and over again?

As I was sitting quietly, staring at the message of my elderly cousin's death, I heard a familiar voice speak very softly to me: "So what do you believe in, Dr. A.?"

In response, I rattled off a series of beliefs like the credo in my childhood catechism—except that each belief was modified by the subjunctive:

If all that I have experienced since my sabbatical is valid;
If my inner self is part of God;
If my newly-found spirituality is authentic;
If we live in a world of illusion, and the real life is beyond all forms;
If the chaos in our lives is caused by our trying to balance our outer world with
    the inner one;
        then I would have to believe in immortality.

"Aristotle said: 'The nonmaterial side of life is a man's true thinking self, with capabilities far beyond his knowing. The physical world and man's physical nature are unspeakably wonderful, but the soul is the real, and the real is the soul.'"

"He was just a small boy when I passed over, of course," Hippocrates said, "but he had some good ideas. A bit rigid, a trifle narrow, but definitely some good ideas."

"Thank you, Hippocrates," I replied, by now used to his sudden entrances, "I'm so glad you approve of Aristotle."

Hippocrates ignored my sarcasm. "But what do *you* make of his words, Dr. A.? Are you convinced?"

"I don't know, Hippocrates. Sometimes I am and sometimes I'm not. It's like a new food that someone describes as sensational. You can anticipate the great taste, but you don't know for sure, you don't own that knowledge until you experience it for yourself.

"If we are really immortal, then death is really nothing but life itself without our bodies."

"It's actually a bit more complicated than that, Dr. A."

"But if it's true, what are we supposed to do with this physical lifetime? Why wasn't the game set up for us to quickly reunite with our creator if that is our purpose?"

"But don't you see, Dr. A., you're here to learn, to grow, and for most of you it doesn't make sense to end your life on earth prematurely. Why sign up for school and then drop out before you've learned most of your lessons?"

That sounded reasonable but it didn't answer all my questions. Why should I bother to fill in this temporary existence with silly business projects? Was it just to pass the time? How do we find our true purpose before the final curtain call? Abraham Maslow, writing some twenty-five years ago, said that self-actualization can only come about once lower needs are satisfied.[1] No one would argue that my lower needs weren't satisfied long ago, earlier in my career, and that I was providing an important service to the community. I seemed to be following Maslow's hierarchy of graduated needs except I had remained enmeshed on the survival level years longer than what was necessary.

And, was it enough that my service to the community was "important?" Important to whom? Certainly to my patients. But was it really important to me?

My eyes wandered over to the Atmos clock, its pendulum silently and gracefully moving back and forth. I had finally gotten it fixed by a goldsmith and watchmaker, Genway Gao, a Taiwanese immigrant who spoke excellent English. I was filled with pleasure that the clock was working again. It seemed to symbolize that I was also moving forward once again, and that the answers which had eluded me for so long would eventually come in their own good time. I seemed to recall that St. Augustine spent a considerable part of his life pondering the nature of time. Augustine had once proclaimed that the world was made with time and not in time, leading to the idea that creation is an ongoing event, changing through time just as we are.

"Fuzzy thinking, very fuzzy thinking," Hippocrates offered.

"Thank you, Hippocrates, your astute opinion is always welcome."

My fear, these days was that I'd drift off course. Although I was being pulled toward deeper and deeper spiritual insights, I kept hitting old familiar snags— business schemes and the road-to-success treadmill. My free time was once again filling up with old rubbish and I seemed to have neither the will nor the sense of direction that I needed to get back on track.

One day, I silently cried out, "Hippocrates, these up-and-down, forward-and-backward cycles are getting to me. Isn't there some clear path ahead? Is there some way of knowing what's really right?"

I sensed Hippocrates' presence but he didn't say anything, though I could tell he wanted to.

"So?" I goaded him, "So tell me."

"I've already told you so many times I must be sounding like...what is your expression? Like a broken record. You know what's right because it feels right. Your problem is that you haven't learned to distinguish between what is simply gratifying and what deeply feels right.

There is no blame if we miss the sign the first time or the second or the third, but if we continually ignore what we are given to understand, then surely it will be difficult to see the purpose of the next test. Truth is not delivered on a silver salver but is distilled within from hard work and good observation.[2]   —*Reshad Feild*

On Saturday, March 5, 1988, I attended a lecture given by M. Scott Peck, author of *A Road Less Traveled,* whose opening sentence reads, "Life is difficult." I had read his book a couple of years earlier and found his premise persuasive that psychiatry and spiritual growth are the same thing. I believed that in spite of doctrinal disputes, they complemented each other in that both lead to unconditional love and transcendent faith as the way to a meaningful life. I had admired Peck's thinking, and I wondered how I might keep in touch with any additional work of his.

I had also been trying to keep track of coincidences, and one of the most obvious was when I saw a small notice in a local newspaper that Peck would be lecturing at St. Andrews Episcopal Church, in Saratoga, about a mile from my home. I chuckled at this coincidence and offered a silent "thanks" to whomever had arranged it.

Peck's book had sold over 2.5 million copies—an astounding number. He talked about how he had wrestled with the changes in his life, and how he had finally become so moved, so passionate about the subject of spiritual growth that he simply had set everything aside to write a book. I thought, *"If only I felt so passionate about something, and so clear about it. That's the only way I could do it. I would have to be willing to drop everything else—everything—and just take the time to do it."*

I left St. Andrews Church feeling better than when I had entered. Peck had confirmed for me that confronting and solving problems is a painful process that most of us tend to avoid. But it is possible to open oneself to new challenges in life and to live in fulfillment, even with constant change.

Only if the event has been frightening enough, a revelation out of the heavens themselves, does it come to dominate the meaning of our lives.
—*Loren Eiseley*

On the California Coast, the rainy season starts in mid-winter and acacia trees and broom herald spring with bright yellow blossoms. Then we see crocus, daffodils, freesias, tulips and all the other bulb flowers. By the beginning of March, the distinctive blue blossoms of the ceanothus tree are evident and succulents are in full bloom. The beautiful hills of Northern California, so dry in the summer, are lush and green. Though the winter nights are cool, the days are brilliantly sunny and warm.

Tuesday, March 22nd, 1988 was one of those glorious days. I had two surgeries scheduled. The first was uneventful. During the course of the second, a bunionectomy, I dropped the drill handle. This necessitated replacing its plastic sleeve with a new, sterile one to protect the surgical wound from possible contamination. I removed the bunion and obtained an X-ray image with the lixiscope which verified that the procedure had been successful. Two stitches closed the small incision. I dressed the wound with surgical pads and compression bandages, and a final post-operative X-ray was taken. The patient was then fitted for a surgical walking shoe, given a mild pain medication, instructed in how to care for her foot until it healed, and sent comfortably on her way.

I then had a few moments alone. *It's one thing to spill milk at home,* I thought, *but quite another to drop a drill during a surgical procedure.* Whether it was stress or possible carelessness on my part, I couldn't be certain. That night my back bothered me more than usual, and my sleep was fitful and uneven. There was also a new sensation, a tingling in both hands and fingers, especially in my right hand, where it had worked its way up to my elbow. I shook my hands vigorously for a few moments, rolled over, and managed to get to sleep. The next afternoon, I had a complex surgery scheduled on Mrs. Reyes deformed foot, which included a bunionectomy, repositioning of the big toe, straightening the hammer toes of the fourth and fifth digits, and surgically raising a dropped metatarsal bone by inducing a controlled fracture.

To enable Mrs. Reyes to be at ease, I administered nitrous oxide gas and then used a Mada-jet to insert a small amount of local anesthetic painlessly under the skin. This made the injection of the lidocaine anesthetic less uncomfortable. Halfway through the injections, my right hand began to tremble and I was unable to maintain a firm grip on the needle. I stopped and readjusted Mrs. Reyes' chair to gain better leverage over the foot area, and I repeatedly stretched the fingers of my right hand. My right hand felt tight and cramped in my surgical glove.

I was uncomfortable not only because of the trembling but because I didn't want my assistant, Lydia, to notice I was shaking. I looked for all the world like an alcoholic with *delirium tremens.* I couldn't understand what had caused it. I hadn't felt nervous or uncertain. Then, as suddenly as it had come, the trembling stopped.

While the anesthesia was taking hold, Lydia prepped Mrs. Reyes and I saw some other patients. When I got the call that Mrs. Reyes was ready, I tried to reassure myself that what had happened was a fluke. I felt perfectly normal as I went about my pre-op scrub and donned my gloves and mask. This was second-nature to me, a ritual I had performed thousands of times.

Mrs. Reyes was waiting quietly, sedated yet alert, listening to music. I began with the hammer toes. It was gratifying to see toes that had for years been deformed in a contracted, claw-like manner suddenly lay flatter and more normal. The miracles that could be achieved through minimal incision surgery always helped sustain me through difficult times.

I began to work on Mrs. Reyes' dropped metatarsal bone. The goal of the procedure was to induce a controlled bone fracture which would raise the position of the metatarsal bone, relieving the pressure on the ball of the foot. Utilizing the minimal incision technique, the procedure was actually quite simple and could normally be completed in a few minutes. Even after performing thousands of these operations, I was amazed at how efficient and successful it was. The procedures were completely painless.

Next I approached the bunion deformity at the base of the big toe. Bunions are bumps that are commonly seen bulging through women's shoes like small golf balls. I was about three-fourths of the way through the procedure when I began to experience a series of hand tremors and contractions that were beyond my ability to control.

"Oh Christ," I thought, *"I should never have performed the surgery! I should have known something was wrong when I dropped the drill yesterday!"* All at once, things began to make sense: spilling the milk, the tight glove, the tingling in my hand and arm. *"What if I have some dreadful disease? What happens to my family? What happens to me? Why is this happening?"*

I had two choices: close up the wound and reschedule Mrs. Reyes to complete the procedure, or try to finish right now. I realized that most of the tremors had occurred when I was tightly grasping the surgical file and rasping the bunion smooth while applying strong counter-pressure at the same time. The fact that Mrs. Reyes had especially hard bone stock had made the task all the more difficult.

The ease with which bones can be sawed, filed or fractured varies considerably from individual to individual. Surgeons have to have strong arms, wrists and hands. In carpentry, by way of comparison, pressure is generally exerted in one direction on a saw, file or drill. In surgery, sometimes the arms and hands are pitted against one another. Motions are controlled, and pressure must be carefully balanced with counter-pressure. It can be very demanding work, and it requires that the surgeon's hands, wrists and arms be in good shape.

"You can do it. Just take it easy and you can do it." I tried to psych myself up to finish. *"Help me,"* I said silently, *"Whoever can hear this, please help me. Whatever my fate is to be beyond this point, I'll accept. Just see me through this case."*

I took a deep breath, gathered myself together, and decided to go for it. I was wet with perspiration. My hand felt a bit unsteady, but by taking my time and not straining, I was able to do the finishing touches on the bunion removal, complete the tendon and ligament release and then straighten out the deviated toe. This was the easy part—it required accuracy but not much strength. I made a final, small incision at the top of the base of the big toe, created a fail-safe drill hole through the bone, cut a thin, pie-shaped wedge from the bone, cranked the toe over onto itself, thereby closing the wedge space and leaving the toe in a normal position. Then I allowed myself a few deep breaths and a huge but inaudible sigh.

X-ray images showed that all surgical objectives had been met. The surgical sights were copiously flushed with sterile solution, a few sutures followed by sterile dressings and an immobilization splint, and it was all over. Mrs. Reyes was still comfortable and relaxed, never realizing that her work came close to being postponed. No purpose would be served in mentioning anything about it to her—the procedures were well done and should heal rapidly and correctly.

Somehow, I made it through the rest of the day, seeing a dozen or more patients. None of them required procedures that taxed my hand, and the tremors did not reappear. But I ended the day physically and emotionally exhausted.

"Where do I go from here?" I asked no one in particular, as I sat in my office for what seemed an eternity of horror. There was no answer, not even from Hippocrates. Once again, my livelihood hung precariously in balance. I had been at the crossroads before—I wasn't exactly a novice at confronting challenges. But this was different because I had no idea what was wrong.

I had realized the surgeon's worst nightmare. The use of my hands was threatened, hands without which I could not practice my trade, hands which I had so casually depended on. In my most pessimistic moments, I had never thought something like this would happen. And again, there was the same question, repeated so many times now that it was sounding like an echo: *"Why... Why... Why... Why... Why?"*

On the wall above my desk was a painting of a sea captain dressed in a naval uniform and possessing striking blue eyes that seemed to follow me. In the background, the sea heaved, all-pervading, ominous and powerfully compelling. I stared forlornly at the painting, and my eyes met those of the captain. His look bore directly into my soul. His face and the churning sea behind him seemed mobile, as if the entire scene had come alive. Suddenly, the distance between myself and the painting vanished, and I felt lost in the sea, my essence dissolving into its infinite depths.

The sea was within me, lashing about furiously. I had broken up into shining droplets, conscious particles of ocean with no center, no focus that could be called Dennis Augustine. My fear was absolute. It penetrated my being so thoroughly that there was no room for anything else.

I'd once had a similar episode while under the influence of LSD. The thrashing waves and white foamy caps of the seashore became a pack of giant cats. Their claws extended, they tried to drag me into the ocean. In the fantasy world brought on by the hallucinogenic, I thought I would die of fear. But this fear was greater. It was beyond the fear of mere death. It was not the fear of any *thing*—it was fear itself.

I sat, transfixed, staring, a silent observer, as fear stilled the sea and drained the light from the sky, leaving only dim shadows behind. Then I felt it touch me. Beginning with my hands, it crept into me and I felt my body, piece by piece, abandon itself to its possession.

Pure fear is completely still. Beneath that stillness was my calm observer self, not knowing or caring whether I would survive. As great as the fear was, it could not touch the Watcher.

I watched, for what seemed a very long time. Then the fear began to slowly recede from my body and return to the painting. The sea remolded itself into its original churning vista and the captain took his place in the foreground. His face hadn't changed, but he seemed to be inwardly smiling, as though he and I were partners on this voyage.

I could feel my body once again, and I opened and closed my hands, to make sure they still worked. I felt very ancient, as though the experience had dragged me to the beginning of time and back again.

Awareness of my disabled hand returned, with all the ramifications of ending my career as a surgeon. It was still threatening, still a real problem. But I had just been to the depths—no earthly problem could compare.

The way I was treated was worse than a dog. Every five years, every doctor should be a patient. —*Elizabeth Kubler-Ross*

The tremors and tingling in my hands worsened. I lay awake at nights, hoping that the numbness and burning in my hands would go away so I could sleep. There was no way I could perform delicate surgery. Fortunately, my associates, Dr. Jeremy Perlman, and Dr. Bill Moulder, were able to step in and perform the most necessary procedures on my patients—the ones that couldn't be rescheduled. And I? I spent the next few weeks with the shoe on the other foot, learning what it's like to be a patient.

Bill Moulder recommended that I see Dr. Fogerty, an orthopedist who specialized in deformities of the spine. Dr. Fogerty worked in Bill's office on Saturdays, seeing workman's compensation patients with back injuries, a good place to start. At Bill's office, I had to wait for over an hour before Dr. Fogerty saw me. When he did, he greeted me with, "Sorry to keep you waiting, but I'm very busy and I'm doing you a favor seeing you at all today."

Dr. Fogerty put me through a series of movement tests and was equally gruff throughout. His whole bearing said, "I have to put up with you, so I will!" So much for "bedside manner." It made me realize how important it is to be polite and considerate with each patient, no matter how rushed you are.

Dr. Fogerty's recommendation was quick and definite: "You must undergo wrist surgery. No 'ifs, ands or buts'—surgery is required!"

Jeremy Perlman recommended that I see Dr. Chatsworth, a chiropractor who shared Jeremey's office space. Since I was becoming more aware and appreciative of holistic, noninvasive medicine, I thought the chiropractic approach might be the best way to go—besides, it couldn't hurt to get another opinion.

Unlike Dr. Fogerty, Dr. Chatsworth was friendly. He needed a complete set of X-rays of my spine and of my right arm. For all the years that I had my patients undergo X-ray evaluation, I had done my utmost to convince them it was in their best interest and safe. Now that I was undergoing a complete set of arm and back X-rays, I was the one who was concerned about excessive radiation.

"Here," Dr. Chatsworth said, while reviewing the developed film, "see the spurring and narrowing that's developed in the cervical area? Either you sustained some damage from your original back injury or it's occurred from overcompensating for that injury. That would explain the symptoms in your right hand, arm and wrist."

"Do you think I need surgery?"

"No way!" he said, countering Dr. Fogerty's recommendation with an opinion that was equally firm. I was starting to understand how helpless a patient feels when he receives conflicting medical advice from doctors.

Dr. Chatsworth believed that with chiropractic treatments performed at least three times a week to start, I would see an improvement. But with all the physical therapy, medications, splints, braces and even yoga that I had used since my back injury, I had little confidence that chiropractic treatments would be the answer. But as I pondered what to do, I realized that, like many other patients, I was carrying some baggage in the form of biases. I knew that, in many cases, chiropractic patients are given a similar treatment regimen…a regimen that requires many repeated treatments and makes a lot of money for the chiropractor. Although there might be temporary improvement, I wasn't willing to become a professional patient like so many people I had seen in my clinic who had undergone chiropractic treatment over the years—addicted to their never-ending treatments.

Still hoping for a clearer diagnosis, I next went to my orthopedist, Dr. Appleton, whom I had seen for my back injury.

"You don't look too well," were his opening words. I wasn't surprised. After a difficult night I had greeted the morning with dark patches under my eyes, and my face had a gray pallor that made me look older than my years.

"Yes, I'm aware of that," I said, trying to hide the sarcasm. "I can't seem to get a good night's sleep. Every time I doze off, I wake up with burning and tingling in my hand."

"Your right hand is cyanotic," Dr. Appleton said. (Cyanotic is medical jargon for blue.) "This whole thing may be no more than tendonitis."

I doubted that—I had treated tendonitis myself many times, and my symptoms seemed too severe for that. But then I thought, *"Doctors are notorious for being poor patients. Stop second-guessing your doctor. You're consulting him for his expertise, not yours."* But the other side of my dialogue retorted with: *"Yes, but sometimes a patient has the best idea of what's wrong with him, and a good doctor learns to listen to what a patient thinks about his condition."*

After more X-rays, and an analysis of them by an expert radiologist, I was informed that I had torn and degenerated discs in my lower back from my previous injury, but the symptoms in my hands could not be conclusively tied to my back problems.

And so it continued. I was advised to see Dr. Richard Farina, a neurologist. Dr. Farina seemed friendly and competent, but he had the distinctive air of the doctor who has a large and successful practice. That is, there was a subtle air of anxiety about him that I recognized only too well; while he was giving me his full attention, he could not let go of his awareness of how much time was passing. You spend too much time with a patient and you fall a step behind in your schedule; you fall one step behind and you spend the rest of the day trying to catch up. Your patients are frustrated and grumbling at having to wait. Your staff is tense from trying to keep patients from boiling over. The answer is simple: see fewer patients, but you don't want to do that because it means less profit. So everything has to march along on schedule; if anything unforeseen delays you, it's going to be a bad day.

After a fairly thorough exam I was asked to disrobe and put on a patient gown. Then I was escorted to a dark room and told to lie down on my back on a flat examination table. A heated electrical blanket was then placed over me. I could see it was going to be a long morning. And there I lay, for more than an hour, waiting for the doctor to see me.

Half a century ago, when most doctors made house calls, the doctor spent more time on each patient than the patient spent with the doctor. That's because it took extra time for the doctor to travel from home to home. Doctors made modestly good livings, but not many grew rich.

It was not the switch from home to office visits that radically increased the doctor's potential income so much as the use of multiple patient waiting rooms and the widespread availability of medical insurance. Multiple waiting rooms allowed patients to be neatly stacked up to await the actual presence of the doctor. This procedure, adopted by almost all present day physicians, clinics and hospitals, resulted in two important shifts: 1) the aggregate amount of time wasted by patients waiting for doctors greatly multiplied, and 2) doctor's incomes rose dramatically. And the relative, widespread insurance coverage allowed patients access to elective surgical procedures for which doctors could command high fees—which patients might otherwise not afford.

The assumption, in modern medicine, is that a doctor's time is always more valuable than a patient's. In addition to technological advances, one of the miracles of modern medicine is how doctors have led patients to docilely accept this system with only minor grumbling.

A heated blanket kept my body temperature at a level high enough to get accurate readings on the EMG test (*electromyograph:* to record the flow of electricity in the muscles). I tried to keep myself from apprehension and despair while I waited. If I was feeling this way, I could only imagine how patients were who were not familiar with the medical terrain must feel. I could hear the muffled voices of patients and staff in nearby rooms, and I had plenty of time to think.

A movement in a corner of the dark room startled me. "Who's there?"

There was a soft clearing of a throat. "It's only me, Dr. A., don't be alarmed."

"Don't be alarmed? You may be used to it where you are, but I find it hard not to be alarmed when you think you're alone in a room and suddenly someone is in it with you!"

"Well that was the best I could do. Would you prefer I enter with a crash of thunder and a bolt of lightning?"

I couldn't think of an immediate reply to that, so I said nothing. Then a wave of self-pity overcame me and I blurted, "Where were you when I was going through that...that symbolic death...or whatever it was in my office? That's when I really needed you."

"Why, Dr. A., I was there with you. Didn't you recognize me?" As he said this, Hippocrates' eyes took on a different look—stern, confident, controlling. His features rearranged themselves into the visage of the sea captain in my painting. For a moment, the fear I had experienced surfaced again, and chills raced up and down my back. Then his features became familiar again.

"You mean...you mean that you mobilized that painting, you caused that whole experience?"

"Not at all, Dr. A., it doesn't work that way. I was simply the agency that allowed you to do what you needed to do. It was not my intention to frighten you. In fact, I had no intent at all. Whatever happened to that painting was directed by you, not by me."

It was too much for me to comprehend. I lay on the table, under the heated blanket, numb and unthinking. Then Hippocrates' voice, began again, whispering softly. "I feel your sense of despair, Dr. A., but despair has its positive aspect also."

I came out of it enough to say "What do you mean?"

"When despair is not solely directed toward one's self and includes compassion for others, it becomes a positive force. These experiences you've been having as a patient have kindled a deep compassion within you."

"You're right, Hippocrates. My heart is aching for all those who have afflictions far worse than mine—people with permanent paralysis, cancer, AIDS, kidney disease. It's true what they say: we take our lives and our health for granted—until disaster strikes."

"Your compassion has grown markedly in the past year, Dr. A. And I believe you've recently learned something about yourself you hadn't admitted before—that in terms of earthly activities, you are rather expendable."

Again, Hippocrates was right on target. I had stopped performing even minor surgery at my clinic. Following consultation with a patient and a review of their X-rays, I would say, "Mrs. Jones, you have a moderate bunion deformity. Here's what needs to be done." After explaining the benefits, risks and possible alternatives, I would say, "If you're ready to go ahead, Dr. Moulder (or Dr. Perlman) will be assigned to perform the surgery." To my surprise, I discovered that patients would accept this. My practice could get along just fine with me playing a lesser role. It was both humbling and a relief.

"Of course," Hippocrates said, with the merest hint of malevolent humor, "there is considerably less profit since you have to pay other doctors substantial fees for their services."

"That is to be expected," I said, not rising to the bait.

I heard some shuffling noises outside the room, and Hippocrates' form rapidly vanished as Dr. Farina and his assistant entered the room. After connecting me to the various recording instruments, Dr. Farina began inserting fine needles into the muscles of my right arm and hand. It was uncomfortable, to say the least, and the feeling was not helped by surges of electricity into the needles that caused my muscles to contract. It was like continuously experiencing the brief tremors I had felt while operating on Mrs. Reyes. The test lasted nearly an hour, and I didn't like it one bit. While the sensations were endurable, the apparatus reminded me of a torture instrument designed to shock the truth out of political prisoners. Not only that, but I was paying a specialist for the privilege of being repeatedly shocked.

Seeing four specialists to find out what was wrong with me and how to cure it apparently wasn't enough. Dr. Farina decided to obtain the opinion of Dr. Prime, a professor of neurology at Stanford. At this point, I was starting to feel like I was being passed through a revolving door from one doctor to another with no real gain. It was easy to see why people get so fed up with orthodox medicine.

Dr. Prime gave me a very careful and thorough examination but, once again, the results were inconclusive. He ended up by recommending more EMG testing (Oh no, not more of that!) When I pressed Dr. Prime for something more definite, he responded in an impatient and defensive manner, and I realized that he really didn't have any answers. I'd gone to Stanford to take advantage of their state-of-the-art technologies, to be sure, but I also needed a helping hand to assist me in mobilizing my body's own capacity to heal. And I wanted to be reassured and encouraged along the way. Isn't this why most people go to doctors?

I wondered how often I'd failed my own patients in this regard? I remembered reading a newspaper interview with the pioneering psychiatrist and author, Elizabeth Kubler-Ross. Following a stroke, Kubler-Ross concluded that she had learned a far more practical lesson than just getting in touch with her own mortality. As a doctor, she got to experience medical care from the patient's point-of-view for the first time in her life. "The way I was treated was worse than a dog. Every five years, every doctor should be a patient."[3]

Specialist number six was Dr. Robert Goldman, a San Jose neurologist. Something I liked immediately about his practice was his system of preregistering new patients by mail so that they didn't have to sit in his office to fill out lengthy background and financial responsibility forms. But by this time, I was sick to death of the paperwork involved in seeing a new doctor.

Again I went through the insertion of needles and the electric shocks. Dr. Goldman then recommended that I see Dr. Foreman, "the foremost authority in the field." A week later I was in Dr. Foreman's office. By this time, I was so used to being poked and shocked that I hardly noticed it, except that Dr. Foreman's assistant, a resident-in-training, performed the test incorrectly and the whole thing had to be done over again, needle by needle, shock by shock. It was a good object lesson in patience and tolerance—after all, this was how doctors learned, and I had been in the same situation years ago.

I kept demanding clear answers and kept getting passed from doctor to doctor. In my own practice, I was often unsure of my diagnosis, in spite of my best efforts to understand the problem. There were times when I simply had to make my best guess and go with it. Now, as the patient, I was demanding a specific, unambiguous diagnosis, and I wouldn't settle for less. If I couldn't get this problem resolved successfully, it meant that my career as a surgeon was finished. As I tallied up the life-altering events of the past few years, I began to feel like Job saying, "God, why have you forsaken me?" Without my ability to perform surgery, I saw only a black hole in the middle of my life, with nothing to fill it. If I could no longer be a surgeon, what was I? What else was left?

The hardest thing to accept was that these events were being forced upon me. I had always thought that if the day ever came when I decided to hang it up, it would be *my* decision—never, never did I imagine that I might be forced to quit due to the vagaries of fate. That might happen to a professional athlete, an entertainer, or a scandalized politician—but not to me!

While at low ebb, I decided to look into whatever rights I had under the terms of my insurance policies. I called my broker, John Lipsey, in San Diego. "Well, doctor, it's been a long time," he said. "How are you doing?"

"Not so good," I replied, trying not to sound too despondent as I brought him current on all the problems I'd been having.

"I'm sorry to hear that," John said. "You know, you should have filed for office overhead benefits last year as soon as your back went out."

"But I was still working; I just wasn't able to work up to capacity."

"But that's just what your overhead replacement policy is for, Doctor," John said, matter-of-factly.

It started to hit me, then, just how ignorant I was about my own insurance. I could practically quote the book on my patients' insurance benefits, but I was virtually illiterate about my own coverage. John continued: "I'll check your policy and let you know one way or the other."

Let me know? *Let me know?* A significant amount of insurance money, enough to cover all my overhead expenses if I couldn't continue, might be riding on someone's interpretation. That was the hardest part—not knowing. I felt control slipping away from me, someone who until recently had controlled everything in his life, including his feelings. Life seemed to be demanding more and more release. The reason, the purpose and the goal were unknown. I'd scaled down my investments, taken time off for a sabbatical, cut back my work schedule and was spending more time with my family—and it apparently wasn't enough.

A soft whisper deep in my consciousness offered: "There is absolutely no holding back now." But the ante was much greater than it had been before. My career—the main focus of my identity, my accomplishments and my pride—was in jeopardy. I hadn't realized until this moment how closely I was bound to my professional image. It felt as though I was holding onto the edge of an abyss, a flick of the will away from falling either to freedom or annihilation. I was being asked to acknowledge that I was completely powerless.

"I can't!" I cried. "I can't do it!"

CHAPTER 13

Emerging From the Labyrinth

There were new endeavors and fresh disasters, for they are the way of life; and the art of life is to save enough of yourself from each disaster to be able to begin again in something like your own image.

—*Murray Kempton*

A friend once told me how the cosmos had toyed with him. Absurd coincidences over which he had no control kept occurring. Then one morning he stubbed his toe as he climbed out of bed and accidentally dropped his wash cloth into the toilet, which his young son hadn't flushed. He suppressed his anger while he groped to remove his pajama top. For some reason, the buttons didn't want to come undone. Still standing near the commode, he pulled harder, and suddenly two buttons popped off. One fell into the still-open toilet and the other arced into the sink and fell down the drain.

That was the last straw. He raced through the hall, opened the back door and ran into the back yard. He looked up and glared at the clouds. Raising his fist to the sky, he screamed at the top of his voice: "Stop it, godammit, stop it!"

It worked. For the rest of the day and for a considerable time after that, everything went well. The question is, was the cosmos chastened by his harsh invective or, having gotten the reaction it was seeking, was it temporarily satisfied?

I was feeling really down. Between my injured back and my hand, I felt like a walking disaster area. I'd been dropping things and spilling things all over the place, and not even the story of Saint Ineptus, who established in the third century a reputation for spilling his food, bruising himself and tripping over nonexistent objects, could lighten my spirits.

I'd seen six specialists already and had an appointment to see a seventh, and I still didn't know what to do about my problem. It wasn't just the loss of my income from performing surgery, it was that I was starting to feel useless. It seemed that life was doing quite well without my participation, that it was passing me by. Then I opened the day's mail.

I was about to throw away a piece of junk mail when a headline caught me. "Disability is a reality! It can happen to you…and when it does, your income stops!" Another caption read, "What would happen to your family, your plans, your future?" Lower on the page was a statistical chart. I found the column for age thirty-seven and read, "For every one hundred deaths among persons thirty-seven years old, there are 350 long-term disabilities."

"Great," I thought, "and I'm one of them."

When I finished the mail and completed my business correspondence, I watched a television dramatization of the life of Julio Iglesias. I had heard and enjoyed his music but didn't know that Iglesias had been a professional soccer player in Madrid when he was seriously injured in an auto crash which left him paralyzed for a year and a half. To help him pass the time in the hospital, a sympathetic nurse gave him a guitar. Although Iglesias had never previously thought about a musical career, he went on to become an internationally-known pop singer.

That night after going to bed, I picked up a book I had borrowed. One of the pages was dog-eared and a line had been highlighted with a yellow marker: "In the seed of seeming tragedy lies the fruit of good fortune."

Signs like these kept appearing to me. However, it's one thing to notice a sign and another to know what to do about it, especially when the signs are conflicting. It felt like I was enrolled in a school where answers only invited more serious problems.

Do signs and omens appear at critical times in our lives, or are they always present but unseen because of our preoccupation with the nitty-gritty of daily life? And when we become aware of their presence, how do we interpret these signs? If we stumble along our paths, does it mean we should stop what we are doing or is it a test of perseverance through which we must pass to reach our goal? Is there some basis, some consistent law, on which to base important life decisions?

The questions were too heavy, too portentous, so I decided to visit Bob Goodheart in Santa Cruz. When we were comfortably seated, I said, "Coincidences occur to me more frequently now. I feel that they contain important signs, but how can I know if I am interpreting them correctly?"

"Why, Dennis, you already know the answer to that. It's just that your scientific training is getting in the way."

"What do you mean?"

"Well, let's talk about intuition again. Do you ever get hunches that turn out to be true?"

"Sure, lots of times."

"Okay, and do you ever get hunches—gut feelings—that turn out *not* to be true?"

"Well...yes, of course I do."

"Now let's see if we can find an observable difference between hunches that work and those that don't."

I really enjoyed this kind of conversation with Bob, and I followed his comment with my own: "If we could isolate the differences, we might know whether or not to follow a particular hunch, right?"

"That's right, Dennis. So, how can we tell if our hunches are genuine or, shall we say, red herrings?"

I paused a moment, then said, "I guess it would be something about how they feel deep down."

"Right again. Here's an example that fits in with your present life. Let's say you're reading a magazine on business and you see what looks like a great investment opportunity, a chance to make a large profit. After making a few calculations, you sense, you have a hunch, that this scheme would really work. How do you react?"

"You mean the 'old me'?"

"Yes, the 'old you.'"

"I would become very interested!"

"All right, how do you *feel* about going ahead with it?"

"If all the numbers made sense, and if I could get the financing in place, I'd feel like I had to pursue it and I'd do whatever it took to make the deal fly."

"That sounds almost like a compulsion, Dennis. It's as though you feel compelled to go after it."

"That's true. If the idea really grabbed me, the old me would find it extremely hard to let go of it."

"But in your overview of your life, now, when you calmly reflect on your long term goals, do you really want to plunge into another investment? We're talking about the 'new you' now."

"No, in fact it's just the opposite. As you know, I'm trying to divest myself of these obligations as much as possible."

"Okay, fine. So that urge, that desire to get involved…let's say in that surgicenter deal you were so hot on not too long ago…that urge was there even though you knew that direction wasn't right for you."

I nodded in agreement, and Bob continued. "Okay, now let's look at another kind of hunch. Say that you're walking along a downtown street and suddenly sense that you should walk into a store, let's say a book store. You follow the feeling and, when you walk in, you see an old friend you have lost track of and have been trying to locate for a long time. Both of you are happy about the chance meeting.

"Now, Dennis, what's the difference between these two kinds of hunches—that is, in what way do they *feel* different?"

"I think I see what you're getting at. When I got the hunch about going into the store, there was no compulsion about it—I just did it spontaneously."

"Right on, Dennis. The difference is pressure or lack of it. In the first example, about finding a new investment opportunity, there was pressure on you. You could feel the tension behind your urge, pushing you to get involved. But when you had the hunch to go into the bookstore—imagine yourself there now—was there pressure on you, driving you to go inside?"

"No, not at all. The feeling just came to me. Somehow, I *knew* I should go into the store, and I went in."

"Okay, I think we're now ready to make a generalization about this."

Just then I thought, "Searching for truth through questions and answers is very much in the mode of Socrates, and he and Hippocrates were contemporaries. I wonder why—"

"I *am* here," a soft voice spoke inside me. "It's just that I am loathe to give Socrates more credit than he has already received for ideas that were actually taken from Anaxagorus and Heraclitus. Socrates was so puffed up, especially after the oracle at Delphi declared him the wisest man in Greece. Sticks in the craw a bit, you know."

Bob was looking at me in a strange way. "Are you all right, Dennis? You just sort of dropped out for a little while."

"I'm fine. I was just talking to Hippocrates about Socrates."

"Oh," Bob said, and without another word he picked up where we had left off. "I was saying we're ready to make a generalization about hunches and intuition. Care to take a stab at it?"

"Well, from what we've just covered, hunches and ideas that feel like they're

179

pushing you, driving you forward, aren't really valid. They're…they derive from something else, perhaps from needs and fears. Right so far?"

Bob nodded, and I went on. "And hunches that are lighter, easier, so you don't feel pressured to follow them—they are the valid ones. You feel a sense…a sense of, well, of *rightness* about them. You know, somehow, that what you're feeling is right."

"Exactly, Dennis, exactly. Intuition in its purest form doesn't push us or force us to do anything. We just have an easy sense of knowing…that something is *right*. When an idea or urge comes to us forcefully, it's not pure intuition—it's some need or fear driving us."

"So our intuition—pure intuition—is…how can I say this…is the repository of cosmic knowledge, of wisdom. When we get in touch with our intuition, we're getting in touch with a kind of cosmic knowledge bank." Just as I said this, I had an insight. "Wait a minute, wait a minute! This is what Jung was talking about when he said, *'For the unconscious self in others is the same self in us all, and part of the greater self called God.'* If that's true, then intuition, pure intuition, is a form of contact with God, a kind of divine knowledge."

"Dennis, that was beautiful. You know, moments like these make the counseling business worthwhile."

We both sat back in our chairs to reflect for a moment on where our conversation had brought us. Then Bob started again. "Well, this brings us around to what you really want to do now."

"Even though I'm trying to simplify my life, I'm still collecting newspaper and magazine clippings on a great many subjects. My resource files keep growing bigger and bigger, but I don't feel like I'm accomplishing much. You know, when I was going to college, I started out as an accounting major. Maybe I should have kept it up—at least in the accounting profession being a stickler for detail would have been an asset. But what I really want to do is to write. I think that's the real reason I've been collecting all this data in the first place. I really believe it will come in handy someday."

"Well, in light of the conclusion we've just come to, how do you feel about writing? Are you feeling pressured to write? Do you think it's your intuition speaking to you, or is it another misguided goal, like your preoccupation with material success was?"

"Nice of you to put that in the past tense, Bob. This thing about writing, though…it feels right, as though everything I've accomplished up to now is for the purpose of writing about it."

"There's an old Hassidic saying that goes: 'Carefully observe what way your heart draws you and choose that way with all your strength.'"

"I know! I know! But I just can't seem to get started."

"What would be the ideal circumstances to get you to sit down and actually do it?"

"I keep having this mental image of some island where it's peaceful and quiet. All I have to do is to write, and I do so all morning right on through to early afternoon. The rest of the day I swim, snorkel and fish with my family in the surrounding emerald blue waters. But the reality is that I still have responsibilities, not the least of which is to find out how to get my hand able to perform surgery again."

"Do you think you could write in an environment that is less than that ideal?"

"I don't know. I don't seem to be able to. I think it has to do with the fact that all my life I've had an all-or-nothing mind-set. When I get serious about something, anything less than perfection seems to be a half-hearted effort. Also, I feel distracted. No, more than distracted. I actually feel my mind is about to burst. Losing the ability to do surgery has really gotten to me. It's like I'm going through all my earlier problems all over again. Only this time, the consequences are greater."

My emotional flood-gates seemed fully open now, and everything seemed to be pouring out. "You see, I may qualify for office overhead compensation if my condition doesn't improve—or I may not. There's a lot of money at stake on that one. Meanwhile, my practice is going downhill, and I'm not generating enough income. Then there's this constant back-and-forth to specialists, and the truth is, I'm worried sick about it. My worst fear, a real possibility, is that I'm becoming a chronic patient. Indecision, not knowing, it's getting to me!"

Quick as that, all the good feelings arising from my insight and the conversation with Bob had gone. I was down again. But a certain objectivity remained. I had never before seen so clearly that I was riding on a roller coaster. That up-down, up-down, was the nature of life, and while it would become less volatile from time to time, it was never going to change. All that could change was how I felt about it. What was it Hippocrates had said? "Bad things happen sometimes and good things happen most of the time, It all depends on how you look at it."

Bob waited for me to calm down before gently suggesting that not all stress was bad. "Sometimes it helps us move on through life. But in your case, I think you may be making a fundamental error and missing a golden opportunity." I waited patiently for him to continue, and after awhile he said, "Good writing doesn't occur when everything is calm, orderly and in place—in fact, it typically happens when you're in the thick of things, when you're feeling strongly about life. Don't drown out that inner voice with logic and analysis—that's what caused most of your problems in the first place. You don't need to wait for an imagined, perfect writing environment to be created—you already have it right now."

We were both quiet for a while. Then Bob said, "Dennis, you *are* going in the right direction. And even if you sense that, overall, you're on track, you're going to have to constantly remind yourself that the *right* direction isn't always a comfortable experience."

Bob rose and came over to me, his arms outstretched. We hugged each other—not a meek little hug, but the hard hug of two strong men who enjoyed it. On the way home, I admired the mountain views and gave thanks for being able to live in such a beautiful area. It was May, and the tall grasses were still green, but showing signs of turning to their summer gold. The hillsides were covered with golden poppies, blue and purple lupine, and brilliant yellow flowering mustard. As the road rose toward the summit, the redwood trees gave way, first to pine, then to oak, and finally to dramatic, red-trunked madrone.

I knew, with an intuitive, easy certainty, that I had passed some kind of milestone this day. Life was indeed a roller coaster, and there was no way of stopping it. I could only change how I viewed the ride. I also knew that this was the last time I would seek Bob's counsel. We had both sensed it, and the finality had been expressed in our hug. Bob was a true wisdom figure—a life guide for me. And he had done his job well: he had made himself unnecessary.

I thought of something Joseph Campbell said to Bill Moyers about the need of going it alone. In discussing the ceaseless task of confronting one's fears and supposed needs, Moyers had asked, "When I take that journey and go down and slay those dragons, do I have to go alone?" Campbell replies:

> If you have someone who can help you, that's fine, too. But ultimately, the last deed has to be done by oneself. Psychologically, the dragon is one's own binding to one's own ego. Thought captured in the cage. The problem of the psychiatrist is to disintegrate that dragon, break him up, so that you may expand to a larger field of relationships. The ultimate dragon is within you; it is your ego clamping you down.[1]

I thought about my hand, my career, my future. I was still uncomfortable with all the uncertainty, but there was an added note of objectivity to it all, even to the beautiful vistas of the drive home. My viewing position had been elevated—not too high, just a notch up. I found myself repeating a little phrase, as if it was a mantra. It went: "Don't try to stop the roller coaster, just observe and hold on and try to enjoy the ride."

Every illness has its own remedy within itself… A man could not be born alive and healthy were there not already the physician hidden in him.

—*Paracelsus*

The specialists had decreed that "it might be" or "I'm pretty sure," or "I think you ought to see…" and charged more than four thousand dollars for visits and tests. I had spent countless hours in waiting rooms and examination rooms. And after all this, none of the doctors had diagnosed my problem with any certainty. The strangest thing about it all was the dichotomy within myself—on one level I was extremely anxious and concerned about my future; on another level, it was all a game and I was watching myself participate with mild amusement. I had no idea which level would be dominant at any particular time. It gave me some idea of what people with multiple personalities must feel like when they cannot control who gets to be on center stage.

My seventh specialist was Dr. Vincent Randolph Heinz, Associate Professor of Surgery at Stanford. Both the professor and his staff exuded absolute confidence and a sense of aloofness. I had seen this demeanor in the halls of political power—here it was being displayed in the form of medical power. Perhaps it was justified. Muscles, tendons and nerves were as familiar to Professor Heinz as a Wurlitzer is to a juke box repairman, I thought as he twisted the palm of my right hand so that it faced up, bent my elbow to ninety degrees, and rubbed his thumb along my ulnar nerve on the inside of my elbow.

Immediately, a sharp, tingling sensation shot into the little finger of my right hand, duplicating the symptoms that had been plaguing me, and accompanied by a wave of intense nausea. "Well," he said casually, after he had released his grip, "we're definitely dealing with a nerve entrapment. There are two places—one in your hand, right here, and one in your wrist, here. In addition, your ulnar nerve has become hypersensitive near your elbow and needs to be surgically moved to a more protected area."

Dr. Heinz advised me that I had three choices: surgery, cortisone injections or wearing a wrist splint. I had already been wearing a splint without improvement, and there was a danger that injections into the tightly-packed wrist area might cause scarring which could exacerbate the problem. That left surgery.

"Surgery is my recommendation. Think about it and let me know how you wish to proceed." That was all. It was very simple. This is my recommendation. If you want to do it, fine. If you don't, it's also fine. End of discussion. No mention was made of possible complications from surgery, or the healing time involved. In my own practice, when I recommended surgery, I always went to great lengths to describe the procedure, possible complications, the typical time required for healing, and so on. I wanted my patients to be able to make informed decisions for themselves, based on objective information.

How different institutional medicine is, I thought. In private practice, the doctor is responsible for educating and encouraging his patients as well treating them. He has to be fastidious in record-keeping and his mind is always on justifying everything he does, in case his performance should ever be called into question by his peers. At Stanford, in contrast, there was a certain mystique, a reverence about the place and its people. It was one of the best medical facilities in the world, with the finest staff that money, prestige and ultra-modern facilities could entice. I suppose that no discussion was really required. These specialists knew whereof they spoke, and they were not particularly interested in debating the issue with patients even if the patient happened to be a doctor. It was, "take it or leave it." Still, a bit of bedside manner would have helped.

Surgery can and sometimes does cause complications and unpredictable results, even with the finest of surgeons. And for a surgeon who was so sure of himself when he was doing the cutting, I was a cynic when it came to my being placed at the end of the scalpel. In fact, now that I was on the receiving end instead of the dispensing end, I found myself critical of many aspects of the medical delivery system: the interminable, repetitive paperwork, the long waiting periods, the impersonality of the doctors who didn't seem to understand that patients are real people with emotional as well as physical needs. Whatever faults I had in my own practice, impersonality wasn't one of them, not since I first watched Dr. Seymour chat warmly with his patients and make them feel comfortable.

I had a big decision to make. Somehow I knew it would all come to this: to undergo surgery, which might mean the end of my surgical career, or to avoid surgery, which, since my condition was worsening, would definitely mean the end of my career. It seemed as though invisible forces were tying events more and more closely together in my life, pushing me into a corner where there was less and less room for maneuver or procrastination. Was my hand problem a blessing in disguise, an omen to push me out of my medical career and into something else? Or was it a test to see if I could overcome yet another obstacle, to "hang in there?"

"Find out what you really want to do with your life, and do it!" Hippocrates had told me. But how could I tell if my wish was an escapist dream or a true goal? So many books I read advised me to "go with the flow." But how could I tell what was "flow" and what was simply taking the easiest way out of a dilemma?

"You just need to learn to let go," Nana Maynard had told me on the Isle of Man. But after I let go of everything, what was I to do? How could I go with the flow without getting washed out with the tide? Wait around for a cosmic wind to blow me in the right direction?

There was another element to letting go that I had the chance to witness close at hand: bravery. My seven-year-old son lost his treasured Popeye blanket for good. It must have been lost a hundred times during the past seven years but had always managed to resurface. This time "blankey" was gone forever. When the realization of this hit Jason, he was grief-stricken, but he was soon able to turn to me and say, "Don't be sad, Daddy, it's okay." What courage! I wished I could show such fortitude in letting go.

There was also the "listen to your inner voice" message in so many of the books I had read. But which inner voice? Bob Goodheart had said, "Intuition, in its purest form, doesn't push us or force us to do anything. We just have an easy sense of knowing...that something is *right*." When I returned home, after seeing Dr. Heinz, I decided to spend some quiet time in meditation. As usual, my mind was abuzz with thoughts of all kinds, and it took a while for things to settle down. Gradually, I felt my body start to relax. First, my breathing became more shallow and regular, then the tautness in my shoulders and abdomen softened, and finally, my jaw slackened and the fine twitching of my eyes stopped.

I listened. At first I heard nothing. Then, gradually, the words of a speaker became distinct. The voice was Hippocrates', but his manner of speaking was formal, as though he were delivering a lecture to a large group.

That the Cnidian School,[2] among whom I count several of my good friends, has developed superb diagnostic techniques there can be no doubt. Their classification of diseases also has no equal, and for these achievements, they may be justly proud.

Like the Cnidians, our Hippocratic School teaches that disease occurs when there is an imbalance in the four humors.[3] The balance of the humors, in turn, is controlled by the glands. This much we know. But if we place too much importance on the mechanics of bodily health, we miss the most important point, and that is to attend to the whole patient.

So when we speak of human health as determined by the humors, we must include the more fundamental elements of diet, hygiene and attitude, and when we treat a patient, we must begin by looking at these fundamentals and only as a last resort should we resort to medicine, surgery and other invasive curatives.

In many cases, the most effective cure and healing occur when the patient decides to heal himself. In our written works which are known as *The Aphorisms and Airs, Waters and Places,*[4] we have recognized the link between the health of a patient and his environment, and, accordingly, as physicians, we strive to...

The voice of Hippocrates began to diminish and finally disappeared altogether. I was left with the distinct impression that one point had been meant for me: *the most effective cure and healing occur when the patient decides to heal himself.*

How little we doctors know about healing. We know, in many cases, how to aid the body in healing itself, but we know so little about the whole picture—about all the factors that are involved with healing. "Physician, heal thyself" Luke declares in the Bible, but doctors are notorious hypochondriacs, probably less able to heal themselves than are lay persons. "Heal thyself" was another interesting avenue open to me. On the other hand, I had a serious problem; was this a time to fool around with notions of self-healing?

I felt like the character, Tevya, in the popular musical, *Fiddler on the Roof.* Tevya spends much of his time philosophizing. But as soon as he comes up with an idea or plan, he reflects and says, "On the other hand..."

Alternatives, possibilities, avenues, glimpses of "right" and periods of great doubt and anxiety. Was life to be always like this? How much simpler and easier it would be if the answers were unambiguously announced by some cosmic scribe: "Do thus and so, and that's it." I envied the simplicity of a bumper sticker on a car belonging to a fundamentalist Christian: "God said it, I believe it, that settles it!"

My longing to "settle it" was growing. I would simply have to make some crucial decisions and accept the results. On the other hand...

Forget safety.
Live where you fear to live.
Destroy your reputation.
Be notorious.
I have tried prudent planning long
From now on, I'll be mad.

—*Rumi*

In India, Hindu tradition divides life into four distinct stages: student, householder, seeker and renunciate. The student period covers all the formal learning that will be needed in order to live in the material world; the householder stage is for building and maintaining a family; the seeker, having provided for his family, once again turns to learning—this time, spiritual learning; and the renunciate gives up all material possessions and goals to devote the remainder of his life to communion with God. Because these stages of life are well established in Hindu culture, individuals, family and government all anticipate them and support the individual as he makes the change from one stage to the next.

In the West, there is little or no cultural support for changes of this kind. Rather, someone who drops his career in mid-life, for example, is looked upon as disturbed or inferior. The stages of life in America should not necessarily correspond to those in India, but how much easier and more pleasant it would be if we approached changes in our lives with the full support of family and friends, not to mention banks and the IRS.

I suppose each of us marches to a different drummer, and we are affected by outside influences in varying degrees. I was deeply affected by Richard Bach's book, *Illusions: The Adventures of a Reluctant Messiah.* In it, Bach describes his alter ego by way of a character named Donald Shimoda. Shimoda is an American messiah who one day disappears in front of 25,000 eyewitnesses.

> "I didn't know the Messiah could just turn in his keys like that and quit," I said.
>
> "Of course you can quit!" Shimoda replied. "Quit anything you want, if you change your mind about doing it. You could quit breathing if you wanted to."
>
> "So I quit being the Messiah, and if I sound a little too defensive, it's

maybe because I am still a little defensive. Better than keeping the job and hating it."[5]

Immediately after I read these lines, I felt a faint pressure, a slight insistence in my head, then a familiar voice saying, "If you follow it back far enough, you'll find that the word *messiah* is derived from the Greek word *christ*. What you may not be aware of is that the idea of a redeemer has been common among a broad diversity of peoples around the world. Ancient scriptures from the Middle East and Central Asia predict the coming of a savior, sent by God. The Zoroastrians of Persia—what you now call Iran—believed in the coming of a messiah. Why, even the Chinese Confucians believed that a godly figure would arrive to bring about a golden age."

"Thank you, Hippocrates," I replied dryly, "your erudition is beyond reproach."

"Now, now, Dr. A.," Hippocrates responded, "tether your sarcasm. I was about to make a point."

"Which is?"

"If a messiah, with all the pressure and obligations on him, can quit, why can't you?"

"What do you mean, 'quit'?"

"You know very well what I mean. To use a colorful and quaint old American expression, I mean the whole kit and caboodle!"

"You mean, quit my practice, just give up my career, just like that? Do you know how hard I've worked to create it? How many battles I've fought to keep it going? Just give up a lucrative money-maker that has provided so well for my family and me? You mentioned Confucius; even Confucius taught that there should be moderation in all things. Look, Hippocrates, there's plenty of middle ground—why do I need to give up everything? What's wrong with being an overseer, for example? I could just come in occasionally...keep the stress level very low."

"Come, come, Dr. A., why are you deluding yourself? Your profession no longer challenges you. Hasn't it become just a job?"

"Well, maybe it..."

"And look at what you're doing to your body. First you became mentally and emotionally exhausted, then your back gave out; now it's your hand. What greater tragedy will it take to make you see?"

"But, Hippocrates, why does it have to be so total?"

"Because, Dr. A., *you* will not settle for anything less. No one is imposing this on you—you're imposing it on yourself. Think of Shimoda's words in the book you just cited. Besides, Dr. A., you must admit that the idea of quitting appeals to you."

"I do not admit that. What are you talking about, Hippocrates?"

"For all your past materialism, you're a romantic, and this idea has a dramatic elegance about it. Just think, a noted surgeon doesn't just ease off, he...how do you say it? He 'packs it all in.' He doesn't bother to sell his Park Avenue Foot Clinic, though he could receive a hefty price for it, he just ends his creation, his baby; he simply puts it to sleep as the universe snuffs out a shining star when its time has come."

"But...but..." I uttered, unable to verbalize a response.

"But what? Can you look yourself in the mirror and tell yourself you're doing, at this moment, exactly what you most want to do in the world?"

I was quiet for a moment and did not respond, and Hippocrates had the good grace to let me be. He was right. Fear and habit would have me answer, "Of course I am!" but the truth was that I was living a lie. Though throwing in the towel was impractical and ridiculous on one level, on another it was appealing. In *Illusions,* Richard Bach says, "A good messiah hates nothing and is free to walk any path he wants to walk—that's true of anyone, of course." And it was true for me. I could simply walk away from it all. I could just do it, just like that...just like that.

Perhaps the decision had already been made, somewhere, on a deeper level within me. And now I was going through a reasoning process so my conscious mind could "catch up." I didn't want to undergo the risks of surgery in an attempt to remedy my tremors, and practicing medicine was no longer enjoyable.

I stopped reading the medical journals in my field—a time-consuming requirement—and, while I continued consulting with my patients, I felt more like someone who just worked there rather than the owner-operator of a foot clinic. In a way, it was liberating to feel I was just punching a time card, just putting in my time.

I thought about my old alcoholic friend and guide, Bob Goldsack, who was forced out of his career when he got his hand caught in a food-processing machine. With my disabled hand, was I following in his footsteps? One thing was certain, I had more time for reading what I really wanted to read. One of the next items on my reading list was *The Secret of the Golden Flower,* a Taoist scripture in which C.G. Jung tells of his own mid-career crisis and credits the German theologian, Meister Eckhart, for introducing him to the art of "letting go." In commenting on the Taoist text, Jung poses the question: "What did people do in order to achieve the development that liberated them? As far as I could see," Jung said, "they did nothing but let things happen. The art of letting things happen, action through non-action, letting go of oneself, as taught by Meister Eckhart, became for me the key opening, the door to the Way." Jung continues, "Consciousness is forever interfering, helping, correcting and negating, and never leaving the psychic processing in peace."[6]

There was not much television in my life these days, but one evening I felt a strong urge to turn it on, as though an electrical signal had been aimed at me. While randomly flipping through the channels, I stopped on the public broadcasting station and found myself in the middle of a discussion of mythology between interviewer Bill Moyers and mythologist, Joseph Campbell. After watching the lively and passionate Campbell for a few minutes, I realized that something very special was going on. Campbell had the uncanny ability to describe myth as an active, relevant and important part of our lives in the here and now. To him, mythology was "the song of the universe." Campbell was saying, "Myths are clues to the spiritual potentialities of human life," and he made his point with several utterly fascinating, probing examples.

Campbell introduced the idea of saying "yes" to life's inevitables—all the difficult things we can't avoid. "Thinking in mythological terms helps to put you in accord with the inevitables...You learn to recognize the positive values in what appear to be the negative moments and aspects of your life."[7] Then, "The black moment is the moment when the real message of transformation is going to come. At the darkest moment comes the light."[8]

To determine the right course for our lives, he observed that "Life is not a problem to be solved, but a mystery to be lived."[9] This made me look at my own trials from an entirely different angle. What had appeared to be a disaster—my inability to perform surgery—I could now see as the advent of a positive restructuring of my life.

Campbell believes that mythology has the ability to liberate one's faith from the cultural prisons of his or her past. At one moment in the PBS program, he managed to reconcile the positive and negative aspects of my birth religion, Catholicism. "Every religion is true one way or another. It is true metaphorically. But when it gets stuck to its own metaphors, interpreting them as facts, then you're in trouble..."[10]

"If you read that Jesus ascended to heaven in terms of its metaphoric connotation, you see that he has gone inward—not into outer space but into inner space, to the place from which all being comes, into consciousness that is the source of all things, the kingdom of heaven within."[11]

Campbell went on to cite chapter and verse from scripture of every major religion to show how they all relate to a single myth—a *monomyth,* the story behind all the stories. Monomyths, he says, can be traced as far back as 3000 B.C. "Truth is one," he said, "though the sages speak of it by many names."[12]

Campbell's advice, *follow your bliss*—the injunction to give up the suffocating life of security in exchange for the creative soul's quest for an authentic life—rang true, and at the end of the series I felt the absence of fear for the first time in my life. It felt strange and wonderful at the same time, as if a benign, protective cloud had enveloped me. Everything just seemed "okay." Beyond that, there was some kind of life force emanating from Campbell that had the effect of greatly energizing and enhancing my own spiritual search.

Campbell helped me to understand things I had read before but had not understood; for example, St. Augustine's "Do not plan long journeys because whatever you believe in you have already seen. When a thing is everywhere, the way to find it is not to travel but to love." When Campbell declared that the Ultimate Mystery could be an impersonal god, an energy source that is the life of the universe, I heard words spoken by another that confirmed my own intuitive feelings. Campbell's wisdom, so transforming and timely in my life, had not come through any effort on my part—it was just there when I needed it. Jung had said, "What did people do in order to achieve the development that liberated them? As far as I could see, they did nothing but let things happen." I couldn't force the occurrence of these events any more than I could force the sun to rise, but I could make decisions that seemed right, and allow events to unfold themselves. And one thing seemed certain. I *would* take the Jungian gamble—risk everything by doing nothing. I would not be resuming my career as a podiatric surgeon. I had reached a decision—the final cord would be cut.

The release from uncertainty was like an elixir. I experienced an unexpected pleasure like an electrifying current that made me strikingly alive and buoyant. I floated through the remainder of the day as if on a magic carpet. That night, while everyone else in the house was asleep, I had a vision of Joseph Campbell. He'd been in his eighties when the TV series had been taped (they were aired after he died at eighty-seven), but in spite of his advanced years, his expressions and gestures seemed alive with energy and youthfulness, and his boyish smile was infectious. In the vision, Campbell turned and addressed me directly, and said, in the voice of an Old Testament prophet, "Thou shalt no more be termed forsaken. Neither shall thy land be turned desolate. *(Isaiah, 62:4)* Bon voyage, Dr. Augustine." Then he smiled that infectious smile and the vision was gone.

CHAPTER 14

Cracking the Cosmic Code

So every bondsman in his own hand bears the power to cancel his captivity.   —*Shakespeare*

I continued my prolific reading, and from Father Fran Dorff's *The Art of Passingover*,[1] I learned the concept of "let it go, let it be, let it grow." To illustrate the idea, here is a condensed version of the Catholic priest's delightful story.

> One day, a mountain climber reached the halfway point to the top of a mountain but then lost his footing and fell. As he fell, he grabbed the branch of a tree, and there he hung, halfway between heaven and earth. He looked down and shouted, "Help! Is there anyone down there who can help me?" But there was no answer. Then he looked up to the top of the mountain and again cried, "Help! Is there anyone up there who can help me?"
>
> "Of course I can help you," a voice answered, "just do as I say."
>
> "I'll do anything you say, if only you will help me," the climber said.
>
> Then the voice said "Let go." The mountain climber was silent. Then he looked around. He saw people from every time and place stuck on the mountain just as he was. Among them were Abraham, Moses, Jeremiah. John the Baptist, Jesus and Mohammed. The mountain climber called out to them, "Did you hear what the Lord said? He must think I'm crazy!"
>
> The mountain climber watched in disbelief as, one by one, those who were with him let go and disappeared from view.
>
> Once again he was alone. "Well," he thought, "at least I'll be in good company." Then he let go.

I received a request to meet with Robert Seidman, the regional manager for my insurance company. My claim was not only a year late but was complicated by the fact that my back injury had merely reduced the amount of income I could generate; it had not put me out of business completely. By this time I was more curious than anxious. I thought, *"Well, they'll offer me a token settlement and that will be it."* And then I let go of the whole thing.

At his office, Mr. Seidman got quickly to the point. "Dr. Augustine, your maximum allowable benefit under the terms of your office overhead policy, due to your back injury, is $12,500 per month for a total of three months. The company has found that your income reduction for the months of May, June and July of 1987, qualifies you for that full amount. I've already made out the checks for you. Here they are."

There was no struggle, no negotiating, not even the slightest hint of begrudgment. He just smiled and handed me a check. I didn't know if I should laugh or cry. If my hand hadn't become disabled, I would have never known that I was entitled to benefits resulting from my back injury; and not having known, I would never have received this serendipitous windfall. How strange and mysteriously interlocked everything was. Having decided to quit wrestling with the forces of fate, I had let go of something really big, something that once seemed so vitally important, and almost immediately, the invisible forces of the universe had compensated me in a way I hadn't expected.

The universe had been speaking to me for a long time—through the anguish in my mind and the pain in my body. The difference was that now I was listening. But I wasn't really doing anything. My decision about my surgical career was to do nothing, to let things be. Jung and Eckhart were right. "Letting go of one's self," in the midst of personal crisis, and letting things happen—as they sometimes must—was the way. It wasn't just an agreeable concept any longer—it really worked. It was the practical key to finding my true direction. Somehow, by letting things be, and having events take their natural course, the invisible forces that direct individual progress become unfettered...the doors open and the way is made clear.

This was utterly marvelous. It was one thing to read about a profound idea and quite another to experience it in your own life. I had a strong sense that the insurance windfall was one more bit of the magic that was happening to me. As I left Mr. Seidman's office, I kept repeating to myself, "It works! My God, it works!"

There is more to Father Dorff's story of the mountain climber. He had, if you recall, just been told by God to let go—and he did.

As he fell, the mountain climber was frightened nearly to death. But as he continued to fall, he somehow became used to falling, and his descent became more pleasant. He began to experience a sense of freedom in his falling, a freedom he had never experienced in climbing. Suddenly, he found himself enveloped in a cloud, stationary, no longer falling. He was suspended and could neither see nor feel anything around him.

"We made it, Lord," he called out, "We made it! What do I do now?"

A voice replied, "Let it be."

The climber waited for a while, then waited some more, and some more. Finally, he called out, "This is boring."

"Let it be," came the voice again.

"I thought you were going to say that," replied the climber, and he remained there for quite a while.

On June 17, four and a half months since making my last diary entry, I felt the urge to start again. After writing a general update of events, I summarized my status:

- I feel I'm progressing farther on the path to becoming one with my true self.
- My need to impress people is not gone but it is steadily decreasing.
- Chasing dollars and wearing expensive jewelry is no longer necessary.
- I am giving myself permission to relax.
- I am developing closer bonds with my family.
- Blessings spring from misfortune.

During this time I felt I was in a position midway between two states of being. The first state was my past, which was over and could not be recovered; the second was my future, which I could not see. All I had was each present moment, and I was learning, or trying to learn, to let things be. It's not easy for a habitual controller to give up control of life. In fact, it's very hard, and the old habits come surging back at the slightest dropping of one's guard. There were a thousand things that I wanted to initiate, fix, modify or otherwise involve myself in. But at the same time, this period of passivity felt like the welcome calm after a perilous storm had played itself out. It was comforting.

Meanwhile, after what seemed a very long time, the mountain climber was still "letting it be."

Then the Lord spoke. "Are you still there?"

"Yes, Lord," he replied, "even though I am doing nothing, I am at peace now. It is good to be here."

"Listen," the Lord said, "I need your help. Will you help me?"

"Of course I will help you, Lord. What do you want me to do?"

"One of my friends is stuck on the mountainside.

"Will you go and help?"

"But I don't know the way." "Don't worry, I will raise you up and show you the way."

"But," said the mountain climber, "I don't know what to say."

"Don't worry, if words are needed, I will speak for you."

"But..." said the mountain climber, and he continued to find reasons why he could not go. When his other reasons were exhausted, he said to the Lord, "I'd like to help you but I'm not much good at mountain climbing anymore." But finally, he knew he had to continue on to his next step. "So be it, Lord," he said, and felt himself moving.

Then the mountain climber burst into full daylight and saw beneath him a more breathtaking view of mountains, hills and rivers than he had ever seen before. Far below, he noticed someone stuck on the mountainside. As he drew closer, he saw that it was a woman, hanging onto the branch of a tree. She was unable to climb up or down. All she could do was hang on for dear life.

The mountain climber grabbed onto a nearby tree and hung there, without saying a word, until the woman noticed him. "Thank God," she cried, "I thought I was alone here. Did you hear what the Lord said? Let go! He must think I'm crazy."

The woman watched in disbelief as the mountain climber let go and disappeared from her sight. "Well," she thought, "at least I'll have company."

Then she let go.

We shared a weekend vacation at the Sonoma Mission Inn with Jeremy and Jody Perlman. The high point was to be a ride in a hot-air balloon, but Cecile had no desire to be suspended thousands of feet in the air, and Jeremy and Jody felt that only one of them should go up, for the sake of their children in case of a freak accident, so Jody and I went together.

At 5:15 a.m., we were picked up by a driver who took us to the balloon field in the Napa Valley. As we got closer to the launching area, the sun began its rise. In the distance, a field of brightly-colored balloons were being readied for flight.

As we stepped into the gondola, Pilot Jim opened the burner. Flames and hot air rose up into the balloon. The ground crew released the tethers and we were away, in total silence except for the occasional roar of the burner.

I learned that Jim had left the high-pressure world of publishing to start the hot-air balloon company. While he told me how he had tried and tried to make the switch and then finally did it, I kept thinking of the character of the reluctant messiah in Richard Bach's *Illusions*, and how he had said, "Of course you can quit! Quit anything you want, if you change your mind about doing it." It seemed as though wherever I turned, I was finding support and confirmation of my own decision to quit.

Up in the air, floating silently with the wind, feeling hardly a breeze because we were going with the wind, watching other colorful balloons sailing nearby, I experienced a wonderful sense of well-being. I had no need to think about it, and no desire to construct an intellectual concept about what was happening. I realized that the continuing effort of the mind to rationalize life's purpose was self-defeating—that the very process denied the experience of being alive. "This is it," I thought, "this is the precious moment of being alive. This is life's meaning and its purpose and its fulfillment—just being."

"Let it be, let it be," Father Dorff had said, and I understood. At least here and now, I could let it be.

Beneath us were mile upon mile of vineyards, their leaves bright green. In a few months—October, harvest time—the air would be filled with the thick, heady aroma of fermenting grapes, and the vines would be bent to the ground with heavy clusters of fruit. Below us the Russian River wound through the Napa Valley and we could see canoeists paddling through the quickly flowing waters. When we began our descent, it seemed as if the ground were moving toward us, and we were motionless. It reminded me of how every consciousness is its own center, around which everything else revolves.

As Jody and I were driven back to the Sonoma Mission Inn, I had a memory of the previous day when the four of us—Jeremy, Jody, Cecile and I—had strolled through downtown Sonoma and spotted something unusual painted on the door of a brown Chevy pickup truck. It was a large yellow circle, and inside it was a human figure with arms and legs outstretched so that they touched the edge of the circle. Painted around the perimeter of the circle were a bird, rabbit, dog and dolphin, and beneath the circle were some words:

"Until he extends the circle of his compassion to all living things, man will not himself find peace."　　　　　　　　　　—*Albert Schweitzer.*

A year ago, I would have dismissed such a statement as a trite platitude, an unrealistic dream unworthy of serious consideration. Now, I understood that it was the true reality, and that reality was surrounded by multitudes of unawakened beings who traveled through their lives like race horses with blinders, unable to see anything but the narrow path down which they continued.

The weekend contained one bit of magic after another, unplanned, unsought, occurring like the orderly unfolding of a blueprint whose plans were meant to be executed one after the other, in their own good time. By contrast, I simply could not hold in my feelings. I was so enthused with the spirit of Jung, Father Dorff, Richard Bach and, especially, Joseph Campbell that my innermost thoughts and feelings came tumbling out.

Like a child who runs home to tell mummy or daddy what has just happened, I blurted out the ideas I had been absorbing, how they related to my life—to all our lives. I was the newly-converted zealot so full of ideas and passion that they had to be shared. Eckhart and St. Augustine, Judaism and Catholicism, Hinduism and Buddhism—here was a Dennis Augustine no one, not even my wife, had ever seen before.

The following week, Jody Perlman phoned to let me know that my ranting discourses on life and spirituality, far from displeasing her, had strongly inspired her to re-examine her own life. One of the books I had recommended, Eswaran's *Formulas for Transformation* or *The Unstruck Bell,* as it is now called had become her bible.

In making the decision to give up my medical career, I think I was finally able to "let it go." When I decided to do nothing about my disabled hand, to let events take their own course, I was getting some good practice in "letting it be." Now, things were moving ahead quickly in my life. and I would try my best to "let it grow."

Once you understand symbolic things, you, too, will see symbols everywhere.   —*Joseph Campbell*

Growth comes in unexpected ways. One afternoon at the clinic, Jeremy gave me a copy of Joseph Campbell's *The Hero With a Thousand Faces.* Campbell equated the hero's quest in mythology with the spiritual quest on which each of us ultimately must set forth. He established a general sequence of events usually encountered by man in this inner journey, and outlined them this way:

The Adventure of the Hero

Departure

The Call to Adventure
Refusal of the Call
Supernatural Aid
The Crossing of the First Threshold
The Belly of the Whale

Initiation

The Road of Trials
The Meeting with the Goddess
Woman as the Temptress
Atonement with the Father
Apotheosis
The Ultimate Boon

Return

Refusal of the Return
The Magic Flight
Rescue From Without
The Crossing of the Return Threshold
Master of the Two Worlds
Freedom to Live[2]

The effect of reading about these sequential episodes—a road map of the inner realm—was dramatic. For years I had been trying to find a pattern in my own experiences, without much success. Now I realized the experiences I had been undergoing were not only normal, according to Campbell, but predictable as well. I was no longer a lone interpreter, trying to fathom the invisible forces of the universe. I was a part of a recognizable, definable process that is shared by all humankind.

It was while pouring through Campbell's cartography of the Hero's Journey that I realized the same stories that gave the answers to other people and other tribes, could very well unlock the secret caverns of my own myth by finding out the answers to life's fundamental questions:

Who am I?
Where do I come from?
What is expected of me?
What is my life's purpose?

Why is there suffering in the world?
How can I heal myself?
Who can guide me?
Whom should I emulate?

This was not something I took lightly; it was something I had to know, and it occupied most of my time. I now understood what Jung must have felt when he asked of himself, *"What is the myth I am living? I took it upon myself to get to know 'my myth,' and regarded it as a task of tasks…I simply had to know what unconscious or preconscious myth was forming me."*[3]

I soon realized that by cross-referencing my own experiences with these ancient myths—which are a type of blueprint outlining the mysteries of the universe—I would be able to develop my own personal working myth. In fact, I had been doing just that, rather haphazardly, without knowing it. Thanks to Campbell, I felt I was becoming reacquainted with a silent, invisible, yet potent foreign language I had long since forgotten, which was waiting to be liberated and redeployed.

The stories I read in *The Hero With A Thousand Faces* included inspiring accounts of the struggles and heroics of climbers who succeeded in reaching the loftiest peaks of their spiritual quest. In time it became apparent that there is no fundamental difference between the top and the bottom of the mountain. The descent from the mountain is as difficult as the ascent. The mountain is the mind of man, and what he learns from the climb and the descent belongs to all who step foot on the mountain. And one cannot speak of success until one reaches the bottom after experiencing the top, and integrates the experience into his own life.

Where was I now on this Journey? I knew that I had returned from "the yonder zone," the "other world," where my consciousness had been transformed by surviving the trials that had been put before me during my own climb and descent. I knew that I was in the process of performing a re-enactment of the mythological journey. And I saw that in attempting to reconcile two worlds, the human and the divine, I had been shown the paradox that the two worlds are separate and, at the same time, one and the same. In attempting this reconciliation, the perilous mountain trail is pulled out from underneath us, and we are forced to suspend our rationality.

It is then that chaos and hopelessness dominate us. And it is then that we find ourselves devoid of any purpose or meaning in life. What has seemingly given meaning to our life—our "reality props"—have been dashed to pieces, and we are powerless.

The state of powerlessness leads, sooner or later, to surrender, a glorious surrender that Thomas Merton describes as: "An intuition of a ground of openness...an infinite generosity which communicates itself to everything that is."[4] It is through the gate of surrender that we are introduced to the world of the divine, and it was here that I came to an understanding of the paradox. From the view of daily existence, our physical surroundings are real and our spiritual nature is unreal, or at least invisible and undetectable. But while in an illumined, cosmic state of awareness, the spiritual world is the real one and our physical surroundings and events are the unreal, background shadows. Thus, both the physical and spiritual worlds are real or unreal, depending on the state of one's consciousness.

Or so it seemed to me.

In describing the cave of illusions, Plato illustrated the seductiveness of unreality when he described a people who believed that their own shadows, cast upon the walls, were more real than they were. Obsessed with the shadow-play, the people neglected their own lives and became prisoners of their fantasies by their self-neglect.

Unfortunately, most us dwell within the cave of our own minds, unable to discern the real from the unreal. It is only when we tire of the illusory shadow play of our daily lives, finding ourselves no longer fulfilled by its deceptive form, that some of us take the existential risk of venturing out towards the light. When we do, we discover another reality, said to be more real than anything we have previously known. Without awakening to this fact, we don't live—we merely exist. We don't grow, we merely react.

During these days, it didn't take much to escape my everyday reality. Something as simple as seeing the way the morning light fell upon the multi-colored pebbled courtyard, or listening to the wind rustle through the Brazilian pepper trees, mimicking the light tap of a tambourine.

I had enjoyed this same spot for years, but my pleasure had been limited to little more than a passing pride of ownership. Now, the scene engulfed me. All other things in life seemed secondary, and during these occurrences, it was difficult to imagine returning to a "normal" life and a "normal" routine.

Campbell's words brought me back: "The first problem of the returning hero is to accept as real, after an experience of the soul-satisfying vision of fulfillment, the passing of joys and sorrows and the banalities and noisy obscenities of life."[5]

Each experience, heightened my sense that things would continue to work out properly in my daily life as long as I did not attempt to resist, challenge or control them. This giving up of all volition in everyday affairs was very foreign to my nature. But at the same time, I "knew" that things would go well because these external events were merely a reflection of my inner harmony.

During the spring, summer and fall of 1988, I was engrossed in a new way of learning and a new way of gaining knowledge—or perhaps it's more accurate to call it understanding. I wasn't gaining detailed knowledge the way I might from studying a medical book. It was more like the intuitive unfolding of a radically new concept.

The new way of knowing that I had begun to experience carried with it a certainty beyond all certainties of physical reality. To feel, to experience a spiritual truth clearly is to know, beyond all question, that it is true, and that it cannot be untrue. One may doubt the established laws of physics, mathematics or even of logic. But the experiencer of spiritual truth can never doubt his experience. It is *he* who brings truth and meaning to his life. Perhaps that's what Campbell meant when he said, "I don't need faith, I have experience."[6]

I had reached a new level. I *knew* in a way that I had not experienced before. And, somehow…somehow, this new way of *knowing* contained within itself the kernel, or basis, of knowledge of all things. Another way to say it is that all things have an essence. And once that essence is sensed/felt/understood, all things are known.

There could no longer be any question whether or not God is omniscient. *We are all omniscient.*

CHAPTER 15

Apart But A Part

The game is not about becoming somebody, it's about becoming no-body.
                                                        —*Baba Ram Dass*

Dr. Ed Marlowe and I had our differences but it was good to see him again. It had been a long time since we'd been in each other's company.

"Denny, the word has gotten around that you injured yourself and that you've been forced to cut way back. What's really going on? How are you doing?"

I told him about my back injury, the intense psychological pressure I had felt, the disabling of my hand, and finally ended with, "Yet with all things considered I feel fortunate to be where I am at this point in my life. It's been a blessing in disguise in many ways. I've never known such peace. You know, in some ways it was great to be a high-flying surgeon and entrepreneur, and in other ways it was awful. I finally decided enough was enough already, and the disability only hastened it. Deep down in my gut I've really wanted to quit for some time."

"I know what you mean," Ed said with a sigh. "My practice sure isn't what it used to be. I cut back some myself. You know, I'm still flying model airplanes and jogging ten miles a day and all...but my mind is always on the office. You know the routine. Is my secretary billing correctly? Is she getting the insurance forms mailed on time? Is my rear end sufficiently covered, or have I left out some critical documentation? Does that nasty phone call from the lady with a bunion problem mean she's going to sue? Is my colleague down the street bad-mouthing me? Man-oh-man, it never ends. Surgical procedures are down, and so are my billings.

"But you know, Denny, even with all the hassle I don't know what I'd do if my hand went out on me now."

Little by little, the word had gotten around the profession that I had some health problems. Friends and acquaintances like Ed were curious and concerned about how I'd been stricken in the prime of life. Of course, underlying their concern was their fear that it could happen to them.

It was interesting how people seemed to want to make my predicament bigger and more hopeless than it actually was. It became sort of humorous to observe all the reactions to the changes I had made. They couldn't understand my calmness and couldn't believe that I was experiencing creative feelings about my disability and my future.

Relatives called to ask, "What on earth are you going to do now?" Colleagues phoned to ask, "My God, Dennis, is it true? You mean you won't be able to operate ever again?" None of them understood that I was not a mere victim of circumstance, that I had made a conscious choice not to undergo surgery and to quit being a surgeon myself. Nor could I get through to them that I could still lead a quality life.

In fact, I had what one medical management magazine called a "friendly disability." It was friendly in the sense that it wasn't life-threatening or massively disabling. I was still able to swim, ride my bike, enjoy family outings, travel and generally function pretty well. The fact that I couldn't perform surgery, play tennis, jog or engage in heavy aerobics was a small price to pay—I was more alive now then I could remember, and a lot happier and healthier overall.

People are intensely interested in the plights of others. Why else are there such huge audiences for television soap operas, and why else does the media overwhelm us with bad news? We are a nation of inquiring minds. But for all this interest, we don't like others to change. We expect a certain amount of predictability in those we know (or know of), and when that predictability is shattered, we are quick to condemn. Take Edward VIII of England. He abdicated his throne in December of 1936 to marry an American-born commoner. The scandal that ensued has not yet died down, and today's tabloid journalism thrives on reporting the continuing saga of Britain's royal family.

Spiritual growth is a type of transformation that is even more incomprehensible to others. Perhaps Rumi was right when he said, "Those on the way are almost invisible to those who are not." But even more than this, these kinds of changes are incomprehensible to others who have not yet experienced them. Often, those closest to us—*especially* those closest to us—cannot comprehend the changes we are experiencing. We threaten their sense of familiarity and permanency, and for most people, the sense of familiarity and permanency is their main security. So when we start to be transformed, we are unwittingly tearing down the security of those we love.

That may be good for them in the long run, for security based on any notion of permanency is always a false security. They may need to be jolted out of that false security. But the short term result is suspicion and fear.

Part of the suspicion and fear stems from one person not knowing what is happening inside the mind of another ("Is my husband flipping out?" "Has my friend gone over the edge?") But there are also practical consequences. Rare is the spouse who can say "It's wonderful, dear, that you're giving up your career to follow your spiritual path. I honor your quest and we will respect and encourage it regardless of the financial consequences." Or the friend who says, "That's a courageous move and I support your decision."

All life is a spiritual journey, and all growth is spiritual growth whether the individual realizes it or not. But rarely are husband and wife or close friends or acquaintances on the same part of the spiritual journey at the same time. This may explain at least some of the lack of harmony in the world. And unless the persons involved have all traveled far enough along the path so that there is an appreciation and respect for the process, spiritual growth can and often does cast relationships asunder.

Thus the irony. As those on the spiritual path grow in their ability to love, beloved ones who are on an earlier stretch of the path may be unable to receive it and may even turn from it in confusion, alarm or hostility.

How does the line of that "spiritual" go? "You got to walk that lonesome highway. Nobody else can walk it for you. You got to walk it by yourself."

But the funny thing is, I didn't feel alone. How could I? I had tapped into a deep well of cosmic "presence," and found the greatest bliss I had ever known, indescribably vast, possessing me in each fiber of my being. I was grateful for *all* my experiences; for what they taught me and how they guided me. I knew without a shadow of a doubt that the spirit has a power to transform every fear into bliss, and that fear is the truest friend of the human spirit, directing it, compelling it to find the right path.

I didn't hear God speaking to me (unless it was through the agency of Hippocrates—and Hippocrates was definitely ungodlike) and, as far as I knew, I hadn't spoken directly to Him. But that deep place within me did not feel isolated—on the contrary, it seemed somehow connected—more connected than I had ever felt before.

It was interesting to listen to the reactions of people around me. Some said "You're lucky! Most people don't have these kinds of experiences until they're older." These were all middle-aged or older people who, more than I, were in a stronger financial position to change their lifestyle—wanted to, in fact, yet for their own reasons they continued leading high-stress, achievement-oriented, self-destructive lives. Others, inwardly driven by unexamined compulsions and fears, awkwardly confided they knew no other way to live than on the fast track. They seemed like flies on a window pane racing along familiar tracks, searching fruitlessly for some avenue of escape.

One morning I had a meeting with David Shuman, my malpractice attorney, to review one of the few remaining lawsuits filed against me. David knew, as much as anyone, the pressures I had been under during the last several years.

"You look the most relaxed I've ever seen you," he said spontaneously as I came in. "What's going on?" After I shared some of my experiences and insights with him, David, the son of a cardiologist who knew about the dangers of stress, felt free to talk about his own situation. "I wish I could slow down, but look—look at this backlog." He gestured around himself. There were files piled sky-high on his desk and on several long tables in the office. I began to feel compassion for this bright, overworked attorney who had become a slave to the system as I had been. The stacks of files represented hundreds of thousands of dollars in revenue to his law firm; they also represented strife, stress and personal bondage. Like so many other hard-driving professionals, David had painted himself into a corner. His place in the pecking order of the law firm depended on how much business he could generate and how many cases he could successfully settle.

Listening to David's lament reminded me of one of Richard Bach's aphorisms: *Argue for your limitations and, sure enough, they're yours.*[1] Bach had found out that if you say it can't be done, then it won't be done. By arguing for our limitations, we place a limit on our choices. And by limiting our choices, we deny ourselves access to real change.

I didn't try to convince David that he had other choices. He, like everyone else, would have to be ready for that realization before words could make an impression. As I left his office, I felt relieved that I was no longer arguing the case for my own limitations. How could I? The whole world had opened up for me in a way I could never have imagined possible.

Hippocrates once referred to my obsession with work and habit as the Sisyphus Syndrome. He said "Sisyphus, as you may recall, was condemned by the gods to shoulder his rock up the mountain again and again, forever. Perhaps it never occurred to him that he could step aside at any moment and let the rock of his troubles hurdle to the ground."

"But if everyone withdraws from their respective roles in life," I had argued, "society would fall apart."

"Yes, I agree with you, Dr. A.. but the phrase, 'Many are called but few are chosen' applies here—there simply isn't going to be a mass exodus from the workplace."

"Hippocrates, must change always be sudden and dramatic or can it be gradual for some people?"

"You know from your own experience that your changes have come about gradually—you have held on to your current situations until the bridge was made secure for your next crossing. Others are called upon to make the move more abruptly, abandoning all paths of security and reasonableness, casting themselves into uncharted territory and trusting that they are on the verge of a great personal discovery. But regardless of whether the changes are gradual or sudden, there comes a point where a final commitment must be made—and that is always dramatic. Most important of all, if those of us who are called don't make the necessary changes, we will die in spirit."

Or, to paraphrase William James, *We and God have business with each other. Our lives take a turn genuinely for the worse or the better in proportion to how each one of us fulfills or evades our inner calling to change. In opening ourselves to His influence, our destiny is fulfilled.*

Walking to my parked car, I looked around at the buildings, the trees, the passing people, and I was filled with a gentle tranquillity and a reverence for all things. My spirit danced with Zorba the Greek on the beaches of Crete. It was a time of awesome unfolding—a new beginning. All I could think of was how ironic it was that I was experiencing such a surge of creativity at the same time my surgical career was ending.

I thought of the book I had begun writing. And I sensed that there was something far deeper here than just one man's desire to map the experiences of his life. I felt the pull of a higher agency…could I, dare I, was I now free enough to call it "God?" Whatever it was, it was calling me. As I drove home, I let myself go quiet, passive and peacefully expectant. I thought, "Come on, God, I'm listening." What was He saying? I wasn't sure, but there was great pleasure, even in the listening.

I will not reason and compare; my business is to create!

—*William Blake*

Shortly after midnight on Friday, August 19th, I opened my eyes and found myself in some sort of half-sleep. I was alone—Cecile and the children were visiting relatives in Chicago. It felt like being in a semiconscious coma. I didn't know if I was in control of myself or not, but there was no fear—on the contrary, the feeling was very pleasant. I lay there for a while, feeling mildly vigilant, as if I sensed something was going to happen. And then I began to receive a series of mental impressions in the form of dictation. I didn't hear a voice inside of my mind speaking words; rather, the words came out of nowhere and suddenly popped into my mind without any volition on my part.

As soon as the transmission stopped, I found myself leaning over (again with no conscious intent), flipping on the bedside lamp and grabbing a pen and piece of paper. It was a poem, a short poem titled *Change*.

After jotting it down, I felt drowsy and rolled back onto my bed and immediately fell asleep. In the morning, when I reread it, the poem seemed simple, even childlike. But what was fascinating to me was how clearly I could recall the experience. It was not at all like trying to recapture the confused details of a dream—the words and my memory of the experience were clear and lucid.

Later that afternoon, when I was resting for a moment with my eyes closed on the love seat next to my bed, I felt again expectant. Once more, words suddenly came as if from nowhere, and I quickly wrote them down.

Once again the words I had heard were expressed as a poem—a poem called *Choices*. "What fun," I thought to myself. "So this is how poets get their flashes of inspiration." The process continued for a few days. Each time it happened a new theme was expounded in poetic verse.

About a week later I awoke in the stillness of predawn and felt myself rising above my body as a luminous body outline. Sometimes "I" seemed to be levitating slightly above the bed looking up; at other times, "I" was near the ceiling looking down at my body. Where the inspired writing experiences were novel and exciting, this was frightening.

As I was trying to figure out what to do, I heard the voice of Hippocrates whisper: "Relax Dr. A., there's nothing dangerous to any of this. As you can see, your body is resting comfortably between the covers on your bed, while you're up here with me."

I peered around the room and everything seemed about the same except there was a warm glow in the room allowing me to see clearly.

"I thought this only occurs when you're having a near-death experience," I said, caught somewhere between rapture and fear.

"On the contrary," Hippocrates replied, "most people do this in their sleep, when all their conscious monitoring functions are relieved of their duties. But by morning when they awake they lose all recollection of the experience."

Still a bit scared I asked, "But don't I run the risk of not being able to re-enter my body? "

"Not at all," he said. "You're perfectly safe. As I said earlier there is nothing to be alarmed about. You've allowed yourself a great privilege. Most people force themselves to awaken prematurely out of panic, and miss a grand opportunity. Just let yourself experience this."

I looked across at Hippocrates and as if reading my thoughts again, he said, "You see, we have mental bodies as well as physical ones. Our mental bodies are not subject to time/space/density requirements. This is what allows us to move about more freely."

"Is that what allows you to visit me and then depart?" Hippocrates smiled and nodded affirmatively.

As our conversation was taking place, I found myself floating...hovering above my bed, looking down at my body, peacefully asleep. I wasn't afraid any more and I was starting to enjoy it.

"Tell me something, Hippocrates. I've been receiving flashes of poems in my mind. How do I get these poetic transmissions without an audible verbal exchange taking place? For that matter how do you read my thoughts?"

"Oh that!" he said casually. "Well, your mental body is transmitting and receiving thoughts at the speed of light. Well, actually, the speed of thought is faster than that. It's much akin to receiving an instantaneous fax copy (I was always surprised at Hippocrates' knowledge of modern life). In other words as soon as thoughts are directed, they are received. This is happening all the time—constantly, in fact. It's just that your senses are usually too busy paying attention to other things or too fogged up to hear them."

"It seems miraculous."

"If you understood universal laws, you would see miracles for what they are. It was not too long ago people were referring to the 'miracle' of commercial aviation. Yet flying is commonplace today. But more importantly, flights of any kind are governed by universal laws. Something poor Icarus had to find out the hard way.

"Hippocrates, can you tell me more about some of the states I've been experiencing?"

"Well, Dr. A., you have intuitions. You know, those fleeting moments of inner knowing. Second, there are visionary experiences.

For example, do you remember what happened to the painting of the sea captain and the turbulent sea storm following Mrs. Reyes' surgery?"

"Remember? How could I forget? That was more like a near death experience."

"Well, in a manner of speaking it was, but only in a symbolic sense. It was a vision—a peak into the future. A preparation for what was ahead.

"Another common state is called 'witnessing.' It is not the Christian form of 'witnessing,' but a process described by a business associate of yours from San Diego."

"A business associate of mine? Who are you talking about?"

"Pearson, Dan Pearson, the gentleman who I understand spent eighteen months meditating at a monastery in India."

"Dan? You know Dan?"

"Let's just say I know of him, yes! Leonora is his psychic guide. She's quite gifted you know. Our frequencies often cross, although we have no direct dealings with each other. It's a pity that you and Mr. Pearson don't talk more often. You two have a lot in common."

Being at a loss for words, I let Hippocrates continue.

"Anyway," he said, "Do you remember Mr. Pearson's interview that appeared in *California Magazine* over a year ago?"

I hesitated a moment, having just a vague recollection of Dan recounting his experiences in India. Then suddenly, I said "Oh, yes, I remember he *was* talking about 'witnessing.' To him, it's a state where the body is asleep but the mind is awake and alert. I remember he said that gurus in this state would lie in bed and have others read to them all night while their bodies slept. The monks in the monastery called it 'going to the movies.'[2] Not to change the subject, Hippocrates, but this poetry I'm receiving…don't get me wrong, I really enjoy it. I really do. But the poems seem so…so amateurish. They—"

Before I could go on, Hippocrates interrupted. "Yes, and what did you expect? Did the spiritual progress you're now enjoying come to you suddenly?"

"Well, no…"

"And your understanding of mythology, of symbolism, and of the invisible forces that surround you; did they suddenly come upon you?"

"No, as a matter of fact I'm still…"

"Well, for Zeus' sake, Dr. A., what do you expect with poetry? To begin at the top?"

"But I didn't write it! The words came from somewhere else! And I assume that before someone else recites poetry through my head, they would surely have had some literary experience of their own!"

That was the first time I heard Hippocrates really laugh. It was a deep belly laugh that degenerated into a series of snorts and wheezes, as if he was trying to catch his breath, nonphysical though he might be. I waited politely until he had recovered. "Dr. A…" he began again but was forced to pause until his chuckling stopped, "…Dr. A., who did you think was reciting it—Euripides or Aeschylus perhaps, or maybe Sophocles? Of course my favorite poet is Sappho. She was…"

"Excuse me, Hippocrates, but is there a point to all this?"

"A point? Well, let me see. Yes, of course there is a point. Blake, William Blake, the English poet. By the way, did you know he engraved all his poetry himself? He—"

"The point, Hippocrates—"

"The point is, Dr. A, that Blake was often asked to interpret the meaning of his poetry and how it compared to that of other poets. But Blake was an artist. He disdained all that. His reply was 'I will not reason and compare; my business is to create!' That is the point, Dr. A. Your business is to create! Don't get stuck in form! Simply enjoy the child-like beauty of it! Think of all this as part of your healing process. Good poetry like good healing takes time."

And, having come to his point, Hippocrates departed, perhaps to attend to an emergency elsewhere. I once asked him, "Why do you so often leave without saying good-bye?" "Because," he replied, "I seldom know when or where I am going until I arrive there." For the first time since we met I understood what he meant.

Although I'd read many poets, I knew almost nothing about composing poetry. Even so, some newer aspect of the spirit within me had been awakened, and as my poetry improved I confirmed the French poet, de Musset, who said "Know that there is often hidden in us a dormant poet, always young and alive."

The nighttime out-of-body episodes continued, always followed by the transmission of a short poem relating to my own, recent growth experiences.

At these times I felt myself to be in some higher state of consciousness, and I didn't want to leave it. It was comforting and safe, like being in the womb of the cosmos.

Between out-of-body forays, I continued reading books on spirituality. My physical therapist and congenial friend Maureen Lister gave me a copy of Gurdjieff's *Meetings With Remarkable Men*,[3] and I was able to delve more deeply into this enigmatic and powerful teacher who stressed-the need to be really awake .

Georgy Ivanovitch Gurdjieff was born near the border between Turkey and Russia around 1866. At first intent on becoming a doctor and priest, he decided instead to become a seeker after truth. Man is like a machine, he theorized, a mechanical puppet twitched by a bundle of external influences. An ordinary man does not know himself, and only when he does come to know himself does he become responsible for his actions.

Gurdjieff believed that man in his usual state of consciousness is asleep—sort of a walking dead—and unaware of what is going on around him. When he is intensely moved or shocked, he may be able to shift to a more awake state which makes him feel that he had never really been fully alive before. Gurdjieff tried to awaken the disciples who clustered around him by shocking them with his intense and bizarre behavior. He was a fascinating personality—part guru, part showman and part clown.

"Just like Hippocrates," I said, smiling to myself.

I was still reading Gurdjieff's book when it was time to meet Cecile and the children, vacationing in Chicago with relatives, so I took it on the plane. During the flight, I was interrupted by a woman's voice from the seat next to mine. "Sorry to disturb you," she said. "My name's Maureen O'Connell. I couldn't help notice the book you're reading. I'm familiar with Gurdjieff's work myself—how do you like it?"

"Hi," I said, introducing myself. "The book is fascinating. Coincidentally, it was given to me by a friend named Maureen."

As we talked, I found out she was an attorney who worked in an office above the California Cafe in the Old Town complex in downtown Los Gatos, a town close to my home. I had been to the cafe the day before the flight to celebrate Jody's birthday. A flurry of entertaining coincidences began to accumulate. Maureen was going to a class reunion of students who once studied in Rome. I had spent much time in Rome throughout my life, and we quickly found out we shared a passion for Italian food, art, music and history. "Where do you live?" Maureen asked me.

"In Saratoga, on Chesterfield Avenue."

"No kidding," came the response, with a laugh, "I can't believe it! I go by your house every day on my morning walk."

Part of me was dying to say, "Well, why don't you come in and say hello some time," but I didn't think Cecile would take kindly to the idea.

The time went by quickly; we soon landed in Chicago, wished each other well, and parted. I thought of Longfellow and

> Ships that pass in the night, and speak to each other in passing,
> Only a signal shown and a distant voice in the darkness;
> So on the ocean of life we pass and speak to one another,
> Only a look and a voice; then darkness again and a silence.[4]

What is it that attracts us to certain people and makes us feel we have known them for years? Perhaps we have. A majority of the world's population believes in reincarnation. Have we been one another's lover, brother, sister, father, mother, boss, teacher or student before? When a man and woman meet and feel an immediate closeness, they often believe that their attraction is romantic. This can result in a tragic mistake, for they may well be remembering an entirely different kind of relationship.

Realizing how temporary our relationship was to be, I wanted to get close to Maureen. That's what I really wanted with all my friends and acquaintances—a personal connection. I wanted to love her for herself, just like I wanted to love everyone else for themselves, and I wanted to be loved that way in return. I'd had so many enemies over the years from my professional battles that I now wanted to compensate for it by finding as much love as possible. And by giving it freely, by giving what I myself wanted, I began to understand that by the very process of giving love we receive it. In my mind, the progression went something like this:

> When we love others, we love ourselves.
> When we love ourselves, we are being our true selves.
> When we are being our true selves, we are at one with the world.
> When we are one with the world, all things are possible.

The advice, "Thou shalt love thy neighbor as thyself"[5] and "This above all: to thine own self be true, and it must follow, as the night the day, thou canst not then be false to any man."[6] merged and became one to me.

CHAPTER 16

Are the Dice Really Loaded?

The nearer we come to great men
the more clearly we see
that they are only men.
They rarely seem great to their valets.

—La Bruyère

While in Chicago, Cecile and I had dinner with Jay Seymour and his wife, Jan. Jay's critics claimed he had sold his soul to the devil in order to build his financial empire, and that he deserved the "fall" he had taken. My relations with Jay had always been good, and I would never forget all he had done to assist me and boost my spirits throughout the years of my Med Wars.

In fact, only a few months earlier, when I was struggling with trying to decide between hanging up the scalpel or risking surgery, Jay had counseled, "There is no shame, no losing face in walking away from a lucrative career, especially if your physical and emotional health are in jeopardy. You've earned the right to slow down. You don't have to prove anything to anybody anymore."

But despite losing his license to practice medicine, Jay himself had continued on the fast track. After we had embraced and exchanged small talk, he said, "You know, Denny, I'd really like for us to do a 'deal' together. I think it would be fun.'"

"I'm done doing deals!" I said, and Cecile and I proceeded to share with them the latest changes in our lifestyle which included no longer encumbering ourselves with debt.

"I'm no longer addicted to deal-making," I offered, "I've kicked the habit."

"You're right, Denny! That's what it is—an addiction," Jay exclaimed, as though I had just diagnosed his own condition.

There was no one I knew who was so obsessed and driven to strike a lucrative deal than Jay Seymour. Jay sought out deals as if his life depended on them. "I am addicted to deal-making," he said in a moment of rare candor. "I can't seem to stop myself. I like the action. It's a game to me; always has been. Besides, at fifty-six, I'm too young to retire, and even If I did I wouldn't know how to pass the time. At least you have your writing and working part-time at the clinic to keep you busy."

Jay was shrewd and tough—at least that's the image he projected. He always seemed to be on top of everything. So it was surprising to hear him speak of any weakness or inadequacies. In fact, the last time we had spoken by phone he had boasted of his currency trading deals with Japanese banks, his popcorn concession at O'Hare Airport which was netting him $200,000 a year, and the fact that he owned a piece of the Chicago White Sox.

Now, he displayed another moment of candor. "I can't tell you how glad I am to be out of the podiatry business, Dennis, especially now that the Illinois four-year statute of limitations has passed. At least I won't be an easy target for any new malpractice suits." Jay went on to describe the massive amount of litigation against him that was still to be settled. When the television show, "The Walking Wounded," had been aired four years earlier, it seemed like everyone he had ever outwitted, bested, insulted or taken patients from had turned on him. As a result, Jay had been hit by just about every malpractice lawyer in town in a legal feeding frenzy that ultimately drove him out of business.

Now, years later, he still had to attend legal depositions every Wednesday as lawyers continued to pressure him and his insurance carrier for settlements. All but eight of the claims against him were covered by insurance. But, he also ran the risk of noncovered punitive damages. In spite of Jay's wealth and deal-making, his only hope for remaining solvent at the time was to negotiate a class settlement for all lawsuits pending against him. I don't know anyone who would have wanted to trade places with him.

Jay Seymour had once dazzled me with his surgical skills; he'd shown me how to create a medical empire. He had broken with conventional wisdom and proven to those whose minds were open that what critics called impossible could in fact be done, and done well. And I had followed in his path. But while I had eventually tried to make peace with my colleagues, Jay had not. He'd recently filed a major lawsuit against several of his adversaries. Maybe the essential difference between us was that he still genuinely hated his enemies, while I was leaning more towards reconciliation.

Seeing him again, this time within the framework of the things I had learned in the past few years, I realized how much I had outgrown my dependency on my former mentor. Jay had once been larger than life to me, but I was my own person now. The mentor/protégé relationship had served its purpose. It hadn't been entirely one-sided, for Jay had gotten the satisfaction of having a following—seeing his techniques become more and more popular, helping more and more people. But our professional relationship had gradually and amicably come to an end. I no longer needed Jay's guidance or approval.

I still loved him, but now it was a different kind of love. I could no longer share his battles, could hardly even converse on his level of continuing confrontation. All I could do was be forever grateful, remain a loyal friend and wish him the very best.

News of some of my other podiatric colleagues had filtered down to me through various sources. One of the letters I received was from Dr. Morris Keppler in Phoenix. Morris had sent me an expose article from the Miami Herald on Dr. Jacob Levine. The headline read: "Podiatrist Being Sued for Malpractice Dozens of Times." The main thrust of the article was that in spite of sixty-one lawsuits against him to date, his license to practice had not been revoked (at the time when Jacob and I had both been board members of the Academy of Ambulatory Foot Surgery, his total had been only twenty-eight). Jacob ran two of the busiest foot clinics in Southern Florida, making him an easy target. Only a small percentage of the malpractice suits against Jacob were justified, but the mere existence of the highly-publicized suits helped bring about his downfall.

The Miami Herald focused on Jacob's ostentatious style of living. The last sentence in the newspaper article read, "Levine drives a blue Rolls Royce convertible and lives in a big pink waterfront home in Miami Beach."

By this time, even the master of all self-promoters, Dr. Louis Needleman, the prominent Madison Avenue podiatrist, had taken a fall. The fast-talking, hard-driving entrepreneurial doctor who had once commanded my respect by surviving at the very top of the dog-eat-dog podiatric profession, who had been unrivaled in the income he generated and in the clever deals he made, had panic in his voice when he called. "I've been swindled, Dennis!"

"What? What happened?"

"My investment advisor took me and a score of other investors for over fifty-five million dollars!" Lou said.

It took a moment for the thought to register. The notorious Lou Needleman, one of the brightest, fastest and most ingenious operators in New York City, the skilled surgeon who had built perhaps the most enviable surgical center in the country, had been swindled?

He was the surgeon to whom movie stars, TV personalities, famous politicians and corporate executives flocked for treatment. In terms of fame, prestige and income, Lou Needleman had been on top of the world. Now this doctor/personality had been taken to the cleaners by a trusted investment adviser who represented one of the top brokerage firms in the country.

I didn't know what to do, or even what to say. Lou Needleman had certainly taught me a few things on the business side of practice, and for that I felt partly in his debt. But there was nothing I could do. "I'm really sorry, Lou," I said, "I wish I could do something, but I'm climbing out from under my own losses and I've had to stop doing surgery. I'm just not in a position to help."

Then there was Brad Newton, the OBG (obstetrics/gynecology specialist) who made a million bucks a year, invested in an Alaskan fishing lodge, and watched it lose his fortune instead of sheltering it. Even Dr. Richard Drummond, the New York City plastic surgeon who had ordered his chauffeur to leave Cecile and me stranded in a rough New York neighborhood in the pouring rain, had ended up being sued for everything he had. Gary Wyatt was still afloat and living in his sumptuous mansion in Southern California despite being sued by the state of California, but was that what life was all about? Managing to stay afloat? Fighting the establishment? Losing one's soul in the battle for the marketplace? For what? An extra zero at the end of a balance sheet?

We would rather die in our dread
Than climb the cross of the moment
And let our illusions die.

—*W. H. Auden*

One by one, the high rollers of the medical profession as well as the corporate "moneyed men" of the era were biting the dust, through scandal, swindle, injury or ruinous litigation. Whether they were rightly or wrongly pursued doesn't seem to matter in the end, when the dust settles.

The ruins of every civilization are the marks of men trying to transcend themselves. Ancient dark cave drawings, the footprints left by children in the drying cement of a newly poured sidewalk, as well as the carving out of careers and empires all reflect a deep, unconscious yearning for immortality. Wisdom, foolishness and creativity stem from the same source from which all natural phenomena arise, and require an outlet of expression. The fact that men are sometimes leveled in the process, for what appears in hindsight to be poor judgment, shouldn't blind us to our common need to reach beyond ourselves.

The truth is, nobody escapes this life without encountering some misfortune. The face of misfortune differs widely in appearance, and when it occurs, it stops us in our tracks. forcing us to take notice of the truth of our lives. In hindsight, misfortunes of others seem obvious—it seems obvious what they should have done to change their lives. But when the misfortune happens to us, and we are in the midst of it, life seems to be presenting us with a series of cryptic messages.

Those who are quick to judge need to be reminded that last year's vices may become this year's virtues; those held in esteem today may be ridiculed tomorrow. Everyone, rich or poor, wise or foolish, is fallible, and those at the top of the heap at any moment may fall.

When we strive to get ahead, most of us are motivated by a deep conviction of our individual importance. This often drives us to prove to the world and to ourselves that we really are important. We attempt to demonstrate this importance not inwardly and gracefully, but externally and willfully, through second-rate props like money, power and fame.

It's been this way for millennia. All lives and all generations recycle history. Seen in this light, Ecclesiastes' admonition that there's nothing new under the sun take on a renewed meaning.

Before leaving Chicago, I spent some time with Cecile's cousin, Dr. Victor Conway. Like two Greek philosophers discussing life and meaning, we talked about the personal setbacks of our colleagues.

"In his essay, 'The Laws of Compensation,' Emerson says that there is a compensating balance for every tragedy that befalls us, and every act we commit. So that each time we experience a setback, there will be a compensating kernel of good fortune; and that earlier setbacks will then be seen as a blessing in disguise."

"Sounds like he's speaking directly to me," I offered, "for I do feel blessed in many ways."

"Emerson also said—and I believe this is a direct quote: 'The changes which break up at short intervals the prosperity of men are advertisements of a nature whose law is growth.'"[1]

I had never heard a finer, clearer definition of the price one pays for wisdom.

I learned as much from the plights of my colleagues as I did from my own experiences, and to the extent that I have been spared many of their travails, I offer each of them my gratitude and acknowledge my debt for all they have taught me. They, too, have been Life Guides.

My colleagues also affirmed for me that there is no perfect life, except the one that is in keeping with who we really are at our core. I can only hope, whether one judges them as villains or victims, that they will come to know themselves and discover that state of inner harmony and peace that I had come to enjoy—to find their own God within.

What is important...is not the right doctrine
but the attainment of the true experience.
It is giving up believing in belief.

—Alan Keightley

Just after Labor Day, my attorney, Frank Lynch, called to advise me on my insurance claim for total disability payments due to my disabled hand. Frank had previously told me of one New Jersey surgeon who had lost the use of his right hand and was denied benefits because of an ambiguous escape clause.

"Dennis," he said, "disability policies are notoriously riddled with fine print provisos that often protect the carrier rather than the injured party. But I'm happy to report that your claim has been approved. It could just have easily gone the other way, so thank your lucky stars. Whoever your advisor was that recommended the policy apparently made sure the agent included all the appropriate riders. Congratulations."

That quickly, yesterday's villain became today's hero. Mike Maglia—the man who had sold me on the Onyx Building—was the same man who sold me a disability policy against my ardent objections.

"I'd rather invest the money in real estate," I'd said.

"But you need to protect yourself and your family in case something happens to you."

"I'm too young for anything to happen, Mike," I said stubbornly. He was right of course. "Something" did happen, and the rest, as they say, is history.

The pendulum of chance had once again gone in my favor. The feeling I experienced was not based on the arrogant expectation that I was entitled to this boon for all the pain I had gone through. On the contrary, it instilled in me an abiding faith that no matter what the circumstances, life never abandons life. The experience reinforced the idea that there truly are no accidents, except the accidents of timing and chance which converge to produce meaningful results in our lives when they're most needed. As Campbell said, "Chance, or what might seem to be chance, is the means by which a life is realized...it is the ultimate backing of life..."[2]

Despite all my sophisticated reasoning—grounded in logic—the universe continued to go it's magical way. Besides Campbell, I was in good company in believing that the invisible forces around me had been at work. St. Augustine, I believe, said, "Nothing happens at random in the world." Spinoza said, "Nothing happens by chance," and Einstein added, "God does not throw dice."

I was also learning that taking responsibility meant accepting the "bad" with the "good", and the difference between hindsight and insight came to me. Over the past few months, hindsight had enabled me to see why certain events in my life had happened. Now, insight allowed me to widen the circumference of my inner vision. Insight is the ability to accept events and to learn from the process of life, as it unfolds.

How many persons, having won a huge lottery or other great prize, have stopped to ask "Why me?" When good things happen, we seldom question how the invisible forces of the universe work to our advantage or to whom or what we owe our bounty. We may give thanks to a benevolent God, or to fate, but by and large we just accept it and do not question the fairness of our good fortune.

How different when something bad happens to us: "Why me?" we ask. "Who is responsible?" and "It isn't fair!" and "Why did this happen?" and "What kind of God would allow this to happen?" and we voice countless other comments and questions.

It is said that true enlightenment occurs when one is able to accept miracles and miseries with equal detachment, knowing, feeling and responding to them as one and the same—voyages of the human spirit.

It was an exciting time, and it was hard to keep all these ideas bottled up within me. I needed to share them with someone. I wanted to talk about fate, predestination, God, heaven, karma and a host of other subjects.

One Friday evening we had dinner with Jeremy and Jody. Jeremy, like Cecile, was Jewish; Jody, like me, had been raised Catholic. Since Friday evening is the beginning of the Jewish Sabbath *(Shabbat),* which extends through Saturday evening, we soon got into discussing Judaism and Catholicism, and the significance of raising our children in a particular tradition.

Jody had agreed to raise her children in the Jewish faith. When Cecile and I got married, I was not interested in religion—my vision was on building a financial empire. Since I held no strong religious beliefs and had not been close to the Catholic church or its teachings for some time, and since it seemed fitting that our children should have the benefit of some tradition—it didn't matter too much to me which tradition it was—I had agreed to let our children be raised in the Jewish faith. But as the years went by, and particularly in the last year, the feeling of wanting our children to experience a cultural diversity—more than a single religious viewpoint—had grown stronger. Although they were being given the comfort of growing up within a rich Jewish heritage, I now felt that a more eclectic upbringing would allow them to feel connected to other people in the world.

Jody, on the other hand, was considering converting to the Jewish faith, so that she and Jeremy could present a unified approach to raising their children. The conversation between us tended to get steamy. "For me, it's important to get back to my roots," Jeremy had said. "When I was growing up in Brooklyn, I had no choice in the matter—I had a Bar Mitzvah. But aside from that my family didn't do much in the way of following Judaism. I want our kids to have more than that."

"Okay, but take this evening's ritual for example," I countered, "Because the prayers are said in Hebrew, it makes non-Jews feel as though they're on the outside and they can't get in. In fact, the main effect of religious ritual—not just Jewish ritual but all ritual, it seems to me, is to remind us of our differences rather than to celebrate our similarities."

"That's crazy, Dennis," Jody said, "Would you have all ritual be the same for everyone? What kind of tradition would that leave us with, a mono-tradition where everyone's the same? Some kind of universally-acceptable pabulum?"

"Well, my point is that I'm uncomfortable having the kids labeled or identified exclusively as Christian, Catholic, Moslem, Hindu or Jew. I feel that we're all God's chosen people.

"I agree with Jeremy and Jody," Cecile added. "What would we have left? If everyone agreed on a common ritual and doctrine, wouldn't that leave us with the lowest common denominator, like television has become?"

"I understand," I pleaded, "I'm not denying that ritual has a place in religion, I'm just suggesting it be redefined. Valid ritual should help eliminate walls between people and culture rather than create them. The great religions are rich in tradition, but when I look at elements of, say, Hinduism, I see knowledge and wisdom lacking in Western religions, knowledge and wisdom that our kids will never know if they have to conform solely to Judaism or Catholicism."

"So now," Jody said, "he wants his kids to be Hindus!"

"No! Jewish, Catholic, Hindu—those are just labels!" I said, my voice growing sharper. Jody, who had claimed that Easwaren's discourses on Hinduism helped her when she was depressed, wouldn't give an inch.

"Look, Dennis," Jody's reply came back, "It's hard enough for me to think of converting to Judaism—I'm not about to adopt other religions to boot!"

"Okay, okay," I said, "but I'm not talking about taking anything away from our kids, I'm talking about adding things to what they already have."

"You can't do that," Cecile shot back. "You can't put all kinds of different ingredients into a blender and mix them all up together—you'll come out with a gray, tasteless mush! It's too confusing for children."

"And it isn't a matter of logic, Dennis. I'm a part of my Jewish heritage and it's a part of me," Jeremy said. "I don't feel a part of all those other religions."

"Okay, everybody stop and please listen, just listen for a moment," I said. "As you know a lot of changes have happened to me this last year. One of the most important of them is that, for the first time in my life, I don't have to manufacture faith in God or try to make myself believe in some divine power—I've experienced it. I know it exists. And it exists...how can I put this? It exists in a pure, a very pure form that doesn't say Jewish or Catholic or anything else. It...it tells me...I know it sounds corny, but it tells me that all of us are one—not just metaphorically, but that all of us are literally one, and that these separations between us are artificial...they're not needed. Isn't the experience of God the ultimate religious experience we're all seeking? Why confine a power that is so dynamic, so all-encompassing to one set of cultural beliefs?"

The room was silent for a while. The others had listened, out of respect. But there were blank looks on their faces that told it all. Finally, Cecile spoke out. "I don't know if I'd want that kind of experience. I hear what you're saying. I, too, believe that our kids should be exposed to the richness of other cultures in an educational sense. But do we have to give up our individual culture in order to find God? I don't think so, I just don't think so."

I realized that we all operate on different levels, ethically, culturally and spiritually. And just as an individual who has never tasted ice cream will be at a loss to understand those who have, so will the individuals who may have never had a direct and profound experience of divinity and oneness be hard pressed to comprehend the experience of one who has. And yet, my desire to share was strong, and I kept trying, hoping not to sound as self-righteous as the people of faith I once found so easy to criticize.

"On the other hand..." as Tevya in *Fiddler on the Roof* would say, on the other hand, it is important for our children to have some kind of spiritual foundation from which to develop and mature into responsible citizens. And since I wasn't planning on returning to Catholicism anytime soon, Reform Judaism (the most liberal of the Jewish sects), whose weekly Sabbath celebrates the creation of the universe, provided an acceptable foundation. Besides, my views were changing so rapidly—day to day even—and I was so caught up in the rapture of my peak experiences that I could not yet give my views the practical intellectual framework and grounding they needed.

In Autumn, more than at any other time, California, the Golden State, strikes heavenly gold. Warm, balmy days with blue skies and bright sunshine, week after week, month after month. I know of an engineer who was forced to move to Seattle. "It was terrible," he said "The weather was so beautiful in California I couldn't stand working inside, so I never got anything done. At the first suggestion, I'd be off to the beach or the mountains. Here, it's nice and gloomy most of the time, and I'm glad to be inside in my cozy office."

One day, in mid September, in spite of the beautiful sunshine, I found myself overwhelmed by a heavy melancholy that wouldn't go away. Ironically, I had planned to spend several hours in the library working on the chapter of my book that deals with happiness. Intellectually, I knew I should just experience the mood and allow it, like all others, to pass in its own good time. But I didn't. I kept questioning it as the day proceeded. I did manage to finish the chapter, which was satisfying because, if I could write under these circum-stances, I could probably write about anything, anytime.

A sense of foreboding followed me from the library to my office at the clinic. When I reviewed my mail, I noticed a letter from an attorney unknown to me. As I opened it, my heart sank into my stomach. It was a request for a review of the medical records of a patient for whom I had done some relatively minor work, which had apparently become infected and delayed the healing. While I had always done my utmost to prevent infection, it was one of the normal risks of surgery (although a rare occurrence in our clinic). I had always carefully explained this to each of my patients, including the patient who had now hired an attorney.

I don't know if other doctors ever become blasé about these things, but I reacted badly—just as I had done in the past when I received word of impending lawsuits. They were legal time bombs waiting to explode. I couldn't get used to them. "Dammit, dammit, things have been going so well. And now this!"

I knew, intellectually, that the problems that seem so serious at the moment invariably become less so with the perspective that comes at a later time. But, right now, the things I had learned didn't matter. I wanted to crawl into a hole. Even though I was no longer performing surgery, I felt that my competence and credibility—in fact, my whole status as a person—was being called into question yet again. The emotional pain, rather than being eased by the knowledge I had acquired over the past year, compounded my misery. After, all, how could I, with all my experiences and all the spiritual wisdom I had acquired over the last year…how could I descend to the depths so readily? What happened to my ability to accept the bad with the good? If I could so easily be cast down by an event, what had really changed? Was I back at the starting gate, having to run the whole race again—and again—and again? And if this was so, would it ever end?

Except there was one big difference. While a part of me was experiencing deep anxiety, another part of me was detached—it just couldn't hurt me like it once had.

A friend of mine once underwent emergency surgery for a hernia repair, with only morphine and a local anesthetic. He said, "It was the strangest thing. I felt the pain; the pain was real and intense, but I didn't care. I casually thought, 'Oh, what pain,' but it was too much of a bother to flinch. I felt it, but I was totally divorced from it."

Some nice things also happened that day, which in the past would have gone unnoticed, buried in all my numbing sadness. I played some fun, nonsensical music with Jason and Michelle; I proudly attended an open house at Jason's school; I took delight in watching "Opera in the Park" on public television; I enjoyed a heartfelt phone conversation with Dad; and I ended the day with a blissful romantic interlude with Cecile.

A full day in a full life. All in all not so bad for a "sad" day.

Higher consciousness does not mean a cessation of physical or emotional pain. We do not become benumbed zombies indifferent to our fate. We still have likes and dislikes. Those who prefer hamburgers and fries to tofu and yogurt will, in enlightenment, still prefer hamburgers and fries. And because we do not become zombies, we still feel anger and fear and excitement and love and bliss—all the normal impulses that move and guide our lives. But there is a difference. There is a seed of knowing, a seed of awareness that understands that none of this is real, that it is a make-believe cloud cover that prevents us from seeing the sun. Our human, worldly experiences will not diminish; rather the seed of our awareness will grow.

The childhood shows the man,
As morning shows the day.
                                                        —*Milton*

One afternoon, I took my son, Jason, to see the movie, "Big." On the way we talked. "What age would you like to be, Jason," I asked him, "if you could be any number of years old?"

"Umm..., umm..., thirteen, no, fifteen."

"How about even older than that? How about twenty?"

"Yeah, Dad, I'd like to be twenty."

"Why, Jason? What's so good about being twenty years old?"

"I could drive, and have my own car..."

"Yes, you could. What else? What else would you have if you were twenty years old?"

"I could do anything I wanted to."

"Well, not quite. For example, you couldn't commit crimes or do other illegal things."

"Yeah, but I could stay up as long as I wanted, and I could eat whatever I wanted."

"I see...guess twenty looks pretty good from your view. That's what this movie's about; it's about a kid who to wants to be big, and it happens—I don't want to tell you any more because I might spoil it for you."

"Okay, Dad, but I'd sure like to be big!"

The movie portrayed a thirteen-year-old junior high student named Josh who fantasizes about being big. Among other things, he has a crush on a tall, blonde girl in his class, and if he were tall, she might notice him. One day, Josh happens by a fortune-telling machine and, as he drops in his coin, he makes a wish to be big. The next day, he gets his wish. As the movie progresses, Josh learns many things and so does the audience. We remember what fun it can be to be a kid, and how adults often spoil things by their seriousness.

The adult-size Josh, who still has the mind of a kid, enters the adult work-a-day world and wins over everyone with his open, carefree, optimistic behavior. But toward the film's end, Josh tires of living in the adult world and longs to be just a kid again. After a difficult search, he relocates the fortune-telling machine and wishes to return to his original kid size. And he is so happy to be a kid again.

Sitting in the theater next to my small son, tears began filling my eyes and overflowing onto my cheeks. This was becoming commonplace—I could hardly go to a movie anymore without crying over something. As I allowed them to come, a soft voice whispered to me, "Why are you crying, Dr. A.?"

"I think, Hippocrates, they are tears of regret for all the things I missed in life."

"Just regret?"

"Forgiveness, too; forgiveness for ruthlessly rushing myself forward so blindly."

"And joy?"

"Yes, tears of joy, and thankfulness that I have been given the privilege of awakening."

"One last thing, Dr. A, don't…how do you say it? Don't…umm, 'lay a trip' on your son about the movie."

"What do you mean, Hippocrates?" I silently asked, but there was no reply. On the way home, I wondered what kind of message, if any, Jason had gotten from it. "Do you still want to be big?" I asked.

"Yes!" he replied without hesitation.

Then I understood what Hippocrates had meant…that I shouldn't expect Jason to get the same message from the movie as an adult would. He was focusing on the fun part, on what a blast it would be to be big—at least for a while. I needed to let him have that, and not to jump on him with a "higher" message as I was prone to do.

For myself, I was focusing on how, as we grow up, we still want to be "big," even bigger than big—and very fast. In the process we lose our child-like qualities. What childlike qualities? I wondered. What did Jesus mean when he said, "Except ye be converted, and become as little children, ye shall not enter into the kingdom of heaven."[3] Was he referring to the way children spontaneously seek their happiness? William Blake said, "unacted desires breed pestilence."[4] I don't think Blake was talking about material desires; I believe he was referring to those desires that spring from our hearts, the creative power that issues from the spirit.

I came away from the movie realizing I did not have to be in a hurry to get "big." I didn't have to worry about how quickly I was making progress, and that if I clung to the need to get ahead, spiritually as I did materially, I would simply be trading one form of slavery for another. In the Afghani tongue, the verb *to cling* is synonymous with the verb *to die*.

Spirituality, so simple in and of itself, can be a complicated maelstrom in the affairs of men, as was demonstrated when word reached us that Rabbi Nathan Weiss, of Cecile's temple, had initiated a controversy.

You never know where a sermon will lead. Sometimes it can be the beginning of a nap, and sometimes it can be the beginning of a journey. On the eve of Rosh Hashanah, the Jewish New Year, Rabbi Weiss had delivered a sermon on what he believed to be a lack of real spiritual understanding and growth among the congregants.

"Yes, you're here for the high holidays, you attend services regularly and you support the temple and its activities, but, I'd like you all to ask yourselves what has this sacred place become? Is it a place to draw closer to God or is it a social club? Is this temple primarily a place to commune with your own soul, or is it a convenient recreation center? There is nothing wrong with recreation centers and with social gatherings, but is the inner spirit that should enliven these places being nourished? And where does your personal commitment to God fit in? For those of you who are willing to ask yourself these questions, I'm inviting you to join me in dedicating our lives to a higher sense of spirituality and personal growth."

Now to some religious groups this kind of sermon would be considered very mild. In fact, the congregants would feel disappointed if they were not severely chastised by their minister. But with Jewish congregations, when the rabbi wanders from preaching from the Torah and starts talking about members of the congregation—questioning their spiritual integrity—he had better tread softly, for he may be starting an intra-congregational holy war.

In the Jewish calendar, Yom Kippur, the Day of Atonement (at-one-ment), the highest of holidays, follows Rosh Hashanah. Because of the controversy the rabbi had stirred up, I was curious what he would have to say on this holiest of days, and I attended the service with Cecile. It was an unusually long service and I was overcome with boredom. Then when Rabbi Weiss began to speak, everyone woke up.

"While I'm deeply saddened that my sermon on the eve of Rosh Hashanah may have caused some of you undue distress, I make no apologies for its content. I'd like to believe that we as a congregation have evolved enough that we can share and respect each others truths without having to fear a backlash of harsh criticism. Having said that, I also believe we need to be able to share the truest part of ourselves with friends and loved ones, even if it's at the risk of uncomfortable confrontation.

"As you know, Jews believe that each of our souls represents a divine spark. If this is so, we must treat each other as sacred receptacles of that divine spark. If we do this in the spirit of love, our lives will become enriched and our community a better place to live."

The sanctuary was so quiet you could hear a pin drop, and after a brief pause the Rabbi continued: "I see my role as more than that of a mere preserver of the faith. I would like to be a facilitator for your spiritual needs, but I can't be expected to be responsible for them. We can walk the same sacred ground—in fact I encourage it—but I can't show you the path to take. Each of us must make that final journey in our own way—create our own relationship with God. It will require going beyond observing the rituals, the customs and practices of our faith—beyond the doing of good deeds and studying the Torah.

"We need to step back from our hectic work weeks, reflect, meditate, reach out to God, reach deeply within ourselves. And while we're given the privilege of seeing the world through Jewish eyes—that provide us with unique layers of meaning—we must also expand our vision to include the non-Jewish world with whom we share a human and spiritual bond."

I understood that Rabbi Weiss was appealing as much to the spiritual needs of his own struggling spirit as to those of the congregation. I intuitively knew that he was undergoing a mid-career transition of his own, that he was standing where I had recently stood. He was no longer willing to play it safe. Sharing his truth—his vision—was as vital to him at this time in his life as breathing. Although our stations in life were very different—he a clergyman and I a layman—it was as if I were listening to a part of myself up at the podium.

Rabbi Weiss was finally speaking from his heart, asking to be respected for who he was rather than what people wanted him to be. There was a sense of urgency in his voice, as if time were running out. Despite his own conflicts and the frustrations he shared with the congregation, Rabbi Weiss delivered a sermon that was wonderfully eloquent and passionate. He was like a lone mystic agitator who rocks the boat, not for the sake of creating discontent as much as to awaken people, even at the expense of inviting their scorn. His call for a spiritual awakening could have been Baal Shem* Calling for a proper balance between traditional learning and intense spirituality. Simple, joyful faith rather than just a strict adherence to fixed doctrinal teachings. The difference was that while taking a strong stand, Rabbi Weiss freely admitted his own pain and doubts as well—the act of a sincere man.

"I can't do it alone," he said. "I must have the full support of the congregation. I've tried to stimulate personal spiritual exploration outside the temple, and frankly I've only gotten a lukewarm response."

Who can tolerate their leader admitting weakness? Apparently not this congregation. They wanted an outwardly strong Rabbi. They wanted a Moses, an authoritarian figure who could do no wrong, forgetting the fact that Moses himself had painful doubts and fears when being called upon to command the Pharaoh of Egypt to "Let my people go." They couldn't handle a rabbi who was a mere man, who demonstrated his vulnerability and unveiled his own inner wounds. By showing his own humanity, he reminded the congregation that they, too, were human. This meant they, too, would have to take stock of their lives and move beyond the protective veneer of their social masks and their proclaimed faith

"Enlighten us, give us religion, connect us to our roots!" they shouted in silent voices. But when the rabbi cried out from the wilderness of his soul to go beyond the mere words, to join with him in experiencing the world beyond all form—they hesitated to follow. They were comfortable where they were, wearing their religion like a warm winter overcoat. *Change? Why do we need to change? Social club? What social club? How dare he treat us like errant children?*

---

* Israel ben Eliezer, also known as the Baal Shem. Founder of the Hassidic movement in the eighteenth century in Eastern Europe.

A man I know once gave lectures on meditation. At first, many members of his audience felt threatened because they feared that meditation would lead them away from their own religion. During his presentation, he strove to show how meditation is not a threat to one's religion, but rather it enhances it. Meditating Catholics become more devout Catholics, meditating Baptists become better Baptists, and so on.

At the end of each lecture, he invited interested persons in the audience to linger on and find out how to sign up for the meditation classes he offered. At every lecture, several in his audience decided to join his meditation program.

One evening, he gave a lecture to a group of Unitarians. The lecture hall was packed, with standing room only. The audience was rapt, and the questions were the most incisive and subtle he had ever heard. There were so many questions and so much interest in the subject was expressed by his listeners that the lecture ran an hour over its scheduled time. They were especially interested in the speaker's idea that meditating before prayer clears the mind of distractions and allows prayer to become more effective. It was what he called "the dynamic duo" of worship.

At the end, the audience saluted the speaker with a burst of applause. Comments like "that was wonderful" and "seems like a really good thing" were heard throughout the hall.

Then, as he did with all the other groups, the speaker invited interested persons to stay a while if they were interested in the meditation program. After the lecture, many among the audience shook hands with the speaker and told him how much they had enjoyed learning about meditation. Then they all slowly filed out. Out of the huge audience, not a single person remained behind to find out about the meditation program.

These were people who were used to talking about matters spiritual, but doing anything spiritual was beyond their scope of interest or appreciation.

Toward the end of Rabbi Weiss' Yom Kippur sermon, he told a story by Father Francis Dorff. The original version goes like this:

> There was a famous monastery which had fallen on very hard times. Formerly its many buildings were filled with young monks and its big church resounded with the singing of the chant. But now it was deserted. People no longer came there to be nourished by prayer. A handful of old

monks shuffled through the cloisters and praised their God with heavy hearts.

On the edge of the monastery woods, an old rabbi had built a little hut. He would come there from time to time to fast and pray. No one ever spoke with him, but whenever he appeared the word would be passed from monk to monk: "The rabbi walks in the woods, the rabbi walks in the woods." And for as long as he was there, the monks would feel sustained by his prayerful presence.

One day the abbot decided to visit the rabbi and to open his heart to him. So, after the morning Eucharist, he set out through the woods. As he approached the hut, the abbot saw the rabbi standing in the doorway, his arms outstretched in welcome. It was as though he had been waiting there for some time. The two embraced like long-lost brothers. Then they stepped back and just stood there, smiling at one another with smiles their faces could hardly contain.

After a while the rabbi motioned the abbot to enter. In the middle of the room was a wooden table with the Scriptures open on it. They sat there for a moment in the presence of The Book. Then the rabbi began to cry. The abbot could not contain himself. He covered his face with his hands and began to cry, too. For the first time in his life, he cried his heart out. The two men sat there like lost children, filling the hut with their sobs and wetting the wood of the table with their tears.

After the tears had ceased to flow and all was quiet again, the rabbi lifted his head. "You and your brothers are serving God with heavy hearts," he said. "You have come to ask a teaching of me. I will give you a teaching, but you can only repeat it once. After that, no one must ever say it aloud again."

The rabbi looked straight at the abbot and said, "The Messiah is among you."

For a while, all was silent. Then the rabbi said, "Now you can go home."

The abbot left without a word and without ever looking back.

The next morning, the abbot called his monks together in the chapter room. He told them he had received a teaching from "the rabbi who walks in the woods" and that this teaching was never again to be spoken aloud. Then he looked at each of his brothers and said, "The rabbi said that one of us is the Messiah."

The monks were startled by this saying. What could it mean? they asked themselves. Is Brother John the Messiah? Or Father Matthew? Or Brother Thomas? Am I the Messiah? What could this mean?

They were all deeply puzzled by the rabbi's teaching. But no one ever mentioned it again.

As time went by, the monks began to treat one another with a very special reverence. There was a gentle, wholehearted, human quality about them now which was hard to describe but easy to notice. They lived with one another as men who had finally found something. But they prayed the Scriptures together as men who were always looking for something. Occasional visitors found themselves deeply moved by the life of these monks. Before long, people were coming from far and wide to be nourished by the prayer life of the monks, and young men were asking, once again, to live with the monks for a lifetime.

In those days, the rabbi no longer walked in the woods. His hut had fallen into ruins. But, somehow or other, the old monks who had taken his teaching to heart still felt sustained by his prayerful presence.[5]

In some parts of the world, treating others as God has long been integral to the culture. For example, in India, when people greet each other they do so with their hands held flatly together in front of their chest, fingers pointing upward. This is accompanied by the greeting, *"namaste,"* which means, "I salute the God within you."

If God is in everyone, then everyone may experience God in his own, unique way. I, who felt that God long ago abandoned the churches, synagogues and mosques where he was still worshipped, had seen an aspect of Him in this rabbi. In this way, I discovered that God can be found not only in beautiful sunsets, in deep meditation, or while engaged in a profound personal trial, but in the very buildings and services that I had assumed were devoid of His presence. There was still so much learning to do.

Following the Yom Kippur service, I found myself deeply moved to correspond with Rabbi Weiss. In revealing a part of himself that I had previously been blind to, I felt an instant kinship, as if our spirits were one in spite of our differing religious and cultural backgrounds. I wrote him a long letter and cited what my experiences had meant to me. I ended by saying, "I was moved, enlightened and enriched by your sermon. I have been having some difficulty in getting Cecile and my close friends to accept my changing beliefs. Your sermon helped me realize that I must reciprocate and accept that their beliefs are just as real to them as mine are to me. This was a barrier I needed to pierce, and I am grateful to you for helping me get through it."

One night, Cecile and I went out to see Eddie Murphy's film, "Coming to America." As we approached the theater, we realized we didn't have enough cash for admission. Since we had thousands of dollars of credit available on our credit cards and would be considered prosperous by most standards, it was ironic and humorous. But it didn't seem funny at the time. Cecile's car had broken down earlier in the day, and a lot of other minor things had gone wrong. This just added to them. In spite of myself, I started to blame Cecile. She was the one who always carried extra cash for contingencies, and I had become dependent on her.

As we drove back home, and I started to get over my anger, I tried to rationalize the situation and look for some good that might come from it. When we got home, at least two people were happy about our foiled plans. Michelle and Jason asked, "What happened?" When we told them, they laughed and their looks said, "See, even mummy and daddy make silly mistakes." A little later, after we'd put them both to bed, Cecile yelled, "Dennis, 'A Leap of Faith' is on!" A made-for-TV movie about a woman who finds out she has cancer, the heroine suffers various indignities and, after she is disillusioned with traditional medicine, undergoes Dr. Bernie Siegal's alternative cancer therapy.

As I watched, I remembered the last time Cecile's car had broken down. We were on our way to Lake Tahoe. While we waited for the car to be repaired, I had watched "People Are Talking" in the customer waiting room. Dr. Bernie Siegal, author of Love, Medicine and Miracles had been the guest. Siegal had spoken about the value of grace that comes our way…how taking a leap of faith allows us to recognize there are no real failures in life—only delays and misdirections, and that the opportunities we create for ourselves are derived from the same raw materials as our so-called failures. Coincidences, he said, are God's way of remaining anonymous.[6]

Dr. Siegal ended his interview by talking of *spiritual flat tires*—events that seem to hold us up but which in truth have occurred for our benefit. He made me feel that perhaps all delays, interruptions and crises in our lives are intentional. Here, I thought, was a doctor I could relate to. From that day on I had become an admirer of Siegal and his work.

Now, on the same day that Cecile's car had broken down again, I was *coincidentally* once again watching Dr. Siegal and learning more about his inspiring methods and beliefs. And because Cecile had used up all her cash to pay for her car repairs, we didn't have enough for the theater and had come home. Now we were viewing another documentary about Dr. Siegal that was wonderfully inspiring to me.

Was there a connection between our car breaking down and my having an opportunity to watch Bernie Siegal? As I pondered these events, I smiled and thought, "Gee, God, can't you choose an easier way of communicating, than causing our cars to break down?"

My day-to-day living now seemed to go easier. I was finding love and beauty in most of the people I met. And then there was Johnny Ortega. Johnny was the kind of man who often mixed Bible quotations with sales pitches. He was the kind of man you loved to hate and hated to love, but sometimes you couldn't help yourself with either.

Socially, Johnny could be quite charming when he wasn't proselytizing. He spoke in calm, whispery tones. But doing business with him made me feel I'd be safer swimming with a barracuda. Johnny was the majority interest holder in a real estate investment in Santa Ana. Ellen Dukakis and I held the remaining shares. Initially, Johnny had set things up so that he realized an immediate $300,000 windfall when we bought it. Years later, when we were ready to close the deal, our attorney discovered at the last minute that Johnny had structured the transaction in such a way that Ellen and I would be liable for paying taxes on his windfall.

We had received a substantial offer on the sale of the apartments, and Johnny would stand to make a nice profit on his investment—a one million dollar profit. But that wasn't enough. Johnny tried to delay accepting the offer as long as he could until he could find a buyer himself, and reap a commission from the sale in addition to the million or so he would receive. Johnny was also trying to set up his own in-house mortgage brokerage company to broker the loan for an incoming buyer and so receive at least a part of the loan fee.

It didn't seem to bother Johnny that he was causing us hardship. From his perspective, he was a hard-working businessman, a decent, law-abiding, mis-understood man. Johnny was a fundamentalist. A charismatic "born again" Christian, and he proudly displayed his fish emblem on the lapel of his coat, on his business letterhead and on the magnetic business sign on the door of his car.

Johnny Ortega was one of the few persons who could make me see "red" and cause me to forget everything I had learned about tolerance and compassion. Maybe he was sent to me as a test.

By his delaying tactics, Johnny also alienated Ellen, both brokers, and a potential buyer for our apartment complex in Santa Ana.

I stayed mad until, that afternoon. we took our kids to Jason's school for the annual Argonaut School Pumpkin Walk. While there, I happened to see our neighbor, Janet Bowers, who asked if I had purchased any raffle tickets. "Why, no," I said, "I don't even know what it's for and what the prizes are."

"It's to help the school continue some special programs. As for prizes, how would you like to own that jukebox?" She pointed to a huge, commercial Wurlitzer, the old-fashioned kind, with brilliant colors swirling around in art deco style. It looked like it had come right out of the 1940s.

"Good grief, Janet, you would actually put that thing in your home?"

"You bet, Dennis! I have the perfect spot for it. John and I bought $150 worth of tickets to increase our chances."

"Well, good luck," I said, as Cecile, Jason, Michelle and I got ready to leave. On the way home, Cecile mentioned that she had bought a few tickets to help out the cause. An hour later we received a phone call from the school. We had won the Wurlitzer!

Actually, it fit very well in our family room, and all of us got a great deal of pleasure from it. Talk about a conversation piece. We also learned that it was a rarity, worth at least $10,000.

Janet had badly wanted the juke box. But we had won it. I had badly wanted to get rid of Johnny Ortega, but I couldn't. Instead, I'd won a juke box I didn't think I wanted. Was there a special message for each of us in all this?

Elizabeth Rivers once said: "When something doesn't go my way, I let go of my idea of how it should be, trusting that my mind doesn't know the larger picture."

Perhaps part of the larger picture for me was forgiveness, and winning the jukebox was God's humorous way of pushing me along. I had a sense that my conscience, in the form of a scolding Hippocrates, was about to appear. I decided I would beat him to it.

"Okay, Johnny Ortega...I...uh...I will try to forgive you."

Then I looked out the window up at the blue sky and the puffy white clouds, suspended, unmoving, and I said to the sky, aloud but softly, "Thanks for the Wurlitzer."

CHAPTER 17

Closed Minds and Open Vistas

The responsibility of tolerance lies with those who have the wider vision.
—*George Eliot*

Rabbi Nathan Weiss was full of surprises—or had I stereotyped him into a "rabbi box" which was much too small for him? While conversing with him after a presentation given by Jason's Sunday School class, we began talking about creation.

"I feel that too many of us are bound by the particular creation myth of our ancestors," I said. "It seems too static, too mechanical, too authoritarian for me."

The rabbi thought silently for a moment, then offered, "I highly recommend you read a book called *The Universe is a Green Dragon*. The author's name is Brian Swimme—here, let me write it down for you. Swimme is a physicist-cosmologist who is affiliated with a group called the ICCS (Institute in Culture and Creation Spirituality) in Oakland."

"Oh, sure," I said, "I'm familiar with their work. In fact, I recently bought a book of theirs called *Original Blessing* by Matthew Fox, the radical Dominican priest who is their founding director."

"Yes, a fine book. I've read it. In fact I followed the controversy surrounding him...how the Vatican silenced him for a year for his unorthodox teachings. I felt great sympathy and admiration for him."

Apparently, the rabbi was far more open-minded than I'd given him credit for. I had a strong urge to get to know him better, which made me feel that a deeper purpose of our relationship was yet to be disclosed. I wondered what it might be. That evening I resumed reading *Original Blessing* and came to the part where Fox calls for a transformation of religions. How can religion be an instrument for change, he asks, if religion itself resists change? He then shows that Jesus, like all prophets, taught people to heal themselves, to become *creative participants in their own salvation.* If "Jesus saves" is the only message, he says, what role is left for each of us in helping to save ourselves?

Matthew Fox's book excited me. This was the first time I had ever heard a religious authority speak to the issues that concerned me during my youth. He also looks at some of the negative contributions of St. Augustine, the emphasis that Augustine placed on "original sin" and redemption, for example. Fox says "Western civilization has preferred love of death to love of life, to the extent that its religious traditions have preferred redemption to creation, sin to ecstasy, and individual introspection to cosmic awareness and appreciation."[1]

Reflecting upon this, I read more about the life of St. Augustine of Hippo, about whom I've always been curious. He was born in the Roman city of Hippo Regius on the coast of present-day Algeria in the year 354 A.D. and died seventy-six years thereafter. He shaped the Christian church and defined much of modern Western thought as well. His advocacy of the critical spirit, intrinsic worth of the individual and the almost-infinite latent possibilities within the self exemplify the best of contemporary thought.[2]

But for all this, my namesake was also the founder and popularizer of the doctrine of original sin. He said that not only humanity but all nature is fallen. To a large extent, he was responsible for instilling in western society the monastic, anti-pleasure theme which still exerts a strong influence. St. Augustine also discredited science and helped cause the split between science and religion that lasted more than a thousand years. How ironic it was that many of the concepts I most admired as well as those I most hated about my Catholic upbringing were initiated by the individual for whom my family was named.

If one of the purposes of organized religion is to inspire and uplift mankind to a more joyous life in God, why has Christianity imbued its adherents with such pessimism? As a Catholic, I felt doomed from the start. I was somehow to blame for sins not of my doing, as well as for sins caused by natural urges and passions. It was not until reading Fox's *Original Blessing* that I discovered that the concept of original sin was on very shaky theological grounds.

While many Christian theologians have claimed that original sin has its origin in the Old Testament, contemporary scholars disagree. Elie Wiesel, the

Jewish writer/philosopher, says: "The concept of original sin is alien to the Jewish tradition."[3] Biblical scholar Herbert Haag states: "The idea that Adam's descendants are automatically sinners because of the sin of their ancestors and that they are already sinners when they enter the world is foreign to Holy Scripture."[4]

The story of the Fall, if believed as a literal fact and not a creation myth, presents the entire natural world as corrupt. I could never fathom why God would allow that to happen. It takes no great stretch of the imagination to realize that it is not God's intent but Man's ignorance and arrogance that attempts to depict the world as corrupt.

In our Western culture, children are taught that they must strive against nature and defeat it. In many Eastern cultures, on the other hand, the child sees himself and nature as one; that to be in accord with nature is a sacred act. If we see the world and all that is in it as corrupt, our acts will be based in fear and guilt, but if we see the world and ourselves as positive manifestations of God, based on acceptance, rightness, and a sense of belonging, our general outlook will be brighter and healthier.

I found places in Fox's book that resonated with the thoughts of Rabbi Weiss. For example, Fox says that Judaism does not claim to have all the answers, insisting instead on the importance of asking questions.

Fox's words also resonated in my heart. His writings offered me the avenue to pursue a deep yearning; I would seek out and embrace the universal truths embodied within the "mystical core" of all religions. It also provided me with the opening through which I could explore returning to Catholicism, should I ever wish to do so. And last, but far from least, his sense of a universal religion helped me to find a common meeting ground between my birth faith and that of my wife and children.

Later that week, Cecile and I were invited to a Halloween party, complete with ghouls, witches and even a choreographed chain saw massacre, at the large Victorian home of some friends. The last time I'd worn a costume was when I went trick-or-treating as a small boy. I later was too much a stuffed shirt to consider doing it, but I was now a "new man," and a new man could do most anything. I went as a sultan, in turban and robe, while Cecile was a Moroccan princess. At the party, in addition to Oliver North, Richard Nixon, Ronald Reagan, Manuel Noriega, Batman, and Jim and Tammy Bakker, I bumped into Cathy Proud, an ex-patient of mine and a devout Christian fundamentalist. She believed with all her heart that everyone around us, our mutual Jewish, unrepentant Catholic and Protestant friends, were going to be eternally damned if they didn't accept Jesus as their personal savior.

In contrast to Johnny Ortega, my conniving, fundamentalist real estate partner, Cathy was a trustworthy, sweet-natured woman. She'd been a pleasant patient to treat and had never proselytized to me or adorned herself with religious icons. I felt comfortable enough with her to share, in a general way, that my life had changed and brought me peace and inner contentment. I told her how this new awareness had helped me forge a closer bond with my friends and family. We must have spent an hour conversing, and I sensed we'd made a deep connection, the kind two people make when they really listen to each other and care about what the other has to say. What a wonderful experience!

A while later, Cathy's husband Steve approached me and said, "Cathy tells me you're on a spiritual quest." We started conversing, and in response to Steve's probing I talked about the works of Jung, Campbell and Fox as well as the teachings of Taoism, Buddhism and Hinduism that had supported my quest. Then Steve's voice hardened and he said, "I studied Buddhism. I thought it was the answer until I accepted Jesus Christ as my personal savior."

It went downhill from that point on. One of the distinctive features of Christian fundamentalism is that there is no room for debate, for give and take. With Steve it was all give and no take. There was not a single concept or experience of mine that Steve could accept as valid. He couldn't accept that the great spiritual leaders, including Jesus, are the messengers and not the message; nor could he accept that more than one prophet could have experienced a divine awakening; and he certainly couldn't accept that there are various life guides that appear in our lives and act as trip wires for our spiritual growth.

From Steve's viewpoint, none of the other scriptures in the world have any validity; the literal interpretation of the New Testament is the only word of God.

When I inquired what he believed Jesus had meant when he said, "In my Father's house are many mansions," Steve replied, "It means just what it says—that there are many mansions, which means that there is enough room for everyone."

"But Steve, isn't it possible that Jesus was trying to tell us there are many avenues, paths, worlds and dimensions still to be known? Couldn't he have been hinting that his illumination was a mystical state that we are all capable of entering, in varying degrees?"

"No! That's not what it says!"

Except for Johnny Ortega, I guess I had never really talked about spirituality with fundamentalists; I'd just had a vague feeling of uneasiness around them. Now I understood why. There was no room for other beliefs. If you weren't with them 100%, you were against them, and they were against you, or, even worse, pitied you for being a lost soul. If you tried to suggest that there might be other possibilities, then the devil was speaking through you, tempting you, and must not be listened to. Voltaire was right when he complained: "Opinions have caused more trouble on this Earth than all the plagues and earthquakes."

In trying to convey what we perceive as truth, our personalities, our egos, sometimes get in the way. We form an opinion, and then we're stuck with it. We feel compelled to defend it, and we may become argumentative and aggressive in the process. The ensuing argument usually has little or nothing to do with the subject being discussed. How can two people talking about the same God, arguing over metaphors, be so far apart?

How do we overcome the impasse? Perhaps by recognizing that the divine word transcends all possible explanations. As Matthew Fox says, "We need to listen to it rather than assume, arrogantly, that our puny words are the only words of God."[5]

The human word is only one of millions of words that God has spoken and that, therefore, emanates from the divine splendor. To make contact with wisdom is to go beyond human words...[6]   —*Matthew Fox*

My conversations with Cathy and Steve, while on the same subject, were as different as night and day. Cathy was understanding and interested while Steve was dogmatic, rigid and unmoved. Yet they were both fundamentalists. Could Cathy show her more sympathetic self and still remain true to her beliefs? Apparently, yes. She didn't need to agree with my ideas and beliefs, but she had listened to them. She didn't need to change her own beliefs, but she had appreciated the way I felt about mine. So two people with identical religious beliefs had reacted very differently to our conversations.

I realized then that to view Fundamentalist Christians as all the same was as illogical as viewing any religious group as an undifferentiated mass, whether or not it had become fashionable to do so.

Before the Halloween party ended, I heard a familiar voice whisper in my ear, "And what of you, Dr. A.?" Standing next to me, in the costume of a Greek nobleman, complete with fig leaf tiara around his head, was my old friend and guide. He was about a head shorter than me but something in the dignity of his stance made him seem larger. He wore a white robe with full sleeves, the cuffs embroidered with what looked like real gold. The square-cut neckline of his robe was also filigreed with gold, and his robe was held in place by a gold clasp in the physician's symbol known as a *caduceus*: two snakes entwined about a staff.

"Hippocrates! What are you doing here?"

"Why, Dr. A., it's Halloween. Hadn't you heard that all 'spirits' were invited?"

"Very funny. Listen, let me ask you a question? Can the others here see you?"

"Of course they can. Would you like to touch me to see if I'm real?" and he gave my arm a mild pinch. "As I was saying, Dr. A., what about you?"

"What do you mean? What about me?"

"I mean, how about your attitude toward fundamentalists? What virtues do you exhibit toward them? What's your tolerance level?"

"Well, not very tolerant. But how can you be tolerant of people who are so intolerant?" I asked.

"Since you've been speaking of Jesus this evening, let's use him as an example. He asked you to love your neighbor as yourself."

"Yes."

"And if you have a nice neighbor, it's easy to love him, isn't it?"

"Yes it is."

"But what if your neighbor isn't so nice? Jesus had something to say about that, too, didn't he?"

"Yes. When confronting our adversaries, he said to turn the other cheek."

"An adequate paraphrase, perhaps, but if I might be permitted to quote: 'Whosoever shall smite thee on thy right cheek, turn to him the other also.' Matthew, Chapter V, Line 29, I believe."

Hippocrates' smugness was both irritating and humorous at the same time. He look so pleased with himself, I didn't know whether to laugh or say something sarcastic.

"Not impressed, Dr. A.? You try quoting from a book that won't be written until hundreds of years after you die! Anyway, we were talking about turning a cheek. It's not easy, is it, to offer your other cheek to your adversary? And what of tolerance and intolerance? It's not so easy to be tolerant of intolerance."

"No, I suppose not, Hippocrates."

"Then your friend, Steve, is a blessing to you, is he not?"

"How do you mean?"

"Because he is allowing you to practice being tolerant of intolerance. This is soul school, my friend. This is how we get to rehearse the virtues we find most difficult to apply."

"Yeah, but this guy thinks he has all the answers."

"A wise man is not fooled by answers, and a fool is not wise for having them," Hippocrates said with a wink.

"But—"

"Oh, excuse me, Dr. A., I believe I see him coming this way."

"Wait, Hippocrates, I want Cecile to meet you."

"Sorry, but that won't happen."

"Why not?"

"Because I've already read the play, and it's not in the script."

I wanted some more answers from Hippocrates, but just then Cathy and Steve approached to say "good night." I shook hands with them both and told Cathy how much I enjoyed talking with her. Then I turned to Steve, looked him straight in the eye and said, softly enough for only him to hear, "For all that I received from Cathy this evening, I received more from you. Thank you, Steve."

Hippocrates was right. Although he hadn't realized it, Steve had done more than just give me practice in being tolerant. He had reminded me that one of the blessings of the path I had taken was that my path, however, imperfect or incomplete, at least had room for other people from all walks of life; that my system of beliefs not only permitted, but sought dialogue with a great diversity and richness of views. In the end, I felt great empathy for fundamentalists who had forsworn so many wonders of creation and in many ways isolated themselves from the rest of the human race by insisting on being the sole interpreters of divine revelation.

I devoured *The Universe is a Green Dragon,* the book Rabbi Weiss had recommended to me, in three days. The author, Brian Swimme calls the universe "green" because it is so alive. "Dragons," in the traditions of Asia, are a metaphorical reference to the power and mystery within the universe which teaches us how to find the "deepest reaches of wisdom."

In one spirited exchange, theologian Thomas Berry tells Swimme, "You scientists have this stupendous story of the universe. It breaks outside all previous cosmologies. But so long as you persist in understanding it solely from a quantitative mode, you fail to appreciate its significance—you fail to hear the music. That's what the spiritual traditions can provide. Tell the story, but tell it with a feel for its music."[7]

And tell it he does, communicating his ideas with wisdom and passion in the form of classical dialogue. Swimme says: "Cosmic allurement is the bond of all matter, the dynamic principle that fuses the material plane, and we humans experience that force as love."[8] He goes on to say, "It is this same (my emphasis) allurement that excites lovers into chasing each other through the night, that pulls the parent out of bed for the third time to comfort a sick child, that draws humans into lifetimes of learning and developing. The excitement in our hand as it tears open a letter from a friend is the same dynamism that spins our vast Earth through the black night into the rosy colors of dawn."[9]

A gifted cosmologist, Swimme made me feel and understand how each of us plays a part through our creativity and love in "penetrating the planet," if we pursue our lives "with the same extravagant devotion of the stars to their own destiny."

He tells us we are not pawns of a God "out there" who is directing traffic. We are the personification of an energy that, collectively, is part of a grand unified energy (divine force) in the same way that the individual notes of musicians come together to create a magnificent symphony.

I felt invigorated and fully alive after reading Swimme's and Fox's books. And I was pleased to learn that these two enlightened individuals who had given me so much had been able to form a powerful, creative alliance. That alliance has taken a giant step forward in bringing religion and science closer together.

In early civilizations, science and religion were on the same team, working together to create an ever more satisfying cosmic myth. In our present age, while science has become the ascendant (and often arrogant) power, religion has become elitist and defensive. But haven't both science and religion become too narrowly conceived? Where is the compassion, the tolerant, open view with which each can admit to the wisdom in the other?

These two groups (sophisticated theologians and sophisticated scientists) seem to be coming closer and closer together in their conception of the universe as "organismic," as having some kind of unity and integration, as growing and evolving and having direction and therefore having some kind of "meaning." Whether or not to call this integration "God" finally gets to be an arbitrary decision and not a personal indulgence determined by one's personal history, one's personal revelations, and one's personal myths.[10] —*Abraham Maslow*

If Maslow was right, a new age is coming, where each person will be encouraged to develop his own, unique beliefs. Can we trust our children enough to allow them to decide these things for themselves or will we continue to force-feed them our beliefs? Can we resist the temptation to tell them and others what we believe is "right?"

Within a few days, due to the God of Good Fortune, I got word of another offer to buy our apartment complex. For some reason, Johnny Ortega had agreed to the sale. Not only that, my attorney was able to negotiate a buyout of Johnny's share in an apartment house I owned in San Jose. In one masterful stroke, I was free of any business entanglements with him. What a relief!

What had caused him to reverse his obstructive behavior? Maybe my practicing being more tolerant of intolerance had something to do with it. Maybe, when I stopped putting up so much resistance to intolerance, the entanglements went away by themselves. I would have to remember to thank Hippocrates for assisting me in that one.

Or perhaps it was thanks enough for Hippocrates to know that I was "doing the work," and that I was now coming around to understanding his own beliefs. I was struck by the timeless sentiments which he had set down in his *De Alimento* two and a half centuries before Christ's birth. In it, Hippocrates had written:

> There is one common flow, one common breathing, all things are in sympathy. The whole organism and each one of its parts are working in conjunction for the same purpose.[11]

In my imagination, I could hear him quoting himself, with great pleasure.

> The most savage controversies are those about matters as to which there
> is no good evidence either way. —*Bertrand Russell*

The lead article in the San Jose Mercury News of November 16, 1988 read:

Priest Meets Death Helping Others:
Santa Clara Priest Slain in the Netherlands.

The victim was Father Lewis Diaz, a former patient who had spent the past three years studying parapsychology at the University of Holland. Killed by a deranged student he'd been counseling.

I was curious about how this warm and loving person had met with such a tragic end. Lewis had been planning to return to Brazil, where he had spent six years of his life helping to run a community clinic for medical and social services. His sister, Mary Roy (who had also been a patient of mine) was quoted describing a postcard Lewis had recently sent to his family. On one side, there was a beautiful peacock; on the other, Lewis had written, "We must be like the peacocks and allow our inner beauty to come out, to enjoy and be grateful." According to the article, Lewis had befriended and was counseling a troubled young student who acted menacing at times. One day the student invited Lewis to go on a walk in a forest preserve, and there he fatally shot him in the head and chest.

After he was captured, the young man said he'd killed Father Diaz because the priest was trying to destroy him, telepathically. After reading this, I shared the family's grief, and it felt as though a close and dear friend had died. During the brief time Lewis was in my clinic, he talked about the missionary work he had been doing in Brazil before he left to continue his postgraduate studies. He told me he'd been helping some poor, uneducated natives overcome their fear of oppressive superstitions that were enslaving them and causing them grief.

At the time, I was ambivalent about religion and tended to oversimplify and overgeneralize. I saw missionaries as merely exchanging one form of enslavement for another. Richard Bach, in one of his books, had spoken for me when he said, "Whoever robs a man in order to rule him is not fit to be his ruler."

Reading about Father Diaz, I realized that he had dedicated himself to helping others in the true Christian sense. He was no pampered, arm-chair priest, but a well-educated Jesuit who spoke seven languages and was always available for support and encouragement—in the most hopeless of circumstances and in the most distant of places—wherever he was needed. I felt guilty about how I had spent almost my whole life making snap judgments and stereotyping people.

As a memorial to Father Diaz, I vowed to try my best to stop, and I promised myself that I would visit with his sister Mary as soon as I could, and offer my condolences. Some family photos I'd recently received were connected with my strong reaction to Father Diaz' death. My sister Josephine had sent me some old, black-and-white photographs of my father in a priest's robe and collar. Dad had been initiated into the Catholic priesthood, briefly, during his young adulthood. When I looked at the photos, I realized that my father's young features were a spitting image of my own. I was sure there was some connection between the photos and Father Diaz's death.

Why had that death affected me so deeply? And why did I frame the photos of Dad in his Catholic vestments and display them prominently on my desk, when I had spent most of my life running away from my birth faith? In my mind, I called for Hippocrates to answer these questions for me, but there was no sign of him. Why was it that when I wanted a question answered, I had to wait and uncover it on my own? When I was sure of myself or otherwise uninterested in receiving advice, it was almost certain to come.

This held true for other aspects of my life. For example, now that I had ceased worrying about it, money seemed to come almost out of nowhere. A few days after mourning the death of Father Diaz, we received a whopping check from the IRS for more than one hundred thousand dollars, covering some of my past investment losses. It produced a strange mix of feelings, thinking about the tragic murder and accepting our good fortune at the same time.

There was a universal principle behind all this, a majestic force operating so complex a matrix of causes, reasons and events that I could not possibly fathom, pass judgment on, or control any one of them.

That evening, as I tucked Jason into bed, he asked, "Dad, who is God? Where does he live?" At moments like these, parents think: "Careful, careful, don't 'blow' this. The kid will be traumatized if I say the wrong thing! If I say that God is a Catholic, or a Protestant, or a Zoroastrian, my kid will believe that for the rest of his life. What a responsibility!"

Most kids probably forget the whole thing inside of thirty seconds.

Anyway, I said, "God is not really a person. He's an invisible energy force, a force so powerful it can be everywhere at the same time. It's as much inside of us as outside of us." As soon as I had said this, I realized I was trying to put the words of a thirty-eight-year-old into the mind of an eight-year-old. I wondered, was that any better or worse than filling him full of the typical

Hollywood image of a personal God who speaks in electronically-extended, deep bass tones?

I hastened to add, "God is the invisible force that gives life and helps everyone to love everyone else." The important thing was for him to feel that God is something good, and not something to be afraid of. Jason's innocent smile told me that, on some level, he had gotten it. After all, a child is closer to the source of his soul than most adults. As I stroked his brow, I thought how we all lose that closeness. Perhaps we need to lose it before we can truly find it.

Jason's last question was, "Why does God care, Dad?" I thought for a moment, then said, "It's built in. God can't help caring anymore than Mummy and I can't help loving you." Then I kissed him goodnight.

How simple Jason's questions had been—I had tried to keep my answers equally simple. Well, there would be lots of other times to do it. Meanwhile, Jason was fast asleep with a peaceful look on his face. That was enough for now.

Another article in the San Jose Mercury-News caught my eye when I noticed Rabbi Weiss's name mentioned. A controversy between the Orthodox rabbis in Israel and the non-Orthodox rabbis in the United States had erupted, with the Orthodox rabbis claiming exclusive rights to convert non-Jews to Judaism. The effect of this battle had profound social effects in Israel, because it could determine citizenship or lack of it; it could split families apart and affect the right to social services and voting. From my perspective, it seemed little different from the street skirmishes of my youth, the controversies in medicine and the long-standing dispute I had seen between the Papal orthodoxy and American Catholic priests. Pure and simple, it was turf war.

No wonder so many people become frustrated and either leave the religion they were brought up in or remain out of fear and come to distrust their own direct experiences and intuition. When I was a boy, I was given my own Missal, but I was never even shown a copy of the Bible. This was to prevent me from getting the notion that I could interpret God's words myself, for this would weaken the monopoly that Catholic priests hold as necessary intermediaries between God and sinners.

The Catholic Church, like most Western religious institutions, discounts the validity of personal experience in religious matters. The church claims that personal experience may be false or even deviltry meant to mislead us. Personal experiences, therefore, can only be sanctioned and validated by the church. In turn, the persons who constitute the church hierarchy are the only ones sufficiently wise to tell which experiences are false and which are true. But isn't individual truth really a nontransferable ticket that bears only one name?

What difference does it really make if an Orthodox or non-Orthodox rabbi presides over your conversion? What real difference does it make if a man or woman celebrates a Mass? Why should we care if members of the clergy are straight or gay? Surely God has enough room for as many expressions of appreciation, tribute and love as the human imagination can create. (But, on the other hand, there's Tevya pointing his finger skyward and shouting, "Tradition! We do it this way because…because this is the way we've always done it!")

Zeal and fanaticism have turned religious theories and doctrines into a vicious personal battleground. All Western religions preach humility but do not practice it when it comes to their own particular doctrine. Eastern religions, at least some of them, do not claim to be sole custodians of the truth. On the contrary, they welcome other views, other gods as a beneficial addition.

Trouble intensifies when a religion has an exclusivity clause. This happened among the Israelites when Jehovah said, "Thou shalt have no other God before me!" Prior to that, the gods were jealous of each other, but none of them claimed to want it all, to be the only God. When the Israelites began to worship Jehovah, The One God, that was the end of divine humility.

Christianity, Judaism's stepchild, continued the exclusive tradition with Jesus as not just a son of God, but the *only* Son of God. Islam, followed with Allah, the one and *only* true God. And the need for divine monopoly has since been bathed in bloodshed and cloaked in terror.

Somehow, along the way, our religious leaders forgot the universal source, the unknown reality, from which all religions spring.

At the same time, in confronting these contradictions, wisdom surrounded me wherever I looked.

I no longer ask the young man's question, "How far will I go?" My questions now are those of the mature person, "When it is over, what will my life have been about?"[12]   —*Rabbi Harold Kushner*

Life is a meeting. We come alive only when we relate to others. Secondly, we are here to change the world with small acts of thoughtfulness done daily rather than with one great breakthrough. Finally, we are here to

finish God's labors. One of the sages of the Talmud taught nearly two thousand years ago that God could have created a plant that would grow loaves of bread. Instead he created wheat for us to mill and bake into bread. Why? So that we could be his partners in completing the work of creation.[13]
—*Martin Buber*

One of the most beautiful works of creation is Hawaii, nature's loving reminder of how paradise can emerge from chaos. In December, Cecile and I took our first vacation alone in seven years. When we arrived, we found that our accommodations were surrounded by a tropical bird sanctuary, and the decor motif was Buddhist. Dozens of impressive Buddha statues were interspersed with statues of Bodhisattvas, enlightened human beings who have come back to earth for the sole purpose of helping others attain that exalted state.

A multitude of birds seemed to be enjoying Buddha consciousness as they perched on the statues, chirping and whistling happily. It was wonderfully peaceful and very conducive to reading, which I did.

One of the books I'd been reading was *God and the New Physics,* by Paul Davies. The new physics cosmology was much more interesting and exciting than the mathematics-based physics I'd struggled through in school, particularly in the ramifications of quantum theory. Quantum theory suggests, among other things, that at every instant the world as we know it splits off into an infinite number of parallel universes. It suggests that every decision, every choice that could have been made and every action made on the basis of those choices, have actually occurred in alternate worlds. This leads to the supposition that different pasts and futures exist. In *God and the New Physics,* Davies asserts that, from the standpoint of quantum theory, although these myriad alternate universes exist in close parallel to our own, they are not accessible to each other.

Are alternate universes ever accessible to each other? This question made me think about my own out-of-body experiences. During those moments, had I been in an alternate universe, or just in a different location in our old, familiar one?

While enjoying a delicious luncheon at our resort, we met Sharon and Vito Borelli, a charming and friendly Italian-Jewish couple who bore an eerie likeness to Cecile and me. They had our dark brown eyes and hair coloring; we were of approximately equal height and weight; we had similar mannerisms of speech.

"You two look so familiar!" they said

"We were just saying the same thing about you guys," I responded.

Further conversation revealed that they, too, lived near San Jose area and had almost bought the house next to one we'd lived in. Sharon who was approaching forty, was our age, while Vito had just turned fifty. They both lived fast-paced, stressful lives and hardly saw each other. This vacation was an attempt to rekindle the romantic flames that had gone unkindled for so long.

"Do you have any children?" Cecile asked.

"No! We're Dinks—double income, no kids," said Vito.

"How about you and Dennis?" asked Sharon, "Do you have any children?"

"Yes! we have two—a little girl named Michelle and our oldest boy, Jason."

As Cecile and I went on and on about our kids, we noticed a hint of melancholy in Sharon's voice as she said, "I'd like to have children. My career in merchandising has been real good to me, but I'm ready to slow down a bit and be a mom. But Vito doesn't want kids. He's afraid we'll lose our freedom."

"You know Vito," I offered, "I had the same fears. I always thought that there was this grand conspiracy out there by those who had children to convince those who didn't that they should—misery loving company and all that. But somehow you overcome those fears and make it work. Our kids really do bring us a lot of joy. We can't imagine life without them."

"Well," Vito responded, "my main priority is building this cable-TV business I own. I have high expectations for the company. It's my brain-child. I work late, and at fifty I'm just not sure I'm capable of being a good care-giver."

I could hear Sharon sigh at that one. For all their success, the loneliness and emptiness in their lives was plain to see. The freedom of not having children, which I had once embraced, now seemed shallow and barren. I got to see what I would be like at fifty had I stayed on the track of just pursuing financial interests.

I believe Vito got something out of our conversation, too. Probably, it was something he had been feeling for a long time but had been unwilling to acknowledge. As we talked, I could see his attitude change to the point where he understood that having children is not so much an obligation as a privilege, and a way of seeing the world through a child's eyes again.

Later that day on the beach, we watched in horror as an overbearing mother told one of her darling little girls that she was "bad! bad! bad!" for committing a minor infraction to be expected of a child that age. Was the mother having a bad day? Had we ever been so insensitive?

"Cecile, are you feeling what I'm feeling?" I whispered.

"What do you mean?"

"Think about our meeting Sharon and Vito, about the insensitive mother yelling at her helpless child, and just look around. Listen to the conversations. Do you feel what's happening?"

For the longest time, Cecile listened and stared, then she said, "It's like we're tuned into everybody...like we know these people."

"That's right!" I said excitedly. It was a joy to feel a deep experience of interconnectedness with new acquaintances and to be able to share it with the one I loved.

To our right were young, doting lovers, oblivious to everything around them but one another. Those awkward, painful years of courtship from our own lives pulsated a wave of instant understanding. To our left, a young bronzed couple in their late twenties shared a blanket with some friends and were telling them that, after three years of living together, they'd finally tied the knot and were planning to move to California.

Behind us, a recently remarried, white-haired couple—he, a former physician; she, a retired school teacher—were confiding to their friends that they regretted not having children along the way. The friends had three grown children and were enjoying all the richness that comes with having a family.

It was clear that, for our path at least, children were an integral part of our growth and maturity. "Isn't it interesting," I said to Cecile, "to see how other people have done it?"

"Yes, it's like we're watching a home movie of our life as it was, and as it could have been," Cecile said.

It was warm and comforting to know we did the best we could, however confusing it might have seemed at the time. My thoughts went deeper, to the idea of predestination. *Does this means that destiny can't be predetermined?* I wondered. *Does anyone—anything—decide our fate? Don't we each make our own choices, every moment of our lives? Taken together, these millions of choices bring us to our Now.*

As if reading my mind, Cecile asked, "Where do you think we'll go in the future?"

"It depends on the choices we make, moment to moment, from this point on," I offered. "I think our thoughts are constrained by habits of the past—but not totally so. They're like old cobwebs; we can wipe them away to see our path more clearly. I'm convinced the future is open-ended."

Scattered thoughts from my memory banks were flooding my consciousness. I was still caught up in the powerful feeling of connectedness—a mysterious link to everyone I had ever known. Hippocrates had once told me that it's hard to pass judgment when it's really ourselves in the spotlight. At the time, I hadn't understood what he meant. Now I knew that the real reason that judging is fruitless is because we are all quite literally the same; the same things motivate us and we all strive, in different, indirect ways, to reach the same goals.

According to Richard Bach, "...Sometimes it seems like...everybody is an aspect of everybody else because consciousness is one."[14]

I once heard President Bush speak of space exploration as the "last, great frontier." But if we think of a frontier as a barely charted region whose conquest demands daring, skill, imagination, courage, and all the mental skills we possess; and if we think of a frontier as a place where boundaries seem infinitely extendable, then the exploration of inner space is truly the last, great frontier.

The next book I read was Synchronicity, by F. David Peat,[15] which deals with the investigation and tracking of meaningful coincidences, something I'd been doing informally for years. Building on Jung's ideas on the subject, Peat believes synchronicity is the point where the objective world of physics meets the interior world of mind and psyche. Peat in turn introduced me to the ideas of Austrian biologist Paul Kammerer. At the turn of the last century, Kammerer collected examples of coincidence and the unexplained clustering of events. From this, he speculated on the existence of an underlying mosaic of nature (what I call the Universal Spiritual Matrix). Kammerer called these underlying patterns "the umbilical cord that connects thought, feeling, science and art with the womb of the universe which gave birth to them."[16] In commenting on Kammerer's work, Albert Einstein called his ideas "original and by no means absurd."[17] I was in good company.

It's very gratifying when your experiences and ideas parallel those of a great historical figure. That's how I felt when I read that Jung conversed with inner wisdom figures which he claimed were independent of himself (Jung related them to Philemon, who in the New Testament was the recipient of St. Paul's epistle; and Inima, who was the spiritual guide of Laotse, the Chinese founder of the Tao. I, of course, had Hippocrates).

What also struck me was that Jung's experience with wisdom guides occurred during his mental breakdown, as mine had begun after my mental burnout. One thing kept leading to another. In *Synchronicity*, Peat refers to the work Jung wrote as a result of his conversations with his wisdom guides, called *Seven Sermons to the Dead*. Jung wrote this in the style of a prophet speaking to his people, and presented a cosmology that integrated mind and matter. In *Seven Sermons*, Jung states that the world of created things emerges from the undifferentiated background and that the created world is not mad and senseless (as he once thought) but highly structured and reasoned.

In conjunction with this, I thought about the occurrence of synchronicities, or meaningful coincidences. I saw them as an overcast sky momentarily parting to let individual rays of the sun through. Synchronicities, then, are merely aspects of the vast interconnected web that we do not normally see; and if we could part the clouds of our psyche, we would see the Universal Spiritual Matrix, the entire universe of interconnections in all its splendor. *Wow!*

Meanwhile, my days were settling down to a regular routine. I took Michelle to her mini-gym classes; I exercised at my health club; wrote for three to four hours every other day; saw patients on a part time basis; and resisted all situations that posed a threat to my serenity.

When my old friend and colleague, Dr. Gary Wyatt, phoned to ask me to lecture the Affiliated Podiatrists of California, all expenses paid, and a fair amount of publicity to boot, I turned him down. They needed a name to pack in the participants. In past years, I'd accepted every speaking engagement, every innovation, every bit of publicity that might help me get to the top. "I'm no longer lecturing on foot surgery," I said.

The more I said "no," the better I liked it. It felt like power, the power of choosing had been restored to me. This ruthless guarding of my serenity had become my top priority. It meant saying "no" to people who either made demands on my time or who invited my participation in something whose potential included emotional and/or financial entanglement.

My life was now quite simple. My priorities were to spend time with my family, learn more, continue to be wholly contained and established within myself, and write my book. These changes in my life style also affected everyone around me. One Sunday morning in February, Jeremy Perlman and I drove to my office to pick up a patient's preoperative X-rays. Jeremy would be performing surgery the next morning on this patient, on behalf of my clinic.

During the ride, Jeremy mentioned that we hadn't been seeing much of each other lately. "You seem inaccessible these days," I replied.

"I apologize, Dennis. Jody has been remiss in keeping up our social calendar."

"Come on, Jeremy, this is me you're talking to. It feels like Jody has been going out of her way to avoid us for some reason."

Jeremy let out a big sigh, then started to come clean. "Well, first, Jody and I have been having some problems between us. And second, Jody sees the way you've been changing, your new life style and all that…she sees that as a threat to us; she thinks you've become a bad influence on me."

"Me a bad influence? God forbid, Jeremy, that you might work a bit less, slow down a bit and enjoy your life more!" I couldn't keep some of the sarcasm out of my voice.

"I know, I know, but Jody keeps pushing to buy the larger house. And me? I'm thinking of going to law school, which would cut down on our income for quite a while. I guess Jody blames you for influencing me."

"So I'm the fall guy because I've influenced you to go in the wrong direction?"

"Something like that, Dennis."

"But I don't get it, Jeremy. Jody's been so interested in these things I've been going through. She's read all the books I recommended, and she loved them. In fact, Jody's the one who's always talking about simplifying her life, about moving to an idyllic farm in Maine or Vermont."

Jeremy shrugged to show he had no real explanation, and we drove on. It hardly seemed real. Jody and I had been so close for so long, and had done things together, just the two of us. Like sharing that glorious ride in the hot air balloon. We'd had many long talks about life, our children, and every other subject. Was it that I was a friend only so long as I was anxiously striving to climb higher and higher on the financial ladder? Now that my financial ship was in dry dock, no longer searching for treasure, I was a threat to my dear friend's standard of living? Apparently so.

This revelation had a strong impact on me. What did it say about the positive influence of my spiritual growth on others around me? If I was indeed becoming more loving, couldn't I expect it to be reciprocated? Or did it mean that the more I developed relative to my friends, the more of a pariah I would become? It seemed the very growth that had allowed me to feel closer to people was pushing me away from them.

"Hippocrates," I thought, "I've found another paradox. How come I get pushed away from others just when I'm feeling closer?"

There was a soft stirring of the air around me, and then I heard—inside of me—his familiar voice. "Tell me, Dr. A., do you count your former medical adversaries as Life Guides?"

"Well, in the sense that they forced me to grow, yes—certainly."

"And while they were guiding you, did you grow closer to them?"

"No, I wanted to be as far away from them as possible."

"They made it uncomfortable for you, didn't they?"

"Yes, of course."

"Very well, now do you understand about your friend?"

"You mean that I—my spiritual growth—is making it uncomfortable for her right now?"

"Precisely, Dr. A."

"And that's okay…it's what needs to happen now."

"You're getting the picture."

"And what matters…to me…is that *I* feel closer, that *I* feel more and more loving. And the rest…is up to…God."

I paused to let my own thought sink in. After a short while, Hippocrates said, "Good bye for now, Dr. A."

"Good bye, Hippocrates." There was nothing more I needed to say.

CHAPTER 18

Kindred Spirits

> Science without religion is blind, and religion without science is lame.
> —*Albert Einstein*

On a Saturday afternoon in February of 1988 I began reading *Uncommon Wisdom—Conversations with Remarkable People,* by physicist Fritjof Capra. The book was, in part, a tribute to the insights of some of the influential leaders of our time. But for me its special value had to do with Capra's own intellectual and spiritual odyssey, and how the discussions he'd had with great thinkers had pushed forward his own development. I hadn't had the opportunity to speak directly with very many intellectual and spiritual leaders, but I was doing much the same thing by reading their works.

And yet, I felt stuck. In spite of my best efforts, my writing had slowed to a plod, and familiar demons of doubt and insecurity had fallen upon me once again: I was wasting away my life; I had foolishly given up the chance to further my professional career by renouncing it; my writing amounted to nothing! My attitude was further darkened by the conviction that I should be beyond such feelings; if I was mired within them, did that mean I'd made no progress at all? Dammit! Why did my confidence and inner knowing come and go so wantonly? Why does certainty falter and reveal our ignorance again?

But then I got to this place in Capra's book:

> I was sitting by the ocean one late summer afternoon, watching the waves rolling in and feeling the rhythm of my breathing, when I suddenly became aware of my whole environment as being engaged in a giant cosmic dance. Being a physicist, I knew that the sand, rocks, water and

255

air around me were made of vibrating molecules and atoms, and that these consist of particles which interacted with one another by creating and destroying other particles.

I knew that the earth's atmosphere was continually bombarded by showers of "cosmic rays," particles of high energy undergoing multiple collisions as they penetrated the air. All this was familiar to me from my research in high-energy physics, but until that moment I had only experienced it through graphs, diagrams and mathematical theories.

As I sat on that beach my former experiences came to life; I "saw" cascades of energy coming down from outer space, in which particles were created and destroyed in rhythmic pulses; I "saw" the atoms of the elements and those in my body participating in this cosmic dance of energy; I felt its rhythm and I "heard" its sound, and at that moment I knew that this was the dance of Shiva, the Lord of Dances, worshipped by the Hindus.[1]

And my mood changed instantly. I suddenly realized that it's not our inner knowing that comes and goes—it's our awareness of its presence that flickers on and off. What we usually see day-to-day is in fact our own personal consciousness. When that's elevated, my, how the mental landscape changes for the better.

Here was the harmonious blending of science and religion I had been seeking for so long. A physicist, using scientific terms to describe his own spiritual peak experience and equating particle physics with religious doctrine. And I, too had experienced the energy of the cosmos; I, too, had felt the "Dance of Shiva." Part of the underlying invisible "reality" I had so often read about and which I had experienced myself had been eloquently confirmed—by a prominent scientist. I felt as if I had suddenly acquired another close friend in Fritjof Capra; another life guide who was trying to describe the ineffable, the pursuit of which has connected truth seekers throughout the millennia.

The visions that Capra and others have described belong to everyone and appear in different ways to thousands, perhaps millions of people around the world. The visions born within us announce themselves to all cultures, all religious traditions, in dreams of ordinary people, artists and clergymen. Everyone is a mystic at heart.

While watching the waves along the shore, Capra recognized with absolute certainty the parallels between science and Eastern mysticism. He revealed this in The Tao of Physics. It took considerable courage for him to do so, for by committing himself to validating mysticism, he placed his own career at great risk.

I, too, had (finally) followed the call. One difference, however, was that Capra was able to integrate his interest in mysticism with his career as a physicist. I, on the other hand, had chosen to give up my career as a surgeon completely. My desire to write was now so strong it overwhelmed all other considerations.

I had been pushed off another plateau. I awoke next morning feeling happier and healthier than ever. That day, words flowed endlessly from me onto paper, but even as I felt once again a part of the flow, I knew that I could not control or sustain these periods of affirmation any more than I could control the ebb and flow of the ocean.

I saw that the latest plateau where I had been stuck was merely one of a long series of plateaus that I had experienced over the years. They were characterized by a long stretch of concerted effort with no discernible progress. Then, finally, after my emotions had been dragged down into the pits, the plateaus would end and be followed by a spurt of accelerated growth. It struck me that we spend a good part of our lives on plateaus, trying to pull free of their grip, desperate to get on to the next positive level of development. This need for control is pervasive. When we cannot, we turn to…what? Unhealthy diets? Overwork? Drugs? Alcohol? Exploitive relationships? Religion? But we never seem to learn that the plateaus are a necessary part of the equation; they are a time of poised stillness which rids us of what is no longer necessary and recharges our batteries and readies us for the inevitable next step. Progress never moves in a straight line. It's a spiral pathway, now going, now returning, holding on and letting go, winning and losing, giving and receiving. Even Shiva's dance of creation is at once a dance of destruction.

Our mental habits and reactions are so ingrained, so stubborn and resistant to unwanted change that knowledge must strike us a hundred times before it dents our defenses. Yet, the spiral of life is such that we return again and again to the same situation, seeing it slightly altered each time until, finally, we grasp its full meaning.

I was long familiar with the concept of accepting the bad with the good. But now, finally, hopefully, it had made a real dent—not in my understanding—but in my ability to really accept life as it is. I vowed to try, as best I could, to experience plateaus, stoppages and reversals for what they really were, and not to wallow in self-pity and doubt. I vowed to try to treat my future plateaus with alertness, and, through my accepting attitude, make myself as ready as possible for the next quantum leap ahead.

Through all these experiences and changes, I somehow had an innate sense of the worth of what I was doing. Sometimes, the simplest things seemed to me the most profound. Not to my acquaintances, however, and I found I was gaining the reputation of having my head in the clouds, of losing my ability to be realistic, to be practical.

One day I spent an hour talking to our gardener, listening to his views on the drought resistance and hardiness of certain plants; how one plant can affect others around it, and how he was going about accomplishing our landscaping goals. His sincerity, confidence and the pleasure he obviously took in supporting the living things he had planted all had an inspiring effect. As they say in est, I "got" it.

All of a sudden I felt what he felt; I was a partner in creating a living system of beauty. Each day my love for the landscape deepened. I felt the glowing abundance of energy flowing through the thousands of green leaves. I understood what the plants wanted, and how they would grow for us if we only attended to their simple needs. In it's own way, it was as profound an experience of being connected as any other I encountered. It may not have been productive by society's measure, but nevertheless it had great value.

"I have sat many hours on the steps of my house, and while I whittled I tasted nature and felt her throb of life. Yet the strangers walking by felt me lazy."[2]
                                                                Chief Dan George

How sad that spending time like this, in what I call solitary refinement, is thought in our society to be idle and wasteful. In her book, *Meaningful Living in the Mature Years,* Charlotte Buhler says:

> The deeper reason for people's disinclination toward leading a contemplative existence lies, however, in the fact that action ranks so high in the value system of our culture that contemplation, like all other forms of passive participation, is apt to be little appreciated.[3]

In addition to working on my book, I was making more or less regular entries into my journal. A journal, to my understanding, is not the same as a diary. A diary is a record of the events that happen to us each day. A journal, on the other hand, is an expanded record of thoughts, feelings or events that we deem particularly significant. Whatever the distinction, I sometimes wondered if it was worth the effort.

During one of these bouts of gnawing indecision, the universe conveniently came to my assistance in the form of Dr. Ira Progroff's Life Context Workshop, which utilized an Intensive Journal® method to promote personal growth. The program was sponsored by Cecile's temple, and Rabbi Weiss had organized it.

The program was curiously tailor-made to fit my needs:

> Through this workshop you're peeking into experiences that make it possible to see your whole life in nonjudgmental perspective. It helps answer the question, "What is my life trying to become?" and makes it possible to progressively restructure your life goals at your own tempo and on your own terms. Intensive Journal work has served as a modern approach to spirituality without dogma.

That bait was powerful. *What my life is trying to become...restructuring life goals at my own tempo, on my own terms...spirituality without dogma.* What intrigued me further was that the person conducting the course was Father Fran Dorff, the author of *The Art of Passingover,* which I had so enjoyed. I had to take the course. It not only fit like a glove—it was as though an unseen force was guiding my hand into that glove.

With his great breadth of knowledge and openness, Father Dorff, was a far cry from the priests I had known as a boy. After the first meeting had ended, I introduced myself to Father Dorff. He was of medium height and build, with sandy blonde hair and blue eyes filled with serenity. When he looked at me, his gaze invited closeness and suggested mutual understanding.

I told him I was writing an autobiographical book with spiritual overtones. "I feel compelled to write it," I said, "but I also feel I'm too young to write an autobiography."

"You know," Father Dorff said in a hushed and gentle manner reminiscent of the confessional, "your namesake, St. Augustine, wrote his famous *Confessions* early in his life, and the Trappist theologian, Thomas Merton, wrote his autobiography, *The Seven Storey Mountain,* in 1948 when he was only thirty-three.

"But I'm neither a saint nor a monk," I said.

"True, Dr. Augustine, but Merton was the first to admit that his vocation did not make him special and separate from the human race. He knew that the stories we tell about our lives are the very lifeblood of the religious experience. God is the ultimate story—and the life story of God is that human beings have lived. Elie Wiesel says, 'God made man because he loves stories.' If Wiesel is right, and I believe that he is, then one's spiritual autobiography is a point of contact with God. Merton realized that we can never know what the result of one's work will be until we take up the 'call' to find our true identity."

Then Father Dorff asked me about my life, and I described what had been happening as briefly as I could.

"But of course," Father Dorff said, "you're at a transition point. Your life as you have known it has come to an end."

What Father Dorff was referring to when he said my life had come to an end may best be illustrated by quoting Thomas Merton: In 1953, at the age of thirty-eight, he wrote, "It is some time in June. At a rough guess, it is June 13th which may or may not be the feast of St. Anthony of Padua. In any case, every day is the same for me because I have become very different from what I used to be. The man who began this journal is dead, just as the man who finished *The Seven Storey Mountain* is also dead; and what is more, the man who was the central figure in *The Seven Storey Mountain* is dead…"[4]

In the Life Context Workshop we were encouraged to share our journal writing with the group. I screwed up my courage one day and read something about my childhood experience with the Catholic church. I aimed it all at Father Dorff.

> Everything was rules, rules, sins and punishment! Give in to God's will! Stop being obstinate, you bad boy! Do this, do that! You're not worthy! God will punish you for that! When you're damned to Hell for all eternity, what will you do then, you wicked child?
>
> Did God tell you to hurt children who don't stand straight in line? Did God order you to hurt children who talk when they aren't supposed to? Did God tell you to embarrass us, to humiliate us and to hit us with rulers and umbrellas and whatever else is handy? Did God tell you to hurt children at all? Did He? Did He?
>
> Damn it, damn it! What did you want from me? I was a kid, a child! Why couldn't you leave me my childhood? You had to take all the fun away, all the pleasure, all the joy from life. And you weren't satisfied unless you had us crawling on the ground, bowing and cowering—not to God, but to you, goddammit! To you! What gall you have! What unmitigated gall, to treat people this way.
>
> And where was God in all this? How should I know? You drove Him away from me. You made me hate Him and hate his church and everything about it! And you didn't do it for God. Oh no, you didn't. You did it because you, yourself, aren't filled with God, you're filled with anger and hatred. You're filled with guilt about your lives, and you think that maybe you can get rid of it if you make others feel guilty, too.
>
> You look so pious, you walk so piously, with your hands carefully

folded in front of you. But your lives are so devoid of God in spite of all your prayers and rituals that you're filled with spite and bile, and all you can do is try to make everyone else feel the same! Goddamn you, you hypocrites! You mean, nasty, shriveled up priests and sisters who ruin life for everyone else. You leave a trail of broken souls behind you, not saved ones, and you nearly broke my soul. You nearly broke it. I wanted to be a good boy, but I couldn't meet your standards, your stiff, rigid, unrelenting standards. I wanted God to like me...I wanted to like him. But you drove me away from Him for so long.

But souls are too strong to stay broken forever. They find God on their own, in their own time, without your rules and your hurtfulness and your hypocrisy, and they are healed.

And I am being healed. Finally, I am rid of you. I don't need you anymore. Perhaps, I won't even need to be angry at you anymore. What are you? What are you? Just silly robots, trying to find your way like everyone else. You want to find God, but you haven't found Him in the church, and you're afraid to look anywhere else.

Deep inside of me, somewhere, I know I wanted to love you. Even as a boy, I felt the mystery, the wonder...I knew something special was going on inside the church. Maybe someday...I don't know when... maybe someday I will learn to love you again, and maybe you will learn to love me too.

It was over and I was completely spent. There was total silence in the room. It seemed I had forgotten to breathe during the ten minutes of my tirade, and now I sucked air into my lungs and let it out in a series of deep sighs.

Father Dorff was the lightning rod—I had tossed it all to him. I had heard the word "transference" in the lexicon of psychiatrists, but this was the first time I had been able to direct my anger toward a priest. This was the first time I had said anything like this to anyone, let alone a whole roomful of people.

To his great credit, Father Dorff had listened without passing judgment. He looked as though he could absorb my anger but allow it to pass through him and be unaffected by it. It seemed to me that, even though he was a priest, he understood.

I had been carrying my anger against the church for thirty years. Would the emotional purge finally free me of it? Later that night, in the dark quiet of my bedroom, Hippocrates gently, circumspectly, made his presence known. In the dim light I could barely make out that he was dressed in a suit and tie, perhaps the same outfit he'd worn when I first saw him at the clinic years earlier.

"How are you, Dr. A.? Feeling okay now?"

"Yes, Hippocrates, but I'm wondering, is this thing I have with the church...is it all over now? Have I really made peace with it?"

"Ask yourself, and feel what answer you get."

"Okay...the answer I get is...that it's like everything else in spiritual growth. We go forward, then backward a bit, then forward again. Like everything else we need to learn, it's as though we have to experience the lesson over and over until we finally own it." I paused to let my intuition do the work for me.

After a moment, Hippocrates spoke again. "There's more, isn't there?"

"Yes, there's more. Each time we experience the lesson, if we don't resist, if we surrender, we get through it more quickly, more easily. And gradually, gradually, it turns in upon itself...it turns in upon itself and devours its own energy until it is nothing...nothing is left of it, and we are free of it, free to go on."

Again there was a quiet moment. Then Hippocrates rose slowly, walked toward me and looked down at my reclining figure. He clasped my hands in his and said, "You are starting to become a wise man. I am proud of you."

And this road is full of footprints!
Companions have come before.
They are your ladder.
Use them!

—*Rumi*

"Kindred spirit," a term familiar and pleasing, suggesting "kin," suggesting someone with whom we feel "kinship." Originally, it did mean family member—someone to whom we were biologically related—but it has come to mean much more. Now, it means someone with whom we share deep feelings, and by virtue of these shared feelings, someone we feel close to, even though we may have never met.

That's how I felt toward Richard Bach, whose *Bridge Across Forever* echoed my experiences, including our mutual, deep distrust of organized religion, our apprehension about being trapped by marriage and our huge financial losses. In Bach's case, after becoming a successful author and amassing a small fortune, he entrusted it to an editor friend turned investment counselor and had ended up losing almost one and a half million dollars—coincidentally, the same amount I'd lost on the Onyx Building. Worse than my situation, Bach lost just about everything he had and was deeply in debt to the IRS.

Like me, he had faced some hard decisions when his world began to collapse around him. He realized the incredible waste of the money and all the years of work that had been poured "...down rat-hole offices of attorneys and accountants and advisers and counselors and consultants paid in desperation for help."[5] But when I felt him most to be a kindred spirit was when he faced that awkward and frightening moment when one either decides to take a stand in all the muck or obtain freedom by flight. "My freedom," he said, "is a choice now between escape to some other country, and careful, slow working out of this heap of broken crockery that was my empire."[6] Boy, could I identify with that. Like me, Bach chose to remain, and he recovered from his financial setback, stronger than ever.

What a gift to be able to write a book based on one's own experiences that will uplift the heart of another and make him feel better than he did before. I had surely made people feel better through my years of medical practice, but Bach's book had literally been read by millions. And he had not merely treated their bodies, he had reached into their souls.

I knew it didn't come easy for him. I recognized the same signs of change, the deep painful longings for a more meaningful life, the rapturous days of bliss, the intermittent episodes of wild irritation with oneself and others that one feels when under the stress of real transformation.

The strange and marvelous parallels and visions I shared with Bach and others who painstakingly took the time to recall their experiences reminded me of the passage in J.D. Salinger's *Catcher in the Rye,* when the teacher says to his pupil:

> Many, many men have been just as troubled morally and spiritually as you are right now. Happily, some of them kept records of their troubles. You'll learn from them—if you want to. Just as someone will learn something from you. It's a beautiful reciprocal arrangement. And it is an education. It's history. It's poetry.[7]

There are many areas of commonly shared experiences that can be relayed—from the most profound to the most subtle. For example, an event that occurs over and over again in the life of a parent. It was Spring Break, and with Jason out of school we headed for Hawaii. One day, Jason was running through some muddy landscaping in his eagerness to get to the swimming pool, when he slipped and scraped himself. I scolded him. It was an instinctive parental response that I immediately regretted. After all, he was only eight and he was having fun, being enthusiastic...being a boy. So the next day, when we were together at the surf, jumping into the waves, he was so dear to me I could barely stand it. I had to tell him, so out of the blue, without preamble, I said, "I love you, Jason," and kissed his wet, salty cheek.

"I love you too, Daddy," he responded, before again losing himself in the experience of the sun and the pounding surf.

I could not recall ever having an experience like that with my own father, and that made this tiny episode with Jason seem even more precious. As I write these words, a warm glow comes over me. I relive the moment and am doubly blessed.

I did something I'd been wanting to do for ten years. I signed up with the Maui Downhill Bicycle Tour Company for the thirty-seven-mile guided ride down 10,000-foot-high Mt. Haleakala. I hadn't done it before because there wasn't anyone to do it with; the altitude might cause problems with Cecile's sporadic heart arrhythmia, and my children were still too young. But I decided to do it anyway.

After we were issued rain gear and given an orientation, we were picked up by a van and began our ascent to the top of Mt. Haleakala. It was warm and raining when we started down, and, since we were high enough to be among the clouds, visibility was poor. A journey like this is taken with several precautions, including a good ability to ride a bike, and speed governors that limit speed to twenty miles per hour. Even so, it was thrilling right from the start, as we cruised downhill and rode through constant sharp curves. Riding through the warm rain made us all feel like kids again, especially when one man spontaneously burst into a joyous rendition of "Singin' In the Rain."

No pedaling was needed, just coasting, steering and frequent braking, and there was plenty of time to gaze at the views. At one point we spotted a perfect double rainbow. Snug inside our rain gear, with a cool mist washing against our faces, silently gliding down this beautiful mountain, the sensations of pleasure were so intense the whole feeling was orgasmic, except that it didn't stop.

As we descended, the rain forest gave way to more open spaces and finally opened to large meadows with cattle grazing peacefully among scattered eucalyptus trees. Moments later, the Goddess Pele graciously granted us a reprieve from the rain, and we burst into brilliant sunshine to see again a perfect double rainbow from horizon to horizon. Toward the end of the ride, we occasionally pedaled, just for fun, as the land began to level out. When we arrived at our destination, Paia, an old Hawaiian cowboy town, and got off our bikes for the last time and rubbed the stiffness out of our rear ends from the long trip, we noticed that we all bore a black, vertical stripe along our backs. This was caused by the road dirt being thrown up by our lightweight, fenderless bikes. It gave us the comical appearance of belonging to a fraternity of raccoons.

So many lessons to be learned, and I learned another one that day. It had taken me three years to take the initiative and sign up for this journey with twelve perfect strangers. As things go, we probably would never see each other again. But the bonds we forged that day made us feel as if we had known each other all our lives. I thought about how many times in my life I had denied myself potentially rewarding experiences because I would be forced to be among strangers. Or that I had complained to myself that I was tied down by family when the real issue was my own timidity and inertia. I vowed that no longer would I allow myself the excuse that "there was no one to go with," when opportunities like this came along.

I thought, "I've made such great progress, and then I realize how much there is to learn, and I wonder…on a scale of one to ten, where am I?"

As soon as I had asked the question, I heard the clearing of a throat, and an oh-so-familiar voice replied, "Make the scale from one to a thousand, Dr. A. Call the spread from zero to number one, 'human civilization up to this time.' Place yourself at number one, and place me close to you. We can then both look ahead to the 999 parts yet to be experienced."

"Okay, Hippocrates, I get it," I said, and got ready to rejoin my family at the hotel.

Angels can fly because they take themselves lightly.   —*Chesterton*

In 1988, we celebrated the Jewish holiday of Passover by inviting Jeremy, Jody, and several other guests to our first traditional *seder* dinner. In Hebrew, the word *seder* means *order,* referring to the orderly, ritualized meal that commemorates the Israelites' liberation from slavery in Egypt. Time has brought innumerable variations to the ritual. In addition to the traditional *seder,* there is a *seder* for vegetarians, a feminist *seder* that emphasizes the role of Moses' sister, Miriam, and even a ritual for humanists who don't believe in God.

The dinner conversation turned serious when someone asked Jody if she was planning to convert to Judaism. Jody was caught between a rock and a hard place on this issue. In Judaism, in mixed marriages the children are not considered Jewish unless born to a Jewish mother; further, they are denied entrance to religious school if they are not considered Jewish. Since Jeremy badly wanted their children to be given an early Jewish orientation, plans were made to have them convert. This presented Jody with a dilemma: convert to Judaism herself, or remain a lapsed Catholic.

I'd recently read a book about the complex relationship of the Catholic church to its congregants, which I thought might be helpful to Jody. "It's called *Once A Catholic* and in it the author, Peter Occhiograsso, interviews twenty-six prominent persons who are practicing or lapsed Catholics, including journalist Jimmy Breslin, comedian George Carlin, musician Frank Zappa, film director Martin Scorcese, former governor and presidential candidate Eugene McCarthy, and even Bob Guccione, the publisher of Penthouse Magazine, who once attended a seminary. It helped me," I told Jody.

"How did it help you, Dennis?" she asked.

"It started with something George Carlin said, something like, 'The trouble with Catholics is that we take it all so seriously. We become so oversensitive to apparent contradictions that we lose sight of the purpose of it all.'"

"Well, that's right on."

"Also," I continued, "when I read the book I was thinking about paradoxes...the inconsistencies that are inherent in all religions, in all life, for that matter. If I'd known that when I was young, maybe I wouldn't have built up so much anger against the church.

"One of the reasons I recommend the book is that it gives some very good reasons for sticking with your birth faith and it also gives compelling reasons for conversion. At the very least, it gets you off the fence and helps you to make a decision one way or the other.

"Tell you what: my copy is all marked up and dog-eared; I'll pick up a copy for you and give it to Jeremy the next time I see him."

"Save your money—I can buy my own copy," Jody replied sharply. I was taken aback, but I bit my tongue and said nothing. There seemed to be a lot of accumulated resentment behind her acid comment, and the dinner party wasn't the right place to air it. I realized that, no matter how well intended your motives, you can't help someone who doesn't want to be helped. And even when they want your help, sometimes you're resented for helping.

As for Jody, she'd been drifting toward making choices by default, as events forced her into corners, and that's the way she would likely continue, even though it at times strained her marriage.

While dessert was being served, Cecile's cousin Susan, asked me how the book was coming along. Relieved to change the subject and distance myself from Jody, I said, "Pretty good; I just finished chapter four."

But Jody apparently wasn't finished with me, for she said, caustically, "He'll be on TV one day and have his own show, like Jim and Tammy Bakker."

That did it. She had gone beyond the mild ribbing of a friend. I didn't respond, but I was surprised how much it hurt. Comparing my experiences and the trials I had undergone to those of a defrocked televangelist may have been funny to Jody, but it wasn't funny to me. Later that night, I wrote her a four page letter, setting out my grievances but doing it in as positive a light as I could muster. I folded the letter and started to address the envelope.

"Are you really going to send it, Dr. A.?" Hippocrates asked softly, and he appeared in his dapper, well-tailored suit and tie, his white, wavy hair lending him an air of great dignity.

"I'm not sure," I replied. "You know, she really got to me."

"Yes, I know. The question is, 'Why?'"

"Because she's mocking me in public when she knows how serious I've been about what's happening in my life."

"Serious? Serious? But, Dr. A., weren't you telling Jody, by referencing a book, not to take her Catholic past so seriously? Didn't you, yourself, say that you wished you hadn't taken it so seriously when you were a boy?"

"Yes, that's true, Hippocrates, but…"

"Yes, Dr. A.?"

"…this is different. This is the most important thing in my life, and I don't take kindly to being made the fool over it."

"Let's look at it from another angle. Suppose Jody had publicly mocked you about your, ahh, former capabilities as a surgeon. Suppose she claimed you had carved up all your patients ineptly. Would that have angered you as much?"

"It would have irritated me…but, no, Hippocrates, it wouldn't have bothered me as much."

"I see. And why not, do you suppose?"

"Because…well, because I'm not vulnerable on that count. I know, Jody knows and the others at the table know that I've been a very competent surgeon."

"Precisely, Dr. A., precisely. And I think you can now anticipate my next question."

"I think so. 'Why am I so vulnerable to the recent changes I've made in my life? Why am I so sensitive to the path of spiritual growth I have undertaken?'"

"And what is your answer, Dr. A.?"

It was hard to admit, hard to put it into words, but I was encouraged by Hippocrates' gentle persistence as he waited, calmly waited, until I'd gathered my thoughts. "I am vulnerable and sensitive because deep down I'm not sure that I've done the right thing. In spite of all the wonderful experiences I've had, in spite of everything I've learned, there is a part of me that questions if my old life was not really the better one, and which views spiritual growth as one big joke. And when I am ridiculed, that cynical part of me sits back and has a big belly laugh."

"Dr. A.," Hippocrates said, "that was a brilliant analysis. I must say I'm impressed." Then he did something out of character, undignified even. He snickered, then snorted, kind of a giggle-snort. Not just once. In fact, he lost control and the snort burst into a full-toned laugh that might have been heard throughout the house.

"Shh, shhh, you'll wake everyone up."

I don't know about you, but when I'm in close proximity to someone who is really laughing, I can't resist laughing myself. I tried to maintain my dignity, but it seemed to be evaporating…there was nothing to hold onto, and I started chuckling. Just a little at first, then more and more until we were like two kids, rolling on the floor and bursting our bellies over something deliciously funny.

"Dr….heh-heh-heh-heh, Dr. A., you are soooooooo serious!" Hippocrates could barely get the words out between guffaws.

"I know!" I responded, holding my sides, "I know!"

"Dennis, Dennis, are you all right?" Cecile's voice came from the living room where she was watching TV.

"Ye-yes, yes…I'm fine." I managed to blurt out.

We wheezed and puffed together and finally got hold of ourselves and wiped the tears from our eyes. Hippocrates took out a large handkerchief and blew his nose, the fog horn sound of it making me laugh uproariously all over again.

"I have never…" I tried to say, "I have never heard a spirit blow his nose before."

"A subject for your next book," he responded and we laughed some more.

When all was calm again, Hippocrates asked, "What are you going to do with the letter to Jody?"

"File it."

"What are you going to say to her?"

"I'll have a talk with her, but…"

"But what?"

"But I'm not going to take myself quite so seriously."

Hippocrates placed his hand on my shoulder and squeezed it. "You know, Dr. A., your case was assigned to me—no, never mind by whom—and not once have I complained about the assignment, but… there were moments when I might have wished to be somewhere else. I have always loved you, because you're closer to me than you know and because you're trying your best just like everyone else. But now, something else has happened. I have begun to *like* you as well. And that's a whole different story."

As he faded from view, I realized that, although I had long respected Hippocrates, I was beginning to like him, too.

Two days later, in my home office, I debated over how to confront Jody. I wanted the issue between us resolved once and for all. I was startled out of my concentration by the ring of the telephone. It was Jody. "Hi, Dennis, can I come over and use your fax? I have some documents I need to get to our builder right away."

"Why sure," I said, wondering if she had picked up my thoughts, if I had picked up her thoughts, or if telepathy worked that way at all.

Telepathy experiments, especially those performed in Eastern Europe during the past few decades, have demonstrated "statistically significant" results over pure chance, but they have never been dramatically successful in terms of replication—that is, giving the same positive results when repeated under exactly the same conditions. In these experiments, one person is often given the role of "transmitter" and another person, some distance away, is asked to be the "receiver."

But the sages tell us there are no causes (transmitters) and effects (receivers), just simply a psychic melting pot—psychologists call it a *gestalt*—where everything happens at once. With telepathy we are simultaneously transmitters and receivers. Jody hadn't picked up "my" thoughts, nor had I picked up "hers." Rather, we had together formed an invisible bridge which spanned "our" thoughts.

The fascinating extension of this idea is that no one's thoughts are his own. Thoughts do not originate in one mind; they are the results of an infinite number of spontaneous connections. That is why new inventions and theories often occur simultaneously in different parts of the world—because they are occurring in more than one mind! This takes Jung's concept of the collective unconscious a step further. We can call it the *collective consciousness.*

When Jody finished transmitting her documents, I told her that I felt humiliated during the *seder* and that I was concerned about her feeling that I was a threat to her and Jeremy's lifestyle. I told her I was disturbed by the way she was avoiding us; it indicated that our friendship was on the rocks.

"Dennis, I suppose I've been misinterpreting messages as far back as I can remember. I get this complaint from Jeremy all the time. I'm not always the most sensitive person to other peoples' feelings. But I didn't mean to humiliate you, and I'm sorry, although, you know, sometimes you're hard to be around."

"How do you mean?"

"Well, you've gone ahead and made all these changes to transform your life, while we only sat around and talked about it. What that means is that you're a constant reminder that we haven't got our lives together, and that doesn't make it easy to be around you."

Change threatens people in many ways, but those who are growing cannot retreat. No relationship can stand in the way of growth once it has begun. Loved ones either rise to the challenge of understanding, and offer their support, or are left behind.

The process is inherently bittersweet. The more you grow, the more people you leave behind. After a while, you will notice that you have not really left them completely, for your influence has nudged them a few steps forward, as you have been moved forward by others throughout your life. Whether your paths remain together or diverge, that influence is your legacy.

How should men know what is coming to pass within them, when there are no words to grasp it? How could the drops of water know themselves? Yet the river flows on.   —*Saint-Exupery*

Vesak, more commonly known as Buddha's Day, was being celebrated on the grounds of Stanford University. Several different Buddhist sects from Northern California were represented, and celebrants included Vietnamese, Tibetan, Japanese, American and Thai Buddhists. There was plenty of food, dancing and singing, as well as the traditional Japanese bathing of the baby Buddha in sweet tea, a display meant especially for children.

The featured speaker was Thich Nhat Hanh, a Vietnamese monk who had once been nominated by Dr. Martin Luther King for the Nobel Peace Prize. Westerners usually think of Buddhists as passive and fatalistic, but Hanh spoke of a kind of Buddhism he called *engaged Buddhism* which, during the Vietnamese War, meant treating and comforting the wounded and the displaced, as opposed to remaining isolated in a monastery.

When he got to the subject of spiritual growth, Hahn said something I hadn't heard before. All the books I'd read on the subject of enlightenment agreed on one thing—we are already enlightened, if we could only see it. This is not only confusing, it is downright irritating to be told, "You silly humans, you're striving for something which you already have. So stop striving." It's the old *damned if you do, and damned if you don't* paradox. We haven't found enlightenment, and we have an innate craving for it, so we try to find it. But we cannot find it through trying. And if we stop trying, we still do not have it but we still crave it!

Anyway, Hanh said there is no way to enlightenment... enlightenment is the way, and that one means of clarifying one's enlightenment is "mindfulness," being more mindful of what is going on around us.

Aldous Huxley, by way of encouraging mindfulness, wrote of a city whose streets were lined with talking mynah birds, trained to repeat "Attention! Attention!" when anyone passed by. In other words, "wake up!" Wake up to the fact that the mystery of life is revealed not in pondering it, but through living it while wide awake.

Hanh continued by saying that the more we are able to live in the present moment, the more enlightenment is experienced, without a struggle, without striving, without trying to achieve anything. In this way, the future takes care of itself.

Westerners view God as the controller, the boss of the universe. In contrast, Eastern religions see creation as an immense organic being of which we are all part. They recognize the oneness of everything as the true reality. Everything else is *maya,* or illusion, a dream from which we are all capable of awaking. The Buddha taught that the aim of religion should not be the appeasement of an angry deity, or obedience to beliefs that promise immortality; rather, the aim should be transcending the whole dynamic by which human knowing creates the world of experience.

In The Lens of Perception, Hal Bennett tells us that our experience of life is not determined by external boundaries but by boundaries shaped by our internal filtering device—the lens of perception—which alters everything we consciously perceive, think or feel. But the passage of perceptions through our lens is not necessarily bad. For example, Bennett says that in the shamanic traditions, the lens is seen as a positive resource: "You may receive through your lens 'visions' that broaden your understanding of yourself and the world in which you live. These insights can direct you in your 'right path,' the path through which you will fulfill your personal destiny."[8]

What I got from this is that we cannot discount the individual ego…that would be throwing out the baby with the bath water. Jung says that once the ego is subjected to the unconscious, deeper self, it becomes a conscious participant in the rich world of the inner self.

How do we relate the ego's usefulness with the Eastern view of One Reality? How do we reconcile Jung's findings with Hanh's advice to live in the moment? Stop trying so hard. Relax, and, in relaxing, be aware…be calmly attentive. Don't try to slay the dragon of the ego; give it its due, but watch it. Allow it to sense our higher aims and, in sensing our higher aims, the ego's passion is subdued. The more we acquaint our ego with our higher aims, the more it is one with our deeper self. And, finally, the more our ego is one with our deeper self, the more we are one with everything.

Ironically, the aim of Buddhism is not the achievement of some holy ideal but the destruction of all viewpoints. From there, enlightenment will follow of its own accord.

Was it really meditation that brought about the Buddha's enlightenment? The Buddhists are curiously playful regarding this paradox. Meditation in and of itself, they assert, can no more bring about enlightenment than polishing a floor tile can make a mirror. It's simply a process to empty and still the mind. And while it can lead to enlightenment there are no guarantees—this from a tradition that employs meditation as a common practice. A Zen drawing makes this point splendidly by depicting a bullfrog sitting on a lily pad, with the caption: "If sitting could make a Buddha, I, foolish old frog, would have been enlightened long before now."

So how close were any of us to enlightenment? Was there any way of knowing, before it happened? Was there any way of gauging how much farther there was to go? While I suspected that there would be no answers immediately forthcoming, I had caught several glimpses along the way of some Reality or Truth that was of a completely different order than what was readily apparent. Perhaps this was "it"—no more and no less. Perhaps the lesson was that no explanation of this reality will ever be right, there's just too much to know. And perhaps what Hippocrates was trying to alert me to was that so long as we don't take them too seriously, we are free to choose, for entertainment's sake, among the many explanations of life.

As we departed from the Buddha's Day celebration, I felt a bit easier, a bit less need to strive for anything...a bit more Buddhist.

CHAPTER 19

Unfolding Theories and the
Presence of Magic

*What you may do may seem very insignificant, but it's very important
that you do it.*
—Mahatma Gandhi

How does one write a book about spiritual growth while in the midst of
spiritual growth? I think Joseph Campbell would answer, "It's simple!
Writing the book becomes a part of the process."

"But," I said to him in our imaginary conversation, "I'm still uncertain
about so many things. I don't have enough experience to know if what I'm
saying is right."

"That's not important," Campbell might well reply, "just express the
uncertainty. Get in there and do your own thing—don't worry about the
outcome. Remember, you're not the only one who's uncertain—everyone's
uncertain at times. Unenlightened states cause uncertainty. For that matter, if
you ever meet anyone who claims to be completely certain about life, than
only one thing *is* certain—you've met a fool."

As I thought about what Joseph Campbell might say, I picked up my
heavily highlighted copy of *The Power of Myth* and began leafing through it. I
found that Campbell had actually said, "Anyone writing a creative work
knows that you open, you yield yourself, and the book talks to you and builds
itself."[1] A bit further on, he says, "To a certain extent you become the carrier

of something that is given to you from what has been called the muses—or in biblical language, 'God.' "[2]

"But," I say, "what do we give the reader when we are in the midst of the process ourselves?" To which he says, "Since the inspiration comes from the unconscious, and since the unconscious minds of the people of any sin-gle...society have much in common, what the shaman or seer brings forth is something that is waiting to be brought forth in everyone. So when one hears the seer's story, one responds, 'Aha! This is my story. This is something that I had always wanted to say.' "[3]

I thought about all the *literary shamans* responsible for the many spiritual '*aha*'s in my life and in the lives of others, sharing the best gift they had to offer humanity—themselves. Had any of them completed their spiritual growth? Is it possible to ever complete one's spiritual growth? Hippocrates had said that if there are a thousand steps to ultimate enlightenment, than he and I had just passed Step One.

Maharishi (great seer in Sanskrit) Mahesh Yogi, guru of Transcendental Meditation, teaches that there are four stages of enlightenment that usually, but not always, develop sequentially: cosmic consciousness, God conscious-ness, unity consciousness and Brahman consciousness. These are experiential states not easy to describe but, to oversimplify, perhaps: cosmic consciousness refers to that state when one becomes a purely objective observer of all the thoughts and events occurring in one's life; when one is of the world but not in the world. God consciousness is when one becomes acutely and perma-nently aware of God's presence behind everything that is. Unity consciousness is when one's awareness has assimilated total knowledge, and that the sum of all knowledge is that everything is, literally, One. And lastly, Brahman con-sciousness is that ultimate stage of awareness when one's individuality has disappeared into God's (Brahma's) greater awareness so that one says, "I am God, you are God, all is God."

I did not feel qualified to be a *literary shaman,* but if I could simply let my book be the process, the instrument of my own continuing growth, I could stop feeling inadequate. As Joseph Campbell might say, "Everyone has a story to tell, and, to a much greater degree than we imagine, our stories are the same. Should someone else, at some point, read your story and say, 'Aha,' why that's just icing on your cake!"

In this context of sharing knowledge, I again met with Rabbi Nathan Weiss. "Dennis," he began, "I have an offer for you. I've been interested in starting up a committee—"

"Oh no, Rabbi, not another committee. I've just spent the last two years of my life getting out of committees!"

"Well, not exactly a committee; actually, more of a forum for presenting ideas from other disciplines that will help science, philosophy and religion come closer together."

Rabbi Weiss knew this topic was dear to my heart, but my initial reaction was to beg off. I was too involved with writing my book. But his pleas gradually became more enticing. "Why not," he continued, "invite a Jungian psychologist, philosophers, theologians, writers and poets? Dennis, you will have a completely free hand to bring in speakers, and this will enhance your writing by giving *you* the opportunity to meet remarkable people.

I was interested, but not yet willing to accept the responsibility for getting The Educational Forum, as it was to be called, off the ground. From my view, the whole point of the exercise would be to demonstrate that spiritual truths are not limited to any one sect or discipline, and that they may encompass secular as well as religious activities. I felt that perhaps if diverse people could agree on a new cosmology, a new working myth that enhances all the creative possibilities of life, rather than opposing them as so many of our institutions do, it would be a worthwhile exercise.

Before we parted, Rabbi Weiss recommended I read *The Hundredth Monkey*, by Ken Keyes, Jr. I had heard of the concept but only vaguely remembered it. All the rabbi would tell me was that it was a perfect metaphor for how human beings can effect change in the world. Unfortunately, I was unable to find it in any bookstore, and it wasn't listed in the "in print" catalogs.

I planned to spend time alone the following Sunday, but at the last moment I changed my mind and joined Cecile and the children at the Jewish Community Center, where the annual celebration of Israel's statehood was in process. While browsing a table of used books, I was drawn to a book lying askew. It was *The Hundredth Monkey*. I laughed and thanked the *invisible network* for bringing the book to me, or me to the book. I then agreed to help organize The Educational Forum.

My sense of stewardship was growing. By "stewardship," I meant contributing to the greater good of the entire planet—not just in big, abstract terms, but in ministering to people, and easing their pain. In *The Art of Loving*, Eric Fromm calls this "standing in for the other."[4] This was in such contrast to my former, self-centered lifestyle that I seemed to have become a new person. I was even starting to think of the old Dennis Augustine in terms of "him" and not "me."

I had spent many years ministering to people's ills as a doctor. Putting aside the question of motive, there had always been a doctor-patient barrier between us. I wanted to be with people without that barrier, but in what role? Within formal faiths, lay ministries serve this function, but what do we do when we don't belong to such a group? Do we open a shelter à la Mother Teresa and invite the poor and homeless to come? Or do we stay with people with whom we feel comfortable? Should we limit ourselves? In *The Art of Passingover,* Father Dorff says, "Unless we are formally trained, ordained and missioned by a specific religious community to serve its people, many of us do not think of ourselves as being called to ministry."[5] Dorff's theme is that we are *all* called to ministries of various kinds, and we find our particular ministry when our work in the world becomes a heart-felt desire, and gives great fulfillment, through service to others.

Father Dorff sets out a fourfold view of the spiritual stages, the archetypal experience for growth in human beings. I paraphrase it as follows:

1) compassion: learning how to endure life—leveling experiences in a creative, humanizing way. For if we can't humanize our own experiences, how can we have compassion and understanding for others in our life—known and unknown.

2) contemplation: a heartfelt acceptance of life's beauty and its brokenness, until we experience that inner vision of what our life is trying to become.

3) communion: feeling at one with all creation, and joining and giving birth to its next phase. For, if it's true that "man is the measure of all things," then man is the microcosm in which the whole universe is reflected.

4) creative commitment: allowing that inner vision to take hold in our world and expressing it in the best way we can (e.g., career change, re-prioritizing one's life, volunteering, taking up writing, music, art, science or politics, etc.). Beginning with a new slate following some tragedy can also be a part of creative commitment.

Saint Theresa had said "Whose hands are God's hands but our hands?" All my life I had left it up to some god "out there" to cure the ills of the world. Now I understood that it is the god within us that is called upon to act; that service need not be grandiose, and that it requires no credential. Moreover, service can be a powerful tool even to the small circles within which we move.

Mahatma (great soul) Gandhi's emphasis on the importance of seemingly insignificant service fit nicely into *The Hundredth Monkey.* The phenomenon, you may recall, concerns the eating habits of a tribe of macaque monkeys on a small island. One day, an observer noted a female monkey washing her sweet potato before eating it to rid it of sand. Other monkeys within her social group, observing the process, soon began washing their sweet potatoes. When about one hundred monkeys had adopted the practice, a striking phenomenon occurred. Overnight, the entire colony of thousands of macaques all began washing their potatoes before eating them.

Applying these observations to human behavior, Keyes suggests there is a critical mass to ideas. When a certain number of people think the same thing, and the critical mass for that particular idea has been reached, the thought suddenly spreads throughout the entire population. Fads and rumors find acceptance this way, a war psychology comes into being, a drive to improve health care, or the rapid desire of tribal groups to form a nation. Here was why Rabbi Weiss had recommended Keyes' book: it confirmed the value of The Educational Forum.

So the *invisible forces* had contrived to bring me another opportunity to further develop my passion and to help others at the same time. I could nurture the idea of how and why our culture was moving toward a more universal view of spirituality, one in which the division between science and religion was slowly disappearing. And the vehicle for this opportunity was The Educational Forum to which I had committed myself.

On the evening of May 18, 1989, I came out of the spiritual closet. After being introduced to the Education Committee members of the temple, as the new co-chairman of The Educational Forum, I attempted to summarize all that I had come to understand about the cosmological shift taking place in our society.

I spoke of religious elitism, and how it had to be eliminated in order for true spiritual activity to grow. I pleaded for more ecumenism among organized religions, to keep pace with the cultural and economic ecumenism rapidly occurring throughout the world. Even as the world economy had already driven past national boundaries, so too are the boundaries between religious doctrines lessening.

At the end of my presentation, I said, "We all agree that there is a higher force at work. Can we honor not only our own tradition, heritage and beliefs, but those of everyone else as well? If we wish to work with that higher force, does it lessen our sincerity and our effect if we call that force by a different name or if we package it in a different way? After all, what is God if not a short hand symbol for our attitude toward the universe?

"As you may know, *Shir Hadash* means 'new song.' I believe this is the age of *Shir Hadash,* and that there is indeed a new song in the air. The question is, can we open ourselves to hear the song of the universe? If we can, I believe we will also hear the message behind the song. I believe that message is: we need to learn to sing together in as many languages as possible. Thank you."

My words were well-received by most of the members, with a few hard-liner exceptions who complained about "new age" ideas eroding the very foundations, etc. Equally important, I had begun doing something I believed in within my small circle of influence, and it began to bear fruit almost immediately, judging from the changed attitudes of some of the participants, and in my own personal life. For example, Rabbi Weiss introduced me to the person who would be co-chairing the group, Judith Hurley, a professor of multilingual education at San Jose State University. This gave me the opportunity to work with a woman as an equal—something I had never done before.

About a month after giving my presentation to The Educational Forum, Cecile and I were invited to dinner by Judith Hurley. As we conversed with Judith and her husband Michael, we found, once again, many parallels. For example, they had both been interested in Buddhism, as I was, and they had both kept journals of "meaningful coincidences," as I was doing.

Judith told us her son had recently been learning about the Japanese tea ceremony in a social studies class, and for a while we discussed this highly stylized ritual, and its meaning. On my side, I had attended a festival at Stanford in celebration of Buddha's Day, where I witnessed the ritual bathing of the statue of the baby Buddha in sweet tea. I had also recently visited a local Japanese tea garden.

We were talking excitedly as Judith served us tea, when the tea cup she was holding suddenly exploded and shattered into pieces, spilling the hot tea onto the floor. Fortunately, no one was burned, though we were all momentarily stunned. One can say the tea was too hot for the cold cup, and the difference in temperature caused it to break, but Judith had been holding the cup for a while, and hot tea had been poured into the cup a hundred times before without incident.

It felt as though something very unusual and eerie had occurred, but none of us had any idea what or why. Breaking the silence, I offered, "Were Carl Jung here, he would characterize the exploding tea cup as a catalytic exteriorization. Jung theorized that such events are the result of a burst of mental energy that is propagated outward into the physical world during times of heightened creativity and emotional intensity. We just got a bit too creative," I added. On the other hand, Freud had called Jung's theory "sheer bosh," just one of the many conflicts they came to have as Jung came into his own and challenged many of the ideas of his former mentor.

Anyway, I came away from the evening feeling more alive. The tea cup incident, aside from its drama, seemed just one more instance of being able to tune into the Universal Spiritual Matrix, the invisible web of forces and occurrences that create, support and maintain all the events in our lives.

A few days later I attended my first Bar Mitzvah. As rituals go, it had some advantages over the Catholic confirmation service with which I was familiar. The Bar Mitzvah was more personalized, acknowledging personal achievement, the culmination of several years of intensive study in Hebrew School. In the ceremony, a thirteen-year-old boy enters manhood and is no longer treated as a minor by Jewish law. It's a one-on-one experience in which the boy addresses God, his rabbi, the guests, relatives, and the entire congregation in a public speaking debut.

It is a challenging and profound experience for the boy and elicits memories of ancient rites of passage. I'd had a lingering resistance to Jason's Bar Mitzvah, not many years away now, because of my old dread of being tied to a limiting, single doctrine. But after watching the entire ceremony, it now seemed that this was a very positive experience for a boy and…yes, I admit it…the religious traditions do have value and are worth preserving. Besides, I heard another good reason on behalf of Bar Mitzvahs.

The Bar Mitzvah boy's father was not particularly a believer. I asked him why he had put his son through all the years of study and now this elaborate ceremony if he, himself, wasn't a practicing Jew. "It gives him something to rebel against," he said.

The answer was simple, direct and full of wisdom. And it had a profound impact on me, but deep down I had a memory and a connection to ritual that now, in some strange way, was helping me to find my way.

We've all seen children who have inherited their parents' bigotry and narrow-mindedness in matters of religion. The children grow up wearing the same pitiful blinders their parents wore. But is it more important for children to have some religious experience—no matter how narrow—than no religious experience at all?

Does our childhood faith provide us with a beacon of experience, of light, by which we are better able to make the journey back? Does the very religion we rebel against provide us with the future pathway of return or of access to a new and powerful spirituality? Then what of the parents who, in their wish to give their children an eclectic religious education, are depriving them of a great gift? For among the parents who want their children to have a broad experience of religion, how many actually take the time to give their children any religious experience at all?

Is the unconscious desire to experience oneness with creation so strong, so determined that it will seek it out and find it regardless of past experiences, or lack of them? If that is the case, aren't we all heading toward the same goal...a goal which we will all eventually reach, no matter how long it takes? And if we will all reach Oneness eventually, should we, or can we, push it?

Muddy water, when allowed to stand becomes clear.

—*Lao Tse*

On a Saturday morning in July, 1989, a *bodhisattva* arrived at my home—not a real Buddhist saint, but an attractive replica. When I was a teenager in Hoboken, Mr. Gonzalez, my parents' Filipino friend, accompanied us into a shop selling Oriental artifacts. "Denny, pick out anything you want," he'd said, and I chose a black, two-foot-high likeness of *Quan-Yin*, the Goddess of Mercy, who had been worshipped in seventeenth Century China. The *bodhisattva* had been stored in my father's attic for twenty-five years, like a medieval monk asleep in its coffin.

Because of my readings in Eastern philosophies, I wanted to have it close to me once again. I'd pleaded with my parents to ship it to me, and it had finally arrived. The sight of it affected me deeply. So real and vital was its presence that I sensed on some level it was speaking to me.

It was a striking object and, after placing it at the foot of the fireplace in our family room, the whole area around it seemed to glow with a peaceful radiance, as if this inanimate object could actually raise the vibrations of the space around it. When it was first unveiled after being in seclusion for so long, I felt the way Count Keyserling, author of *The Travel Diary of a Philosopher*, must have felt when he wrote: "I know nothing more grand in the world than the figure of the Buddha; it is an absolutely perfect embodiment of spirituality in the visible domain."[6]

There it sat in meditative pose. To me, it was a vivid manifestation of man's true mind, emanating the poise and equanimity, the sensitivity and compassion, and the strength and the unity that are within each of us. Its mysterious aura, and the aura I felt radiating about me, convinced me that my own essential nature and the Buddha's were inseparable.

Each day I grew more convinced that different spiritual traditions are essentially complementary rather than antagonistic—different languages for similar ideas. After *Quan-Yin* was settled into place, I attended the advanced Progroff workshops at a Catholic retreat called *Vallombrosa* (Shady Valley) in Menlo Park. Originally purchased in 1947 by the Catholic Church, the buildings and ground were now used for religious and educational workshops and seminars.

Enlightenment aside, every man is to a large extent hostage to the cultural milieu in which he is raised. He cannot deny his relationship without doing violence to his spirit. So it was with me. In spite of the fact that I was more and more coming to terms with Catholicism, being in a Catholic setting, with Catholic symbols and icons—it even smelled Catholic—brought up old, powerful feelings from my childhood and my Sicilian ancestry.

There was something poetic about the fact that the workshop was located at a Catholic retreat and was being taught by a Jewish psychologist. Ira Progroff was a well known psychologist and former Drew University professor who had studied with Carl Jung in the '50s and had developed a dynamic way of journal writing. Rather than a passive record of one's life, the journal became an active instrument which helped participants clarify current dilemmas, seek out inner wisdom and search out future direction.

The principal idea behind Progroff's journal process is that no matter your state of mind— depressed, sad, annoyed, angry or confused—you can write a dialogue from it. This creates an atmosphere where important new insights can be gained that help to resolve the problem.

A bespectacled man in his mid-sixties with a gentle, scholarly countenance, Ira Progroff had a disarming boyish grin and a twinkle in his eye, as becomes a man of wisdom. He sat in a comfortably padded lounge chair on an elevated platform in front of us like we were guests at his home. He began softly with, "I want you to envision yourself going down deeply into a private well. When you go deep enough, you will reach an underground stream that is the common source of all wells." Progroff spoke like some tour guide of the soul. "The idea here is to have you connect with that part of the self that is capable of deep inner-knowing. Since there is a tendency for the conscious mind to resist, I will facilitate the process with an opening or entrance meditation."

Progroff then read a passage from *The Cloud of Unknowing:* "In a word, let this thing deal with you and lead you as it will. Be the tree; let it be the carpenter. Be the house, and let it be the householder who lives there. Be willing to be blind, and give up all longing to know the why and the how, for knowing will be more of a hindrance than a help."[7]

During the orientation session, Progroff said, "The results of the Life Integration Workshop are designed to help answer the following questions: Where am I in the movement of my life and what is my life trying to become?" The timing of these questions was very significant for me. I had just decided to let go completely of being a doctor-surgeon—to stop seeing patients altogether. Now, Progroff's entrance meditation was another method of letting go, and it seemed custom-tailored for me.

While in the meditative state, I envisioned myself in the hands of a great master who, like a skilled fisherman, doesn't pull his catch in all at once. Instead, he patiently reels the fish in slowly, tempering its resistance on the way. "In the end you must learn to lie quietly, to surrender everything," a voice whispered. I imagined myself the catch of a benevolent fisherman, and I allowed myself to surrender. The feeling was delicious, and I held on to it for several minutes.

Then the process was over and we were quietly encouraged to make an entry of our impressions in our journals.

In another important exercise we were asked to spontaneously list our past experiences in ten to fifteen steps called "stepping stones."

"Take a trusting look at each event and experience whatever feelings come up for you," Progroff said.

I had never looked at my life in terms of major transition points before. I was amazed that by plotting out my life in this way, I was able to fill in the blanks and see my past in a way that was clearer than my previous attempts had been. Central to the Intensive Journal® method is the use of a dialoguing technique. We were asked to draw up a list of people—dead or alive—who played an important role in our lives. "I want you to speak to them, and let them speak back to you as if you're having a conversation,"

I had imaginary conversations with Bob Goldsack, Dr. Carmine Sippo, John Dempsey, Dr. Seymour, and with such wisdom figures as Bob Good-heart, Hippocrates, Joseph Campbell, Carl Jung, Matthew Fox, Richard Bach and others. The thing I liked most about Progroff's method, aside from the deep insights it flushed out, and the camaraderie I felt with those in attendance, was that it was a nonthreatening practice, with no dogmatic theological underpinning. So it was with some surprise that I found out that the program appealed to Roman Catholic priests and nuns, some of whom, apparently, had begun using it in their religious communities. This seemed to be a tacit admission that some members of the clergy were struggling to find meaning in their lives and made me feel more compassionate towards them.

The Program Coordinator for Vallombrosa was a Catholic who was openly critical of many of the Pope's positions. She was deeply interested in Taoism and Buddhism and wore a *yin-yang* button on her lapel. During breaks between workshop sessions, we were invited to the center's library to view two videos, "The Tao" and "Zen," both narrated by Alan Watts.

The openness of everyone at Vallombrosa surprised and delighted me. What a far cry from the harsh, narrow-minded Catholic slave masters of my youth. I thought that either Catholicism had come a long way in the last few decades or California Catholicism was a breed apart, like so much else in California. Whichever was closer to the truth, I felt that I was no longer a religious orphan.

Non-Catholics have a hard time understanding the intense love-hate relationship that Catholics have with their church. We swing from one extreme to the other and are rarely, if ever, indifferent. *Once a Catholic, always a Catholic.*

During a workshop session, an ex-Jesuit priest named John Leider described how difficult it had been to free himself from the image of his former title. In response, Ira Progroff said, "You can take the person out of the Jesuits, but you can't take the Jesuits out of the person." I understood completely. In my own way, I had been "hooked" to my profession as tightly as the ex-priest was to his. Now, I experienced a feeling of great, great relief; I could once more be comfortable—at least at Vallombrosa—within the ambiance of the Catholic Church.

On the last day of my stay at Vallombrosa, I was lying in my bed, resting. The austerity of the small, plain room was in sharp contrast to my spacious, luxurious surroundings at home and, in the comparison, this small room seemed more pleasing—at least for contemplation, if not for raising a family. Thinking about this, I fell asleep and began to dream. In the dream, persons unknown to me were planning to kill me. I was awakened by the soft voice of Hippocrates. This time, he appeared as an ethereal figure, barely visible, and surrounded by a delicate aura of light. His presence felt consoling, after the troubling dream.

"Dr. A., the struggle of becoming a new person isn't an easy one, but gradually, ever so gradually, the struggle gives way as you become that very person in truth. Notice…are you awake now? Good… Notice that I said 'the struggle gives way.' You see, as you become that new person, as you align yourself more and more with the cosmic flow, or, as you put it, the Tao, the less you need to struggle. Indeed, unneeded struggling becomes an obstacle, and that is one thing I've come to caution you about."

I was fully alert now. Something in Hippocrates' voice sounded more serious than usual, and I paid close attention. "You have left your old life behind you, and something is needed to replace it. Well and good. But your new life, like your old one, will be based upon living, and not upon fleeting transcendental experiences. The esoteric experiences you have had serve a purpose but they are not an end in themselves—always remember that.

"A spiritual…uh…what is your term? Oh yes, 'junkie.' A junkie is one who is addicted. Although an addiction to harmful drugs is a very bad thing, so is an addiction to *anything*. One of the greatest dangers on the spiritual path is to become addicted to spirituality.

"Dr. A., enjoy the esoteric pleasantries when they come your way, but do not seek them out; otherwise, you'll end up with a closet full of spiritual collectibles that will confuse and hinder you rather than enlighten you. Remember the basics. Continue trusting your own intuition, that inner guide which has served you so well thus far."

I could sense that Hippocrates had not come for a conversation this time but to impart information, and it was to be one-sided, which was fine with me. After a brief pause, he continued. "The second thing I have come to caution you about pertains to your dream. It was symbolic, and you needn't worry about anyone killing you. The old you was killed off long ago. But the spirit senses deception and treachery long before the conscious mind becomes aware of it, and your spirit has sniffed it in the air. My purpose in coming this time is not to warn you about treachery, for you are perfectly capable of taking care of yourself in this regard. My purpose is to caution you about overreacting to it.

"Understand! The danger to you is not from the deception that will occur—the danger is that you may be deterred from your path by your dramatic tendency to feel yourself victimized, and to philosophize endlessly on why something has happened. Remember what you have learned. Every situation, every event, every relationship occurs for the good of *all* participants.

"Stay alert, Dr. A., but stay loving."

Of course, I wanted to ask, what is the treachery? Who is involved? When will it happen? But I knew that Hippocrates wouldn't provide those answers.

I had to overlook the questions and focus on my trust of the process—and it was hard.

In spite of our frank conversations to clear the air, Cecile and I weren't seeing much of Jeremy and Jody. I knew they were having difficulty juggling two careers and dealing with the challenge of trying to raise a young, growing family.

Then there was the lawsuit. A Mrs. Anatoya had filed a malpractice suit against both Jeremy and me. Then, suddenly, she had dropped her suit against Jeremy and focused on me. This was strange because Mrs. Anatoya had needed only a minor surgical revision to alleviate her foot problem, which Jeremy and I had jointly performed. However, a complication later arose—which happens in a certain number of cases no matter how careful you are—and it necessitated further surgery.

Jeremy recommended a radical procedure, potentially more debilitating than anything up to this point; a procedure that was beyond what could or should be done on an outpatient basis. With Mrs. Anatoya's consent, Jeremy agreed to take full responsibility for her care. She was hospitalized and Jeremy performed the surgery. After a series of mishaps and gross complications, including several recurrent infections, which were never divulged to me, Jeremy was forced to turn the patient over to another surgeon. The unfortunate end result was that Mrs. Anatoya's foot was severely damaged and had to be partially amputated.

What was strange about Mrs. Anatoya dropping Jeremy from her lawsuit was that Jeremy and I had an agreement. He was legally responsible for any procedures he did on behalf of my clinic—we were jointly responsible for any cases on which we worked together. So in this case, it appeared the responsibility was clearly his. When I questioned him about it, all he could say was that Mrs. Anatoya had decided to drop him from the case, and that a letter stating that fact was forthcoming.

Since Jeremy had assumed total responsibility for this patient, since he had performed the procedures and since he had not told me about the continuing complications he was facing, it was hard to see why the plaintiff would drop *him* from the case rather than *me*.

"Something is rotten in the state of Denmark,"[8] I thought. Hippocrates' warning about treachery seemed about to be fulfilled.

When something like this happens, we tend to question all the scenes from the past that might have had some bearing on the issue. Had this lawsuit been the real cause of our estrangement, or was it because Jeremy and Jody were preoccupied with their own problems? Had Jeremy somehow arranged a deal with the plaintiff's attorney to save his own skin and leave me holding the bag? Several months ago, when I had talked with Jeremy about our distancing, he had said, "You should trust and respect the fact that Jody and I intend to do the right thing by you when it comes to honoring the sanctity of our friendship." Could someone say that and then turn around and betray you? Was Jeremy still worthy of my trust?

Was my bad dream and Hippocrates' visit simply a precognitive vision of an event that was preordained? And what about his warning that the real danger to me was in being swayed from my path? "Stay alert and stay loving," he had told me. I had been overly quick to blame others in the past? Was this another test of my tolerance? The best course seemed to retain cordial relations and hold my opinions in abeyance until I understood more about what was happening.

In some ways, those persons who are spiritually mature have a harder time judging their fellow man than those who are less mature. Consider those individuals who are unencumbered with "spiritual values." They allow their intuition spontaneously and automatically to size up any relationship; and they "know" when something is wrong because they can "feel" it.

But what of those who are somewhat spiritually developed? There are so many things to evaluate. Should we ignore the wrongness we feel in a relationship because we should be loving and tolerant? And after we consciously imagine an adversary's heart filled with love, and we deliberately send him beautiful thoughts, should we ignore evidence to the contrary? What should our actions be based upon?

There is some profound advice in the most famous of all Hindu scriptures, the *Bhagavad Gita* (Divine Song). It tells us not to concern ourselves with deciding right and wrong, Rather, we are told to first establish our awareness in God; and from that state, we will always spontaneously do what is right.

Then does the question arise: is our awareness sufficiently in God to insure that our decisions will be right. Perhaps the asking of this question provides the answer.

From above a layer of cloud, individual peaks appear to stand majestically isolated and alone. From below the clouds, they can be seen as rocky prominences of the same mountain range…An awareness of synchronic-

ity allows one to look below the clouds. It allows one to connect all the
details of life.   —*Toby Johnson*

Hugh Weir thought the ecumenical Educational Forum might start by
talking about Abraham Maslow's pyramid of human needs. At the bottom of
the pyramid are the most basic needs such as food and shelter. Each level
upward represents higher needs. Near the top are man's spiritual needs.
Maslow placed "aesthetic" needs at the very top of the pyramid and stated that
man's lower needs must be met before the ones above them can be pursued
and satisfied. I thought it interesting that Maslow made a distinction between
spiritual and aesthetic needs, and that he believed aesthetic needs, rather than
spiritual, were at the apex.

Hugh commented that "most people fall on the lower level of Maslow's
scale—survival. Consequently, they don't have time to look into issues of
spirituality. On the other hand," he added, "many people are actually above
the survival scale, but run their lives as if they are not." That one hit home,
because even when I was making more than a million dollars a year, I somehow
felt as though I was still operating on the survival level.

From there, the conversation turned to the need for each adult to establish
a balance between the inner and outer lives. And in speaking of an inner life,
we weren't referring to religious training per se, but to the development of a
spiritual awareness that would improve one's life. We all agreed that our
primary goal was to transform the community by helping individuals to
operate from their own center.

The next day was August 26th and my birthday. It was filled with many
synchronous events, but I couldn't stop thinking about Maslow's hierarchy
and aesthetic and spiritual needs. For me, the two seemed closely related,
perhaps aspects of the same thing, and a series of events embodying both
aesthetic and spiritual needs seemed to bear me out.

All the events had to do with poetry. That morning I had finished reading,
in *Creation* magazine, some works of a poet named Iverson, which had
whetted my appetite for more. During breakfast in our backyard, the children
asked me to read from Shel Silverstein's, *When the Sidewalk Ends.* When I had
finished reading, Cecile brought in the day's mail and we opened a package
addressed to Michelle. It was a gift from her Uncle Laury, and it was a copy of
the same poetry book I'd just finished reading. Later in the day, Cecile gave
me two beautiful books of poetry. And when I turned on the public television
station, Maya Angelou was being interviewed by Bill Moyers.

Of *thematic coincidence clusters,* there were poetry days and music days;

accidentally-meeting-old-friends days and surprising letters-in-the-mail days. They weren't all positive; there were also car trouble days, children's accidents days and late-for-every appointment days. These synchronous events were so far above the limits of probability that I was continually dazzled by their occurrence. It felt as if God was saying to me, "Like patterns? Check this out, kid."

In our society, many people become irrational when confronted with paranormal phenomena. Some people naively accept *all* traditionally-unexplainable events as supernatural and valid; many others ignore *rational evidence* in support of those events that may well be valid. Synchronicities are a case in point.

Everyone has experienced their own synchronicities—clusters of connected events whose occurrence together is beyond any statistical probability. Yet many of those who have experienced these synchronicities for themselves continue to deny that they are anything more than chance happenings. It is ironic that those who pride themselves on their logical thinking become so lacking in it when evaluating anything beyond what is acceptably normal. Take, for example, the remarks attributed to the renowned nineteenth century physicist Hermann Helmholtz about an inexplicable phenomenon: "Even if it is true, I don't believe it."

The great Einstein wasn't immune to being perplexed by this. He did not believe that "God throws dice with the universe," and so remained uncomfortable when Quantum Theory exploration—a theory filled with chance, randomness and paradox—became popular. Yet the possibility exists that God does throw dice. The fact that they may be loaded is often overlooked by the orthodox scientific community. Yet we now have a generation of scientists who are quite comfortable with the laws of uncertainty.

As David Peat says, "Synchronicities are the jokers in nature's pack of cards, for they refuse to play by the rules and offer a hint that in our quest for certainty about the universe, we may have ignored vital clues."[9]

In my own view, synchronicities are not so much an occult phenomenon as they are creative cracks through the barriers of our thinking and living which allow us to perceive a deeper level of awareness. As we become more aware of their occurrence, and are more sensitive to their possible meaning, we find that the weight of evidence increasingly shifts to viewing them as meaningful events. Perhaps they are unexpected fax messages from God. They remind me of the time when it was believed that the universe was benign and all things worked together for the good. I welcomed synchronicities, respected them, and thought they were fun, demonstrating that we live in a world where everything can be an instrument of revelation.

A few weeks later, Cecile and I attended a special program in San Francisco put on by the Creation Center for Spirituality. The event was called, "Freeing the Imagination," and was in honor of poet, potter, teacher and writer M.C. Richards, a lovely lady in her seventies. There were several luminaries present to pay tribute to Ms. Richards, including composer John Cage and choreographer Merce Cunningham.

It was a celebration I'll never forget. The sense of love in the hall was all-pervasive, as though the individual goodwill of each attendee had been vastly multiplied, and had saturated the air. We had been seated in the second row. Coincidentally, seated in the front row, directly in front of us, was the well known, liberal priest/theologian Matthew Fox, whose book, *Original Blessing,* had done so much to help me reconcile myself with Catholicism and religion in general. Coincidentally seated in the third row, directly behind us, was author Brian Swimme, whose book, *The Universe is a Green Dragon,* had shown me a way to connect with the cosmos. Afterwards, I was able to meet these two Life Guides. After we returned home late that night, I made some journal entries and was pondering the evening's events when a familiar voice said, "Hello, Dr. A. Nice evening?"

"Very enjoyable, thank you, Hippocrates. To what do I owe the honor of this visit?"

"It's this idea you have of synchronicity. Incidentally, the term *synchronous,* like so many of the really important words you use, derives from the Greek— *syn* meaning *with*, and *chronos,* of course, meaning *time.*"

"Ahh, Hippocrates, you didn't come to give another discourse on Greek civilization. What's your point?"

"You keep speaking of probabilities, Dr. A.. but there is something you don't understand."

"What's that?"

"Let's approach the subject by way of the authors you so serendipitously met this evening."

(It was now my turn) "Of course, Hippocrates, you recall that the word *serendipity* is derived from a fairy tale called *The Three Princes of Serendip,* by Horace Walpole, which was about the accidental good fortune of these—"

"Yes, yes, of course I know that, Dr. A. There is no way I could *not* know it."

"What do you mean?"

"You'll see, you'll see. Now, may we—"

"Get back to the point? Yes, Hippocrates, certainly."

"I was speaking of your, uh, serendipitous meeting with the two authors this evening. You think it was statistically improbable?"

"Yes, Hippocrates."

"On the contrary, Dr. A., it was almost inevitable! You see, a book is more than knowledge and the paper on which it is printed. A book—every book—contains within itself...let me see, how can I say this in words? It contains a piece of the author's soul, or essence. And when you read a book, you are contacting not only the author's ideas—you're also contacting the author himself."

"You mean that literally, Hippocrates, or just metaphorically?"

"No. no, Dr. A., I mean it literally."

"But, Hippocrates, the implications of that are enormous. If it's a two-way street, that means that in addition to the author affecting the reader, each reader affects the author as well."

"Precisely, Dr. A., precisely. Now when you read Mr. Fox's and Mr. Swimme's books, you felt an affinity toward their thoughts and, by extension, toward them as well, did you not?"

"Yes, I did."

"That affinity was, and is, a real thing: an energy that seeks out its targets and weaves strands of connections which, themselves, are alive. These strands of connections, between you and the authors, work to bring you together, like magnets attracted to each other over a distance. If you go with the flow, if you follow your intuitive inclinations, it is not at all improbable that you will meet—it is highly probable, almost inevitable.

"A book acts as a kind of psychic data link, a transmitter/receiver for all the mental energies of its author, its readers and of everyone else who has an interest in it. Thus, each book (or any medium of communication) forms a vast corps of resonant souls whose numbers swell and wane in correspondence with the degree of interest and emotional connection of each person to that book. As a matter of interest, Dr. A., the psychic vibrations in a library are nothing less than overwhelming."

I was momentarily speechless. Finally, I said, "Hippocrates, that is one of the most remarkable things I have ever heard in my life."

"Thank you, Dr. A. I thought you would like it."

CHAPTER 20

The Order Behind the Chaos

The deepest words of the wise man teach us the same as the whistle of the
wind when it blows or the sound of the water when it is flowing.
—*Antonio Machado*

In October of 1989, Cecile and I attended Yom Kippur services at her
synagogue. It was a time of fasting. As he started his sermon, Rabbi Weiss
sipped a bit of water. This was against the fasting rule for Yom Kippur.
Although Judaic law states that health concerns take precedence over ritual,
Rabbi Weiss asked for the congregation's understanding because his throat
was hoarse and he would not otherwise be able to speak. Nevertheless, several
members of the congregation complained about this modification. Ironically,
I saw some of the same people wolfing down some sweets in the parking lot
following the service.

I was surprised at this outburst against the rabbi. After all, this was a
"reform" temple, where rituals and practices were being constantly redefined
in the light of current needs. The irony was that the protesters had missed
the whole point of the rabbi's sermon, which was practice tolerance and
don't be quick to judge. They believed that the rules of fasting were more
important than the sermon. The conflict brought back many of my old
dislikes of organized religion, especially how form is of greater concern
than content.

Nevertheless, I liked Rabbi Weiss personally. Cecile and I had invited him
and his wife, Shana, to join us in San Francisco for a talk that was to be given

by the Dalai Lama at the Fairmont Hotel. Four days prior to this event, the Dalai Lama had been awarded the Nobel Peace Prize, and there was great excitement at being able to be with him. Rabbi Weiss and I had been working together on The Educational Forum—our presentation of a varied, ecumenical program for the temple congregation—and the Dalai Lama's philosophy seemed appropriate for our purposes. During his talk, he said:

> No culture, no ethnic group, no government and no religion should put itself above human happiness and compassion. Today the world is smaller and more interdependent. One nation's problems can no longer be solved by itself completely. Thus, without a sense of universal responsibility, our very survival is threatened. Basically, universal responsibility is feeling for other people's suffering just as we feel for our own. It is the realization that even our enemy is entirely motivated by the quest for happiness. We must recognize all human beings want the same things we want. This is the way to achieve a true understanding.

At the end of the luncheon following his talk, as the Dalai Lama made his exit, he greeted each of us individually. I had seen other spiritual leaders up close, and they had shown different character facets. Although they had seemed congenial, some appeared to be in a different space, as though they weren't really connected with the world and weren't interested in it; others had been standoffish. But what they all had in common was that they seemed to be apart from me, spiritually, and from everyone around them.

The Dalai Lama was different. He had no airs about him. When he looked at you, it felt like an intimate look, as if he had known you for a thousand years, and had liked you for each one of them. His eyes and face were filled with intelligence and happiness. His manner didn't make you want to revere him or be in awe of him—it made you want to be friends and to get to know him better. And when he humbly bowed to each of us, expressing his respect for the God within us, it made me love him.

Rabbi Weiss, too, was exhilarated by the experience. He told us it was more moving than when he was ordained. "I feel reordained as a teacher of peace," he had said later. Rabbi Weiss may have had Jewish roots, but in the Dalai Lama's presence he had experienced what it was like to have Buddhist wings.

Meeting the Dalai Lama confirmed my long-standing attraction to Buddhist ideas. The Buddha statue that now sat serenely on our fireplace hearth was perhaps the first harbinger of my affinity for Buddhism. Twenty-five years ago when I had first seen and admired it, I'd had no idea of why I liked the statue so much. But if time is of no consequence to our inner selves, then my inner self already knew of my Buddhist affinity, even though it had not yet developed in my conscious mind. And that inner knowledge came through as a feeling, a desire for things Buddhist.

Isn't that how it works for all of us? As we grow older, we begin to see the pattern that has shaped our lives. And all the arbitrary or ambivalent decisions we once made are now seen as part of that pattern.

I believe this was part of what the Dalai Lama was conveying to me when he looked at me. I like to think he *had* known me for a thousand years but had the good grace not to mention it, to allow my awareness to ripen in its own good time.

It was quite a week. The luncheon with the Dalai Lama at the Fairmont; then an interfaith service at San Francisco's Grace Cathedral. A few days after that had been an "Education For Life" presentation by Dan Millman, author of *The Way of the Peaceful Warrior,* followed by folk dancing and singing from around the world by Montessori School children. And the week wasn't over yet. On Saturday I met my friend Chip at the University of California, Santa Cruz, for a full-day course given by the famed science fiction writer, Ray Bradbury.

Bradbury's challenge for us to "put yourself in the way of experience to see what appeals to you" and have a "life with many loves" struck a strong, resonant chord within me, for this is what I had been passionately doing over the past two years. Bradbury described this as the "root system" that opened up a whole new way of life for him. "Don't ask yourself what you're doing— just do it," he said, "then decide if what you've done is worthwhile. You throw up first, and find out later what you threw up," he added graphically. "You can't live intellectually; it's got to come from here," he said, pointing to his heart. "You can't think about it, otherwise you won't perform. It has to be explosive. It's like sex in the heat of passion. Love comes first. Love is the lubricant."

Bradbury recommended that we feed ourselves with good people—people who share our same interests—and good ideas. "Compare your truth with other people's truth," he said. "Think of all that you have read and the sum total of all your experiences as mulch for you to work with. Pretty soon, your ideas about life and art will begin to take root and birth themselves. Above all, remember, that whatever you do, for God's sake and yours—it must be fun."

I have a friend who met Bradbury in his younger days, in the late 50s. He claims Bradbury told this story about himself:

> It was fun to take walks down Wilshire Boulevard in Beverly Hills to see the wealthy, the famous and the ostentatious parade past the exclusive

shops. Movie stars and aspiring movie stars would go out of their way to attract attention, and a possible news story. One way they did this was to walk unusual pets on leashes. In addition to many glamorous dogs, you might pass pigs, giant lizards, chimps and an occasional alligator being taken for their daily stroll.

But the most fun was the women. There were so many attractive ladies walking down that stretch of Wilshire that I could hardly keep my eyes off them. Unfortunately, they weren't interested in me. So I developed a technique to overcome this shortcoming. Each time I passed an attractive woman, I would stop and smile, and in my most polite voice, say "Pardon me, would you go to bed with me?" I got a lot of disgusted looks and an occasional slap, but every now and then…

That evening Cecile and I, and our off-again, on-again friends, Jeremy and Jody Perlman, had been invited to dinner at the temple by Rabbi Weiss and his wife, Shana. Our host and hostess provided all the food, which was served under the *sukkot,* a thatched hut created for the Jewish festival of the tabernacles which, in ancient times, signified the time of the harvest of fruits.

I hoped this intimate gathering would help to heal the strained relationship between the Perlmans and us. The setting couldn't have been better. The stars were pitched out against the dark sky and shining with quivering brilliance; the air was fresh and mild; and I felt a satisfying sense of history and symbolism, seated under the *sukkot.* I, a non-Jew, felt completely at home in the religious setting.

At one point, Jody asked Rabbi Weiss, "How did you happen to become a rabbi?"

"I was a secular teacher at one time," he began, "but then one day I attended a lecture in Berkeley by Rabbi Zalman Schecter, a very wise rabbi, one of the wisest men I've ever met. His words had the effect of nonphysical open-heart surgery on me. I experienced this intense feeling of love, of truth and of understanding, as if this man standing in front of me was a conduit for a higher power and had signaled me out for some special transmission.

"In time I decided to attend rabbinical school to pursue my spiritual development. I hadn't met Shana yet. That came later. At first, there was no intent to become a rabbi; I just wanted to learn about the other side of life, sort of like Dennis is doing now…searching, exploring, taking new and exciting courses and workshops, and meeting some interesting people along the way. Then the rest sort of…just happened, and I became a rabbi. Meeting that wise rabbi and deciding to change my life was the best thing I ever did."

The evening was delightful, and I hoped the harmony would continue. As we sat there, looking up at the stars, Rabbi Weiss's story made me wonder whether my future life would be secular or religious. Before my father had married, he had searched his soul, trying to decide whether or not to remain in the priesthood. Now, I understood his experience. Each of my days was filled with intense but inconstant feelings of faith, love and connectedness. It felt as though I was looking into a sensitive telescope whose images are now clear, now fuzzy, as the focusing knob is turned.

A few days later I was listening to a tape called "Life and Spirit," by Dr. Bob Goodheart, when the phone rang. I picked it up and was only mildly surprised when I heard Bob Goodheart's greeting—synchronicities like this had become commonplace. It was good to talk to Bob again. Suddenly, without warning, there was a loud roar, the earth began to tremble like a thick wave of liquid concrete. The swimming pool began to rock like the tilt-a-whirl carnival ride that used to visit Hoboken, sending the water splashing violently from side to side. It was a powerful earthquake. Was it the "big one" tabloid psychics had been predicting for years? As I attempted to run inside, I lost my balance and stumbled, dropping my yellow writing pad and the cassette tape player onto the patio floor. A wave from the pool splashed over it. I regained my balance and rushed through the screen door. Lita our Filipina housekeeper was kneeling on the floor, covering her head with her arms. "Where's Michelle?" I yelled, unaware that Cecile had gone out and had taken our daughter with her.

Our neighbor's teenage daughter, Julie, appeared in the driveway. She had been home alone and was panic-stricken. I comforted her and led her into our house to call her parents. Then I thought about Jason and picked up the phone. It was working perfectly. I dialed the temple where he was attending Hebrew School, only to hear a shaken man at the other end say, "All the children are accounted for and safe. Everything is okay."

After an hour of waiting, Cecile returned home with Michelle. They were badly shaken up. The house they were visiting was closer to the epicenter of the quake and had been severely rocked. Michelle was sent flying against a wall, but other than a bad fright, she wasn't injured. Cecile had injured her knee while attempting to shield Michelle from objects falling from shelves.

Moments later, our neighbor Janet Bower and her two daughters sought safety and comfort with us. Her husband and son were at the World Series baseball game in San Francisco. Like many others, our neighbors had felt the need to congregate with others in the face of potential catastrophe, and our house turned out to be a refuge. We had a full house, and I kept all the children entertained by setting up drawing projects for them in our living room. I offered a prize for the best representation of the earthquake they had just experienced. The drawings were quite creative and told of each child's state of mind after the quake. One that stands out in my mind was of lightning bolts striking the earth and causing big cracks in its surface. After they had finished, I declared a tie and gave each child a dollar prize.

The rest of the afternoon was spent looking for damage, answering phone calls and trying to help find accommodations for visiting friends. We were fortunate in that we lost only a few pieces of crystal and some figurines, which had toppled over. For all the rocking and rolling, there was no apparent damage to our house. That evening, after all our guests had departed for their own homes and things had quieted down, I had some time to reflect on the events of the day. The news services had not yet reported the deaths and injuries from a collapsed freeway and a section of the Oakland Bay Bridge, and I was unaware of any severe injuries in our area.

I realized that, although this quake was not a gentle little teaser, my feelings about the mighty ground shaker had bordered on the sublime. I felt in awe of the overwhelming power of nature, the same kind of feeling I had experienced during my sabbatical when I watched the fury of a raging ocean storm from the cabin porthole of a cruise ship off the Amalfi Coast; the same kind of feeling I experienced in my grandmother's arms as a child when I watched Mt. Etna erupt in Sicily.

Why the sublimity? I'm not sure. Perhaps it was because I felt at one with the awesome power, safe and secure within its flow, just as I was becoming safe and secure within my own self. Or perhaps because I had tasted life's slings and arrows, and nothing could shake my euphoria.

Earthquakes are nature's way of dealing with its own mid-life crises. As with people, the stresses and strains build up to a critical stage within the earth's fault lines and then, suddenly, they adjust! A new life cycle begins, often at the expense of everything in its path. We humans who pride ourselves on being at the pinnacle of creation have a hard time accepting this. We forget we are part of nature and receive no special treatment from it. An earthquake is not carried out as a matter of vengeance; it is a natural inclination of the earth to change to a new, altered state and to then reconnect itself to the universe.

Many people were angered and scared by the October 17, 1989 earthquake. My Israeli friend Itzik told me he was angry with God and nature for disrupting his life and his sense of order.

"It's unfair!" he exclaimed. "What do you think of it?"

"To me, it's not so much that it's fair or unfair but that our expectations cause us to see life as unfair."

In contrast to Itzik, I was in accord with it. Unlike those who saw their lives flash before them with their goals and dreams unmet, I was now content with who I was, with what I had, and with the eternal, present moment. I had no more "could haves" or "should haves" or "if onlys." I was living the life I wanted to live. And while the earth trembled, I had a stable platform to fall back on.

"Establish yourself in God!" the Bhagavad Gita implores, "Then all else is possible." I was not arrogant enough to believe that I was fully connected with God...or to even begin to know what that meant; but I felt a strong enough connection to know that I was safe, that I was home, and that I would be safe and at home no matter what happened.

Little deeds of kindness,
Little words of love,
Make our earth an Eden
Like the heaven above.

—*Julia F. Carney*

In the Hebrew language, the word mitzvah loosely translated means "an act of kindness." It's a nice word and I use it often. Like most of us, I'd done my share of good deeds, or at least I thought I had. But there was always a string attached. Maybe it wasn't as blatant as "What will I get out of it?" Maybe it was just the knowledge that I would be recognized in some way...perhaps a brief newspaper headline, "Dr. and Mrs. Augustine have made a generous contribution toward the building fund." Or perhaps a mere expression of gratitude from the recipient, so that I could feel like the benefactor.

Now I was having a new experience—giving with no thought or care about benefit, prestige or respect. Just giving, for the sake of giving, or simply being a *mensch,* a decent man, to use another popular Yiddish expression. Like on Halloween evening, when I took Jason and one of his friends trick-or-treating. One of our stops was at the residence of the Bowers, our next-door neighbors. While chatting with Janet, I learned that her mother was scheduled for an exploratory operation for cancer, and I mentioned Dr. Bernie Siegal's book, *Love, Medicine and Miracles.* Since Janet was a born-again Christian, I didn't want to get hung up in the spiritual aspects of the book. Instead, I mentioned that it helped the reader understand the stages one goes through with an illness of this magnitude. Janet seemed open to the idea.

The next day I felt compelled to do a *mitzvah,* and I purchased the gift package which contained the book and cassette tapes. I included a small card on which I wrote, "One day at a time," and presented it to her.

It felt wonderful to be able to perform these simple *mitzvahs* outside the family. It was as though my energy, my gift of life, was finally being used in the way it had been meant to be used—more fully and selflessly. From giving a book to a neighbor, I moved on to giving a sack of lemons from my tree to another neighbor; then there were several modest acts of good will to help me reconcile with my former professional adversaries; there was comforting the bereaved and the sick; visiting elderly friends; serving on committees to help promote understanding and good will.

While I had never been an ornery, mean-spirited person, nevertheless I identified with Dickens' character, Ebenezer Scrooge, who wakes up on Christmas morning filled with love, and for his first act, buys a large turkey for Tiny Tim and the whole Cratchet family.

Like the awakened Ebenezer, I, too, could now see the potential for doing good everywhere around me. Instead of dwelling on all the things that were wrong in the world, I was thinking of all the opportunities available for helping to balance them out. For the first time, I realized that everyone wants an opportunity to contribute to their fellow man. We hesitate because we are either too self-absorbed like old Ebenezer or we fool ourselves into believing that our contribution won't make a difference. This short-sightedness reminded me of the timeless quote by Jan de Hartog in The Lamb's War: "Do not commit the error, common among the young, of assuming that if you cannot save the whole of Mankind you have failed."[1]

One opportunity was a program I had been working on for our mixed-marriage group. It was to be a formal event held in the large den of my home and featuring several speakers and a brilliant artist, Sid Stave, who would be showing slides of his powerful, controversial religious paintings. I had even arranged for the event to be professionally video-taped.

During the week preceding the event, my mom and dad arrived for a visit, bringing presents for the children and my favorite Italian deli food (so good that fellow Hobokenite Frank Sinatra has food from Fiore's air-shipped to him wherever he goes).

Dad is always a good sport, and the evening he arrived, jet lag and all, he accompanied me to Stanford University for a Buddhist ceremony called

Shomyo. The *Shomyo* ceremony dates back to an era as ancient as Hebrew psalms and Brahman hymns, and until that evening it had never been performed in the United States. Dressed in sumptuous, saffron robes, the monks entered and sat before an altar and a large brazier filled with charcoal. Special seeds and plants were then ignited in a formal fire ritual called *Goma,* whose origins can be traced as far back as Vedic India prior to 1000 B.C. As a priest fueled the fire, the others began a hypnotic chant accompanied by gongs, bells and symbols. With the flames soaring, the monks prayed for enlightenment, peace and happiness as they scattered symbolic paper flower petals into the fire as offerings to the Buddha.

Rather than carry on about "that foreign nonsense," Dad was very interested in the ceremony. He commented how the incense burning reminded him of Catholicism, and we agreed that religions tend to borrow from each other; there are common elements within all the world's great religions. Best of all, we both felt the sacred atmosphere during the ritual. This was a special time for us, for most of our lives had been spent in conflict with one another. Now, we both realized how much we had in common: our constant curiosity, our fascination with religions, history and current events involving religious freedom and persecution. For a while, father and son distinctions were no more—we were united in one spirit.

In the past, while my days were active, they were just days. One day might be better or worse than another, but life just went on against a constant background of anxiety, striving, planning and pushing. Now, life felt like the words in *Flower Drum Song:*

> *A hundred million miracles are happening every day,*
> *And those who say they disagree*
> *Are those who cannot hear or see.*
> *A hundred million miracles,*
> *A hundred million miracles,*
> *A hundred million miracles*
> *Are happening every day.*

For example, on the day after the Shomyo presentation, we went to the Hakone Tea Gardens where there were displays of several Japanese arts and crafts, including brush painting, origami, calligraphy, bamboo flute making and bonsai cultivation. Artist-in-residence Ami Wada patiently demonstrated the art of Sumi-E brush painting by guiding us with brush in hand.

Within minutes, We were each able to produce an image we could proudly call a bird—or as a Japanese artist might put it, the essence of bird. I was absolutely thrilled. It touched some chord within me, and I instantly knew that someday I would draw and paint for my own satisfaction. I also understood that the theme of a bird was not arbitrary but was meant to quicken something, to enliven some dormant area within my life. In this way, each day presented its miracles; each day had its profound moments. And living was…it was just pure, great, clean fun.

Over sixty guests were expected for our mixed-marriage, interfaith social. I was happy to present the artistic work of Sid Stave. When I first met him during the Progroff workshop at Vallombrossa, I sensed we would be seeing more of each other. Sid lived in Salinas, some sixty miles south of San Jose, on Augustine Drive. As I introduced him to our assembled guests I was struck by who I was and what I was doing here. The Dennis Augustine of two years ago could not have conceived of orchestrating and speaking to a gathering of this kind. I would have deemed it too "hokey," too disgustingly religious to even waste my time attending such an event. But now I had things to say, experiences to share and a message to get across.

If I were introduced to the Dennis Augustine of two years ago, he would reject me. That's because a lower state of awareness has had no experience of the higher state yet to come, and thus cannot really understand or appreciate it. They are quite literally worlds apart. But could I appreciate that my earlier version was in a state of preparation, preparing to blossom even though no bud could yet be seen?

Once we have arrived at a given state of awareness, we look across the chasm of humanity at others who do not share our views, and we have a tendency to be impatient with those who have not progressed sufficiently to appreciate where we are. Yet when we look at our own earlier selves, we find we were the same way. And when we look back in time, we do not disparage and curse our former selves—we accept them as an earlier stage of what we have now become.

Why, then, do we not view others with the same tolerance? Aren't they also an earlier stage of something that will become finer, more profound and more tolerant? Aren't they also in a stage of preparation even though the bud cannot yet be seen?

When Jesus implored his followers to love their enemies, perhaps he could see not only the seedling but the fully grown tree yet to come. Having seen the whole tree—that is, having seen the fully developed souls which our enemies are in the process of becoming—who among us would still wish to strike the seedling?

During the course of the evening, I spoke about Giordano Bruno, a passionate poet, philosopher and Dominican priest who conceived the idea that all cultures had one single, underlying tradition. His universal views of spirituality suggested that God consists of one totality which manifests in all living things. "God is not an external intelligence," says Bruno, "it is more worthy of Him to the be the internal principle of motion."

However benign these statements may sound to us, they cost Bruno his life. Refusing to retract his teachings, Bruno was burned at the stake by the Inquisition.

From Bruno I leapt to Spinoza, the Dutch Jewish philosopher who taught that God must be too great to have revealed Himself to just one people. Consequently, he believed that our separateness in the face of God was impossible. Spinoza, too, was declared a heretic, excommunicated from the synagogue for his views on spirituality and banned from Jewish life; at that time, this was a fate equivalent to a living death.

"That's the bad news," I said. "The good news is that times have changed. Respected theologians are becoming committed to interfaith dialogue; and many of them are beginning to believe that all the world's great religions have a uniqueness that is at the same time complementary. The emphasis is being placed on a God-centered living faith, rather than a prophet-centered one which claims exclusivity and often incites violence."

From there I went into the subject of interfaith marriages and how rituals are even now being redefined in order to sanctify the mixed marriages of couples who are in love. I spoke of the children of interfaith marriages; that what confuses them is not the experience of grappling with the different faiths within the family unit, but the problems of divorce, verbal and physical abuse, drug and alcohol addiction, and neglect.

A series of speakers followed, presenting ideas on interfaith rituals, the purpose of modern-day, institutional religion, and the necessity of learning to view the earth and its inhabitants as a whole. Then our featured guest, artist Sid Stave, showed his slides. It was a powerful portrayal of a man's love of his work and his god. Most appreciated his work; some found it extremely unsettling, several to the point of abruptly leaving.

On the other hand, Steve Proud, the same Steve who had so dogmatically refuted my ideas and beliefs at last year's Halloween party, now stayed for the entire presentation and I overheard him having a spirited but pleasant dialogue with the artist.

Many other guests found their own beliefs brought into sharp question. Some of the Jewish people present were forcibly reminded of their people's persecution, and the fact that the artist was a Jew who openly embraced other faiths and doctrines as valid avenues of the human spirit made it even more uncomfortable for them.

It would be some time before I had a sense of what we had accomplished, although there could be no doubt that many seeds had been planted. Whatever the effect upon my guests, the program marked a turning point in my own life. In a sense, it was my own Bar Mitzvah or coming out party, where I and others unashamedly bared our souls. I had been called upon to do it—it was part of my new covenant with God.

I later read the words of a Sufi mystic that seemed to describe how I had been "called." The Sufi was Abdul Qadir Gilani, and he said:

> When he has renounced the world so that he does not take to it on account of his (own) desire, nor in compliance with his own urges, but does it to fulfill the commandment of God, he is then commanded to talk to the world and establish contact with it; for now there is a portion for him in it which cannot be discarded and which has not been created for any other person.[2]

The next day, as Cecile and I were perusing the guest book, we happened to notice that Jason, had signed it. As soon as I saw it, a flood of happiness washed through me and tears came to my eyes. Jason had wanted to be a part of the event, and this was his way of showing it. I hadn't done anything to coerce him in any way, but he had sat in the first row, like a little gentleman, and closely watched the slides of Sid's artwork. I could tell that he had been affected by them. It had never even occurred to me that I might be planting a profound seed in the mind, if not the spirit, of my own son.

A few days later, Jason brought out a stack of papers. They were sketches of his impressions of Sid Stave's paintings. I don't think Jason noticed my eyes shining with pride and wet with happiness. I had done a *mitzvah* and it had come back to me tenfold.

Creation is so much grander than we can ever imagine, and its *invisible means of support* are so much more complex than we can ever know.

> Like many of the finest things of life, like happiness and tranquillity…the gain that is the most precious is not the thing sought, but one that comes of itself in the search of something else.[3]

CHAPTER 21

Vital Connections

If we could read the secret history of our enemies, we should find in each man's life sorrow and suffering enough to disarm all hostility.

—Henry Wadsworth Longfellow

"How do you love your enemy without condoning what the enemy does, without accepting his aggression?" Bill Moyers asks Joseph Campbell.

"I'll tell you how to do that" says Campbell. "Do not pluck the mote from your enemy's eyes, but pluck the beam from your own. No one is in a position to disqualify his enemy's way of life."[1]

My article, "A Time for Reconciliation and Change," appeared in the Central Coast Podiatry Newsletter. It was to-be the first of a monthly series. In it I suggested that podiatrists emphasize the humanistic side of the profession, including ways for dealing with intra-professional relations.

Stan Tobin had been one of my staunchest enemies. He now said, "Dennis, I think you have something important to say. It'll be a pleasure to write an introduction for you."

There was a lovely irony here. I'd been the whipping boy of certain influential members of the society. I'd even been threatened with bodily harm (Cecile had received an anonymous, menacing call at our office: "Tell Dr. Augustine we're going to blow him out of his little red car"); now I was writing editorials for their newsletter.

Reconciliation with my former enemies came about naturally and without a struggle. It required no effort to get rid of my resentments. Rather, I felt a deep soul-level communication, as though I'd entered into the mindscapes of my enemies without their conscious awareness. It was like entering a secret passageway that bypassed their defense systems. There was no feeling of separation or conflict as long as the experience lasted. It made me see that when our awareness is raised, compassion flows as freely as a riverbed is nourished by an underground spring.

We're all "tuned in" to other people's minds, because we are all part of one mind. But human beings, misled by their bifurcating intellects, lose sight of this basic communion. Out of this estrangement grows the unconscious longing for reconciliation. In fact, this communion is never really lost, and a signal much like a homing device eventually brings about a turnabout in the deepest cradle of our consciousness. Those who "awaken" to this fact become the beneficiaries of one of the great healing mechanisms of the universe. For forgiveness is man's highest achievement, long recognized by spiritual masters as enlightenment in action.

I've always favored the underdog, but I hadn't been aware I was living the myth, that I had created and attracted the events that allowed me to play out the myth. By becoming an underdog, I could justify my plight, creating anger, blame and hatred in the process so I'd have someone to hold accountable. Vengeance was the fuel that fanned the flames that propelled me forward.

My enemies reacted out of fear and an absence of love in their own lives. My counter-reaction was also based on fear and lack of love. For practical purposes I now saw them as having been *good* enemies. Although that may seem a contradiction in terms, Karl Jaspers, a major nineteenth century existentialist philosopher, dispels this inconsistency when he says that a good enemy provides the "loving combat"[2] through which we can test and refine our values. How can we ever clarify and refine our values without putting them to the test?

There are no accidents. Everyone who crossed my path, regardless of whether I chose to hate or admire that person, was a guide and a teacher. If a person is perceived as an enemy, it's hard to own that the hostile emotions we carry are projections of our own thoughts. We carry them like a handcuffed briefcase wherever we go. And, since the energy of all thoughts is returned to the sender, negative feelings towards others return to weakens us.

We were planning a family vacation to New Zealand and Australia, but first I had to see Dr. Bill Moulder. Bill had helped care for my patients when my hand first became disabled. He had proven to be competent, efficient and dependable. He had a warm, winning way about him that made patients feel comfortable and trusting.

For a long time, I could not believe Bill was real. I'd never met someone so self-effacing, considerate and generous. As time went on, I began to understand that Bill had been placed in my life to disarm my apprehensions, to help me get rid of my "wait and see" attitude, which made me reluctant to trust any but a select few.

When Bill and I met for lunch, I presented him with a bottle of champagne to help celebrate the coming New Year. To my surprise, he had gotten me an attractive personal grooming kit for travel, along with the latest *Fodor's Guide to New Zealand and Australia*. The gifts were totally unexpected and much appreciated. I then asked Bill about his plans. "I've sold my branch office, and I'm available to put in more hours at your clinic if you like," he replied.

"Bill, I need to know something. How long are you intending to stay on with me?" This was the first time I had broached this subject.

"I'm willing to commit myself to you for five years," he said, to my surprise and great relief. "Whatever you decide to do in the interim is okay with me. If you decide to sell or close the clinic sooner than that, I'll understand. Feel free to do what you need to do. Don't worry about me."

I looked at Bill with some embarrassment, still feeling timid about showing my feelings in public. I wanted to hug him. As if sensing my hesitancy, he hugged me first. "I love ya, Denny," he said. "Have a great trip and don't worry about a thing."

Bill had just given me a great gift. He had shouldered my responsibilities as well as his and relieved me of concern about the clinic. His attitude was, "I am here to help, and that's all there is to it—there are no strings attached."

Bill Moulder was a Bodhisattva in the flesh—an incarnation of a caring soul come to earth not to seek his own further enlightenment but simply to help others achieve theirs. He wasn't on a pedestal, and he had no large, adoring following. He had been right beside me all along, and I hadn't noticed.

A friend of mine has had the good fortune to have lived with several different *pundits* and *gurus* (respectively, "learned men" and "spiritual teachers" in Sanskrit). Asked about relationships, each of these revered men and women said much the same thing: *Find those persons with whom you are comfortable. Find those persons in whose presence you feel more energetic, more creative and more able to pursue your life goals. Stay away from persons who make you feel apprehensive, or who influence you to doubt yourself. Especially, stay away from those persons who drain you, so that your energy is all used up in trying to maintain the relationship.*

Trees and animals, humans and insects, flowers and birds: these are the active images of the subtle energies that flow from the stars throughout the universe. Meeting and combining with each other and the elements of the earth, they give rise to all living things.   —*Lao Tzu*

Flying across the Pacific Ocean, I dreamt of flying. In my dream I had the clear, sharp sight of a hawk looking down upon the world.

Birds had been the theme of a number of recurrent synchronicities I had recently experienced. Each time I saw a bird, I noticed something new, the subtle coloring around the head, or the way it lighted on a branch. I had no idea why, but the bird theme continued during our trip.

Even Jason was getting excited by synchronicities. When we passed a red telephone booth, Jason shouted, "Hey, Dad, here's another one!" As I came closer I saw that the name "Jason" had been carved into the side of the booth. The whole family was starting to notice meaningful coincidences.

In Christchurch, the largest city on New Zealand's South Island, our hotel bordered on the Avon River, swarming with ducks and gulls. One beautiful black bird stood out from the rest, standing atop a piling, alone, facing into the wind, totally still. It was so elegant and looked absolutely content. I moved slowly closer, not wanting to frighten it, and then I just stood still, looking at its eyes. What kind of consciousness does a bird have? There is certainly not the related-species feeling you get from looking into the eyes of a primate, or even a dog. But there was some connection, some mutual acknowledgment that we both belonged here, even if for different reasons and with different viewpoints.

In the center of Christchurch is Hagley Park, a 350-acre natural wonder that includes an extensive botanical garden. Strolling through the garden, we all seemed drawn to a large bird bath the size of a swimming pool. A few children were wading in it. A brightly-colored, sparrow-sized bird alighted on the bench beside us and began hopping closer to us. There is nothing more pleasing to a child (or to most adults) than to see a small, wild creature, spontaneously approaching. The children were delighted and Michelle was hard pressed not to reach out and try to grab it. After filling its beak with our bread and satisfying its curiosity, it flew off as suddenly as it had come.

Cecile and the children went on through the gardens while I lay down on the grass to take in the songs of birds, the sweet smells, the sparkling blue sky, the colorful flowers and the canopy of branches. What a wonderful vacation this was. It wasn't just the physical beauty; it was the absence of anxiety: no background worries about paying bills and work piling up at home; no concern about the dire problems of the world; and no doubt about my purpose for *being*. The feeling was delicious—a "high" without drugs.

Gazing at the slow-moving clouds, I reflected on how I had gotten here. It had taken me two years to learn how to live and enjoy life—

"Wrong, Dr. A," said the familiar voice of Hippocrates. I turned my head to see him sitting on the grass next to me, and I laughed out loud.

"What do you find so amusing?"

"I've seen you in dapper suits and in your native dress and sandals, but never in sneakers, shorts and a T-shirt."

"Yes, well, you know the old saying, 'When in Athens....'"

"Umm, yes. To what do I owe the honor of *this* visit?"

"It was that last thought you had that attracted me to you...about how it's taken you two years to learn how to enjoy life."

"Yes, what about it?"

"How many years, Dr. A., did you live on this earth prior to the last two?"

"Thirty-seven."

"Very well. Thirty-seven plus two equal thirty-nine. That's how many years it has taken you to learn how to enjoy life, Dr. A."

"I assume you mean that the first thirty-seven years were learning years as well."

"That's what I mean. But they weren't only *learning* years; they were *earning* years, too."

"Certainly they were earning years, Hippocrates. They were striving, pushing years with no time for anything else."

"Yes, but don't you see that those years of striving enabled you and your lovely family to be here today, enjoying this extended and rather expensive vacation? Moreover, if you now had to scrape for a living, how much leisure time would you have to enjoy life the way you are now doing?"

"Well, that's true, Hippocrates, but what's the point?"

"It's this. A spiritual path has no ending, but it has a beginning and a prolonged middle. Like most people who have experienced rapid changes, you think of your past two years as the beginning and the middle of your sojourn. But the changes you have undergone over the past two years would not have been possible without the previous thirty-seven. Those thirty-seven years— and for that matter, several thousand that went before them—should be recognized as just as valid and important as the last two."

"What 'several thousand' are you talking about?"

"I think you already know, Dr. A. But look, your family is returning, so I'll just leave you with this."

As he said this, a strange thing happened. One moment, I was lying on the grass looking at Hippocrates; the next moment, I was seated looking across at Dennis Augustine! And, I was saying to him, "Whatever you are now is the result of everything you have ever been. And no single experience is more valid than any other in its ability to propel you forward. Each one has been a part of the invisible web which you have talked about at length. No one can say whether any of your experiences have been 'right' or 'wrong' for you—but in the aggregate they have made you what you are today."

As soon as I had completed *my* thought, *my* awareness returned to "normal," and I watched Hippocrates slowly rise from his seated position on the grass, and with a straight face, say, "Ouch. These 2400-year-old joints are getting stiffer every year." As he walked away, I saw that the back of his T-shirt had the image of a large, bright green parrot on it. Underneath were the words, "I (heart) New Zealand."

The whole thing had been smooth and uninterrupted. Except that for about…what? Half a minute or so? I was Hippocrates! Let me try to be as clear as possible about this. The *me* that was Hippocrates felt no different from the *me* who was Dennis Augustine! I was not in Hippocrates' mind—I *was* Hippocrates!

From New Zealand we cruised to Sydney, Australia. With its high-spirited culture and sunny, semitropical landscape, Sydney seemed every bit as open, forward-looking and innovative as California. I took notes for my book, and I discovered something about writing that I had only been vaguely aware of before. As I wrote about an experience, I could see and feel aspects of the experience that hadn't occurred to me when it happened. The experience became fuller and richer as its subtleties were unveiled to me.

For example, Sydney harbor teemed with gulls. A coveted perch was atop the cruise boat's flagpole, just above the Australian flag that whipped in the breeze. As we floated along, I watched the gulls screeching and forcing the previous resident off the pole. The notion of "survival of the fittest came to mind." But later, while writing about it, and visualizing the gulls in my mind's eye, I was struck by the regularity of it. Now it seemed to me that the gulls, rather than competing for domination, had been cooperating the way children do when they take turns climbing to the top of a playground slide. Yes, some of the children stay longer at the top, showing off, but by and large they all have fun sliding down. The raucous gulls were also taking turns and having fun. Otherwise, wouldn't the dominant gull simply have remained on the flagpole, undeterred by its rivals?

Naive speculation? Wishful thinking? Perhaps, but it opened up possibilities I hadn't considered before.

We visited my Sicilian relatives who had settled in Western Australia. One evening, they took us to an open air market with all the mystery and charm of a Humphrey Bogart movie. It was like a stateside flea market, but with exotic products from around the world. As we strolled along I noticed a crowded shop emanating Middle Eastern music. I normally shy away from crowded places, but I was lured inside by a compelling sense.

I had just finished reading You'll See It When You Believe It. In it, author Wayne Dyer talks about how books, tapes and even people appear in our lives at just the appropriate moment. And he quotes from The Last Barrier, by Reshad Feild. Feild's book seemed to hold real potential, too, and I was anxious to get a copy when we returned home. But none of this was on my mind when I entered the crowded shop. It was filled with craft items and merchandise from a range of Middle Eastern countries, but to one side was a table of books for sale and, yes, Feild's book was there. The novelty never wears off synchronicities; it's not just the convenience of suddenly finding things, it's the knowledge that whatever I desired, something else was causing it to happen. If I deviated from my intuitive feelings about the best direction to follow, the synchronicities dropped off. When I again followed my feelings, they became more noticeable and more frequent. "What excitement will tomorrow bring?" I wondered.

The next morning, Thursday, December 28, 1989, I was doing some last-minute packing when I felt a strong jolt that was followed by a series of rumbles for about half a minute. It was an earthquake. I felt unsettled for a moment but quickly got over it. I looked up at the sky, laughed aloud, and shouted to whomever was listening in the heavens, "Thanks for your quick response!"

Cecile and the children were downstairs eating breakfast. I ran down and asked them, "Did you feel the earthquake?"

"Yes," Cecile said, "but nobody here believed me. When I told the waitress, she said, 'You Americans are so paranoid—it was just a passing train.'"

The epicenter was in the city of Newcastle, about one hundred miles north of Sydney, and it registered 5.6 on the Richter scale—a moderately hard jolt, but at the airport the customs inspector insisted, "There are no earthquakes in Sydney." But there are. We had been in Sydney's first earthquake.

We had spent several days being hosted by cousins, uncles and other relatives, many of whom I'd never met. There was cousin Guido, who insisted on treating us each time we went out, because, "We're family!" There was Guido's seventy-year-old father, Gaetano, the dark-skinned, leather-faced patriarch of this family of Sicilian Australians. Gaetano, or Guy, as he was called, had started in Australia as an impoverished fisherman and had worked his way to becoming the owner of one of the most successful of the Western Australia fishing fleets. Then there were Theresa, Bruno, Charlie, Ianno, Rina, Nino and Katherina, to mention a few. I was proud to be a member of the clan—an American relative of this hard-working, close-knit family who were living creative, fully-engaged lives and contributing to the spirit of this vast, southerly continent. I loved them as much as if I had been with them all my life.

It was a wonderful experience for Jason and Michelle to meet people who lived on the other side of the world, wonderful to be received with such warmth and acceptance, and to know how much we all shared with our far-flung family. I thought of what J.D. Salinger had said about life being a journey from one piece of holy ground to the next.

A holy place is created by a state of mind. Profound spiritual experiences can come from the simple celebration of earth's treasures and the friendship of good people. A holy place is a playground for the soul.

In spite of everything life is good.

—Anne Frank

We decided to stop over in Hawaii before returning to California. Sitting at poolside, relaxing in the warm sun, I noticed a middle-aged Japanese man in the pool with his daughter. The girl was about ten years old and a quadriplegic. With infinite gentleness and patience, her father held her and guided her through the water. I tried not to gawk, but I was struck by how much pure joy this disfigured, helpless girl displayed—she was having the time of her life!

After a while her father carried her out of the pool and eased her onto a lounge chair, next to her wheelchair. Then he began to feed her some cereal with a spoon. The girl couldn't control her spasmodic, jerking motions, and as I watched she cracked the plastic spoon.

My instinctive reaction was to fetch another spoon at the snack bar, so the father wouldn't have to leave her side. But I didn't budge, immobilized by inhibitions. What if I appeared to be intruding on a private affair? If I got them the spoon wouldn't that give away the fact that I had been watching them all along? I was ashamed of my sudden inertia. It's amazing, I thought, how emotional handicaps can sometimes be as disabling as physical ones. Yet we manage to cover them up so nicely because they are invisible.

The girl was at first unaware of what had happened. Laughing gently over it, her father explained to her what had happened. She responded with a series of shrieks and grunts, her way of laughing. Then her father walked to the snack bar and returned with two fresh spoons.

While the girl was being fed, she suddenly began to cough and choke. Was it serious? Was this a common occurrence? I couldn't tell by the father's outward calm. Then, as suddenly as it had come, the girl's choking stopped. Meanwhile, the other hotel guests were busy swimming, snorkeling or sunbathing. I noticed that many of the guests had deliberately turned away from the Japanese man and his daughter. Their actions said that they would prefer not to witness this often-concealed part of life, which is why the parents of severely disabled children avoid taking them out in public, especially to a popular tourist hotel during the peak season.

Research shows that the typical American father spends only five minutes each day bonding with his children (for that matter, the typical Japanese father doesn't even see his children during the six workdays of the week). Yet this Japanese family had elected to let their daughter experience some of the wonders of the world, whatever the sacrifice. I have seldom seen, even in the best of families, the love and affection that this frail girl was receiving from her father. After she finished eating, he carried her down to the surf and gently lowered her body so she could feel the warm waves splashing against her. Her pure joy and exultation was expressed in cackles and screams. No one nearby was having such a good time.

I was reminded of how to turn a crisis into an opportunity, how to accept what life dishes out nobly and courageously, and how we can learn from all people, no matter what their race, background, affliction or station in life.

In a little while, the sun began to set, and the entire sky was soon aglow with fiery reds and golds so brilliant you think the world is ending—or beginning. From poolside, I could see the silhouette of the Japanese father, sitting at the edge of the surf with his daughter on his lap, watching the unfolding drama of the sky. The girl's constant jerking motions had stopped, and both figures were completely still. I was no longer inconspicuously glancing—I was staring at them, caught up in the drama and beauty of their togetherness.

Then the father leaned over and kissed his daughter on her cheek. And I could no longer control myself. My heart opened and tears flowed from me in profusion. The love I felt for these two people whom I had never met overwhelmed me. I felt so privileged, so honored to share their experience. And that kiss...was the sweetest kiss I have ever seen.

I think of compassion as the fundamental religious experience and, unless that is there, you have nothing.   —*Joseph Campbell*

A few days after returning from vacation we were invited to dinner by Jeremy and Jody Perlman. Cecile was driving, and as she turned onto their street, a car coming from the opposite direction attempted to turn onto the street at the same time. There was a mad screeching of tires, and we stopped just inches apart from one another. We looked at the driver in the other car and he looked back at us, and we were all aware of how close we had come to a serious, possibly fatal accident.

How ironic! We had just traveled halfway around the world without harm, narrowly avoiding serious injury at home. How unexpected and fickle life can be. It doesn't matter who or what you are, what you are doing or where you are going—when it's time for that final curtain call, there's no place to hide. But in contemplating my mortality a change had come over me. Somehow, I had learned to accept death as part of life, as part of the creation I now understood more intimately. I certainly didn't relish the idea of dying, but neither did I dread it. It no longer seemed like an end, the gateway to oblivion;

now it seemed like another change, sharing with birth the status of life's two most profound transformations.

> There are persons who shape their lives by the fear of death, and persons who shape their lives by the joy and satisfaction of life. The former live dying; the latter die living. I know that fate may stop me tomorrow, but death is an irrelevant contingency. Whenever it comes, I intend to die living.[3]
> —*Horace Kallen*

We arrived at Jeremy and Jody's house bearing gifts from our trip, ready to resume a spirit of real friendship, but our hosts seemed fidgety and preoccupied. The pleasantries of small talk seemed forced. The entire time together felt stilted, and I kept asking myself, "Why keep on with this charade?"

The reason became clear within a few days, when I received a letter from my attorney. Now I knew for sure why Jeremy had been acting strangely for several months. I remembered Hippocrates telling me, "the spirit picks up the deception that the mind doesn't see."

A deal had been struck some time ago on the malpractice lawsuit that had been initiated against us. Jeremy had agreed to some legal maneuvering that enabled the plaintiff's lawyers to extend the statute of limitations on the case which, in effect, allowed them to include me as the target. In return, in a legal maneuver that allowed him to save his own neck, Jeremy had immediately been dropped as co-defendant in the case.

It was patently unfair. The patient had been under Jeremy's care for a year after I had referred her to him. While he had told me about the radical surgical procedures he was going to perform on her, he hadn't informed me about the resulting series of infections, her hospitalization and the subsequent partial amputation that became necessary. On top of that, Jeremy and I had a personal agreement to share responsibility in any cases where our treatments overlapped.

So Jeremy had sold me out—pure and simple—with the complicity of the plaintiff's lawyers. Perhaps they felt that I was a bigger fish, with larger assets, so that they could win a larger award. Or more likely, Jeremy conned them—as he did the patient, into thinking that I was solely liable and he was merely the white knight whose attempts to rescue her had backfired. Whatever the reason, it became apparent the fix was in.

One Saturday afternoon, after I finally confronted him about the matter, Jeremy paid me a visit to try to justify his action. "I never saw myself as being selfish," he said, "but I guess in this instance I was." In response to my accusing him of lying, he said, he hadn't told real lies, just "shades of lies."

I looked at Jeremy, my intimate friend and colleague of so many years, and asked him directly: "What would you do in my shoes? How would you respond to betrayal by a close friend?" Jeremy shrugged and was unable to answer. I hadn't really expected an answer. I would have to determine that for myself. Should I forgive and forget or retaliate? Should I turn the other cheek or force Jeremy to be accountable for his performance? All I could think of was Marshal DeVillars famous line: "God save me from my friends, I can protect myself from my enemies."

I suppose I had always known about Jeremy's potential for jumping ship in a crisis. I had seen him do it before, all the while crying out it was someone else and not he who was to blame.

And what of my own role? Why had I condoned it all along? Maybe for the same reason I hadn't jumped up to replace the broken spoon for the Japanese father and daughter—my inhibitions about interfering. Or maybe I thought Jeremy's allegiance couldn't be questioned when it came to *me*. After all, he had made a considerable amount of money by working in my clinic and through my referrals. But even more than that, Jeremy, Jody, Cecile and I had done so many things together; we'd been friends since the late 1970s, when I had already established myself and they were just starting out.

Beyond that, Jeremy had been intimately aware of all the changes I had undergone over the past two years. Since we first met, he and I had engaged each other in literally hundreds of profound discussions where we had bared our souls to each other. Jeremy had been my male soul-mate and confidante. But he had his own agenda, and in the end that seemed more important than our relationship.

It was hard for me to understand. I still do not understand it completely. We can never put ourselves in someone else's mind and know all their motivating fears and desires. But at least the months of ambiguity over his culpability were over. One thing I couldn't take away from him is that Jeremy had been, in many ways, a true friend. He had a marvelous ability at clever repartee—it was fun to be around him. Also, he had done many little kindnesses for me. But I had long overlooked his complex patterns of unde-pendability, of small lies and contradictions.

"Why did you overlook them for so long?" asked Hippocrates in his ever-gentle tone. I was no longer surprised by his unexpected entrances, and I immediately replied, "I suppose it's because I'm so dumb."

"Come now, Dr. A., disparaging yourself doesn't help. More importantly, it isn't true."

"Then why *did* I go along with so many of Jeremy's foibles?"

"For the same reason so many others overlook the faults—often very serious faults—of their friends. Remember what you've learned these past years...that the essence of the creation is love, and you, as a more and more attuned part of the creation, are an expression of that love. You didn't overlook your friend's faults because you're dumb or insensitive, Dr. A., you overlooked them because you wanted to express love, and true, loyal friendship is a way of expressing it.

"For that matter, Dr. A., I will remind you of something you've known all your life even though you may not have always been aware of it. You are a loving person, a deeply loving person. Even when you were acting out the role of a tough kid on the streets, it was more important for you to show friendship and loyalty then it was to ever hurt anyone. Do you remember the time you got stabbed? When you were lying on the street, bleeding, until the ambulance came to get you?"

"I'll never forget that."

"What got you stabbed, Dr. A.? Hatred for the young Puerto Ricans? No, it was loyalty to your friend who was in danger. We've had—I mean, you've had that all your life, Dr. A., and it's a wonderful trait, not a weakness."

"Then what—?"

"Get on with living, Dr. A., get on with it. As my friend, Diogenes, says, 'When two friends part. they should lock up each other's secrets and exchange keys. The truly noble mind has no resentment.'"

Hippocrates was right, though I had my doubts I could do it fully. And yet, there was no room for game-playing, no time to put myself down or to entertain thoughts of resentment, hatred or retaliation. It would cancel out everything I had come to learn about love, compassion and forgiveness. Sure it hurt—it was unfair. Then, I remembered something Bob Goodheart had once said to me: "Expecting the world to treat you fairly is like expecting a pit bull not to attack you because you're a vegetarian."

Find those persons with whom you're comfortable. Find those persons who, as a result of being with them, make you feel more energetic, more creative and more able to pursue your life goals. Stay away from persons who make you feel apprehensive, tense, or who influence you to doubt yourself. Especially, stay away from those persons who drain you, so that all your energy is used up trying to maintain the relationship.

Jeremy and Jody, Cecile and I would continue to be cordial when the occasion demanded it, but our close relationship was finished. Our friendship was no longer worth all the awkward adjustments we had to make in order to maintain it.

What had its purpose been? What did—?

"Just one more thing, Dr. A.," Hippocrates said, "remember that *all* relationships are for the benefit of *all* parties to them. You have done a great service to Jeremy...one that he will come to know when he is ready to know it. And in return, he has done you an equal service. I think you know what it is."

I did know. I knew without any doubt how firm my resolve was to go forward on my journey. No one, no relationship, no obligation, no disappointment could deter me. Suddenly, the anguish of betrayal passed over me and I was finally at peace with what had happened between Jeremy and me.

"What a precious gift!" I thought to myself. I then wrote a brief letter to Jeremy, one which I would never mail:

Dear Jeremy,

Thank you for being a Life Guide to me. Wherever you go, whatever you do, I wish only good things for you. May your life become blessed and filled with love. And know that while my path now moves away from yours, the higher aspect of you, the part that is most truly you, will always be close to me.

Your friend, Dennis

The path of spiritual growth is littered with the residue of discarded relationships. That doesn't mean the relationships were wrong or unwise—it simply means they outlived their usefulness. Just as continents break apart, so do relationships. As a friend says, "Where does the path take us? Sometimes together, sometimes apart, and all directions leading to ourselves."

CHAPTER 22

The Site Of Enlightenment

It's time to speak of roses and pomegranates,
And of the ocean where pearls are made of
Language and vision,
And of the invisible ladders
Which are different for each person,
That lead to the infinite place
Where trees murmur among themselves.

—Rumi

John Hipsley was a member of the Educational Forum project who seemed to come out of nowhere to play an important role in my life. He inspired and validated my spiritual experiences, partly through a series of programs called "Scriptures and Myths—Their Lore and Legend."

John was skillful at sifting out simple wisdom from complex, esoteric teachings. His programs were stimulating, challenging and inspiring. One of his topics was "States of Enlightenment as Experienced by Persons Throughout the Ages." He went to great pains to distinguish between intellectual understanding and direct personal experience of the divine. In addition to historic evidence, John drew on myths, fairy tales and fantasy literature, then brought them all together to show the importance of symbology. He defined the creative source as a truth that is unknowable and whose "love is so fine as to be bruised by the rough wrappings of words."

John called himself an independent searcher with no ties to organized religion. He felt that set beliefs don't bring about experiences of the divine in and of themselves. He liked to say that "belief is secondary to the direct experience of one's awakened state"; and, "It's not the Truth we are looking for—that can never be known—but an openness to levels of experiences that stretch out to infinity."

John's comments made me realize that the whole point to the mystic vision is that it inspires this sense of openness to greater realities, and that opening oneself to the possibility that everything can be true has the power to transform lives.

We began our class one evening in a candlelit room of the church with Gregorian hymns playing softly in the background. John had a sense for dramatics, and I had the feeling I was participating in some secret rite. It felt good. "As breath gives life to the body," John began, "so there is a spiritual pulse which throbs through the human organism, sustaining the cosmic rhythm and universal harmony, linking every man and woman with their soul and with each other...

"This course will explore the sacred language...a language that reveals a sense of truth to the inquirer. For example, 'the opening of doors' and 'the lifting of veils' are mystical metaphors which poetically describe a spiritual process. They describe the passage from the mundane world into the world of depth. The concept with which we are dealing in this course is the basic oneness of the world. Without this concept we cannot advance from the known to the unknown. And truth, as we are seeking it, has no other meaning than the reduction of plurality of phenomena to an essential unity."

Together, we delved into the meaning of parables. "Parables," John said, "are short stories based on human experience, used to illustrate a moral, religious, or spiritual truth. We all know that Jesus, like all great sages of their time, used parables to explain the mysteries of 'The Kingdom of Heaven.' He told his disciples that he did so 'because they seeing see not; and hearing they hear not, neither do they understand.'"

Continuing, John said: "What Jesus called the Kingdom, if taken metaphorically, can mean the mystical realization of the ultimate unity of all things—rather than the more common literal reference to some afterlife. So we can consider the parable a 'symbolic narrative of comparison' which illustrates the laws of the inner world by reference to the outer. 'I will open my mouth in a parable; I will utter dark sayings of old'" *(Psalms 78:2)*.

I had been drawn to symbols and myths for some time, and hearing the way John put it—that the inner world can be illustrated by references to the outer world—confirmed that I was on the right track. Far from being simplistic stories to entertain and perhaps capture the curiosity of the uninitiated, myths with their rich and varied symbols are the language of the soul.

Then we got on to the subject of spiritual growth, and one of the participants, a retired school teacher, asked: "What did you mean when you said that evolutionary change is slow and arduous but transformation is inevitable? It doesn't seem to offer much hope of it happening in my lifetime. I'm sixty-five years old, for God's sake."

"The pace at which it happens," John said, "is up to you—it's your choice."

"But how on earth can I choose to have an act of grace that only touches a few?"

"Ah, but that is a different sort of myth—a very false and harmful one at that—that keeps you outside the circle. Remember, 'The Kingdom of the Father is spread over the earth and men do not see it.' While there are no guarantees, the question we need to ask," John added, motioning to the audience, "is not what our chances are in the cosmic lottery; that is, will I be one of the few to receive Grace? The questions we need to ask ourselves are: when that door opens—when that veil lifts—will I be ready? When the opportunity presents itself, can I accept what's there?

"Ultimately, each one of us is responsible for the image of God we allow to dominate and guide us. This is what I mean when I say that only through choice is the way shortened. Not only does it mean we must recognize the transcendent experience, but we must be prepared to respond to the call. This is where free will comes in. The ancient Hebrews became the Chosen People not because they were uniquely chosen, but because out of all the tribes they *chose* to enter into a direct covenant with God."

By the look on the face of the elderly school teacher who asked the question, I could see he was in a sea of confusion that was just begging for clarification. "The answers to your questions," John said, "won't come from any words I can utter. No one can logically predict when these opportunities will come to you, what choices you'll have to make or how you should make them.

"You have to unlearn a lifetime habit—that of processing everything through your intellect. As a beginning, just listen to this poem for a moment, without trying to analyze it.

> To every man there openeth
> A Way, and Ways, and a Way,
> And the Low Soul gropes the Low,
> And in between, on the misty flats,
> The rest drift to and fro.

But to every man there openeth
A High way and a Low,
And every man decideth
The Way his soul shall go.

—John Oxenham

Somehow, the right poem or story seems to do the trick every time. Its words provided no logical answers to relieve the older man's anxiety, but nevertheless his features seemed to soften, his eyes grew misty as if for a fleeting moment he understood, and he acknowledged his understanding by nodding.

That evening as I helped Cecile tuck in the children, Jason asked, "Daddy, what kind of class did you go to tonight?"

"Oh, it's too hard to explain right now," I said, choosing the easy way out.

"Daddy can you read us a story?" asked Michelle.

"Sure," I said, not admitting I was feeling very tired.

"Let's see what you have here? Hmmm, here's *The Fish that Looked for Water.*"

As Jason, Michelle and I cuddled in bed together I began reading: "One day a fish was swimming close to shore. 'Water is the most important thing in the world,' he heard someone say. 'Without water there can be no life.'

"'I wonder where water is?' thought the little fish. He began to swim around looking for it. He looked close to the bottom of the river. He looked close to the top. He looked behind the plants and under the rocks.

"'Where is the water?' he called to another fish. But that fish said, 'Where can I find water?' He did not know either.

"Farther and farther the little fish went out into the ocean. He asked fish after fish. But no one knew. The little fish went deeper and deeper into the ocean. There he met a wise old fish. 'Did you ever hear of water?" he asked.

"'Sure,' said the wise old fish. 'You can't live without it.'

"'That's right!' said the little fish. 'But where is it?'

"The old fish blinked. 'It's all about you and around you.'"

As I kissed the children goodnight and tucked them in, I realized that the story was as much for me as it was for the them. I thought of how the retired teacher had yet to find what he was looking for. I thought about what John Hipsley said in his reference to Jesus: "The Kingdom of the Father is spread all over the earth, but men do not see it."

Opportunity had knocked on my door that night, in the form of a child's request and a simple story about a fish. I'm glad—this time at least—I had been ready.

Why do some people experience enlightenment and others do not? The literature is replete with stories of seekers who spend their whole lives at it but have never become "finders." They are like the fish in the story. They are lost, said priest-philosopher Teilhard de Chardin, in the "divine milieu" that nourishes them.

What methods or qualities does a person need to have in order for enlightenment to come about? Some sages have spoken of the necessity of faith, others of discipline or God's grace. Some yogis claim it is a matter of refinement of the physical nervous system—a biological basis, while Zen masters suggest that the nervous system must be shocked out of its normal state. Other recommended paths to enlightenment are through devotion, fasting, meditation, prayer, the acquisition of wisdom, the guiding force of a guru, or the activation of Kundalini energy,* to name a few. Sometimes it occurs by some quirk of fate—an accident, an act of grace through which enlightenment shines.

Nobody knows for sure why some people experience enlightenment and others don't. It is one of the great mysteries. And for all our vaunted contemporary knowledge of the human condition, and for all the wisdom stories of the ancients and their contemporary counterparts, we are no closer to knowing than people were thousands of years ago.

Why aren't we any closer? Maybe it is as simple as accepting the possibility that for many of us our time has not come yet; perhaps it is in recognizing that there are those who, for whatever reason, choose to keep their true identity a secret.

Joseph Campbell, in *Hero's Journey,* tells the story of a tiger raised as a goat whose quest is to discover his true identity. "When Hallaj or Jesus let the orthodox community know that they were tigers, they were crucified," he said, "And so the Sufis learned the lesson at that time with the death of Hallaj, around 900 A.D. The lesson is: You wear the outer garments of the law; you

---

* An intense and powerful spiritual energy, described in the teaching of Kundalini Yoga, said to become activated after long and disciplined periods of yogic practice.

behave like everyone else. And you wear the inner garments of the mystic way. Now that's the great secret of life."[1]

With the memory of Jeremy's betrayal still fresh in my mind, I decided to drop my own lawsuit against the condominium in Hawaii where I'd injured my back in April of 1987. The lawsuit was justified on two counts: the equipment had been poorly positioned in the workout room and there was insufficient space to use the exercise machines properly, and these were factors in causing my injury. When I initiated the lawsuit, I didn't know how severe my injury was or whether I would be able to continue working. Filing the lawsuit had been an instinctive act of survival, but I didn't need the money and it would be hypocritical to pursue it now. My injury was not an accident. And, as it turned out, it wasn't even the major cause of my disability. Now, I wanted to remove as much negativity from my life as possible.

I tried to apply this new state of mind to other concerns. A friend was considering suing a local hospital and her attending physician for what was supposed to have been a routine hysterectomy for fibrous tumors. Marilyn's case had been a tragedy of errors—which sometimes happens. After the surgery, an infection got pretty serious and her physician had left an associate on call. The prescription for her pain medication proved insufficient to allow her to be comfortable, and the hospital had some difficulty getting hold of the doctor on-call in order to augment it.

What was supposed to be a three-day hospital stay turned into ten days, with Marilyn's parents sitting vigil until their daughter's fever finally broke and the infection was under control. Marilyn's experience was complicated by the fact that her parents were paying for the surgery—it was a preexisting condition that wasn't covered by insurance—and the cost came in at more than ten thousand dollars over estimate.

I recommended that Marilyn hold off filing suit until I had a chance to speak to one of the hospital administrators. Dan Dunne was second-in-command at the hospital, and Dan's son Brian was Jason's good friend. That was the opening I needed to help present Marilyn's case. I wasn't an attorney, but I had been through the medical lawsuit quagmire so many times I understood how to make the system work.

In the end, Marilyn agreed to a greatly reduced bill and the threat of a lawsuit was dropped. Everyone was reasonably satisfied, which was my compensation for the time and effort I had put in. It helped me understand how truly satisfying the role of peacemaker can be. Once again, I saw that doing a *mitzvah* without any thought of reward makes you feel great.

The next morning I had a temporary relapse. It was a rainy winter morning, dark and dreary. As I lay in bed, I was suddenly overwhelmed by anxiety. Would the mail bring another medical complaint or, even worse, a legal summons? Would I be able to perform adequately, or would I make an error in judgment and cause a patient some unwonted complication? Would I be able to make the large balloon payments coming due on my leveraged investments? And would I be able to maintain the lead on my competitors?

It was the same litany of concerns that used to keep me from wanting to get out of bed in the morning. Unable to shake the mood, I managed to stagger down the hall to my office. Still half asleep, I rested my head on my desk momentarily. Suddenly, I was aroused by a familiar voice.

"Dr. A., Dr. A., don't fall for that. Get hold of yourself. Those feelings are just echoes from the past. We—I mean, you—have been out of practice for more than six months now, and you've gotten rid of most of your troublesome investments. You don't have to dread another day at the clinic; you can relish this wet, windy day from inside your snug home, or you can go outside and enjoy it!"

That snapped me back to reality. "But Hippocrates, why would these echoes from the past come back to haunt me—when everything is going so well?"

"It's because the old ways are very seductive. As a result, you're still prone to slipping every now and again into striving for what you think is perfection. For example, whenever the weather does something you don't like, you call on everything negative you can think of to verify that it's a bad day, even if it means resurrecting old worries that are no longer valid."

Hippocrates was right. I had always had a tendency to project my deep unhappiness of the past onto any day in which the weather was less than perfect. As a consequence, I had spent most of my adult life living in frustration, painstakingly trying to fit life into an unattainable ideal.

"You see, Dr. A., your urge to make things perfect didn't spring from anything bad—it's simply energy, and energy isn't bad or good—it's neutral."

"Maybe I should have had less energy."

"If you'd had less energy, you'd have spent even more of your time moping around, lamenting the imperfections you saw around you. The difference would have been that you'd just mope—you wouldn't have tried to do anything about it."

"So what's the difference? Why have more energy if we don't use it correctly?"

"Ahh, Dr. A., there's a big difference, a very big difference. You see, if you have little energy, you haven't as many options, there's not much you can do to change your situation. In contrast, if you have lots of energy, you have the potential for doing great things. It's just a matter of learning how to use your energy wisely."

"Hippocrates, are you equating my energy level with spiritual development? Does an individual gain energy as he or she grows, spiritually?"

"Yes, Dr. A., but not necessarily in the way you mean it. In some Eastern countries there are people called 'masts' who stand stiffly erect like the masts of boats. These people have followed a spiritual practice whose purpose is to put themselves in touch with divinity by shutting out all external influences. They have begging bowls slung from their necks, and devout attendees feed and wash them. These 'masts' are thought of as holy men, communing with God. But their energy is directed inward. From an observer's view, they are doing absolutely nothing—*merely* existing.

"Your energy, on the other hand, has been outwardly directed. It's up to you to determine what to do with your energy, but having been blessed with prodigious amounts of it, you have the potential to accomplish much in the world if you choose to do so. Which brings us back to this rainy day. Is it really dreary? Take another look."

"Well, the cloud formations are actually rather beautiful."

"Of course they are. Remember, the worst things are always imagined, and the calamities hardest to bear are those that never happen."

Just then Jason and Michelle came into my office, and Hippocrates vanished. I put my arms around them and together we walked over to the window and looked out. Several birds had taken refuge in the tree outside the window, and we could hear their loud chirping through the glass. As we watched, a line by Karl Durkheim came to me: "By allowing ordinary consciousness to darken, we can at last see the light of life." As I looked out into the darkness of the day, I saw a subtle rainbow in an area of light among the clouds. I pointed it out to the children, and Jason pointed out the rays of the sun that came cascading down toward the earth.

The names of people who had been influenced my life in one way or another kept popping up with negative connotations. Cecile's cousin, Jeffrey Berkowitz, who helped me get out of the Onyx Building and who had built up the family wealth from a real estate investment to an empire was checking himself into the Mayo Clinic with chest pains. All his money, resources and prestige had not given him the security and peace of mind he wanted and needed.

Then there was California State Senator Joseph Montoya, formerly one of the most powerful politicians in California. Senator Montoya had helped level the playing field between minimal incision podiatrists and hospital-based, traditional podiatrists, but he'd been forced to resign his office after a scandal had erupted. Shortly after his resignation, he was convicted on federal charges of extortion and racketeering. Senator Montoya had the distinction of being the first California lawmaker to be convicted of political corruption in more than 25 years.

When I phoned Dr. Louis Needleman, instead of a warm reception, all I got were questions about my personal finances. It only took me a few minutes to realize that he was only interested in what I had, and not how I was doing. If I had expected a humanistic mellowing in Needleman's attitude, I was sadly mistaken. Despite his failing health, his sole preoccupation was in regaining the fortune he had been swindled out of, and once again becoming a top gun.

I also heard from Jay Seymour. He had managed to keep much of his wealth intact. But his days consisted of preparing for and attending to litigation matters. Defending himself had consumed all his energy and, in my opinion,. taken over his life.

Dr. Gary Wyatt was also in trouble. Gary's aggressive marketing had created the most successful, free-standing, podiatric facility in the U.S. His efforts made mine appear paltry, but now he was deeply embroiled in a suit with the state of California for alleged "business practice violations." He had so far agreed to pay four hundred thousand dollars in fines plus an equal amount in attorney's fees, and it wasn't over yet. He was spending almost all his time digging up documentation and researching the medical literature to support his case, just as I had once done.

Then I heard of the death of Malcolm Forbes, multi-millionaire and chairman of the board of Forbes Magazine. Forbes was the very symbol of capitalism, a man who made the possession of money and conspicuous consumption the mantra of the corporate world. Perhaps his most often-quoted saying is, "Whoever dies with the most toys wins."

Around the same time, the infamous Michael Milken pleaded guilty to a host of charges including securities violations in the Drexell-Burnham junk bond scandal. Even Donald was at least temporarily out-trumped, not so much by his impending divorce from Ivana as from his over leveraged empire, which was teetering on the brink of ruin.

The signs and omens kept accumulating and one evening, after eating with Cecile and the children at a Chinese restaurant, I opened a fortune cookie and read it aloud. "Depart not from the path which fate has assigned you." I chuckled, but it made me think about the parade of misfortunes I had been witnessing among the masters of materialism, and what Joseph Campbell had to say about those with whom I had long identified. "If you follow your bliss, you'll always have your bliss," he said, "but if you follow your money, you may lose it at some time."[2]

I had experienced the latter and was grateful to be following the former.

When I was a boy, I used to hear the phrase, "money is the root of all evil." I hated that phrase. It railed against all I wanted to do, and it stymied my efforts to prove myself in the world. Only now do I realize that the complete phrase, from the Bible, is: "For the love of money is the root of all evil."[3] This corresponds with spiritual teachings from all over the world, which claim it is one's thought, one's intent, that does more harm or good than one's actual deed. As Bertrand Russell said, "It is the preoccupation with possessions, more than anything else, that prevents men from living freely and nobly."

Thus it isn't their actual wealth that hobbles men, it is their continuing lust for wealth that eventually leads them to ruin.

Several days later, while dictating some notes, Jason ran into my office and said, "Dad, Dad, come outside. There's a bird in our lamp." I let myself be pulled out to our courtyard. Sure enough, there was a little sparrow in the lamp of an alcove. As I approached the lamp to get a better look, the sparrow flapped its wings wildly against the glass and brass fixture. Then it flew out the bottom and into the trees at the edge of the lawn.

We went back inside and continued whatever we were doing. But the same thing happened the next day, and the next. It was just a little bird trying to find a nesting spot, or something like that. But it felt like more. It was as though something was trying to speak to me through a symbolic language, using birds as symbols for the transmission. And I was now beginning to feel that there was some connection between this incident and all the birds I had been noticing over the past few months.

Then, ever so suddenly, the little bird no longer appeared in our light fixture, and the message went untranslated.

I was still involved with the series of workshops given by John Hipsley. At the close of the series, he left me with these words of wisdom:

Some people go through life's experiences like the fragility of a piece of paper and are consumed by them.

Others go through life's experiences like a rubber band, flexible up to a point; then they snap and become obliterated.

Some people go through life like a candle and are melted away.

Still others go through experiences like a paper clip and show no outward appearance of change at all.

Finally, a few people go through life's experiences like an incense stick; while appearing to be extinguished, they leave a powerful essence wherever they go.

John's words raised some questions in my mind. Who among us will go through life as rubber bands, candles or incense sticks? On what basis is our fate determined? Considering the whole issue of enlightenment, what degree of control, if any, have we over our own spiritual development? Do we call on God, does He call on us, or must it be a reciprocal arrangement?

In *The Winged Life* by Thoreau as edited by poet Robert Bly, Thoreau makes the following comment when referring to his own experiences:

> There comes into my mind such an indescribable, infinite, all-absorbing, divine, heavenly pleasure, a sense of elevation and expansion, and (I) have had naught to do with it. I perceived that I am dealt with by superior powers. This is a pleasure, a joy, an existence which I have not procured myself. I speak as a witness on the stand, and tell what I have perceived.[4]

One of the nicest and simplest explanations of how divine influence operates comes from the Vedic tradition. God is a sun, an immensely brilliant sun that shines all the time, indiscriminately, everywhere. It shines on everyone, whether good or bad, and it shines on everyone regardless of whether they believe in it or not.

We humans are as tiny planets, each of us surrounded by our own cloud system. Some days when we are fraught with anger, fear and doubt, our clouds are thick and little divine sunlight gets through; other days when we are confident, joyful and enthused, our clouds thin, and God's radiance shines through more clearly. Is God aware of these changes in our individual weather systems? And if He is, does he care? Yet, for most people, these are not the most important questions.

The most important question becomes: who controls our cloud cover? The same Vedic tradition suggests that we, ourselves, have accumulated our individual clouds through all the experiences we have ever had; that we have been twisted by our own strong emotional reactions to events. The degree that we are able to relieve ourselves of these deeply-rooted tangles is the degree of sunshine we will perceive.

The same question keeps pursuing us in different form. Now it is: how do we relieve ourselves of our emotional twists and tangles? The answer is utterly simple: once again—let go.

Let go? Which, of course, raises many new questions.

CHAPTER 23

Behind the Face of Myself

In all faces is shown the Face of Faces, veiled and as if in a riddle.
—*St. Nicholas of Cusa*

Saratoga is the most westerly part of the Santa Clara Valley whose rolling hills rise to form the Santa Cruz Mountains. Although it is only about ten miles from the techopolis known as Silicon Valley, it feels quite rural and still has many fruit and nut orchards of the kind that once covered the entire valley. Like most of Coastal California, Saratoga has a benign climate; the daytime temperatures rarely vary from their 60-80° range, and most days are sunny and pleasant.

In this area, nature is a friendly, considerate medium, almost unnoticed but for the constant comfort it provides. Maybe that's why the California coast is so innovative—most of its residents don't have to expend their energy protecting themselves from freezing or flooding, or from the lethargy that accompanies intense heat and humidity.

On a balmy day in April, while strolling in the courtyard, I noticed that the little sparrow was once again in our outdoor light fixture. When I took a closer look, it was clear why she was there; she had been nest building over the past several weeks. Her entrance was a small opening, and I was hard pressed to understand how she had managed to get large pieces of twig and leaf into the light fixture.

The fixture was mounted on a wall, about eight feet above ground level. I needed a step ladder to see inside, and when I finally got to peek in, I saw four,

330

small, white eggs in the nest. I showed the eggs to Cecile, and we helped Jason and Michelle to see them. As the days went by, we carefully monitored their progress without disturbing them. We also found five other nests around the perimeter of our home, strategically placed in the trees, in the corner recesses of solar panels and under the eaves.

In fact, there seemed to be an unusual number of birds flying and chirping around our house. Nowhere else in the area had I seen such a concentration of birds of different species. It was as though we'd put out a sign saying, "Bird lovers live here—you are all welcome."

In mid-April, we started a family gardening project that Cecile and the children were keen on doing as an Earth Day program. When I agreed to join in, Cecile happily hugged and kissed me. She still wasn't used to the new me who was now more available for family activities. As our three-and-one-half-year-old Michelle helped Cecile turn over the soil, and Jason and I applied fertilizer, I noticed the birds were still in abundance, singing and building their nests as in some animated cartoon. Everything seemed alive and full of song and good cheer.

The sedate, pastoral setting brought to mind a conversation I once had with Bob Goodheart: "It's not enough to slow down," he'd said, "you must find a way to put the spring gait back in your life and a song back on your lips. Do this, and the answers will follow."

Quoting an ancient Chinese proverb, Bob added: "Birds don't sing because they have the answer, they sing because they have a song."

As Jason and I walked around humming and whistling while gathering tools, we looked at the neighboring houses and could see few birds. We felt so fortunate to be flattered by our little friends' visit and welcomed the opportunity to provide them refuge.

I napped for a while later that day and was awakened from a dream by a kiss on the forehead from my little princess. Michelle had fallen asleep beside me and had awakened before I did. She had been especially affectionate all day. I told her "That was the sweetest little kiss I ever had," and watched as she shyly smiled, her beautiful doe-like eyes shining.

"Did you dream, Daddy?" Michelle asked.

"Why, yes, my darling, I did have a dream." And I began to describe it to her.

I had dreamt again that I was flying, but this time I was flying over Hoboken. I felt compelled to fly just above the rooftops, but I couldn't land. Friends and neighbors marveled at the sight of me but yelled, "Stop, stop, before you get hurt." I was tempted to stop, tempted to believe them, but I didn't stop. Instead of looking downward I looked up, and just then a gust of wind caught me and lifted me up into the clouds, where I was beyond time and space, in a state of wonderful contentment, free of all influences except one—the most perfect one—that came from within me.

I felt like Robert Lowell might have felt when he wrote, "Sometimes I feel weak enough to enter heaven."[1] There was a seductive buoyancy that accompanied this graceful flight, and, looking down at the earth with its people, houses, seas and landforms, I felt a warm kinship to everything on the planet. I was part of it and it was part of me; I sensed we both had a profound effect on each other.

I wanted to fly forever—to be above it all—but something kept pulling on me, a feeling of incompleteness that I couldn't identify. Then, just as suddenly as it had lifted me, the wind brought me down again. I was performing a gentle landing when Michelle's kiss awakened me.

OOBE sounds like a medical specialty but it really stands for *out-of-body-experience*. As OOBEs are studied more thoroughly, investigators are learning that some of them are accompanied by strong feelings of kinship with the earth and its inhabitants. A friend has provided me with an enticing explanation for these feelings; he says we are "attached" to the earth in more ways than we know.

Viewing a single lifetime on earth from the perspective of nonphysical awareness, OOBE gives a unique perspective to the viewer. The aggregate influence of each person's thoughts and deeds while on earth can be seen as a tremendous trail of threads, of effects that reach all over the planet.

The influence of these individual thoughts and deeds can somehow be discerned by the viewer, in regard to how much good or bad they have done to other humans, to other species and even to the planet itself. The overall effect is like viewing a vast, interrelated network of accomplishments of a lifetime.

And while there are a few individuals who have done great harm, almost everyone would be amazed to see how far reaching are their thoughts and acts of good will; how a simple act of kindness stretched and grew, through influence upon its recipients, so as to eventually cause profound effects totally unforeseen and unknowable by their initiator.

In fact, the traces of the thoughts and acts of a single person can be seen to cover the planet in ways that are remarkable in the extreme. Those who have seen the total results of their life cannot help but come away, wondering, "Did I actually cause that?" and feeling better about themselves.

The days following the dream of flight were comfortable and pleasant— and devoid of anxiety. It was a peaceful time…time to reflect, to write, and to realize once again that every experience can be useful. One afternoon, I read in the newspaper that twenty-five of the remaining survivors of the 1906 San Francisco earthquake would meet there the next day for the eighty-fourth anniversary of that great event. The following day, the day of their reunion, three earthquakes hit the San Francisco area. It was as if the meeting needed a bit of authenticity, and the planet obliged by providing the special effects.

Then there was the cane.

When we were in New Zealand, I had come across some exquisitely carved walking canes. Remembering that my Dad had an arthritic knee, and always carried a cane wherever he went, I shipped one to him directly from New Zealand. On a whim, I bought a second one as a decoration for our family room and had it shipped home.

After we returned home I injured my own knee and was hobbling around the house in dire need of a cane for convalescence. That extra New Zealand cane became the perfect walking aid. It's as if a part of me knew I would need a cane before my injury occurred.

What an immense job it must be for the universal intelligence that provides us with our *invisible means of support*, to coordinate the lives of every living creature, back and forth through space and time, and make the system work!

Each synchronous event has multiple ramifications and influences. These synchronicities, these meaningful coincidences, all work so smoothly that it is often impossible to tell at the time they occur that they are in any way out of the ordinary. Only later, in retrospect, does their magic sometimes become fully known to us, and only sometimes are we permitted to see their multiple effects.

We had given up hoping to see the little sparrow eggs hatch in our outdoor light. After all, we hadn't seen the parents for almost a week, and it looked as if the abandoned eggs would serve no other purpose than to provide natural coffins for it's unsuspecting inhabitants. But one Saturday morning we were amazed to discover four tiny chicks, sitting in their nest, their tiny yellow beaks wide open, waiting for a feeding.

Since we could all hear the high-pitched chirps of the hatchlings, I felt confident that their parents would hear them also, and bring food. Coincidentally, I had been reading *The Winged Life*[2] wherein Thoreau talks about marveling at the process of birds hatching their eggs. I, too, felt that something marvelous happening in the tiny drama unfolding in our courtyard, but I wasn't able to interpret its meaning.

Meanwhile, convalescing from my leg injury gave me plenty of time to reflect and to write. Since I couldn't get around well enough to work at the local library, I decided to set up a folding table on our patio which would serve as my temporary outdoor office. I was perfectly situated to observe the birdlife, and once again I found myself in the company of vocalist birds, and spring in full bloom.

When my boyhood friends and I discovered the bluffs along the Hudson River in Hoboken and climbed them for the first time, we felt like the great discoverers of the New World, higher than everyone else and privy to wonderful views and secret happenings. Now, observing the secret life of birds, I was filled with the same glee.

Suddenly, I heard Jason yell. "Dad! Come quick, Mom wants you!" I limped as quickly as I could to our courtyard. Cecile had discovered that the four little chicks in our light fixture were readying themselves to venture into the world, but something was wrong. Their parents had built the nest in such a way that it partially blocked the chicks' exit. They couldn't get out. Several mature birds were flying around the light and flapping their wings as if to say, "Look! This is how you do it. Come on out! Come on out!"

We observed the spectacle as if it had become the most important thing in our lives. The situation grew more and more desperate, with the mature birds hovering like miniature helicopters three to four feet from the fixture, shaking their wings frantically and chirping loudly. But it seemed as though instinct plus the frantic prodding they were getting wasn't enough for the baby birds to squeeze through the fixture opening and free themselves. They reminded me of people who want to do something in the worst way but no matter how hard they try they just can't seem to do it without help.

I understood, then, that I would have to intervene. It was as if all nature was speaking to me through this micro event. The mother sparrow had flown around the courtyard many times over the past several weeks, distracting me whenever I'd approached too closely to the light. But now she had no choice—trust or not, the fate of her little ones was in my hands.

My eyes locked with the stone-hard, unblinking gaze of the mother bird. I hoped that on some level she would understand that, if I could help it, no harm would come to her chicks. Atop a ladder, I removed the brass bolts from the base of the lamp and saw the problem. The nest had blocked three of four exit points. I lifted the outer casing carefully, with all the attention of an obstetrician giving birth to quadruplets.

The four little chicks were completely disoriented. Their tiny, fragile wings were flapping wildly against the frame of the lamp and I was afraid they were going to injure themselves. I turned the lamp sideways to give them a better avenue of escape, then I proceeded to remove bits of the sturdy nest the parents had built. This created a clear passage for the baby birds.

So fast it was a blur, all four chicks, suddenly expert fliers all, flew out of the fixture to safety, rendezvousing with their grateful parents and meeting their extended family in a nearby tree.

Suddenly, I felt as though some new door had opened for me as well, that by clearing a path for the little birds I had uncovered my own path as well. Some constraint, something that had been holding me back suddenly dissolved. Whatever it was, I felt wonderful. I stood on the ladder, bad leg and all, watching the birds in the trees, and grinning like a bird-loving Cheshire cat. I felt freer than I had ever felt in my life.

As I watched the sparrows cavorting, my mind suddenly flashed back to all the bird experiences of the past months and to my dream of flying. I recalled the incomplete feeling I'd had during the dream. It was somehow connected to freeing the little birds and watching them fly away.

That day, I found myself suspended on the "still point of here and now." Like the sparrows, I was perfectly balanced and supported on a shaft of sacred air. I was as free as they were. Hippocrates once said: "Letting go is one side of freedom, freeing others is…how do you Americans put it? The 'flip side' of it." He had told me about Anaximander, or was it Thuycidides, who said, "In order to gain freedom, one must first give freedom."

It struck me that I had been the liberator of the sparrows—their Life Guide—just as they had been mine; that I had been everyone's Life Guide and that everyone who ever existed or would ever exist was also mine. Space and time were now playthings. Just as the warm, clear water of Hawaii is a medium for our enjoyment, so space and time and all the material things of the world are mediums for our enjoyment.

Who was I now, and where was the Dennis Augustine I had been for so many years? He was long gone, on his own adventures. He and his other many selves, those who had made different choices along the way, had branched off into their own alternate worlds and are now beyond counting. But they are not alone. For all our alternate selves exist simultaneously and are in constant communication with each other.

I sensed a Dennis Augustine who had disregarded the advice of one of his early mentors, Dr. Carmine Sippo, to go to medical school, and who remained on the streets of Hoboken, trafficking in marijuana and eventually becoming a hardened criminal. I also sensed the Dennis Augustine who stayed so wrapped up in his own personal needs that he never married, and never participated in the procreation of Jason and Michelle, beautiful creatures who might have adorned his life.

A Dennis Augustine also exists that continued on his driven quest for riches and fame, and who will end up among the fallen masters of materialism. Then, of course, there is the Dennis Augustine who made it to the top—riches in hand—only to be stricken by a paralyzing stroke and unable to enjoy it. And yet another Dennis Augustine exists who continued harboring bitter resentments toward his father and never had a chance to regain the loving relationship he so desperately wanted.

I sense another Dennis Augustine, one who has learned from everything there is to experience in this world. He will face the choice of remaining here or merging back into the infinite. Which of those will *I* become? Both of them, of course, just as I became all the alternate personalities that now exist.

I walked into the bathroom of the house, looked at myself in the mirror, and saw the familiar face that was the outward image of me. The image had changed quite a bit in the past few years. Now it looked friendlier, and I decided I liked it.

But it wasn't the image of my own face that transfixed me as I looked in the mirror. I had seen my own face all too often before: in mirrors all around the country—in hotel rooms, homes of friends and family, and in a thousand photographs. It was something else that rooted me on the spot, inviting me to ask the sixty-four dollar question,

So I asked it: I looked directly at myself and said, "Who are you? I mean, who are you, really?" As I watched, a rapid succession of holographic pictures appeared in place of my own image, flashing by so quickly I could not consciously recognize them all. Each one appeared and disappeared into the vortex of the mirror as if it were a secret passageway to the mysteries of my life and the universe itself.

Look! There was Bobby Shannon. I had tried to protect him and ended up getting us both stabbed. And there was Sister Assumptor, smacking my hand with her hard umbrella handle. There was my father as a young seminarian in his priest's cassock, then Mom, Bob Goldsack, Carmine Sippo, Crazy Jack Malone and his erotic wife Jasmine. There was Carl Jung and Joseph Campbell and Rabbi Weiss, Dr. Ed Marlowe and Nana Maynard from the Isle of Man. And, yes, my cousin Cadina from Sicily, the young girl I loved in my youth.

The motion picture flickered on. There was Richard Bach and Eknath Easwaran. Oh, wait, who was that? Ahh, that was Dr. Milo Turnbo from Chicago, and the quadriplegic girl in Hawaii. There's John Hipsley and Father Lewis Diaz, who was murdered by the crazed student he was counseling. And my mentor, Jay Seymour, and…and…they were coming by so fast I couldn't possibly catch them all: St. Augustine, Matthew Fox, Dr. Bill Moulder, Bob Goodheart, Cecile's mom and her father Harry, whom I had dearly loved. And Jeremy and Jody Perlman and then the faces of Jason, Michelle and Cecile, and now here's Hippocrates looking right back at me.

He didn't speak, but I sensed that this was the most sacred moment of my journey, where the Light of Truth, so well hidden, was in full view. I was standing at the crossroad of an invisible matrix which I intuitively knew existed all along, a matrix made up of all the roads that ever were and all the roads that will be, briefly converging in this place at this special moment.

Hippocrates and I looked at each other for what seemed a long time, our thoughts blending until we were of one mind, one consciousness, and I realized we had always been one mind. Our mind thought, "Hey, we are awake! We have been asleep but now we are awake. We are both in the mirror, just as everyone else is in the mirror with us. And while we are all a part of each other, we are also whatever individual personalities we need to be for as long as we need to be them.

I saw and finally understood how the mind of each of us creates the universe of experience and then reveals its creation to itself. Out of habit, I felt a brief urge to remain separate, to prolong my singular identity as Dennis Augustine a bit longer. But there were still some things I/we had to know.

"What is the most important thing?"

"Love," came the answer.

"What is love?" I asked.

"God," came the answer.

"What is God," I asked.

"We are," came the answer.

"Why do we exist?" I asked.

"To learn to love," came the answer.

"And when we are finished learning?"

"There is no end to learning to love," came the answer

"Then there can be no end to us?" I asked.

"No," came the answer.

And then I thought of one last question.

"Are these questions and answers of any value?" I asked.

"No," came the answer.

We looked at each other and Augustine/Hippocrates burst into loud laughter. "Dennis," Cecile called from the adjacent room, "What is it? What's so funny?" After we had calmed down, I shouted back, "I just shared a joke with Hippocrates." Then, after a moment, I shouted again, "I love you."

My attention returned to the mirror. The image of Hippocrates began to fade, and with it all the dramas of my short, intense life. As I looked into the mirror I saw a light—not a physical light, but a dynamic, vital light that was…alive. The light itself was a presence, a wonderful presence more blissful than anything I had ever felt. The light was intelligent, and it conveyed a sense of completion, of fulfillment. At that moment I realized that we, too, are light—light, compressed into bodily form. We are the divine being we are so desperately searching to meet.

We are the creator of the idea of God, and we create this idea to remind us every now and again of who we really are. And to give breadth to our idea, we also create signs, symbols, omens, visions, dreams, synchronicities, metaphors, stories, myths, scriptures and miracles to enhance the wonder that is our own essence.

Suddenly, I was being asked to make a decision. "I have a choice," I thought. "I can be everyone or I can pretend to be just Dennis Augustine for a while." I listened to several voices within offering sage advice and suggestions. Then, one voice seemed to stand out from the rest. It said, "Be Dennis Augustine for a while. It's simpler."

"Okay," I said, "but just for a while."

There was a silence and I asked myself, "So what do I do now?"

"Go create something," all the voices shouted in unison.

"Anything?" I asked.

"Anything," the chorus responded.

"Okay," I said, "I think I'll finish my book."

And I did.

And the end of all our exploring
Will be to arrive where we started
And know the place for the first time,
Through the unknown, remembered gate
When the last of earth left to discover
Is that which was the beginning,
At the source of the longest river
The voice of the hidden waterfall.

—*T. S. Eliot*

Notes

Chapter 3

1. Richard Bach, *The Bridge Across Forever* (New York: Dell Publishing, 1984), p. 252.

2. Roger Gould, *Transformations* (New York: Simon and Shuster, 1979), p. 81.

Chapter 4

1. Will Durant, *The Life of Greece* (New York: Simon & Shuster, 1939), p. 260.

2. Dennis F. Augustine, *How To Market Your Professional Services* (Footnotes Unlimited, P.O. Box 2043, Saratoga, CA 95070, 1979).

3. Dennis F. Augustine, *The Foot Care Revolution: How to Walk Away From a Foot Operation on Your Own Two Feet* (Footnotes Unlimited, P.O. Box 2043, Saratoga, CA 95070, 1980).

4. Ralph Waldo Emerson, *The Selected Writings of Ralph Waldo Emerson,* ed. Brooks Atkinson (New York: Random House, 1968), p. 175.

5. Zondervan Corp., *The Student Bible,* New International Version (Grand Rapids, MI.: Zondervan Corp., 1987), p. 1014.

Chapter 5

1. Martin Gray, *A Book of Life* (New York: Seabury Press, 1975), p. 171.

2. Jan Halper, *Quiet Desperation* (New York: Warner Books, 1988), p. 51.

Chapter 6

1. Richard Bach, *The Bridge Across Forever* (New York: Dell, 1986), p. 83.

2. Philip Kapleau, *The Three Pillars of Zen* (New York: Anchor Press/Doubleday, 1980).

Chapter 7

1. James Kavanaugh, *Will You Be My Friend?* (Los Angeles: Nash Publ., 1971).

Chapter 8

1, 2. Christopher P Andersen, *Father, the Figure and the Force* (New York: Warner Books, 1983).

3. Alexis de Toqueville, *Democracy In America,* 1st ed. (New York: Schocken Books, 1961), Volume 2, Chapter 13.

4. Viktor Frankl, *Man's Search for Meaning* (New York: Washington Square Press, 1967), p. 106.

5. Walt Whitman, *The Completed Poems,* a critical anthology, ed. Frances Murphy (New York: Penguin Books, 1969), p. 185.

Chapter 9

1, 2. Colin Wilson, *Poetry and Mysticism,* (San Francisco: City Lights Books. City Lights Books, 1970), p. 66.

3, 4. Eknath Easwaran, *The Unstruck Bell* (formerly, *Formulas for Transformation: a Mantram Handbook;* Nilgiri Press, Box 477, Petaluma, CA 94953: 1985).

5. Hugh McCann "Alternative Medicine Sheds Image of Quackery, " The Detroit News (June 25, 1987), p. 1.

6. Fran Dorff, *The Art of Passingover,* (Mahway, NJ: Paulist Press, 1988), p. 17.

7. Jolee Edmondson, "The Allure Of The Amalfi Coast, " *Bon Appetit* (March 1990), p. 24.

Chapter 10

1. Fritjof Capra, *Uncommon Wisdom, Conversations with Remarkable People* (New York: Bantam, 1988), p. 197.

2. Nikos Kazantzakis, *Zorba, The Greek* (New York: Simon & Shuster, 1972), p. 45.

3. Uri Shulevitz, *The Treasure* (New York: Sunburst Books, 1986).

Chapter 11

1. Fran Dorff, *The Art of Passingover* (Mahway, NJ.: Paulist Press, 1988), pp. 48–49.

2. Attributed to the English writer, John Bradford, 1510-1555, who was heard to say upon witnessing a public execution, "But for the grace of God, there goes John Bradford." He was prophetic, for he himself was burned as a Protestant martyr.

3. Carolyn Hyatt & Linda Gottlieb, *Why Smart People Fail* (New York: Simon & Shuster, 1987), pp. 235–236.

4. Peter Swet, *Parade Magazine,* New York (May 13, 1990), p. 8

5. Carl G. Jung, *Man and His Symbols,* 10th ed. (New York: Doubleday, 1988), p. 212.

Chapter 12

1. Abraham Maslow, "A Realizable Ideal, " *The Humanist* (April/May, 1990).

2. Reshad Feild, *Here to Heal* (Longmead, Shaftesbury, Dorset, Great Britain: Element Books, Ltd., 1986), p. 25.

3. Dave O'Brien, an interview with Elizabeth Kubler-Ross, *San Jose Mercury-News* (February 4, 1990).

Chapter 13

1. Joseph Campbell and Bill Moyers, *The Power of Myth;* ed., Betty Sue Flowers (New York: Doubleday, 1988), p. 149.

2. Cnidus was a city of Ancient Greece, located in what is now Eastern Turkey. It was noted for its medical school as well as for other institutions of learning.

3. In the fifth and fourth centuries B.C., when the Hippocratic School flourished, the four humors were known to be: blood, phlegm, black bile and yellow bile.

4. *The Aphorisms* and *Airs, Waters and Places* are two of several works produced by the Hippocratic School of Cos, Greece which have been passed down to the present day.

5. Richard Bach, *Illusions, The Adventures of a Reluctant Messiah* (New York: Dell Books, 1977), pp. 45–47.

6. Carl G. Jung, "Commentary, " in the Richard Wilhelm trans., *The Secret of the Golden Flower* (New York: 1962), p. 93.

7. Joseph Campbell and Bill Moyers, *The Power of Myth;* ed., Betty Sue Flowers (New York: Doubleday, 1988), p. 163.

8. Campbell p. 39.

9. Joseph Campbell, *The Hero's Journey* (San Francisco: Harper, 1990), p. iv.

10. Joseph Campbell and Bill Moyers, *The Power of Myth;* ed., Betty Sue Flowers (New York: Doubleday, 1988), p. 56.

11. Campbell, p. 56.

12. Campbell, p. 149.

Chapter 14

1. Fran Dorff, *The Art of Passingover* (Mahway, NJ: Paulist Press, 1988), pp. 39–53.

2. Joseph Campbell, *The Hero With a Thousand Faces*, 3rd ed. (Princeton: NJ., Princeton Bollingen Series, 1973), Table of Contents.

3. Joseph Campbell, *The Portable Jung,* trans. by R. F. C. Hull (New York: Viking, 1971).

4. Thomas Merton, *Zen and the Birds of Appetite* (New York: New Directions Publishing, 1968), p. 62.

5. Joseph Campbell, *The Hero With A Thousand Faces*, Princeton Bollingen Series, XVII, 3rd ed. (Princeton NJ: Princeton University Press, 1973).

6. Joseph Campbell and Bill Moyers, *The Power of Myth;* ed., Betty Sue Flowers (New York: Doubleday, 1988), p. 208.

Chapter 15

1. Richard Bach, *Illusions* (New York: Dell Publishing 1977), p. 100.

2. Tom Huth, "The Man Who Levitates Hotels, " *California Magazine* (Interview with Dan Pearson, April, 1988).

3. Georgy Ivanovitch Gurdjieff, *Meetings With Remarkable Men* (New York: Dutton, 1974).

4. Henry Wadsworth Longfellow, Elizabeth.

5. New Testament, *Leviticus,* XIX:18.

6. William Shakespeare, *Hamlet,* Act 1, Scene 3.

Chapter 16

1. Ralph Waldo Emerson, *The Selected Writings of Ralph Waldo Emerson,* ed. Brooks Atkinson (New York: Random House, 1968), p. 187.

2. Joseph Campbell and Bill Moyers, *The Power of Myth;* ed., Betty Sue Flowers (New York: Doubleday 1988), p. 161.

3. New Testament, *Matthew,* XVIII, 3.

4. Brenda Ueland, *If You Want to Write* (St. Paul, MN.: Gray Wolf Press, 1987).

5. Francis Dorff, "The Rabbi's Gift, " *New Catholic World,* Vol. 222, No. 1328 (March/April, 1979), p. 52.

6. Bernie S. Siegal, *Love, Medicine and Miracles* (New York: Harper and Row, 1986), p. 214.

Chapter 17

1. Matthew Fox, *Original Blessing,* (Santa Fe: Bear & Company, 1983), p. 33.

2. Langdon Gilkey, "Ordering The Soul: Augustine's Manifold Legacy, " *The Christian Century* (April 27, 1988).

3. Matthew Fox, *Original Blessing* (Santa Fe: Bear & Company, 1983), p. 47.

4. Fox, p. 47.

5. Fox, p. 39.

6. Fox, p. 37.

7. Brian Swimme, *The Universe is a Green Dragon* (Santa Fe: Bear & Company, 1984), p. 19.

8. Swimme, back cover.

9. Swimme, pp. 49–50.

10. Abraham Maslow, *Religions, Values and Peak Experiences* (New York: Penguin Books 1987), p. 56.

11. John Prescope, "Hippocrates on Diet and Hygiene, " trans from *De Alimento,* a tract ascribed to Hippocrates, p. 174.

12. Karen Emmons; Linda Gomez; Peter Meyer and Bureaus, *The Meaning of Life,* quoting Rabbi Harold Kushner, *Life Magazine* (December, 1988), p. 90.

13. *Life Magazine* (December, 1988), Kushner quoting Buber, p. 90.

14. Richard Bach, *One* (New York: Morrow & Company, 1988).

15. F. David Peat, *Synchronicity* (New York: Bantam Books, 1988), p. 9.

16. F. David Peat, p. 9.

Chapter 18

1. Fritjof Capra, *Uncommon Wisdom* (New York: Bantam, 1989), p. 34.

2. Chief Dan George, *My Heart Soars,* 1st ed. (Surrey, British Columbia: Hancock House Publishers, 1990), p. 52.

3. Don Fabun, *The Dynamics of Change* (Englewood Cliffs, NJ: Prentice-Hall, 1969), p. 21-iv.

4. Thomas Merton, *The Seven Storey Mountain* (New York: Harcourt Brace 1948), p. 348.

5. Richard Bach, *Bridge Across Forever* (New York: Dell Publishing 1986), p. 206.

6. Richard Bach, p. 206.

7. Dan Wakefield, *Returning* (New York: Penguin Books, 1989), p. 188.

8. Hal Zina Bennett, *The Lens of Perception* (Berkeley, CA.: Celestial Arts Press 1987), p. 59.

Chapter 19

1. Joseph Campbell and Bill Moyers, *The Power of Myth;* ed., Betty Sue Flowers (New York: Doubleday 1988), p. 58.

2. Joseph Campbell, pp. 58–59.

3. Joseph Campbell, pp. 58–59.

4. Eric Fromm, *The Art of Loving* (New York: Harper-Collins, 1989).

5. Fran Dorff, *The Art of Passingover* (New York: Paulist Press, 1988), p 74.

6. Hermann Graf von Kayserling, *The Travel Diary of a Philosopher* (New York: Harcourt, Brace 1925).

7. Ira Progroff, *The Cloud of Unknowing* (New York: Dell Publishing, 1957).

8. William Shakespeare, *Hamlet,* Act 1, Scene 4.

9. F. David Peat, *Synchronicities* (New York: Bantam, 1988), p. 7.

Chapter 20

1. Jan de Hartog, "The Lamb's War, " *Towers Club U.S.A. Newsletter* (P.O. Box 2038, Vancouver, WA 98668), January 1990, Issue 160, p. 1

2. Reshad Feild, *The Last Barrier* (Dorset, U.K.: First Element Books Ltd., 1985), p. 172.

3. Marcus Bach, *The World of Serendipity* (Marina Del Ray: DeVorss and Co., CA, 1982), p. 8.

Chapter 21

1. Joseph Campbell and Bill Moyers, *The Power of Myth;* ed., Betty Sue Flowers (New York: Doubleday, 1987), p. 211.

2. Karl Jasper, *The Philosophy of Existence* (Philadephia: Univ. of Penn. Press, 1971).

3. Harold Kushner, *When All You Wanted Isn't Enough* (New York: Simon & Shuster, 1986), p. 161.

Chapter 22

1. Joseph Campbell, *The Hero's Journey, On His Life and Work,* ed. and intro., Phil Cousineau (San Francisco: Harper-Collins, 1990), p. 231.

2. John Maher and Denise Briggs, eds., *An Open Life: Joseph Campbell in conversation with Michael Toms,* (New York: Larson Publications, 1988), p 16.

3. New Testament, *1st Timothy*, VI:10.

4. Henry David Thoreau, *The Winged Life*, ed. Robert Bly (San Francisco: Sierra Club Books, 1986), p. 16.

Chapter 23

1. Andrew Harvey, *Hidden Journey* (New York: Arkana, 1992), p. 96.

2. Henry David Thoreau, *The Winged Life*, ed. Robert Bly (San Francisco: Sierra Club Books, 1986), p. 16.

Bibliography

Ackerman, Martin S. and Diane L. *Money, Ego, Power.* Chicago: Playboy Press, 1976

Andersen, Christopher P. *Father, the Figure and the Force.* New York: Warner Books, 1983

Auden, W.H. *Age of Anxiety,* a baroque ecologue. New York: Random House, 1947

Augustine, Dennis F. *How To Market Your Professional Services.* Footnotes Unlimited, P.O. Box 2043, Saratoga, CA 95070, 1979

Augustine, Dennis F. *The Foot Care Revolution: How to Walk Away From a Foot Operation on Your Own Two Feet.* Footnotes Unlimited, P.O. Box 2043, Saratoga, CA 95070, 1980

Baba Ram Dass (Richard Alpert). *Be Here Now.* San Cristobal, N.M.: Lama Foundation, 1971

Bach, Marcus. *The World of Serendipity.* Marina Del Ray: DeVorss and Co., CA, 1982

Bach, Richard. *Illusions, The Adventures of a Reluctant Messiah.* New York: Dell Books, 1977

Bach, Richard. *One.* New York: Morrow & Company, 1988

Bach, Richard. *The Bridge Across Forever.* New York: Dell Publishing, 1986

Bancroft, Anne. *Twentieth-Century Mystics and Sages.* New York: Viking Penguin, Inc., 1976

Bennett, Hal Zina. *The Lens of Perception.* Berkeley, CA.: Celestial Arts Press 1987

Bly, Robert. ed. and trans., *Times Alone: Selected Poems of Antonio Machado.* Scranton, Pa.: Wesleyan University Press, 1983

Bolt, Robert. *Doctor Zhivago; The screen play.* New York: Random House, 1965. (Based on the novel by Boris Pasternak.)

Bock, Jerry. *Fiddler on the Roof.* New York: Crown Publishers, 1965

Brennert, Alan. *Time and Chance.* New York: Tom Doherty Associates, Inc., 1990

Brewi, Janice and Brennan, Anne. *Celebrate Mid-Life.* New York: Crossroad Publishing Company, 1988

Bry, Adelaide. *est: 60 Hours That Transform Your Life.* New York: Harper and Row, 1976

Buber, Martin. *The Legend Of The Baal-Shem.* New York: Shocken Books Inc., 1969

Campbell, Joseph. *The Hero With a Thousand Faces,* 3rd ed. Princeton: NJ., Princeton Bollingen Series, 1973

Campbell, Joseph. *The Portable Jung,* trans. by R. F. C. Hull. New York: Viking, 1971

Campbell, Joseph. *The Hero's Journey.* San Francisco: Harper, 1990

Campbell, Joseph, and Bill Moyers. *The Power of Myth;* ed., Betty Sue Flowers. New York: Doubleday, 1988

Cane, Melville; Farrar, John; and Towsend Nicholl, eds., *The Golden Year,* The Poetry Society of American Anthology, 1910-1960. Fine Editions Press, 1960. (Includes works of R.H. Grenville)

Capra, Fritjof. *Uncommon Wisdom, Conversations with Remarkable People.* New York: Bantam, 1988

Carter, John Mack and Feeney, Joan. *Starting At The Top.* New York: William Morrow & Company, 1985

Chesterton, G.K. (Gilbert Keith). *The Wisdom of Father Brown.* Harmonsworth: Penguin, 1974

Chardin, Tellhard de. *The Divine Milieu.* New York: Harper and Row, 1960

Cone, Molly. *Hear, 0 Israel, about God.* New York: Union of American Hebrew Congregations, 1973.

Cossman, Joseph. *The E. Joseph Cossman Lecture Series How To Make Money.* Palm Springs: E. Joseph Cossman, 1975

Cusa, St. Nicholas of. *The Vision of God.* Trans., E. Gurney Salter. New York, 1928

Davies, Paul. *God and the New Physics.* New York: Simon & Shuster, 1983

Diamond, Harvey and Marylyn. *Fit For Life.* New York: Warner Books, 1985

Dorff, Fran. *The Art of Passingover.* Mahway, NJ: Paulist Press, 1988

Dostoevsky, Fyodor. *The Brothers Karamazov.* Andrew H. McAndrew, trans., Konstantin McChulsky, intro. New York: Bantam Books, 1970

Durant, Will. *The Life of Greece.* New York: Simon & Shuster, 1939

Dyer, Dr. Wayne W. *You'll See It When You Believe It.* New York: William Morrow and Company, Inc., 1989

Durkheim, Karlfried Graf. *The Call for the Master: The Meaning of Spiritual Guidance on the Way to the Self.* New York: Dutton, 1989

Easwaran, Eknath. Trans., *The Bhagavad Gita.* Petaluma, Cal.: Nilgiri Press, 1985

Easwaran, Eknath. *TheUnstruck Bell.* Petaluma, Cal.: Nilgiri Press, 1985

Einstein, Albert. "Autobiographical Notes, " in Paul Schlip, ed., *Albert Einstein: Philosopher-Scientist.* New York: Tudor, 1951

Eiseley, Loren. *The Night Country.* New York: Charles Scribner's Sons, 1966

Eliot, George. *The Best Known Novels of George Eliot.* New York: Modern Library, 1940

Eliot, T.S. (Thomas Strearns) *Four Quartets.* New York: Harcourt Brace, 1943

Emerson, Ralph Waldo. *The Selected Writings of Ralph Waldo Emerson,* ed., Brooks Atkinson. New York: Random House, 1968

Fabun, Don. *The Dynamics of Change.* Englewood Cliffs, NJ: Prentice-Hall, 1969

Feild, Reshad. *Here to Heal.* Great Britain: Element Books, Ltd., 1986

Feild, Reshad. *The Invisible Way.* New York: Harper & Row, 1983

Feild, Reshad. *The Last Barrier.* Great Britain: Element Books Ltd., 1976

Felleman, Hazel, ed. *Poems That Live Forever.* New York: Doubleday & Company, 1965. The Ways: John Oxenham cited.

Fitzgerald, F. Scott. *Flappers and Philosophers.* New York: Scribner's, 1959

Fox, Matthew. *Original Blessing.* Santa Fe: Bear & Company, 1983

Frank, Anne. *Anne Frank: The Diary of a Young Girl.* New York: Doubleday, 1952

Frost, Robert. *Collected Poems of Robert Frost.* Cutchogue, New York: Buccaneer Books, 1986

Frye, Northrop, ed. and intro. *Selected Poetry and Prose of William Blake.* New York: Modern Library, 1953

George, Chief Dan. *My Heart Soars.* Surrey, British Columbia: Hancock House Publishers, 1990

Gould, Roger. *Transformations.* New York: Simon and Shuster, 1979

Gray, Martin. *A Book of Life.* New York: The Seabury Press, 1975

Gurdjieff, Georgy Ivanovitch. *Meetings With Remarkable Men.* New York: Dutton, 1974

Guthrie, William Keith Chambers. *The Greek Philosophers.* New York: Harper, 1960

Halper, Jan. *Quiet Desperation.* New York: Warner Books, 1988

Hanh, Thich Nhat. *The Miracle of Mlndfulness.* Boston: Beacon Press, 1975

Harvey, Andrew. *Hidden Journey.* New York: Arkana, 1992

Hayward, Susan. *Begin It Now.* Australia: In-Tune Books, 1988

Heidegger, Martin. *An Introduction to Metaphysics.* Trans., Ralph Manheim. New Haven: Yale University Press, 1959

Helmholtz, Hermann von. *Epistemological Writings,* ed. R.S. Cohen and Y. Elkana; trans. Malcolm F. Lowe. Boston: Reidel, 1977

Henry, Lewis C. Ed. *Five Thousand Quotations.* New York: Doubleday, 1945

Hoff, Benjamin. *The Tao of Pooh.* New York: Penguin Books, 1983

Hopkins, Jeffrey, ed. and trans. and Napper, Elisabeth co-ed., *Kindness, Clarity, and Insight.* The Fourteenth Dalai Lama, His Holiness Tenzin Gyatso. Itacha, NY: Snow Lion Publications, 1985

Huxley, Aldous. *The Doors of Perception.* New York: Harper & Row, 1954

Hyatt, Carolyn & Linda Gottlieb. *Why Smart People Fail.* New York: Simon & Shuster, 1987

James, William. *The Will To Believe, and other Essays in Popular Philosophy, and Human Immortality.* New York: Dover Publications, 1960

Jasper, Karl. *The Philosophy of Existence.* Philadephia: Univ. of Penn. Press, 1971

Johnson, Toby. *The Myth of the Great Secret,* A search for spiritual meaning. Berkeley, California: Celestial Arts, 1992

Jung, Carl G. *Man and his Symbols.* New York: Anchor Press (Doubleday), 1988

Jung, C.G. *Synchronicity, and Human Destiny: Noncausal Dimensions of Human Experience.* New York: Dell, 1973

Kapleau, Philip. *The Three Pillars of Zen.* New York: Anchor Press/Doubleday, 1980

Kavanaugh, James. *Will You Be My Friend?* Los Angeles: Nash Publ., 1971

Kayserling, Hermann Graf von. *The Travel Diary of a Philosopher.* New York: Harcourt, Brace 1925

Kazantzakis, Nikos. *Zorba, The Greek* (New York: Simon & Shuster, 1972)

Keen, Sam and Anne Valley-Fox. *Your Mythic Journey.* Los Angeles: Jeremy P. Tarcher, Inc., 1989

Keightley, Alan. *Into every life a little Zen must fall.* London: Wisdom Publications, 1986

Keys Jr., Ken. The Hundreth Monkey. St Mary, Kentucky: Vision Books, 1982

Kushner, Harold. *When All You Wanted Isn't Enough.* New York: Simon & Shuster, 1986

Levine, David. *The Fables of Aesop.* Trans., Patrick and Justina Gregory. New York: Dorset Press, 1989

Lindstrom, Marilyn. *The Voice From Inner Space.* Redondo Beach, CA.: Los Arboles Publications, 1990

Longfellow, Henry Wadsworth. *The Complete Practical Works of Henry Wadsworth Longfellow.* New York: Houghton Mifflin Co., 1922

Maher, John and Denise Briggs, eds., *An Open Life: Joseph Campbell in conversation with Michael Toms.* New York: Larson Publications, 1988

Maslow, Abraham. H. *Religions, Values and Peak Experiences.* New York: Penguin Books, 1987

Maslow, Abraham H. *The Farther Reaches of Human Nature.* New York: Viking Press, Inc., 1971

Mayer, Nancy. *The Male Mid-Life Crisis.* New York: New American Library, 1978

Merton, Thomas. *Zen and the Birds of Appetite.* New York: New Directions Publishing, 1968

Merton, Thomas. *The Seven Storey Mountain.* New York: Harcourt Brace 1948

Millman, Dan. *The Way of The Peaceful Warrior.* Tiburon. CA: H.J. Kramer, Inc., 1984

Milne, Alan Alexander. The *House at Pooh Corner.* New York: E.P. Dutton & Co., 1956

Milton, John. *Paradise Lost and Paradise Regained.* Ed. Christopher Ricks. New York: Signet Classic Poetry Series. New American Library, 1968

Moyne, John and Coleman Barks, *Unseen Rain, Quatrains of Rumi.* Putney, Vermont: Threshold Books, 1986

Needleman, Jacob. *Money and The Meaning of Life.* New York: Doubleday, 1991

Needleman, Jacob. *The Way of the Physician.* New York: Penguin Books, 1985

Occhiogrosso, Peter. *Once A Catholic.* New York: Ballantine, 1989

Peat, F. David. *Synchronicities.* New York: Bantam, 1988

Peck, Dr. M. Scott. *The Road Less Traveled.* New York, Simon & Shuster, 1978

Pollock, Sir Frederick. *Spinoza's Life and Philosophy.* London: Duckworth and Company, 1899

Prather, Hugh. *Notes to Myself.* New York: Bantam Books, 1988

Progroff, Ira. *At a Journal Workshop.* New York: Dialogue House Library, 1975

Progroff, Ira. *The Cloud of Unknowing.* New York: Dell Publishing, 1957

Roberts, Jane. *Seth Speaks: The Eternal Validity of the Soul.* London: Prentice-Hall International, Inc., 1972

Robbins, Anthony. *Unlimited Power.* New York: Simon and Shuster, 1986

Rumi (Coleman Barks). *One-Handed Basket Weaving.* Athens, Georgia: Maypop, 1991

Russell, Bertrand. *Unpopular Essays.* New York: Simon & Shuster, Inc., 1950

Saint-Exupery, Antoine de. *A Sense of Life.* New York: Funk, 1965

Salinger, J.D. (Jerome David). *Nine Stories.* Boston: Little Brown, 1953

Sarte, Jean-Paul. *Wall and Other Stories.* Trans., Lloyd Alexander. New York: New Directions, 1948

Schweitzer, Albert. *The Teaching of Reverence For Life.* Richard and Clara Winston, trans. New York: Holt, Rinehart and Winston, 1965

Shakespeare, William. *Complete Works,* Campbridge Text established by John Denver Wilson. London: Octopus, 1983 Singer, Dorethea Waley. *Giordano Bruno: His Life and Thought.* New York: Dover, 1961

Shulevitz, Uri. *The Treasure.* New York: Sunburst Books, 1986

Siegal, Bernie S. *Love, Medicine and Miracles.* New York: Harper and Row, 1986

Smith, Scott. *Coincidences.* Aptos, CA: Living Business Press, 1987

Steinbeck, John. *The Short Novels of John Steinbeck.* New York: The Viking Press, Inc., 1963

Stowe, Harriet Beecher. *Uncle Tom's Cabin.* Literary Classics of the USA. New York: Viking Press, 1982

Swimme, Brian. *The Universe is a Green Dragon.* Santa Fe: Bear & Company, 1984

Tagore, Rabindranath. *Glorious Thoughts of Tagore.* India: New York Book Society of India, 1965

Tart, Charles T. *Waking Up.* Boston: New Science Library: Shambhala, 1987

Thoreau, Henry David. *The Winged Life*, ed. Robert Bly. San Francisco: Sierra Club Books, 1986

Toqueville, Alexis de. *Democracy In America*. New York: Schocken Books, 1961

Tzu, Lao. *Tao Te Ching, A New Translation* by Gia-Fu Feng and Jane English. New York: Viking Press, 1972

Ueland, Brenda. *If You Want to Write*. St. Paul, MN.: Gray Wolf Press, 1987

Voltaire. (Francois Marie Arouet) *Candide*. New York: Dover Publications, 1991

Wakefield, Dan. *Returning*. New York: Penguin Books, 1989

Warner, Rex. *The Confessions of St. Augustine*, a contemporary translation. New York: Nal Penguin Inc., 1963

Whitaker, Julian Dr., editor, *Health and Healing*. Potamac, MD: Phillips Publishing, Inc., October 1993

Whitman, Walt. *The Completed Poems*, a critical anthology, ed., Frances Murphy. New York: Penguin Books, 1969

Wilson, Colin. *Poetry and Mysticism*. San Francisco: City Lights Books, 1970

Winokur, Jon. Ed., *Zen To Go*. New York: New American Library, 1989

Yogi, Maharishi Mahesh. *Transcendental Meditation*. First published as *The Science of Being and Art of Living*. New York: New American Library, 1963

Yoo, Young H. *Wisdom of the Far East*. Washington: Far Eastern Research & Publications Center, 1972

Zondervan Corp., *The Student Bible*, New International Version. Grand Rapids, MI.: Zondervan Corp., 1987

About the Author

After facing a series of life-altering events, Dr. Dennis F. Augustine the founder and director of the Park Avenue Foot Clinic in San Jose—gave up a lucrative career as a board-certified podiatric physician and surgeon in 1989 at the age of 39. Ask him for his business card today, and you will find an assortment of interests ending with the words et cetera—reflecting an open-ended image of what possibilities might be in store for the future. Dennis Augustine has been a former street gang member, gambler, pizza delivery boy, grocery retail clerk and cashier, gas station attendant, U-Haul rental agent, salesman, investor, administrator, entrepreneur, amateur philosopher, poet, artist, saxophone player, motorcyclist, novice hang glider, writer and perennial traveler. His childlike curiosity and eclectic pursuits have lead him to explore the Caribbean and Hawaiian Islands, Europe, Canada, Australia, New Zealand, East Africa, India, and Israel, in search of indigenous cultural experiences. He is an avid reader and collector of anecdotal stories, parables and myths that lift the human spirit. Dennis resides in Northern California with his wife Cecile and their two children, Jason and Michelle.

Here's How To Order
additional copies of

Invisible Means Of Support
(This form may be photocopied.)

Telephone orders (credit card orders only):

Call Toll Free (24 Hour Service):

☎ 1-800-247-6553

Fax orders (credit card orders only):

✳ 419-281-6883

Postal Orders:

✉ Golden Gate Publishing
P.O. Box 2043
Saratoga, Ca. 95070

$24.95 plus $3.00 shipping and handling*
Make check or money order payable to Golden Gate Publishing

Special Offer: No additional shipping charge for multiple copies.
Invisible Means Of Support makes an excellent gift for relatives and friends. To order multiple copies, type or print recipient's name and address on a separate sheet of paper. **Sales Tax:** Please add $8\frac{1}{4}$% ($2.06) for books shipped to California addresses.

- -

Please send_____ copies of *Invisible Means of Support to:*

Name:_____

Address: _____

City: _____State: _____ Zip: _____

Call TOLL FREE and order now for faster service
1-800-247-6553

WANTED

Stories and experiences of
Invisible Means of Support

Share your sense of spirit with the rest of the world. If you've had an unusual experience or have a favorite quote or saying, poem, story, myth, news clipping or account (published or unpublished) that reflects the spirit of *Invisible Means of Support*—Dennis Augustine would like to hear from you.

The author of *Invisible Means of Support* is especially interested in magical coincidences, spiritual insights, life-affirming events or situations, and pivotal life guide stories that have made a positive difference in people's lives.

Please identify the source (author, date and publication) of any previously published material. All submissions will be respectfully considered for a future book on a similar theme, and all contributions accepted for publication will be acknowledged in that book.

Mail or fax your submission to:

Dr. Dennis Augustine
P. O. Box 2043
Saratoga, CA 95070
Fax: (408) 741-0492

With heartfelt thanks,

Dennis Augustine